THE ENCYCLOPEDIA OF
SECRET SIGNS
AND SYMBOLS

ADELE NOZEDAR

THE ENCYCLOPEDIA OF
SECRET SIGNS
AND # SYMBOLS

THUNDER BAY
P·R·E·S·S

San Diego, California

Thunder Bay Press
An imprint of Printers Row Publishing Group
9717 Pacific Heights Blvd, San Diego, CA 92121
www.thunderbaybooks.com • mail@thunderbaybooks.com

First published by HarperCollins*Publishers* 2008
This revised and updated edition published 2022

Printers Row Publishing Group is a division of Readerlink Distribution Services, LLC. Thunder Bay Press is a registered trademark of Readerlink Distribution Services, LLC.

Correspondence regarding the content of this book should be sent to Thunder Bay Press, Editorial Department, at the above address. Author and rights inquiries should be addressed to HarperCollins*Publishers*, 1 London Bridge Street, London, U.K. SE1 9GF.

Thunder Bay Press
Publisher: Peter Norton
Associate Publisher: Ana Parker
Editor: Dan Mansfield

Produced by HarperCollins*Publishers*
Editor: Caitlin Doyle • Designer: e-Digital Design
Author: Adele Nozedar

ISBN 978-1-6672-0076-7

Library of Congress Control Number: 2022939552.

Printed in Bosnia-Herzegovina

26 25 24 23 22   1 2 3 4 5

Dedication

For Adam
and for the seven secrets

"In every grain of sand there lies
Hidden the soil of a star"
Arthur Machen

"I do not need a leash or a tie
To lead me astray
In the land where dreams lie"
Yoav

In Nature's temple, living pillars rise
Speaking sometimes in words of abstruse sense;
Man walks through woods of symbols, dark and dense,
Which gaze at him with fond familiar eyes.

Like distant echoes blent in the beyond
In unity, in a deep darksome way,
Vast as black night and vast as splendent day,
Perfumes and sounds and colors correspond.

From "Correspondences," Charles Baudelaire

CONTENTS

INTRODUCTION

The aim of this book is to seek a true understanding of the secret signs, sacred symbols, and other indicators of the arcane, hidden world that are so thickly clustered around us. During this process, we'll shed light on the cultural, psychological, and anthropological nature of our signs and symbols. We'll also be surprised to discover that many of the everyday things we take for granted can hold hidden secrets, and by having the key to this knowledge we'll gain an insight into the minds and concerns of our forbears who constructed these symbols.

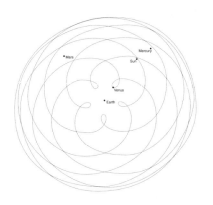

NO BEGINNING, NO END: ANATOMY OF A SIMPLE SYMBOL

Rodin said, "Man never invented anything new, only discovered things." While it's true to say that some symbols have been made by people for a specific purpose, it's equally accurate to argue that everything is inspired in some way by the natural world around us, by the forms of nature, plants, animals, the elements. Even a reaction against the fluid forms of nature is generally inspired by a desire to provide an alternative. Sometimes the revelation of a natural symbol is immediate; other such discoveries are the result of years of painstaking observation.

One of our simplest symbols has elaborate and arcane origins.

On the previous page is a picture, not of a man-made or computer-generated pattern, but of the shape made in the sky by the planet Venus. Venus is the only planet whose dance around the Sun in the depths of space describes such a definite and distinctive form, and we can only imagine the sense of wonder that must have been felt by the ancient Akkadians who first charted the design. They also realized that the Morning Star and the Evening Star, previously considered to be two separate celestial bodies, were one and the same. This discovery had a profound effect, which has cast such a long shadow over the archaeology of symbols that we are still governed by it today. Here's why.

Because of Venus's proximity to the Sun, its light is often obliterated, and so it is visible only in the early morning or in the evening, either just before sunrise or just after sunset. The Greeks called the morning star Eosphoros, "bringer of the dawn" (later, the star would be called Lucifer, the brightest of the angels cast out of the heavens). As the Evening Star, it was called Hesperos, "star of the evening" (which gives us the name of evening prayers, or vespers).

It takes eight years and one day for the appearances of Venus to complete an entire pentagram. These days we can plot these movements relatively easily, but for our ancestors the process must have been elaborate and painstaking, as uncertain and laborious a voyage of discovery as the traversing of any great physical ocean. The goddess that we know as Venus was, to the Akkadians, Ishtar/Inanna, divinity not only of love and harmony but also goddess of war. Incidentally, Venus is the only major planet of our solar system, aside from the Earth itself, to be designated a feminine spirit.

The Mayans determined their calendrical system from the movements of Venus, and chose propitious positions of the planet to determine the time of a war. The five-pointed star that is still used as a military symbol—stenciled onto tanks, for example, or used in insignia—derives from the stately movement of this great astral goddess.

Similarly, the apple given by Eve to Adam contained a hidden symbol within it; the pentagram created by the pattern of the pips. Eve offered Adam not only knowledge of the divine feminine—a holy grail indeed—but offered him a symbol of the true marriage of opposites, the feminine number two wedding to the masculine number three. Eve, therefore, personifies Ishtar/Venus/Aphrodite as the goddess of sensual love (and Venus, incidentally, is the derivation of the word "venereal"). Further, Ishtar was demonized in the Bible as the Whore of Babylon.

So, a seemingly simple thing such as the shape made in the sky by the path of a planet can be full of complexities and contradictions, which not only clarifies some aspects of the symbol but also poses further questions. The truth is that the quest to understand the meaning of a symbol is as much a personal voyage of discovery as a collective one, and it is in the spirit of exploration that I hope you will adventure into this book.

THANKS

There are several people without whom this book would never have been written. I'd like to thank Katy Carrington, Terence Caven, Jeannine Dillon, Chris Wold, Simon Gerratt, Graham Holmes, Kate Latham, Faith Booker, and Laura Summers at HarperCollins. Charlotte Ridings, Martin Noble, and Mark Bolland were the editors. I'd also like to thank Wanda Whiteley.

Any book about symbols would be nothing without the illustrations. Paul Khera has done the bulk of these, with additional thanks to Anat Cederbaum, Myong Hwi Kim, Kruti Sanaija, and Yuki Nakamura for advice and help with some aspects of these pictures. I am also lucky enough to have Finlay Cowan contribute images to this book.

Other illustrators include David Little, Lyndall Fernie, and Kalavathi Devi. I would also like to thank Willa and Milo Seary for their drawings. Thanks are also due to Gavin and Davina Hogg, Sigorour Atlason, Caroline Danby, Tania Ahsan, Hamraz Ahsan, Carla Edgley, Judy Roland, Theo Chalmers, the Order of Bards, Ovates and Druids, Stuart Mitchell, and the good people of Raquetty Lodge, Hay on Wye. Most of all I have to thank starship commander Adam Fuest for putting up with my obsession about this book and my possible bouts of absentmindedness about anything else during the writing of it.

FIRST SIGNS: THE BASIC SHAPES OF SYMBOLS

There are certain elemental structures that occur repeatedly, not only as component parts of more elaborate symbols, but also with rich meanings of their own. In fact, it's probably true to say that the simpler the symbol, the more scope there is for interpretation; ergo, the more meaningful it is and, paradoxically, the more complex it becomes. These primary shapes transcend barriers of time, geography, and cultural context, part of a universal language that goes before, and beyond, words. Don't be fooled into thinking that these basic shapes are as self-explanatory as to need no analysis. A true understanding of what they represent can only add to the comprehension of the more elaborate shapes and symbols that follow in this section.

SPACE

The elements of a symbol are defined only by the space that is a part of its construction. Like the wind, the effect of space is gauged by its effect on the things within it or surrounding it. The concept of space, the void, is a profound part of our experience. To reach a state of "emptiness" is, for many, the ultimate spiritual experience and a way of connecting to the Absolute. When John Lennon wrote "Imagine," whose lyrics gradually strip away the trappings of the material world, it was this idea that inspired him.

To be aware of the possibility of space within a flat, two-dimensional representation is to give that shape substance and a new kind of reality that lifts it off the page and makes it real. Space is not flat and cannot be confined by lines on a piece of paper. The page and the shape on it do not exist in isolation, but are a part of a greater cosmos. This book and you, the reader, are a part of this equation.

The concept of zero is a space. Indeed, the realization that "nothing" can be "something" marked a profound leap forward in man's development. All creation myths begin with a void, symbolic of potential.

Although attempts to explain the concept of space are inevitably faulty, it might help to think of a blank page. Before a mark is made upon the paper, the potential for what might appear there is so vast as to be unimaginable, a consideration which causes consternation for some artists and writers. Without this space, there is no arena for anything else to exist. This absence of any thing means that no thing is the most important symbol in the world.

DOT

A dot might seem to be an unassuming little thing, the first mark on the pristine sheet of paper. In this case, the dot is a beginning. But see what just happened there? The dot, an essential component in the structure of the sentence, closed it, making it a symbol of ending. Therefore, the dot is both an origination and a conclusion, encompassing all the possibilities of the universe within it, a seed full of potential and a symbol of the Supreme Being. The dot is the point of creation, for example the place where the arms of the cross intersect.

The dot is also called the bindhu, which means "drop." The bindhu is a symbol of the Absolute, marked on the forehead at the position of the third eye in the place believed to be the seat of the soul.

The presence of dots within a symbol can signify the presence of something else. A dot in the center of the Star of David marks the quintessence, or Fifth Element. It also acts as reminder of the concept of space. The decorated dots that surround the doorways of Eastern temples are not merely ornamental devices but have significance relevant to the worshippers. Dots frequently appear in this way, acting as a sort of shorthand for the tenets of a faith. In the Jain symbol, for example, the dots stand for the Three Jewels of Jainism. The dots in each half of the yin-yang symbol unify the two halves: one dot is "yin," the other "yang." Together they demonstrate the interdependence of opposing forces.

CIRCLE

The next logical magical symbol is the circle. Effectively an expansion of the dot, the circle represents the spirit and the cosmos. Further, the circle itself is constructed from "some thing" (the unbroken line) and "no thing" (the space inside and outside this line). Therefore, the circle unifies spirit and matter. The structure itself has great strength—think of the cylindrical shape of a lighthouse, built that way in order to withstand the fiercest attack by a stormy sea.

The physical and spiritual strength of this symbol are there because the perfect circle has no beginning and no end; it is unassailable. This power is the reason why the circle is used in magical practices such as spell-casting. The magic circle creates a fortress of psychic protection, a physical and spiritual safe haven where unwanted or uninvited entities cannot enter.

Hermes Trismegistus said of the circle:

God is a circle whose center is everywhere and circumference is nowhere.

Where would ancient man have seen the most important circles? Obviously, in the Sun and the Moon. As the Sun, the circle is masculine, but when it is the Moon, it is feminine. Because the passage of time is marked by the journey of the Sun, Moon and stars in orbit around our Earth, the circle is a symbol of the passage of time. In this form, it commonly appears as the wheel.

Because the circle has no divisions and no sides, it is also a symbol of equality. King Arthur's Round Table was the perfect piece of furniture for the fellowship of knights who were each as important as the others. Similarly, the Dalai Lama has a "circular" council.

ARC

Perhaps the most prominent arc of the natural world appears in the elusive form of the rainbow, which primitive man saw as a bridge between the heavens and the Earth.

As a part of a circle, the arc symbolizes potential spirit. The position of the arc is important. Upright, shaped like a cup or chalice, it implies the feminine principle, something that can contain the spirit. If the arc is inverted, then the opposite is true and it becomes a triumphal, victorious, masculine symbol. As such, the arc can take the form of an archway. The vaulted or arched shape of many holy buildings, from a great variety of different faiths, represents the vault of the heavens. The arc shape often appears in planetary symbols.

VERTICAL LINE

Man, alone in the animal kingdom, stands upright, so the vertical line represents the physical symbol of the number one, man striving toward spirit. This simple line is the basic shape of the World Tree or Axis Mundi that connects the heavens, the Earth and the lower regions. It is not only a basic phallic symbol but also signifies the soul that strives for union with the divine.

The upright line tells us where we are at a precise moment; think of the big hand of the clock, vertically oriented at 12 o'clock.

HORIZONTAL LINE

The opposite of the vertical line, the horizontal line represents matter, and the forward and backward movement of time. This line also signifies the skyline or horizon and man's place on Earth.

CROSS

Here, the vertical and horizontal lines come together to create a new symbol—the cross. There are of course countless different types of crosses, a few of which are covered in this book. Despite any embellishments or devices, however, the basic meaning of the cross stays the same.

The earliest example of the cross comes from Crete and dates back to the fifteenth century BC, although the sign is much older than this,

ancient beyond proper reckoning. It is an incredibly versatile and useful sign with many interpretations. As the convergence of the vertical and horizontal lines, it symbolizes the union of the material and the spiritual (think of the sign of the cross given by Catholic priests). As a geometric tool, it has no equal; if you put the cross inside the circle, then you are able to divide the circle equally. Similarly, the cross is said to "give birth to" the square.

Because of its four cardinal points, the cross represents the elements and the directions.

In the West the cross equates with the number 4, but in China, it is associated with the number 5 since the "dot" in the middle of the cross, where the two arms intersect, is also included.

The cross is sometimes disguised as another symbol, such as a four-petaled flower. All over the world, the cross is a symbol of protection.

SQUARE

Said to be the first shape invented by man, the square represents the created universe as opposed to the spiritual dimensions depicted by the circle.

The square represents the Earth and the four elements. Plato described the square, like the circle, as being "absolutely beautiful in itself." Like the cross, the square is associated with the number 4. A square has four corners; to speak of the "four corners of the Earth" is something of an anomaly since the Earth is round, without corners. All the symbolism of the number 4 is encompassed within the square, and it is interesting to note that, just as the square represents the created universe, in the Hebrew faith the holy name of the Creator is comprised of four letters.

The square gives man a safe, static reference point, and a stable, unmoving shape as opposed to the continual motion of the circle.

Temples and holy buildings are often built in the form of a square, solidly designed to align with the four points of the compass. The Ka'aba at Mecca is a fine example, as is the base of the Buddhist Stupa. Altars, too, are square. Square shapes define limits and create boundaries; to speak of someone as being "square" means that they are fixed and unchangeable.

LOZENGE

A diamond shape often with rounded rather than pointed ends, the lozenge is often overlooked, but is actually a representation of the female genitalia. As such, its most popular appearance is probably as the vesica piscis, the sacred doorway through which spirit enters the world of matter. In heraldry, for example, the lozenge is used in place of the masculine shield, to denote a coat of arms belonging to a woman or a noncombative male, such as a member of the clergy.

TRIANGLE

The triangle shares all the symbolic significance of the number 3, as a shape, and therefore represents the many things that come in groups of three, from the Holy Trinity to the triple aspect of the goddess. Triangles appear in lots of different signs and symbols. In ancient times, the triangle was considered synonymous with light, and the meanings of the triangle vary according to which way up it is. When it sits firmly on its base, then it is a masculine, virile symbol, representing fire. The other way up it becomes the water element, a chalice shape, emblematic of the feminine powers. Balanced on its point in this way the triangle also represents the yoni, further underpinning the goddess aspect. The equilateral triangle is a harmonious form, used to indicate the higher powers, providing a framework, for example, for the all-seeing eye of God.

As a symbol of strength, the triangle reinforces the corners of the square, both physically and metaphysically. The solid shape of the triangle also makes its appearance in yogic positions, for example in the Trikona Asana or Triangle Posture.

DIAGONAL

The square can be divided into two diagonal triangles. Because the length of these shapes has no simple relationship to its sides, the Greeks concluded that the diagonal must be a symbol of the irrational. Therefore, the diagonal, or oblique, has come to be associated with the incomprehensible, occult world. In J. K. Rowling's Harry Potter books, Diagon Alley is the hidden part of London that is a magical high street full of occult devices.

ZIGZAG

However it is interpreted, the jagged shape of the zigzag carries with it the idea of heat, energy, vitality, and movement, the archetypal sign for lightning or electricity. The double zigzag that makes the astrological glyph for Aquarius could be water or it could be the life-force itself. The serpent that spirals up the Caduceus is a softened zigzag shape. There is an inherent danger in the zigzag, and the deities that carry it in their hands do so as a sign of their own authority and power.

Part One

SIGNS AND SYMBOLS OF MAGIC AND MYSTERY

AASKOUANDY

Ironically, the first entry in this encyclopedia is a symbol that is impossible to illustrate because it takes various different forms.

An Aaskouandy charm is any object that is unusual in some way, which appears unexpectedly or is somehow out of place in its surroundings. For example, if a stone is found in the entrails of an animal that was particularly hard to hunt, then this stone is perceived to be the object that gave the animal its power, and so is eligible for Aaskouandy status.

The Iroquois believe that the Aaskouandy, a magical charm of considerable power, has a mind of its own, so much so that if it is neglected it can even turn against its owner. They also believe that the Aaskouandy has trickster tendencies and can change shape at will, so confusingly it

may metamorphose into another object altogether.

Because the Aaskouandy is an independent being, the owner is careful to stay on the right side of it, keeping it happy with gifts and feasts.

If an Aaskouandy appears in the shape of a fish or serpent, then this is particularly potent because of the inherent power of these creatures. In this case, the Aaskouandy changes its name, too, and becomes an Onniont.

ABRAXAS

Depending on your point of view, Abraxas is either an Egyptian sun god who was adopted by the early Christian Gnostics, or a demon from hell who is closely associated with Lucifer, although there is a case for the former, since he was not demoted to the ranks of a demon until the Middle Ages.

Abraxas was no ordinary god, however. As ruler of the First Heaven he had dominion over the cycles of birth, death, and resurrection.

Whatever the case, the symbol for Abraxas is a very unusual one. He has the head of a chicken, the torso of a man, and two serpents for legs. He holds a shield in one hand and a flail-like instrument in the other. The image of Abraxas was carved onto stones (called Abraxas Stones) and the stone used as a magical amulet. Occasionally Abraxas will appear driving a chariot drawn by four horses; these horses represent the elements.

This Abraxas symbol was adopted by the Knights Templar, who used it on their seals. No one knows precisely why this symbol was of particular significance, but a hidden secret within the name "Abraxas" may provide a clue.

In Greek, the seven letters are the initials of the first seven planets in the solar system.

Further, if we apply numerology to the name then it adds up to 365, not only the number of days in a year but also the number of the spirits that those same early Gnostics believed were emanations from God.

Added to the mix is the speculation that the supreme magical word, "Abracadabra," may derive from the name Abraxas, which means "harm me not."

ADRINKA SYMBOLS

Originating in Ghana, Adrinka symbols are now related, in general, to the Ashanti people. There are hundreds of these signs, which were originally printed on the cloth that was used in sacred ceremonies and rituals, funerals in particular. "Adrinka" means "goodbye."

The patterns are created using a block printing method. The symbols are cut into a calabash gourd, and then stamped onto the cloth in ink or paint.

The language of Adrinka is rich and varied, embracing philosophical concepts and sociological ideas as well as straightforward words. The symbols take their influence from plants, animals, the landscape, and the natural world, as well as man-made objects. There is a vast Adrinka vocabulary, with complex meanings attached to what might appear, at first glance, to be simple little doodles.

AESCLEPIUS WAND

Often confused with the Caduceus, the Wand or Rod of Aesclepius is the true symbol of the medical profession. The symbol belongs to the Greek god of healing whose name it bears. Although the origins of many symbols are indeterminate, there is a theory that the Aesclepius Wand came about due to the method of removal of a certain parasite that was drawn gradually from the body by winding it around a stick. However, the serpent is a powerful symbol of healing, despite its toxic nature. In general, the symbol of the serpent rising up toward the top of a pole or tree is representative of matter transforming into spirit and of enlightenment.

AGNUS DEI

Agnus Dei translates as the "Lamb of God," and is also known as the Paschal Lamb. It is symbolized pictorially as a lamb with a halo, proudly trotting along, carrying a banner and a cross.

Lambs were commonly sacrificed during the time of the Passover, the blood sprinkled in the doorway or rubbed onto the lintel, so the connection was made because of the sacrifice of Christ.

Part of the Catholic mass includes the plea, repeated three times:

Lamb of God, who takes away the sins of the world, have mercy on us.

AKHET

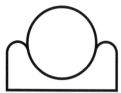

In Egyptian, Akhet means "dawn." This symbol—often made into an amulet by the ancient Egyptians—symbolized the new sun rising over the sacred mountain.

The symbol sometimes features the double-headed lion, or Aker, that guards it, and is also related to the glyph used to denote the astrological sign of Libra.

AKWABA

This is an African fertility symbol belonging to the Ashanti tribe. The Akwaba is a doll, usually carved of wood, which commands the same attention as a real infant. It is dressed, washed, and even "fed" until the human child is actually born, an example of sympathetic magic believed to ensure the arrival of the true baby.

ALCHEMY

Alchemy is an ancient art, at the heart of which lies the manufacture of a mysterious substance called the Philosopher's Stone, the highly desirable and legendary object that is said to transform base metals—such as lead—into gold.

However, the gold in this instance symbolizes not just the valuable metal, but enlightenment and eternal life, and alchemists are concerned with their own spiritual and personal development as well as the pursuit of the seemingly unattainable goal. The Chinese differentiate these different kinds of alchemy as nei-tan (the alchemy of spiritual transformation) and wai-tan (the straightforward "lead-into-gold" type).

The motto of the alchemists is *Solve et Coagula*, meaning "Solution and Coagulation."

The work of the early alchemists was necessarily a secretive and clandestine matter, and its secrets are still held within a rich encrustation of symbols, pictures, oblique references, double meanings, and riddles. Alchemical symbolism features animals, birds, colors, and parables as well as archetypal symbols such as the Cosmic Egg.

The key tenets of alchemy are encompassed in something called the Smaragdina Tablet, or the Emerald Tablet, which is said to have been found by Alexander the Great in the tomb of Hermes Trismegistus (Hermes the Thrice Great) who is the founder of all things alchemical. The alchemical tradition existed in ancient Egypt, China, and India, but its most recent incarnation was in medieval Europe.

Those who dabbled in alchemy include the famous and the infamous, such as John Dee (astrologer to Queen Elizabeth I), Paracelsus, Albertus Magnus, Christian Rosenkreuz, Nicholas Flamel, and Isaac Newton. Some of the chemical treatises are befuddling to even the most learned of scholars, but the very word "alchemy" is almost in itself a symbol, conjuring up images that are magical, mystical, and marvelous.

ALCHEMICAL SYMBOLS

Although some of the alchemical symbols occasionally varied a little between practitioners, the following lists show the most commonly used interpretations. This list is by no means comprehensive but gives a good cross-section of the "feel" of these mysterious signs. It is interesting to see how many of these alchemical symbols have survived to the present day, and how the meanings of the simpler symbols are so universal that they extend well beyond the reaches of this one system.

The four basic elements

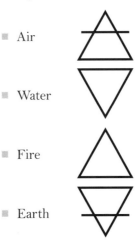

- Air
- Water
- Fire
- Earth

The four seasons

- Spring
- Summer

- Fall

- Winter

The seven planetary metals

- Sun
  gold

- Moon
  silver

- Mercury
  quicksilver

- Venus
  copper

- Mars
  iron

- Jupiter
  tin

- Saturn
  lead

The alchemical spirits

- The World Spirit

- The Spirit of Silver

- The Spirit of Mercury

- The Spirit of Copper

- The Spirit of Tin

ALL SEEING EYE

Probably the best-known use of the All Seeing Eye symbol is as a part of the design of the Great Seal of the United States of America, which appears on the U.S. dollar bill. Set within a triangle, a single eye is surrounded by rays of light; on the seal, the whole rests on top of an unfinished pyramid.

The Encyclopedia of Secret Signs and Symbols

There is something quite sinister about this disembodied, ever-watchful eye, although its symbolic meaning is simple; it represents God watching over humankind, and is also known as the Eye of Providence.

The eye itself is a powerful and popular symbol, and the All Seeing Eye has its roots in the Egyptian Eye of Horus. The addition of the triangle represents all the different aspects of the shape, including the Christian trinity of the Father, Son, and Holy Ghost.

The fact that the Great Seal was a symbol that belonged to Freemasonry and alchemy prior to its adoption as part of the Great Seal of the United States has given rise to many conspiracy theories. That the All Seeing Eye is also the symbol of the Illuminati, a secretive organization within the Catholic Church, has further bolstered these theories.

In Freemasonry, God is known as the Architect of the Universe. The first reference to the All Seeing Eye as a Masonic symbol appeared in 1797, although the Great Seal was designed in 1776 and first used in 1782. It is whispered that Masonic influences must have been at work when the seal was designed; no one will ever know for sure, although those magical symbols that encrust the seal must have been put there for a reason. What is certain is that when the Eye was adopted as part of the design of the dollar in 1935, it was as a direct result of the influence of the president, Franklin Roosevelt, who had no reason to conceal his Masonic affiliations.

ALMADEL

This is a particular kind of magical amulet, made of wax so that the secret names of demons can be written or engraved upon it. The whole is then melted so that its creator need never reveal the secret. The color of the almadel should correspond to its magical intention.

ALTAR

The root of the word "altar" means "high" or "high place," and therefore the altar is symbolic of the Holy Mountain, given that it is raised above its immediate surroundings and is used as a focus for holy rites and sacred practices. Altars, as such, exist in all religions and cultures, the symbolic meaning remaining unchanged across diverse belief systems. Altars certainly provide the main focus within churches, but they are not confined to large public buildings; many faiths have a small domestic altar in the home.

AMULET

Although it is worn on the body as a piece of jewelry, the amulet is different from "normal" jewelry in that it holds a magical significance that is peculiar to its owner or wearer. Generally, the powers of the amulet fall into two specific categories, either to bring luck or to avert evil; either of these qualities arguably reflect a positive or negative attitude on the part of the owner. The talisman is effectively the same thing as an amulet although its name derives from an Arabic word meaning "magic picture." Therefore a charm made specifically and inscribed with the names of the spirits, the Seal of Solomon, and other mystical symbols is more likely to be referred to as a talisman.

Significant symbols for use as amulets include birthstones (or other gems according to their magical powers), astrological signs, specific symbols such as the Hand of Fatima or the cornus, and symbols specific to the religious and spiritual beliefs of the wearer, such as the cross, the star, words, names, and numbers.

Incidentally, both amulets and talismans are referred to as "charms"; the origin of this word has the same root as the Latin word for "song," indicating the link between a magical sound and a magical intention.

ANKH

Essentially the tau cross surmounted by a loop or circle, the ankh is a prominent feature of ancient Egyptian reliefs, artworks, and funerary paraphernalia. Like the tau, the ankh is a letter; specifically, it is a hieroglyph meaning "life."

The volume of meaning that can be squeezed from such a simple symbol is awe-inspiring. The ankh represents the male and female genitalia, the sun coming over the horizon, and the union of heaven and earth. This association with the sun means that the ankh is traditionally drawn in gold—the color of the sun—and never in silver, which relates to the moon.

Putting aside the complexities of these separate elements, though, what does the ankh look like? Its resemblance to a key gives a clue to another meaning of this magical symbol. The Egyptians believed that the afterlife was as meaningful as the present one, and the ankh provided the key to the gates of death and what lay beyond.

Powerful symbols frequently stray across into other cultures despite their origins, and the ankh is no exception. Because it symbolizes immortality and the universe, it was initially borrowed by the fourth-century Coptic Christians who used it as a symbol to reinforce Christ's message that there is life after death. The ankh is used by the Rosicrucians too. Even though its actual invention is shrouded in thousands of years of mystery, the ankh symbol can be bought in any high street jewelry store anywhere in the world. When Elvis Presley was criticized for wearing the "pagan" ankh among his many other crosses, he commented, "I don't want to miss out on heaven because of a technicality."

ANTIMONY

See Gray Wolf.

APHRODISIACS

The Pomegranate Badge of Katherine of Aragon

The Greek goddess of love, Aphrodite, lends her name to an extensive list of foods and other weird and wonderful items that are supposed to increase the libido and enhance the chances of seduction and therefore fecundity. The issue of fertility has always been an overriding concern for humankind, and any substance that either enhances sexual prowess or increases the chance of conception has always been highly sought after.

Ancient people had a limited seasonal diet, and a bad hunt or the failure of a crop could literally be a life-or-death matter. Getting enough food to eat was an overriding concern. Chances of fertility are restricted if nourishment is poor, and so certain foods were given magical powers in the hopes that they might increase both male and female potency despite the limited diet. There is a marked differentiation between the foods that increase fertility versus the ones that enhance sex drive, and given that early people did not know about the chemical constituents of food, many aphrodisiacs were chosen as such primarily because of their symbolic significance. The Doctrine of Signatures—the notion that a plant or a feature of an animal that is similar in appearance or quality to a body part could be beneficial to the organ it resembles—had an important part to play in deciding which foods had aphrodisiac qualities. Rhinoceros horn, for example, still carries a frisson as a stimulant to sexual appetites, as does Spanish fly. Both these ingredients, sort of mystical precursors to Viagra, were ingested by men in eager anticipation of increased virility.

Pliny the Elder and Dioscordes documented many of these aphrodisiacs as far back as the first century, and it is likely that they would have been regarded as such for some time prior to this.

The behavior and lifestyle of certain animals made them fertility symbols, too. For example, the sparrow, a prolific breeder, was sacred to Aphrodite and its blood was a popular ingredient in love potions. Steak was thought to contain all the virility of the animal it came from, the bloodier the better. Ground rhinoceros horn is symbolic of the libido but the power of the rhino is also perceived as the ultimate in male sexual energy.

This ancient, visceral belief in the power of appearances has meant that many of the original foods that were considered to have aphrodisiac powers by ancient people still carry the same meanings today, despite their actual chemical constituents. It is true to say that certain foods actually do have aphrodisiac powers purely because of these old beliefs, and generally owe more to folklore and symbolism than to fact; however, a symbol is a potent force and often the association alone is enough to bring about the desired effect. For example, a dinner date where oysters and strawberries are on the menu will leave no doubt about the intended conclusion to the evening.

To our ancestors, any kind of food that resembled the penis, the vagina, or constituent parts thereof, carried powerful suggestive meanings, although latterly our ability to analyze certain minerals and trace elements has proven that some supposedly aphrodisiac foods may actually deserve their reputation. For example, the fifty oysters that Casanova reputedly managed to swallow every day for breakfast not only resemble the female sexual parts in scent, texture, and form, but it has also been discovered that their high zinc content may indeed help enhance the libido; a large proportion of zinc is spent when men ejaculate.

For ancient people, it was not always necessary for the foods to be eaten for them to have the desired effect. Some of the weird and wonderful things considered to have aphrodisiac qualities were toxic, but could work their magic simply by close proximity. The berries of mistletoe, for example, were a reminder of the semen of the gods and the little crosses on the undersides were kisses, but it would be unwise to eat them.

Seeds, nuts, bulbs, and eggs, because they are full of potential new life, were considered as aids to fertility; snails, too, were considered to enhance sexual appetites because of the viscous fluid of the trails they leave behind, although slugs are not considered to have any aphrodisiac qualities whatsoever.

Here is a brief list of some of the foods that have been considered, at some time or other, to have aphrodisiac qualities.

NUTS, SEEDS, AND BULBS

Aniseed

Falls into the category of seeds. Also aids digestion and sweetens the breath, which could explain why the Romans considered it a useful ingredient for seduction.

Star anise

Because of its shape, the star anise was sacred to the goddess and therefore a potent fertility symbol.

FRUITS

In general, all seed-bearing fruits are aphrodisiacs. Their numerous seeds, their texture, scent, and color make them a naturally sexy foodstuff.

Apple

Infamous as the fruit that Eve gave to Adam, a symbol of sexual awakening.

Cherry

Sensuously red and juicy, and containing a potent symbol of new life inside the stone. "Popping the cherry" is a slang term for losing one's virginity.

Raspberries and strawberries

Libido enhancing because of their color, their many tiny seeds, and their resemblance to nipples.

Tomato

The tomato is also called the "love apple" and is regarded as an aphrodisiac, because of the prolific number of seeds contained within it. However, the name itself is the result of an accidental misinterpretation. Because they were originally a yellow color they were called "pomo d'or" in Italy, the apple of gold. It was also called the "pomo d'Moro"—the apple of the Moors, referring to its Spanish origins. From here, it was just a slip of the tongue to the French, "pomme d'amour," or love apple.

MALE GENITALIA

Many of these are self-explanatory, all considered powerful simply because of their shape. Asparagus, carrots, and cucumber are just a few of the "phallic vegetables."

Avocado

The Mexicans called the avocado tree the "testicle tree," since the fruit dangles down in pairs. The sensual texture of avocado adds to its reputation.

Banana

The banana flower resembles the phallus. Islamic tales say that Adam and Eve covered their sexual parts with banana leaves rather than the more common fig leaves.

Cloves

Because they resemble little phalluses, cloves were considered to enhance male potency. The clove tree was planted to signify the birth of a baby boy in certain parts of Indonesia, the health of the tree reflecting the health of the child as it grew up.

FEMALE GENITALIA

Almond

As well as being the same shape as the vesica piscis, the sacred doorway through which matter emerges into spirit, the almond is a nut and therefore carries the potential for new life.

Fig

The plethora of tiny seeds inside the fig is symbolic of fertility, and the moist plumpness of the fruit has a very sensual, feminine element to it.

Oyster

The oyster's resemblance in form, scent, and texture to the female genitalia is renowned. Oysters have had a long history as an aphrodisiac and their reputation is well known. The pearl that is sometimes found inside the oyster was said to increase the powers of arousal, because it resembles the clitoris.

Other shellfish, such as mussels, fall into this same category.

SPICES AND HERBS

Anything sharp tasting or pungent is believed to stimulate the senses, so spices are often used as libido-enhancing ingredients.

Asafetida

This is the ground root of a fennel-like plant. It has a powerful odor, and despite its folk name, devil's dung, it is used as a sexual stimulant in Ayurvedic medicine.

Cinnamon

The glorious scent of cinnamon was reputedly used as oil by the Queen of Sheba to help her capture the attention of King Solomon.

Coriander

Also comes under the category of seeds. Reputed to stimulate appetites of all kinds.

Fennel

The Egyptians who used this as a sexual stimulant cannot have known that it contains plant estrogens that can help balance female hormones. These estrogens also enhance the breasts.

Ginger and ginseng

Considered to have aphrodisiac powers because of their sharp sensual taste, and because their roots resemble the human form.

Mint

A Greek legend says that Menthe, a beautiful nymph, was transformed into the herb because Persephone was jealous of the beautiful scent that captivated her husband, Pluto.

HONEY

The sweetness of honey made it a rarity for ancient people. It is likely to have given humankind its first instance of alcohol in the form of mead, and its intoxicating effect has distinct aphrodisiac qualities. Bees are themselves symbols of fertility, and honey gives its name to the honeymoon period spent by newlyweds immediately after their marriage.

CHOCOLATE

The melting point of chocolate is the same as that of blood temperature, and so its mouthfeel alone is a sensual experience. Added to this, chocolate contains mood-lifting substances, including phenylethylamine which, when released into the bloodstream, induce feelings of euphoria. Still arguably the most popular food given as a gesture of love. When the sixteenth-century Spanish conquis-tador Hernán Cortés heard about its reputation as an aphrodisiac, he planted two thousand trees.

APOTROPE

This is a word of Greek origin meaning to "turn away," and refers to a specific kind of amulet designed to ward off evil of some kind. The amulet therefore features a protective symbol, such as an eye (which wards off the evil eye, by staring right back at it), or the Hand of Fatima.

ARC

See First signs: Arc.

ARK

There are two famous arks, Noah's Ark and the Ark of the Covenant. Both held extremely valuable objects, and so the ark symbolizes a treasure chest, a secure repository for items of secret or sacred significance. The word comes from the Latin, *arca*. The Greeks described the same item as a chest.

There are also two Hebrew definitions for the ark. One explains it as a wooden chest, the other as a flat-roofed building twice as long as it was high and wide. The ark could also float, and the same word is used to describe the casket that the baby Moses was found in, floating in the reeds.

In the Bible, the ark that God commands Noah to build has a very specific set of instructions as to size, measurements, and materials used. The momentous treasure contained in this "box" was a breeding pair of every animal in the world, a genetic repository to safeguard the future of all creatures on earth after the Deluge had washed everything else away. The ark was God's promise of protection to his chosen people. However, as Barbara G. Walker points out in her *Woman's Dictionary of Symbols and Sacred Objects*, the scale of the ark must have been mind-boggling if its purpose as outlined in the Bible were to be taken literally, since it would have had to hold

7,000 species of worms, 80,000 species of molluscs, 30,000 species of crustaceans, 50,000 species of arachnids, 900,000 species of insects, 2,500 species of amphibians, 6,000 species of reptiles, 8,600 species of birds, and 3,500 species of mammals, as well as food for one and all.

The Ark of the Covenant, similarly, had to be made to strictly detailed plans, as was the building that should house it. Shittim wood—the timber from the incorruptible acacia tree—was specified for the basic construction. The Book of Exodus also describes the other materials that had to be used; gold and silver, brass, blue, red, and purple silk, fine linen, goats' hair, spices, various precious gems, red rams' skins, and "the skins of badgers."

Inside the ark were stored the two Books of the Law, Aaron's Rod, and a pot of the manna that the children of Israel lived on during their time in the wilderness.

There is speculation about what actually happened to the ark when Nebuchadnezzar destroyed the Temple of David in the sixth century BC. However, Jewish faith decrees that the ark will be restored to its rightful place with the coming of the Messiah.

ARROW

Symbol of flight, penetration, and direction. As a weapon, the arrow is a symbol of the power of the person who carries it, along with the bow. As a sacred symbol, it is the attribute of the goddess of the hunt, Artemis/Diana, as well as of Eros, who uses his arrows to pierce the people's hearts with love. Here, the arrow also serves as a phallic symbol and an emblem of masculine power. The symbol of the heart pierced with an arrow, popular on Valentine's Day cards, is a covert symbol of sexual union.

The arrow as a symbol of direction works on a physical level and a metaphorical level. The arrow that shoots high up into the sky is an emblem of the link between earth and heaven, a symbol of an idea, or of a message being carried directly to the gods.

The arrow is used, too, as an analogy for swiftness and sureness, since the arrow travels in the direction in which it is shot. The astrological sign of Sagittarius, the hybrid creature that is always depicted in the process of shooting an arrow from his bow, has a Latin root, *sagitta*; this means "arrow" and is derived from a verb, *sagire*, that means "to perceive keenly or quickly." Therefore, the arrow is symbolic of quick-wittedness and intuition.

Arrows were used by the ancient Arabians, Chaldeans, Greeks, and Tibetans in a form of divination called belomancy. This was practiced by shooting arrows in the air and reading a meaning from the direction of the arrows or their positions in relation to each other. For example, crossed or touching arrows meant "no." Later, the arrows had words written on them to make any answers even more definitive.

ASHTAMANGALA

In Sanskrit, *ashta* means "eight" and *mangala* "auspicious," and the word refers to the eight auspicious symbols of Himalayan Buddhism, although the relevance of eight sacred objects is important in the Hindu faith, too, and also in China. The Ashtamangala of the Tibetan system are, in no particular order, the Vase of Treasure, the Two Golden Fish, the Dharma Wheel, the Conch Shell, the Endless Knot, the Victory Banner, the Lotus

Flower, and the Parasol. These symbols are used both in the home and in public areas and the hidden meanings of the objects are far more significant than their surface value.

THE PARASOL

Represents the sky, and is not only a symbol of protection but a sign of expansion and learning.

THE TWO GOLDEN FISH

These are also a symbol of the eyes of the Buddha, and act as a reminder to be fearless no matter what fate brings.

THE TREASURE VASE

Any representation of a vessel is as important for the space it contains as well as for any material objects it might be able to hold.

The spiritual treasures within this vase include good health and a long life, good luck, wisdom, and prosperity.

THE LOTUS FLOWER

Symbolizes purity of mind, body, action, and speech. The lotus flower rises above the metaphorical "muddy water" of attachment and desire.

THE CONCH SHELL

Because this shell can be used as a sounding horn, it acts as a reminder that followers need to be open to the sound of the Buddha's teachings and that they need to stay awake (in a metaphorical sense), remaining aware and alert.

THE ENDLESS KNOT

Symbolizes compassion and wisdom combined, and the need to unite spiritual and material matters.

THE VICTORY BANNER

Represents the triumph of a positive mind over seemingly negative obstacles.

THE DHARMA WHEEL

Represents the teachings of the Buddha. It is also a mandala or sun symbol.

ASSON

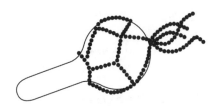

For practitioners of Voudon, the asson is a sacred rattle, made from a large dried-out gourd with seeds inside, and covered with beads and snake bones. It is used in important rites and ceremonies and is itself a symbol of the authority of the Houngan, the Voudon priest who is considered the Chief of the Spirits. The asson is the equivalent of the scepter. It is a larger object than the musical instrument called the cha cha, although they do have a similar appearance.

ASTRUM ARGENTUM SEAL

This is the seal that was designed by Aleister Crowley as the emblem of his Esoterical Magickal Order, the Astrum Argentum, or "Silver Star." The seal uses a seven-pointed star as the basis of its design. *See also* Cancellarius seal.

Athame

This is the ceremonial knife used by a witch. It generally has a black handle, and is used to mark a magical circle, for example, or to direct energy, but is never used to cut anything. For physical cutting, a boline is used. The pointed shape of the blade of the athame suggests the element of fire, which it also symbolizes. The athame is balanced by the chalice, which represents water.

Athanor

A key symbol of alchemy, the Athanor is the furnace of the alchemists. However, as with everything else in alchemy, the Athanor is no simple piece of laboratory equipment. Regarded as the vessel in which transmutation takes place, the Athanor exists on a metaphysical

level, too, as the Orphic Egg or as a place of ultimate creation, a kind of universal womb.

Atheist symbol

Based on the atomic swirl, this is the symbol of the American Atheist Association, although it is used by other such organizations too. It represents the idea that science is the only thing that can show the way forward to a better life for everyone. The broken loop at the bottom of the symbol represents the idea that there are questions yet to be asked and yet to be answered.

Atlantis cross

This symbol, comprised of a cross intersected by three circles, is a sign of recognition among groups who claim an Atlantean descent; that is to say, people who believe that they are descended, literally or spiritually, from inhabitants of the

Each ray carries various meanings, which are equally significant and come in sets of three. They stand for past, present, and future; love, knowledge, and truth; male and female energy and the balance between the two; or the three pillars of wisdom. Another interpretation of the symbol is of the three fundamental letters of the name of God, I, O, and U, which, when pronounced contribute to the actual word "Awen," which can be intoned in much the same way as the Aum of Eastern tradition, used as a meditative focus.

lost island of Atlantis. The crossed circle that forms a main feature of this symbol represents the four elements and the four directions.

The Order of Bards, Ovates, and Druids places the three lines and the three dots within three concentric rings, further amplifying the meaning of the symbol as well as placing it within protective, magical circles.

AWEN

AXIS MUNDI

The Awen is related to many new Druid movements. The actual word, which is Welsh, means "inspiration" or "essence." Related to the Breton symbol called the Triban and with a nod to the Trishul, the trident held by the Hindu deity, Shiva, the Awen is composed of three convergent rays, like paths, leading to a high point, a dot (or three dots) similar to the bindhu.

Quite literally, the Axis Mundi translates as the "World Axis," the axis around which the world revolves and which links the heavens to the earth and the dominions below. It is a universal concept, often defined symbolically as a tree or standing stone, a mountain, the omphalos, the lingam, the Vajra, and the Pole Star. The solstices represent the World Axis in terms of time.

Ba

For the ancient Egyptians, the Ba was the symbolic representation of the soul. It takes the form of a small bird with the head of a human being. The Ba could fly between its owner and the gods for as long as the body was intact. The Ba is twinned with the Ka. If the Ba represented the soul, then the Ka was the "life-force," the spark of life that animated the body and whose departure resulted in death. The Ka was sustained with offerings of food and drink, although it was the "ka" or spirit of the food and drink that was consumed. In the afterlife, the Ba and the Ka would be reunited to form one single entity.

* * *

Baphomet

The Baphomet we recognize today is a winged goat with a masculine torso and breasts; he has a blazing torch between his horns, and cloven feet. Adding to the confusion, one arm is male and the other is female, and all in all this has become a real bogeyman of a symbol, inspiring fright and terror.

The image made its first appearance relatively recently, in Eliphas Levi's *Dogma and Rituals of High Magic* (1854). Although Levi intended the creature (also called the Goat of Mendes) to be an idealized symbolic form, an amalgam of images from all disciplines including the Kabbalah, he actually created something that looks far more terrifying than he may have originally intended. The picture influenced illustrations of the devil, not only in tarot card illustrations but also among latter-day rock bands and, as already mentioned, among Satanists.

The Encyclopedia of Secret Signs and Symbols

Baphomet himself was first described at the trials of the Knights Templar, centuries before Levi's interpretation. When the order began in the twelfth century, it was designed to protect pilgrims traveling to Jerusalem. Because the knights were exempt from taxation, they amassed a huge amount of wealth and, consequently, power. When they became a threat to the establishment, they were persecuted, and part of this persecution included accusations of heresy including the worship of a peculiar-looking goat-headed creature.

BECKONING CAT

A friendly little statuette with a warm welcome found all over Japan and China. What the cat is doing with his paws carries a secret message.

The cute little Maneki Neko or beckoning cat is ubiquitous in Japan and China where he appears in both homes and offices. This friendly-looking cat can also be seen in Asian restaurants all over the world and is for many people the ultimate symbol of prosperity and good luck.

The Maneki Neko comes in different colors, each of which signifies a different meaning. For example, a red cat will protect from illness, and a black one will ward off evil.

The position of the paws also carries a message. With the right paw raised the cat will bring money and happiness to home and workplace. A cat raising its left paw (like the one illustrated here) will attract new customers for a business. And a cat with both paws raised hits the jackpot; both home and business will be happy and profitable, attracting good luck, friends, prosperity, and new clients.

This cat is also the symbol of the small Buddhist temple in Tokyo, where the original incident that shot the cat to fame is said to have happened. Originally the temple was a lowly place, whose impoverished priest would regularly share what little food he had with his pet cat. One day some Samurai were passing and noticed this cat, who had one paw raised as though to say hello. The warriors stopped, intrigued by the beckoning cat, and went into the temple just as a horrendous rainstorm started. They believed that paying attention to the cat's invitation had prevented them being struck by lightning. Thereafter, the fortunes of the priest, the temple, and of course the cat, started to change for the better.

BELL

There is a mysticism surrounding the bell that far transcends its mundane use as a way of getting attention in the schoolroom, for example. The sound of the bell is universally accepted as a way of communicating with the spirits, or as a herald for the arrival of a supernatural, holy power.

The analogy of the bell occurs in language, too, used to symbolize something of sacred origin. In Islam, the "reverberation of the bell" is used to describe the sound of the revelations of the Qu'ran, and in Buddhism, the "sound of the golden bell" is an analogy for heavenly voices. The sound of a bell is a reminder that, like the sound, the world may be experienced, but not possessed.

Pagoda roofs sometimes have hundreds of tiny bells hanging from them, symbolizing, in sound, the concepts of the Buddhist laws as well as frightening away any malicious entities. For the same reason, the church bells of Christian churches, at one time, were pealed not only during processions or as a notice of a ceremony or service, but also during thunderstorms to chase away demons.

The bell is also a sacred object. In the form of the Buddhist Drilbu, or the Hindu Ghanta, it symbolizes the illusory world, because of the fleetingly resonant nature of its sound. It is the feminine principle paired up with the masculine vajra.

The use of these bells largely influenced their European symbolism and use. The sweet reverberation of a bell, rung three times in the silence of a large stone church or cathedral, has a quality of calming the atmosphere, attracting the attention of the worshippers, welcoming in the spirits, and setting the scene for the ritual that follows.

The power of the bell as a way of spiritual communication is carried one step further in the magical bell made of an amalgam of the seven sacred metals that are ruled by the planets. This bell, engraved with the Tetragrammaton and the planetary seals from alchemy, allegedly has the power to summon the spirits of the dead. However, this spell calls for the bell to be put into a grave for seven days and seven nights before it will work properly.

Bell, book, and candle

Singly, these items all have mystical significance. When grouped together, they have a certain frisson, somehow seeming to resonate with dark forces, pagan ideals, and witch-craft in particular. However, this sinister grouping actually comes from the rites of excommunication or anathema in the Roman Catholic Church. Effectively a powerful curse, this ritual is taken very seriously, reserved only for those whose transgressions against the Church are deemed unforgivable.

After the officiating cleric has verbally declared the excommuni-cation, he declares it symbolically with three actions; he shuts the Bible, sounds the bell, and then snuffs out the candle.

These actions are clear. Closing the Bible tells the excommunicant that he is no longer privy to the Word of God. Ringing the bell is symbolic of mourning for the "departed," the excommunicant, who is now effectively spiritually dead to the Church. Snuffing the candle is a universal sign of the "snuffing out" of the soul, now doomed because of its banishment from the faith.

Besom

See Broomstick.

Bindhu

See First Signs: Dot.

Black Sun

The notion of the sun being black runs completely counter to what is generally accepted about it; the simplest explanation for a Black Sun is that it describes what happens at night, when the sun is casting its light on another part of the planet. However, the Black Sun more sinisterly denotes the idea of the world going wrong, destructive forces, disaster, and even death.

Whether the Nazis were aware of this aspect of the Black Sun is open to conjecture. The symbol reproduced for this entry was also called the "Sonnenrad" or Sun Wheel and was based on the design of early medieval brooches, some of which had a swastika in the center. The "rays" numbered between five and twelve, with the twelve-rayed symbol denoting the passage of the sun through the months of the year. The rays bear a great deal of resemblance to the swastika and to the lightning flash symbols used by the SS, themselves the same as a rune known as "Sig," meaning "Sun" or "Victory."

The symbol, used by wartime German occult mystics and still employed by some neo-Nazis, is based on a mosaic set into the floor of the early seventeenth-century castle of Wewelsburg in Germany. Himmler decided that the site of the castle would be the center of the proposed "New World" once victory was achieved. However, the extensive building works planned for the castle were never completed; the ambitious "New World" failed to materialize and the building work that had been started was blasted to the ground in 1945. The mosaic remains, although there is no concrete evidence as to who put it there. The mosaic is of dark green marble, set into a cream-colored marble floor.

For neo-Nazis, the symbol has proved a useful one. The single swastika is banned in Germany, and yet the Black Sun symbol hides three swastikas within it. Further significance is accorded the symbol since it contains twelve of the aforementioned Sig runes from the Futhark runic system. The circular shape of the symbol implies protection and magical powers. Secret signs, indeed.

BLACK SUN IN ALCHEMY

Alchemists and hermeticists believe that there are two suns; one of the pure "philosophical gold" that implies the highest attainment of the spirit, and the other of the baser "material gold." The Black Sun is the symbol of this material form of the sun, and symbolizes the unworked, primal matter that needs to be developed.

BLAZING STAR

See Pentagram and Freemasonry.

BOLINE

The boline is a knife in the Druid and Wiccan tradition. Its specific symbolism is held within its blade, which is shaped like the crescent moon and is silver in color. The boline usually has a white handle, also in deference to the moon.

This boline is a practical, ceremonial tool often used for cutting herbs either for magical uses or simply for cooking. In the case of the Druids, it is also used for cutting mistletoe directly from the tree.

BOOK

It might seem as though the book is such a commonplace object that it should not really have much significance as a secret symbol. However, this isn't the case. Take, for example, the High Priestess card in the tarot. The Priestess holds a book or scroll, half concealed within the folds of her robe. Here, the book symbolizes knowledge and hidden secrets, and in a wider sense the book symbolizes the very universe itself. There are also parallels with the book and the Tree of Life; like a tree, the book has "leaves" that represent individual ideas and concepts and that collectively represent the sum total of all knowledge, occult or otherwise.

If we delve into word meanings, we find more analogies between books and trees. The etymology of "book" comes from the Old English *bokiz*, or the Germanic *buche*, meaning beech. This is likely to be because runes were initially inscribed on beechwood tablets. Similarly, the word "library" originally meant the "inner bark of trees."

A book that is closed is a book that conceals its secrets; sometimes we refer to an inscrutable person as a "closed book." An open book is the opposite, ready to share its information with all and sundry.

The Book of the Dead, for the ancient Egyptians, was the series of magical charms that were interred with the dead in order that they might journey safely into the next world, and that would provide answers to the questions posed by those casting judgment on the soul. This book, effectively, symbolizes the secrets of the divine that are revealed only to those who have undergone the ultimate initiation: death. The Book of Shadows is a sort of recipe book of spells, charms, and rituals, generally belonging to the Wiccan practitioner, written by hand and often in code. This book is the personal property of its owner, and can be a series of traditional texts as well as a personal journal, containing secrets that are passed down from generation to generation.

BRIGID'S CROSS

Corn dollies are frequently constructed in the shape of Brigid's Cross, and although the symbol itself predates Christianity, it was given the name of the saint in order to ease the passage of acceptance of the new religion.

The symbol is reminiscent of the ancient sun symbol, the swastika, its four arms pointing to the cardinal points of the compass. They also represent the elements, with the point at the center indicating the fifth element or quintessence.

BROOMSTICK

The hard and polished elm wood that is traditionally believed to make the handle of the witch's broomstick would help to make it more aerodynamic.

The broomstick, at first, appears to be a simple piece of household equipment. Its form may have changed over the centuries from the traditional dried branch of the broom plant (hence the name) but its use seems to have remained unchanged. However, there's far more to it than that. The very act of sweeping was a sacred task in temples, since to be able to clean something properly the person doing the cleaning must be both clean and pure.

As well as sweeping away dust and dirt, symbolically the besom or broomstick sweeps away other things too; in parts of France, for example, it's considered bad form to sweep up after dark in case good luck is swept away with the dirt. In ancient Rome special broomsticks were used by sacred "midwives" or wise women to symbolically sweep away any negative influences from a house in which a baby had just been born. These broom-wielding midwives are the precursor to the witch that popularly flies about on a broomstick, which has to be the ultimate carbon-neutral vehicle.

The broomstick of the female witch is a very handy object to have around. It is often seen as a phallic symbol, and in pre-Christian societies marriages were often validated by the happy couple leaping together, hand in hand, over the broomstick. It is also a symbol of the liberation of the woman away from domestic drudgery; with her magical broomstick, the witch can fly anywhere, wield her power, and disclose her true identity.

Incidentally, the broomstick is sometimes called a "besom"; this word originates from the old English *besema*, meaning "woman," and has the same root as the word "bosom."

BULL ROARER

An important ritual object for Native Americans, Eskimos, Africans, and the Australian Aborigines, for whom the object is associated with the Churinga.

The Bull Roarer is a long, narrow piece of wood with tapering ends that, when attached to a cord and whirled around the head, produces a sound very much like thunder or the bellowing of a bull. It was taboo for women to see this sacred object, which was used in initiation ceremonies and was regarded as carrying the actual voices of the spirits.

The Bull Roarer was thought to make men invincible and indeed the noise it produces is quite terrifying, especially if it is not expected. It was also used in fertility rites and as a way of calling for rain.

Bulla

Caduceus

This is a special charm or amulet that was given to Roman children when they were born. A sealed locket, the bulla (meaning "bubble" or "knob") contained magical spells specific to the child in question, such as symbols of protection, or wishes for wealth. The bulla was constructed of different materials depending on the wealth of the family, leather for the poorest families and gold or other precious metals for the wealthiest.

Roman boys put aside their bullae when they reached puberty, and the object was offered to the gods. Girls wore theirs until the eve of their wedding. In either case it was considered that the bulla belonged to the child, as part and parcel of their personality.

The bulla is the origin of the name of the Papal Bull, the special edict that hails from the Vatican, which is fastened with an oval seal of the same shape as the bulla.

A rod, staff, or wand generally surmounted with wings. Two serpents entwine about the staff, forming a figure-of-eight shape. The key elements of the construction of this ancient sign are the serpent, the spiral, the infinity sign, the circle, wings, and the wand.

The Caduceus is an extremely ancient symbol, and its earliest recorded appearance is on the goblet of the King of Lagash, dating back to 2600 BC.

The Caduceus is the emblem of Mercury/Hermes and is incredibly rich in meanings: first, the staff or wand is a symbol of power and authority, of magical and supernatural forces, and is the tool of all magicians, medicine men, and shamans. It also represents the Tree of Life or World Axis. Then there are the wings on top of the wand.

Wings signify flight (both physical and metaphorical), intuition, the spiritual, and communication from the heavens or the gods. Mercury is the messenger of the gods. The two serpents, twining in opposite directions, represent opposition and equilibrium. They also signify opposites—male and female, day and night, good and evil, and so represent balance. Serpents also remind us of hidden knowledge.

As the serpents scroll around the wand, they form the figure-of-eight shape, or infinity symbol, which stands for completeness and perfection.

Part of the infinity symbol is the circle, ultimately representing the cosmos, the spirit, and unity.

All these elements combined make for a powerful symbol that has altered very little over the millennia. Together, they add up to supernatural power and hidden wisdom, messages from the spiritual realms, authority, the cosmos and infinity, and the pairing of opposites in harmony and unity.

Perhaps the most common use of the Caduceus, both today and since its earliest appearance, is as a symbol of healing and medicine. Aesclepius, the first physician and the god of medicine, had the Caduceus as one of his attributes because he had the power and the intuition (the wand and the wings)

to be able to use potentially poisonous or corruptive substances (the serpents) to restore health and, reputedly, to bring the dead back to life.

The Caduceus was not only the instrument of Aesclepius, but of the healing god Ningishzida of Mesopotamia (whose symbol is intertwining snakes), and of the Egyptians Ba'al, Isis and Ishtar. It is also found in India where it carries the same meaning.

CAGLIOSTRO SEAL

This curious sigil, the image of a snake, impaled by an arrow but with an apple in its mouth, presses all sorts of symbolic buttons; all three elements of the seal are powerful emblems in themselves. Is this the snake that tempted Eve with the apple, being punished for its transgressions? The snake also makes a curious S shape; is this significant, and if so, how? In addition, the union of the line of the arrow and the serpent seems to make a lemniscate, or figure-of-eight, symbol, meaning infinity. Unfortunately, it seems as though the precise meaning of the seal died with its namesake.

Cagliostro himself seems to be as mysterious as his seal. The self-styled Count Alessandro di Cagliostro was actually born as the much less grand-sounding Guiseppe Balsamo, and lived in Italy in the eighteenth century. The rumors surrounding his life and adventures come thick and fast and there is very little that is known for certain, due in no small part to the dense forest of fantastical stories that Cagliostro seems to have hidden himself within. He said that he had been born into the nobility but for some reason was abandoned on Malta, whereupon he wandered, as a child, throughout Morocco and Egypt where he learned many arcane mysteries, including those of the Kabbalah and alchemical magic. Whatever the truth, he certainly had skills as a pharmacist. It seems that the secure advantages of regular employment held no attraction for the count, his attention being much more drawn to magical and mystical matters. He became

a maker and vendor of magical amulets and talismans, and later, forgeries, including letters, certificates, and a myriad of official documents. He also offered the sexual favors of his beautiful young wife as trade for instruction in forgery.

Cagliostro's seal has been the result of much analysis and conjecture, its appearance so convincing that it was even incorporated into an early Masonic-style organization called the Brotherhood of Luxor.

CALUMET

For the Plains Indians, the pipe, also called the calumet, is one of the most important and recognizable symbols. Although it is sometimes referred to as the peace pipe, shared ceremonially as part of a unifying ritual, the pipe was just as valid a symbol during times of war.

The tobacco used in the pipe is also a powerful magical substance originally intended for ritual use only. The smoke rising from the pipe signifies a prayer traveling toward the gods and symbolizes the sacred breath, source of all life. The fire that lights the pipe symbolizes the sun and the male element. The pipe itself is equivalent to the prayer that is offered up from it.

The calumet is considered so important that in Native American tradition it is described as though it were a person, and each of its components has the name of a body part. In addition, the bowl is described as an altar, and the stem, the passage of the breath extending from the human body.

CANCELLARIUS SEAL

This is one of the symbolic seals of Aleister Crowley's Astrum Argentum, or Silver Star order. As the name suggests, it indicates the position of Chancellor. The symbol shows an Eye of Horus at the center of rays that are set in twelve groups of three.

The Astrum Argentum was started by Crowley in 1907 as an alternative to MacGregor Mathers's Golden Dawn. Although he had initially been enamored of the Golden Dawn and its charismatic leader, it is fair to say that Crowley liked to do things his own way, resulting in his expulsion from the Golden Dawn. Crowley believed that his own personal angel, Aiwaz, approved of his decision to supplant Mathers's brotherhood. The unusual structure of the Astrum Argentum was typical of Crowley's desire to be different. Each member was supposed to know only his immediate superior and anyone he introduced into the order. For Crowley, the sole purpose of the Astrum Argentum was to disseminate his own teachings and mystical beliefs. It was assumed that anyone introduced into the Astrum Argentum would already have had a great degree of magical training, in contrast to the Golden Dawn, which was dedicated to teaching.

CANDLE

A candle symbolizes light in the darkness in a way that a lightbulb simply cannot do. A candle

represents the element of fire as a benevolent force, made even more powerful if the candle is made of wax, a substance made by a magical creature, the bee. The colors of candles are significant in magical practices: for example, pink is said to attract love. Black candles are used in dark magic.

CAULDRON

In understanding symbols, sometimes it is useful to simply look at the shape and see what it resembles. The traditional cauldron represents nothing so much as the belly of a pregnant woman and, unsurprisingly, the cauldron is an important female symbol all over the world. The circular shape of the cauldron

gives another clue; the circle is a symbol of never-ending life and regeneration, and these themes recur repeatedly in stories containing cauldron symbolism.

The way the cauldron is used also gives a hint about its symbolic meaning. Things are put into the cauldron, heated, and something different is taken out; the basic ingredients are transformed. Therefore, the cauldron also symbolizes germination and transformation.

Traditionally, cauldrons have three legs. The number 3 in this instance represents the triple aspect of the Great Goddess, or the three fates. Shakespeare alludes to this when the three Weird Sisters— arguably the most famous witches in literature—cook up trouble at the beginning of *Macbeth*.

In pre-Christian literature, there are countless legends featuring magical cauldrons, and it may be because of this that the cauldron has its witchy associations. Celtic tales tell of cauldrons that contain an unending supply of food or of knowledge. The dead are frequently thrown into a magical Cauldron of Rebirth and climb out the next day, alive once more. Mythical warriors and heroes who died in battle are restored to life in this way. Ceridwen had a cauldron full of inspiration and magical powers. In India, a magic life-giving food, called Soma, was brewed in three huge bottomless cauldrons.

In Greece, there are tales in which an ordeal of initiation involves the person boiling in a cauldron, but after the rite, the initiate emerges with magical powers, including the gift of immortality.

CELTIC CROSS AND SUN CROSS

In the Celtic Cross or Ring Cross symbol, a cross is contained within a circle. Very early versions of this cross, found in Ireland, do not show the arms of the cross protruding beyond the circle; the whole symbol is encompassed inside the circle and in this case it becomes the ancient, universal symbol called the Sun Cross, the Wheel Cross, or Odin's Cross. This sign first appears at the very start of the Bronze Age. Among other

things, it symbolizes the wheel and in China represents thunder, power, and energy. It also appears in the seal of the Babylonian sun god, Shamash.

The Sun Cross symbol also appears in ancient astrology. In modern astrology it still signifies the planet, and element of, Earth; the cross represents the four corners of the planet, the elements, and the directions, and the circle is the planet itself.

Because it was the symbol of the sun, the king and the highest temporal and spiritual powers, it was easy for the early Christians to adopt this pagan sign and incorporate it into the Latin Cross. It is still used by bishops to bless a new church, drawn onto the walls in sanctified water or oils, at twelve different places around the church.

The Celtic Cross is frequently used as a grave marker, or as a war memorial, particularly in Celtic countries.

Incidentally, the hot cross bun, eaten specifically at Easter and popularly believed to represent the Christian Cross, is actually of pre-Christian origin. The Greeks, Romans, and ancient Egyptians all ate wheat cakes to celebrate the coming of spring. These cakes were circular (representing the moon or sun) with a cross that divided the cake into the four lunar quarters or the four seasons.

CELTIC KNOTWORK

One of the most distinctive decorative features of Celtic artwork and architecture are the beautiful constructions of Celtic knotwork. It adorns stonework, illuminated manuscripts, and jewelry; the knotwork has left a distinctive trail that clearly shows all the places in the world that were visited at some point by the Celts.

The knotwork itself would appear to be a purely decorative device. If at one time there were specific symbolic meanings attached, then these have been lost over the centuries. Intertwining shapes and lines, however, generally point toward ideas of connectedness and the harmonious convergence of opposites, male and female, fire and water, heaven and earth, for example. In addition, any sign that

can be made without the pen leaving the paper tends to have strong protective associations, and knotwork, with its continual looping and spiraling, could have been used in this way, perhaps used for amulets and talismans.

Existing symbols—such as a heart, or birds and animals—are often rendered in Celtic knotwork. In this case, the form of the underlying shape carries the symbolic meaning.

The Celtic Knot that is square in form is a protective symbol, called a shield knot.

CHA CHA

In Haiti, there are certain seedpods called cha cha that are used to make rattles for ceremonial music-making in Voudon rituals. The rattle is called a cha cha, too, and the dance of the same name also comes from the name of the seedpod.

See also Asson.

CHALICE

This is a cup or grail that is generally used in rituals. No matter what the religious or spiritual persuasion of the celebrant, a chalice of some form is used, whether it

shapes. Designed by science fiction writer Michael Moorcock, it has been adopted as an emblem by exponents of Chaos Magic, the contemporary branch of magic inspired by the works of Austin Osman Spare.

be the highly ornamented vessel of the Catholic Church or the simpler wooden cup favored by some pagan groups. The chalice itself is symbolic of water or of the spirit, and is used as such in the suit of cups in the tarot, for example. The chalice is also a universal symbol of the feminine aspect because of its shape, its use as a vessel, and its link with water.

Eastern religions use a kind of bell, called a drilbu, in the place of a chalice.

CHAOS WHEEL

The Chaos Wheel, or Chaos Star, is a wheel constructed from eight arrow-headed spokes. Representing the notion of infinite possibilities, the symbol is a recent addition to a veritable galaxy of meaningful

CHESS

Chess originated in India. The checkerboard that chess is played on is, in itself, a secret symbol. It is symbolic of the world that we understand, that is composed of opposing forces. Also, the black and white colors of the symmetrically arranged squares stand for male/female, light/dark, positive/negative, good/evil in much the same way as the yin-yang sign does. It is no accident that the floor of the Freemason temple has the same construction as the chessboard, a constant reminder of both the harmony and tension between opposites. The pieces, too, are black and white, reinforcing this idea.

The chessboard has a further mystery that can be revealed in the number of the squares. Each side has eight squares. Eight is the number of infinity and of completion, and eight times eight makes 64, the number of cosmic unity.

This is the magical number that, in sacred geometry, is the basis of temple construction.

The square shape of the board symbolizes the stability of the earth and its four corners, the directions and the elements.

Superficially, chess might seem to be a relatively straightforward game, a simple series of different moves ascribed to each of the pieces. However, its complexities are only really revealed when the player is so familiar with the rules that he or she can carry them out automatically. Chess is plainly connected to war strategy and the ability to surprise the opponent. A good player will understand the need to sacrifice pieces in order to gain a greater advantage. Although the pawn may appear to be valueless, it is arguably one of the most important pieces on the board, and certainly the most prolific. We even use the word "pawn" to describe a person that we think is insignificant.

In Ingmar Bergman's film *The Seventh Seal*, the knight, Antonius Block, invites the hooded figure of Death to join him in a game, despite the fact that Death warns him that he cannot win. Effectively, chess owes as much to chance as choice, and further underlines the dilemma between the concepts of fate versus free will. The knight knows that he will die, yet he persists in playing the game. Stanley Kubrick, too, believed that his skill as a chess player gave him the discipline to think rationally and to see the bigger picture, an invaluable skill for a film director. The detachment and lack of emotion required by the talented player is synonymous, for many, with an idealized, Zen approach to life.

For the Celts, the game of chess was called "intelligence of the wood." It was the game of kings and the stakes were high. The game therefore symbolizes the intellect of the king, despite the fact that the most versatile piece on the board is the queen.

CHI ROH

See Labarum.

CHNOUBIS

The Chnoubis is a hybrid creature, with the head of a lion and the tail of a serpent. It was carved onto stones for use as an amulet, providing protection against poisons in particular. Amulets featuring the

Chnoubis date back to the first century and it is supposed that this odd-looking creature may be related to Abraxas, whose image was used in a similar way.

CHOKU REI

A symbol of Reiki healers, the Choku Rei is comprised of a spiral that culminates in a hooked stick. It looks a little like the treble clef used in musical notation. The symbol is used by Reiki healers to increase the power available to them, and to help focus this energy. The meaning of Choku Rei is "place the power of the universe here." Healers draw the sign mentally in the air as a form of meditation, generally before and after giving a treatment.

CICATRIX

A cicatrix is a scar, but not just any scar. It refers to a very specific incision that is scored onto the body and carries secret symbols pertaining to the person's religious or magical beliefs. A very painful process called scarification leaves these raised marks on the skin. Until the end of the nineteenth century, Maori men had ritual scarring all over their faces in order that they might look more frightening to the enemy. A cicatrix acts as a permanent amulet that is an inherent part of the person. Its purpose is similar to that of the tattoo; the pain involved in the process is an important rite of passage. Ritual scarring is popular among dark-skinned people because a tattoo is not particularly visible against the skin.

CIMARUTA

In Italian, this means the "sprig of rue." It is an amulet, made of silver in honor of female energy in the form of the goddess, comprising a model of a sprig of rue with various charms in its three branches. The Cimaruta is a very old charm, which evolved from an Etruscan magical amulet. It dates back as far as 4500 BC, although there are more contemporary versions such as the stylized one illustrated here. The charms featured generally include a crescent moon, a key, stars, daggers, and flowers; different regions of Italy produced their own specific symbols. Also known as the Witch Charm, the Cimaruta is favored by witches, and to see one in someone's home might indicate the spiritual persuasion of the owner. It is worn either as a pendant or might be hung over a doorway, a possible reason for the Cimaruta being double-sided. When used in this way as an ornament the Cimaruta is usually quite large in size.

The three silver branches of the Cimaruta relate to the notion of the Triple Goddess. The charm itself takes on all the significance of the rue plant as being both protective and a tool of witches, used to cast spells and throw hexes.

CIRCLE

See First signs: Circle.

CLADDAGH

The Claddagh is a popular symbol, often incorporated into the design of rings, and worn by people as an attractive piece of ornamentation although they may not know what it symbolizes.

Traditionally used as a wedding ring, the Claddagh is so called because it was originally made in a Galway fishing village of the same name in seventeenth-century Ireland. However, the elements of the design are much older, stretching back into pre-Christian Celtic history. The Romans had a popular ring design, the Fede, which featured clasped hands. "Fede" means "fidelity."

The Claddagh symbol features a heart held by a pair of hands. A crown usually surmounts the heart. These features represent love, friendship, and loyalty.

The Encyclopedia of Secret Signs and Symbols

Clothing

Of all the animal kingdom, humans are unique in that they wear clothes. In the Bible, Adam and Eve don fig leaves to cover the newly discovered sexual parts that are a reminder of the lower animal nature. Once we had managed to protect our modesty and keep ourselves warm, our attention turned to the use of clothes as an outward sign of status or of certain religious observances. As secret symbols, clothes have an elaborate history, especially when they are connected to religious beliefs; sacred texts from all religions are full of instructions as to the nature of certain clothes and how they should be worn. This section doesn't claim to be an extensive analysis of these ideas, but serves merely to point out the meanings of some of the most common items of apparel.

CAPE

The cape has a simple design. At its most basic, it is a piece of cloth with a hole in the middle. Often worn by members of the clergy, when it is called a "chasuble," the cape shares the same symbolism as the arc or dome that it represents; the vault of the heavens. This suggests the idea of ascendance. The wearer of the cape becomes a living representation of the Axis Mundi.

CLOAK

As well as being a symbol of religious asceticism, the cloak is the garment of kings. In addition, the word "cloak" has become synonymous with the notion of hiding something; the invisibility cloak is a very ancient idea. The god Lugh had such a cloak that enabled him to pass unnoticed through the entire Irish army in order to rescue his son. Effectively, though, the cloak makes the wearer invisible without any need for magical intervention. A cloak, especially a hooded one, is a mask for the body, covering the wearer from head to foot. A cloak can help someone change his or her identity while at the same time confirming it. In the Bible, St. Martin gives half his cloak to the beggar. This is not only a material gesture but also a symbol of his charitable nature.

The Khirka, a specific type of cloak, originally meant a scrap of torn material. However, its unworldly nature made it an appropriate garment for the Sufi mystic.

It was originally blue, signifying a vow of poverty, in the same way that brown and gray have the same meaning to Christian believers. The Sufi receives the Khirka after three years of training, a sign that he is worthy of initiation. To wear the Khirka, the Sufi must understand the three levels of the mystic life. These are the Truth, the Law, and the Path.

FOOTWEAR

When you put your foot upon the ground, this gesture is synonymous with taking possession of the Earth beneath it.

Because the holy ground at churches and temples is not, effectively, a territory that belongs to people, the jumble of shoes, sandals, and boots outside the doors of holy places all over the world may certainly be a sign of respect. However, the owners may not be aware that they are, literally, following in the footsteps of a more ancient idea, that they have no claim to this sacred territory. The footwear is significant because it is removed.

The children of Israel sealed agreements between two parties by swapping one sandal each. In addition, in northern China the word for "slipper" and "mutual agreement" is the same. This is why slippers are given as wedding presents.

Shoes also symbolize travel, a meaning that precedes the time of motorized transport. In certain northern European territories, children leave their shoes out for Father Christmas to fill with gifts; not only is Santa himself making an arduous journey, but his gifts help in the "journey" of the coming year.

Shoes are also a status symbol. Slaves generally went barefoot; hence, the wearing of shoes was the sign of the free man.

The slipper that Cinderella lost, that later proved her identity to the prince, is an example of the shoe as a sexual symbol. In common interpretations of this tale these "slippers" sound uncomfortable, since they are apparently made of glass. However, it was an old European tradition that a potential suitor would show his sincerity by making his intended bride a pair of fur boots. It is likely that the word for fur, *vair*, was confused with the word for glass, *verre*. The sexual symbolism continues with these kinky boots; the old word for fur shares its roots with a word meaning "sheath."

BELT/GIRDLE

Often the very first piece of clothing to be worn, especially in Asian countries, the girdle or belt is circular, and so it represents the union of spirit and matter, and of eternity. It also symbolizes the binding aspect; the girdle is a synonym for the soul that is bound to the body. Although the girdle is tied around the waist of a baby at birth in some countries, it appears in various other forms. The belts of the martial arts exponent range through the color spectrum from white to black to signify levels of expertise.

The girdle also protects; it acts as a symbolic "wall" through which evil entities cannot penetrate. It's a sort of spiritual utility belt. The girdle, too, represents the idea of chastity. The belt worn around robes of monks and others who are called to a spiritual life carries the greater significance of the girdle. Notably, in the Middle Ages prostitutes were allowed to wear neither belt nor veil.

To talk of "girding the loins" means to prepare oneself, whether for a journey or something else. The ankh is called the Girdle of Isis or the Buckle of Isis, and carries the same notions of the circle and the knot as binding forces.

A sash is also a kind of girdle, used in Freemasonry, for example, as a symbol of office. The knot itself is often used as a reminder, and the knot in the girdle or belt is a reminder of the promise made when the girdle was donned.

Another form of a girdle is the Sacred Thread, or Poonal (in Tamil) that is worn by male Hindus, particularly those from the Brahmin caste. The Sacred Thread ceremony can happen any time after the boy's seventh birthday. The thread is handwoven from three sets of three strands, although extra strands are added to represent marriage and children. It measures about 96 times the breadth of a man's four fingers; this is roughly the same as his height. Resting on the left shoulder, the thread is wrapped around the body, ending under the right arm. It is knotted only once. Once the Sacred Thread ceremony has been carried out, the thread is never taken off although it is replaced once a year. The single knot represents the concept of Brahman, the unity of all things. The numbers of strands in the thread signify various tenets of the Hindu faith.

GLOVE

Freemasons sometimes wear white gloves, not only as a symbol of work to be done, but also to show purity of thought. White gloves are worn for the same reasons in the Catholic Church. They are given to bishops and kings after their investiture, and here they are a reminder of newborn purity. Gloves—especially the highly ornamented kind—are a relatively luxurious item of clothing, emblems of the nobility who used gauntlets as part of the equipment associated with falconry. Gloves on heraldic shields usually indicate some connection with hunting birds.

To "throw down the gauntlet" is still used as a synonym for a challenge, dating back to the days of chivalry, where it was a politer version of a slap but hardly any less shocking.

HEADGEAR

Headgear immediately identifies the status of the owner. The crown, for example, is an immediate recognition of royalty. People in authority wear peaked hats. The beggar goes

"cap in hand." Additionally, headgear itself indicates a relationship with the divine, since the top of the head is effectively the first point of contact with the spirit that descends from above. The symbolic nature of headgear is altogether different from its practical usage. In temples, churches, and other holy places, the feet might be bare but the head is covered as a sign of modesty.

THE CROWN

The open crown, coronet, tiara, or diadem has no practical secular purpose; indeed, the heavier crowns that belong to the sovereignty can be headachingly heavy. The crown is a circle, symbolizing the idea of immortality and eternity, but with the added dimension of a connection between the spiritual and material that is cemented by the ritual of coronation itself, which signifies a blessing, benediction, or union with the divine power that comes from above. Crowns traditionally feature jeweled "rays" signifying sunbeams, an allusion to illumination in all senses of the word.

For the ancient Egyptians, only pharaohs and deities were permitted to wear the crown. The double crowns of the pharaohs consisted of the white conical miter that represented Upper Egypt, surrounded by the red encasement of Lower Egypt. The serpent symbol called the Uraeus, again worn only by pharaohs, was incorporated into this sacred crown.

The pope wears a triple crown, or Triregnum (*see* Papal symbols). The three parts symbolize different aspects of the Catholic faith and of the papal role.

The crown is not always made of princely materials. The crown of laurels is still given as a sign of victory, and for Romans, the highest accolade for a soldier was to be given a crown made of lowly grass. The Corona Graminea signified the ownership of the territory, the right to the land on which the victory had taken place.

The feathered headdresses of Native Americans not only signify the status of the wearer, but the feathers themselves signify the different qualities of the birds they belong to. The most valued of all is the eagle feather. These headdresses epitomize the crown as a sun symbol.

THE HAT

Which single factor is shared by the old-fashioned policeman's helmet from the UK, medieval Jewish hats, the papal Triregnum, and the traditional witch's hat? They all have a tall, conical shape. This has the effect of making the wearer taller than anyone else, more noticeable, and therefore more authoritative. This kind of hat is also a phallic symbol. In addition, the hat of the witch or wizard contains the essence of her magical power in the form of a spiral of energy.

SKULLCAP

Orthodox Jews wear the skullcap (also known as *yarmulke* or *kippah*) at all times; it is stated in the Torah that no man should walk more than four paces without the head being covered. This is because of the belief that the head should always be covered in the presence of God, and since God is omnipotent, then it makes sense that the *yarmulke* is worn at all times.

The *yarmulke* is not only a recognizable symbol of the faith, but covering the head is in itself a sign of respect for, and fear of, God. Many men also cover their heads for the same reasons.

Covering the head as a sign of respect for God is not restricted to the Jewish faith, although many people tend to restrict this practice to the times that they are actually in the place of worship.

HOOD

The wearing of a hood is sometimes viewed with suspicion, because it masks the face of the wearer. Therefore, the hood is a symbol of invisibility, of disguise, of secrecy, and tends to have negative connotations because we assume that the wearer has reason to conceal him- or herself. The figure of Death, with its scythe, often wears a hood, alluding to the fact that no one knows what form death will take.

HELMET

Like the hood, the helmet is a symbol of invisibility. It also denotes power and invulnerability. The Greek king of hell, Hades, wears a helmet, and epitomizes all these powers. The covered-face helmet shares many of the same qualities as the mask.

KHALSAS

The five Khalsas are the dress rituals of adherents to the Sikh faith, and signs by which they can be recognized. The five Khalsas are:

1. Kesa—this is uncut hair. The hair remains uncut as a reminder that harm must not be inflicted upon the body. Male Sikhs wear the turban as an article of faith, and it also makes a practical garment to cover and contain the hair.
2. Kacha—this is a particular kind of undergarment as a symbol of marital chastity. Men and women wear similar garments.
3. Kanga—a wooden comb, symbolizing tidiness and cleanliness.
4. Kara—a steel bangle, which serves as a reminder of the truth and of God.
5. Kirpan—a dagger, for ceremonial use only, and a reminder to protect those who need it.

The Khalsas are sometimes referred to as the "Five Ks."

ROBES

Nuns, monks, and priests of all persuasions wear the plain robes called "habits." As well as acting as a kind of uniform, the habit also symbolizes the rejection of material values in favor of spiritual virtues. Generally colored gray or brown, the wearer no longer has to worry about a choice of clothes since external appearances do not matter. Effectively, the habit removes the individual personality. The sackcloth robes worn by ascetics are an extreme statement of the renunciation of worldly appearance, often worn as a penance.

Robes in general signify the rank of the wearer, and because they are distinctly different from everyday dress, they tend to be the preferred dress of spiritual or religious people. In China, the Imperial Robes were very ornate and carried specific symbolism as a part of their design. The round collar was the heaven, the square hem, the earth; the wearer of this robe was therefore an intermediary between the two. Latter-day Druids of some orders wear green robes to signify the bardic grade, blue for the ovate grade, and the fully initiated Druid wears white robes. Indeed, pilgrims of all faiths, including Buddhist, Muslim, and Shinto, wear white robes. Buddhist monks and followers of Hare Krishna wear robes of the sacred saffron color.

The robes of a shaman, like those of the wizard, are covered in magical signs. They are also decorated with feathers (symbolic of transcendence) and the pelt of the animal whose spirit they wish to connect with.

SHIRT

A shirt is a symbol of protection. To "lose one's shirt" means to relinquish the last vestige of dignity as well as material wealth. However, to give "the shirt off your back" is a gesture of great generosity, indicating a willingness to give away the last of your material possessions. The "hair shirt" is an uncomfortable garment worn by penitents who want to self-inflict punishment.

The tunic is an earlier form of the shirt. The Cathars used it as an analogy for the human body. When they said that fallen angels wore tunics, they meant that they were made of flesh.

VEIL

The veil symbolizes a distinct separation between two states of being, physical objects, or concepts. However, the object effecting this separation is apparently flimsy. It must be remembered that this is a two-way separation; the nun that "takes the veil" to become a bride of Christ separates herself from the world, but also removes the worldly from her relationship with the spiritual.

The Greek word for veil is "hymen." The veil that is lifted to reveal the face of the bride at her wedding not only symbolizes her new status, but also alludes to the tearing of the hymen which is the physical outcome of a marriage. The word "revelation" comes from the Latin *revelatio*, to draw back the veil.

Penetrating a veil, therefore, is symbolic of initiation; hidden knowledge is often described as "veiled." This veil protects us too; in the same way that the light from the sun can illuminate, it can also dazzle or even blind us if it comes too close.

The Qu'ran says that women should be addressed from behind a veil. The hijab is the physical manifestation of this idea. Although the hijab has been interpreted by some as a sign of oppression, devout followers of Islam would argue that not only is the wearing of this veil instructed by the Prophet, but also gives the woman a great level of freedom. Here, a veil of misunderstanding separates two ideas and cultures.

According to Buddhists, Maya is the symbolic veil that separates pure reality from the illusory nature of the world in which we live.

COLOR

Despite the fact that colors have an essential part to play in symbolism and the understanding of it, they are, nevertheless, frequently overlooked. Colors are proven to have a profound effect on the human psyche and on our moods. They resonate with the elements, the directions, the seasons, the planets, and astrological signs, as well as holding huge significance in their own right, for example, in the tarot. Colors, and particular shades of them, confer an immediate identity and make a strong statement. For example, in the green, purple, and white of the suffragettes (green for hope, purple for dignity, and white for purity), or in the red and white stripes of the old-fashioned barber's pole (where the white represented the color of flesh and the red was the blood sometimes drawn by the razor).

Territories use colors to represent themselves on their flags. Sometimes the reasons behind these colors have unexpected origins, such as the bright orange that is so strongly linked to the Netherlands; more of this later.

The simple colors used by children generally represent the most elemental meanings; blue for the sea and the sky, green for growth, brown for the earth, yellow for the sun.

The significance of colors is proven by the high value that our ancestors placed on certain plants or substances that could be made into dyes, such as the imperial purple of Rome that was produced from a mollusk that was valued more highly than gold, or the saffron crocus that produced the sacred color of the same name. Prior to the development of chemical dyes, the creation of colors that did not fade in the sun or wash away was a combination of art, science, and magic, akin to an alchemical process. The impact of the sun shining through stained glass, painting the interiors of churches with living colors that shimmered and danced, in a medieval world where color was often a privilege of the wealthy few, can only be imagined. Warriors in ancient Britain daubed themselves in blue pigments in order to look more fearsome to their enemies.

The power of red was once so powerful that corpses were daubed in red ocher in the belief that the color had the same life-giving properties as blood.

The seven colors of the rainbow—which break down into 700 shades that are visible to the naked eye—are associated with the seven planets, the days of the week, the Seven Heavens, and the seven notes of the musical scale.

BLACK

SYMBOLIC MEANINGS: *night, the absence of light; mourning, sobriety, denial; authority; perfection and purity; maturity and wisdom.*

Technically speaking black is not a "color" at all. This doesn't stop it having a wealth of symbolic meaning.

Black often has negative connotations for the reason that it is the color of the night, or the absence of light. It doesn't require a great leap of the imagination to extend this light/dark, day/night symbolism to good/bad. A fundamentally natural occurrence to do with the orbit of Earth around the Sun, therefore, has had far-reaching consequences, resulting in

fear, racism, superstition, and bigotry which even continues today simply because of skin color.

In the West, black is the color of mourning and funerals. In some cultures, white is used in this context, in which case it carries the idea of rebirth. Black, however, is not so sanguine. It is final, conclusive, the denial of life.

Despite the mirthless sobriety of black, it depends how you wear it. The "new black" is a term applied to anything that is in vogue, since black is also somehow dangerous and sexy as well as practical, therefore always fashionable as a color.

The "black sheep" of the family refers to the one who is a bit of a scoundrel, and the "black dog" means depression. Conversely, a black cat is a very lucky symbol in some parts of the world. A person who holds a black belt in any of the martial arts is considered to be at the pinnacle of their abilities, and indeed, in Japan, black is the color of wisdom, experience, and maturity. In this instance, black is a color of perfection, an idea shared by the Cathars who also saw black as a symbol of completion and purity.

Black is a secretive, mysterious color and used as such in rite and ritual. A polished black mirror provides a perfect, glossy surface for scrying or seeing into the future.

BLUE

SYMBOLIC MEANINGS: *truth and the intellect; wisdom, loyalty, chastity; peace, piety, and contemplation; spirituality; eternity.*

Blue is the color of the heavens and is related to the fifth chakra. Blue is traditionally worn by the Virgin Mary, the very embodiment of all the qualities described above. Whereas the reds, oranges, and yellows carry with them a carnival atmosphere, blue is more sober, even somber, despite its many variations. If we're "feeling blue" then we're depressed or melancholy. And yet the bluebird is a universal symbol for happiness. The color has even given its name to a rich vein of music. The "blues" actually refers to "blue notes." These are notes, either sung or played, that are pitched down a little for expressive purposes. An example is Billie Holiday's heartbreaking rendition of "Strange Fruit."

There's something cool and detached about blue that gives rise to its reputation for spirituality and chastity. Above all, blue is the color of the sky. Like the sky, blue is infinitely spacious. It contains everything, and yet contains nothing. The color is therefore associated with ideas of eternity. When filmmakers and animators want to place a subject against a different background, they film against a blue screen since the color can be made invisible. In Jewish tradition the city of Luz, where the Immortals live, is also called the Blue City. Similarly, the mythical sacred mountain of the Hindus, Mount Meru, is constructed entirely of sapphire on its southern face and it's this that is said to tinge the skies with blue.

To put any color out of context can have an alienating and often frightening effect. Knowing this, early British warriors daubed themselves in woad. These blue-skinned savages must have been an alarming sight for Roman soldiers.

Members of the aristocracy or the royalty are described as having "blue blood," but why? The phrase originated with the Spanish, *sangre azul*, and refers to the pale-skinned Castilian ruling classes who prided themselves on never having interbred with darker-skinned races. Therefore, their blue venous blood was plainly visible underneath the surface of their skin. There's even a particular shade of blue that is meant to represent this color, called royal blue.

BROWN

SYMBOLIC MEANINGS: *poverty, humility, practicality.*

Brown is the color primarily associated with the earth, soil, the raw element before it is covered with greenery. The word for earth, in Latin, is *humus*, which carries the same root as humility. Religious ascetics wear brown as a reminder of this quality and also of their voluntary material poverty.

GRAY

SYMBOLIC MEANINGS: *sobriety, steadiness, modesty.*

Gray is the midway point between black and white, and tellingly the "gray area" is an area of indetermination, indecision, or ambiguity. To be described as gray is rather less than flattering, since gray is such a subdued and neutral color, and implies that the person blends into the background. However, gray is also a color of balance and reasonableness and is the color

used, in photography, to balance all others.

Because people's hair turns gray with age, the word is often used to describe elderly people and is also a color of wisdom.

For Christians, gray is the color of resurrection and is worn when people are coming out of the full black of mourning as the midway point on the journey to other colors.

GREEN

SYMBOLIC MEANINGS: *new life, resurrection, hope; the sea; fertility and regeneration; recycling, environmental awareness; a lucky color; an unlucky color.*

Green is an amalgam of blue and yellow, and is the color of the fourth chakra. Green is the universal symbol for "Go!" to red's "Stop!"

In common with yellow, there seem to be several anomalies in the symbolic meaning of green. To call someone "green" means that they are inexperienced or innocent and obviously refers to fresh young shoots, yet jealousy is also described as the "green-eyed monster." This saying is actually Shakespearean in origin. In *Othello*, jealousy is described as being like the green-eyed monster, the cat, "which doth mock the meat it feeds on." Probably the same origin gives us "green with envy."

Green is a soothing, refreshing color, so it is interesting to discover why it's sometimes believed to be unlucky.

In the Middle Ages, green was meant to be the color of the devil. He's even depicted on a stained-glass window in Chartres Cathedral as having green skin and green eyes, strangely similar to a generally held belief about the appearance of Martians. In this sense the color denotes an alien, non-human, possibly threatening being; no surprise, then, that it's the color of the fairy folk, and it might well be that the color is lucky or unlucky depending on their attitude toward you. If you dressed in green, it was believed that the fairies could claim you as their own.

In Islam, green is the color of paradise, and Mohammed has a green banner. Paradise actually means "garden," and in the arid desert landscape of the Bedouin, any stretch of lush green land must indeed appear heavenly.

The epitome of the nature god in the Western world is the Green Man, the pre-Christian deity whose leafy face peeps out from bosky woods and verdant forests and reminds us that Mother Nature is supernal. However, the Green Man is not exclusive to the West. He also exists in Islam, as Al Kadir. Al Kadir is the patron of travelers, and he's said to live on the very edge of the world where the oceans of heaven and earth merge. Be mindful if you meet Al Kadir that you should do as he tells you, however outlandish the instructions might be.

In alchemy, full of hidden meanings, the Green Lion itself has more than one meaning. It is a symbol for vitriol (sulfuric acid), which is created by distilling the green iron sulfate crystals in a flask. But the life-force itself was symbolized as the blood of the Green Lion, blood contained in a green vessel; this was a reference not to real, physical gold, but to Philosophers' Gold, far more valuable and elusive.

MOTLEY

SYMBOLIC MEANINGS: *wealth; a chameleon personality.*

Not strictly a color as such, but a combination of many other colors. The word is generally used to describe cloth or clothing. The rainbow nature of motley means that whoever wears it has as many aspects as there are colors, a chameleon personality, and it can indicate the trickster or fool (as worn by the jester, or the Fool in the tarot) as well as kings, emperors, and deities. In the Bible, Joseph's coat of many colors is the object of much envy.

ORANGE

SYMBOLIC MEANINGS: *balance between spirit and sexuality; fertility and yet virginity; energy; the sun; like yellow, orange is believed to be an appetite stimulant.*

Orange has two aspects that we see time and time again, pivoting between the material and spiritual worlds, which is not surprising given that the color itself is a balance between red and yellow. As such, it represents the second chakra, the first being red, and the third yellow.

Orange is a vibrant, cheerful color that definitely lifts the spirits. The orange blossom is the traditional flower for brides because the fruit and the flower can appear on the orange tree at the same time, hence the virginity/ fertility symbolism.

Similarly, a Hindu bride has an orange powder smeared on her forehead once she is married, a sign of her status. Hindu places of worship are indicated by an orange flag or banner, which is replaced once a year in a colorful and effusive ceremony.

Why is the color orange so closely associated with the Netherlands? Originally it was because of the Dutch ruling dynasty, the House of Orange. Loyal Dutch farmers who gave the world the first orange carrot further cemented the association. It might be impossible to associate the carrot with any other color these days, but originally they came in black, red, or purple and were a much more bitter vegetable than the modern varieties. By the 1700s, the Dutch had succeeded in hybridizing pale yellow carrots with red ones. It might be a coincidence, but a recent UNICEF survey showed Dutch children to be the happiest in Europe; given that happiness is one of the symbolic associations with the color orange, could there be a link?

PINK

SYMBOLIC MEANINGS: *femininity, innocence, good health, love, patience.*

Pink is the ultimate feminine color, being flirty, girlish, and innocent at the same time. Pale pink is used as the symbol for a baby girl, just as pale blue is used for baby boys. This feminine angle is why the color pink has been adopted as a symbol of gay pride.

Pink is the color of universal, unconditional love.

PURPLE

SYMBOLIC MEANINGS: *royalty and pomp; power, wealth, majesty.*

Purple, or indigo, is the color associated with the sixth chakra.

Since it was first discovered, purple has been *the* color of choice to denote wealth and power. Emperors, kings, and the more powerful members of the clergy—such as bishops—choose the color as a way of defining their status. This is because the dye itself was originally available from one source and one source only: the secretions of a certain gland of an unfortunate sea snail called *Murex brandaris.* Therefore, purple was extremely costly to produce and strictly the color of those who could afford it, since the dye itself was more expensive

even than gold. The most popular shade of the color is called Tyrian purple (named for the city of Tyre, where it was manufactured). Heracles's dog, which had a predilection for snacking on the snails he found along the seashore, is credited with having discovered the dye after his owner noticed the purple staining around his mouth. It is likely, however, that the Minoans on Crete discovered the purple pigment quite some time before Heracles's dog trotted into the picture.

If the Minoan theory is true then the rare purple dye has been with us for at least 3,500 years, so its associations with all things glorious and splendid are well embedded into the human psyche even with the advent of synthetic dye alternatives.

RED

SYMBOLIC MEANINGS: *vitality and life-force; fire, the sun, the south; blood; good luck and prosperity; power and authority; masculine energy; war and anger; passion, energy, sexuality.*

One of the three primary colors, bright red pops out of whatever environment it happens to be in and grabs our attention more than any other color. Moreover, it is the first actual color that is seen by babies. Because it has a lower vibrational frequency than any other color in our visible spectrum, it is associated with the base chakra and symbolizes passion, sexuality, fertility, and animal urges. Red-light districts are so called because of the dim red shades of the prostitutes' quarters.

Red is the color of blood, which means that it is associated with the life-forces and vitality. Hunters daub themselves in the red blood of the kill, which they believe will give them empathy with the spirit of the animal. Red is also the color of fire, the sun, and the southern direction.

The word for "magic," in German, is directly linked to the word for "red ocher." A recent archaeological discovery provided unusual evidence of the reverence in which the color was held by early humans. Lumps of red ocher, as well as tools stained with the substance, were found in early graves in an Israeli cave, indicating its importance as a symbol of vitality, life, and resurrection.

Pure colors used to be very difficult and expensive to produce, and so red cloth was used by people in positions of power, such as the monarchy and the clergy. Byzantine emperors were dressed from head to foot in red. In Rome, red was the color of nobles and generals, and the Holy Roman Church still dresses its cardinals in pure, bright, cardinal red. To roll out the red carpet for someone is to honor their presence.

Red is a color of protection and has been viewed as such for at least the last 2,000 years. Amulets made from rubies or garnets were far more valuable than any other kind, able to make the wearer invincible.

And how about the red planet? Mars has a preponderance of iron oxide in its soil, giving it a red appearance that is clearly visible to the naked eye. This color is partially responsible for its association with war and warriors.

In India and China, red is the traditional color for weddings. Indian brides wear saris of red or pink, and the Chinese happy couple will be surrounded by a veritable sea of red; clothing, souvenirs, and gifts. Even the home of the bride and groom are decorated with red banners and ribbons. Roman brides, too, favored red for their wedding veil, which was called a *flammeum*. This tradition is shared by modern Greek brides.

In ancient Egypt red was synonymous with evil, because it was the color of the god Seth, who haunted the arid desert places, the personification of destruction. Seth was called the "Red God," and an Egyptian charm of the time goes like this:

Oh, Isis, deliver me from the hands of bad, evil, red things!

Similarly, in Christian symbolism, the devil is sometimes depicted as a red creature. Like Seth, he also has a predilection for scorched places.

In alchemy, the Red Stone is mercuric sulfide, a compound of sulfur and mercury that is also called vermilion. The creation of vermilion was a very important primary stage in the process of making the Philosopher's Stone, which is itself disguised as the Red Lion, since this elusive substance was characterized by turning red in its final stage.

SAFFRON

Symbolic meanings: *spirituality, holiness, good fortune.*

Named after the saffron crocuses whose stigmas create the color, the harvesting of these delicate plant parts is a labor-intensive and time-critical matter and so the actual dye is costly to produce. Saffron is an extremely auspicious color for Buddhists, Hindus, Jains, and Sikhs, and a saffron or orange banner indicates a place of spiritual worship. The foreheads of Hindu deities are daubed with saffron paste to denote their celestial status, and although the Hindu pantheon is vast and complex, the use of saffron is a unifying factor across the many different manifestations of the faith.

Saffron is paler and more golden than true orange, and is said to be the color of wisdom, the rising sun, and of Mother Earth.

VIOLET

Symbolic meanings: *knowledge and intelligence; piety, sobriety, humility, temperance; peace and spirituality.*

Violet is the color associated with the seventh chakra.

There are many shades of violet ranging from ethereal pale shades through to the darker mauve, considered the only color acceptable as a relief from the relentless strict mourning convention of black and gray in Victorian times.

Violet is a combination of red and blue, and its association with temperance is indicated in some tarot suits. Temperance is the 14th card of the Major Arcana and is depicted by a woman holding a jug or vase in either hand, one red, one blue, pouring a clear liquid from one to the other.

Violet is often worn by people predisposed toward psychic matters, and is the perfect symbol of the "higher" mind, combining as it does the earthy fieriness of red with the cool reasonableness of blue to forge an entirely different hue. Its association with the seventh chakra, at the crown position at the top of the head, gives violet the power to connect with the world of spirit.

The humble qualities of violet as a color come from the flower. The tiny violet grows close to the ground, hidden modestly in among the grass, yet noticeable because of its striking color.

WHITE

SYMBOLIC MEANINGS: *purity, virginity; death and rebirth, a beginning and an end; in the Far East, mourning.*

White can be seen as the absence of any color and the sum of all colors together, so in a sense it can mean everything or nothing. This combination of all colors has given white the name of the "many-colored lotus" in Buddhist teachings.

Probably the most telling of both ends of white's symbolic spectrum are reflected in its associations with purity and a fresh start (as worn by brides in the Western tradition, as an optimistic sign of virginity) and as the color of mourning in the East, a use that used to be common in Europe, too. Cadavers all over the world are still wrapped in white shrouds and, as death precedes birth, the white here has an optimistic meaning, since in this instance, white symbolizes rebirth. White is also used to denote initiation, another form of rebirth. Children wear white at their first communion, and in Africa, boys smear their bodies with white paste after circumcision to show that they are apart from their main society for a time. When they reenter, it is as men, their bodies painted red.

White is the color of expectation and contains all the potential of the blank canvas. The pristine glory of a fresh fall of snow makes the world look clean and pure but white shows up every mark, hence its usefulness in hospitals and other clinical environments.

White is a symbol of peace, and the white flag is a universal sign of submission and surrender. However, the white feather is a sign of cowardice. This originates in the days of cock fighting when a bird with a white feather in its tail was believed to be a poor fighter. The potency of this particular white symbol is such that, just after World War II, an "order of the White Feather" was started as a method of goading men into joining the army. Women were encouraged to hand the white feather of cowardice to any man not wearing a uniform.

YELLOW

Symbolic meanings: *the sun; power, authority; the intellect and intuition; goodness; light, life, truth, immortality; endurance; the empire and fertility; cowardice, treachery.*

Yellow is one of the three primary colors and is related to the third chakra which lives in the region of the solar plexus. This is apt, since yellow, like red and orange, is one of the sun colors. It could be argued that yellow is the most dazzling of the three, so the association makes good sense. The ancient Egyptians had only six colors available in their pallet, and wherever yellow was used this indicated endurability and timelessness.

In China, yellow was the color of the Emperor. The average man in the street was forbidden from wearing it until relatively recently. It is also the color of fertility, since healthy soil in China is a yellow color. Because of this, all the hangings, sheets, and pillows of the bridal bed were dyed in vibrant shades of yellow as well as red.

However, there are some contradictions with yellow. In some places, to call someone "yellow" or to say that they have a "yellow streak" means that they are cowardly. There are several theories about why this should be. The one that seems to fit best is that Judas Iscariot wore yellow robes, and his own cowardly act was to betray Christ for thirty pieces of silver.

Jewish people were made to wear a yellow Star of David by the Nazi regime during the years of World War II. Similarly, in 1215 the Lateran Council ordered Jews to wear a yellow circle to identify themselves. It was probably small comfort for these persecuted people that they believed yellow to be synonymous with beauty. In tenth-century France, the doors of criminals were painted yellow. Conversely, in the fourteenth century, the yellow chrysanthemum was worn by warriors as a symbol of courage.

Because leaves turn yellow and then to black with the onset of fall, in several places, including ancient Egypt, yellow is a color of mourning. A yellow cross was painted on doors as a sign of the plague, possibly for the same reasons, and even today yellow marks off a quarantined area.

CLAVICLE

See Key.

COMPASSES

See Freemasonry.

CORN DOLLY

These days, the corn dolly generally gathers dust in gift shops, an innocuous souvenir for tourists in rural areas. However, its origins as a powerful magical symbol go back thousands of years to pre-Christian times. It may come as a surprise that the corn dolly hanging on the kitchen wall can trace its roots back to a particularly bloody ritual.

In any agrarian culture, the success of the crop is all-important and in northern Europe the harvest produce was essential to survival during the winter period. It was the generally held belief that the spirit of the harvest—in this case, the versatile grain crop—resided in the plant, and once the plant was cut down then the spirit effectively became homeless. In order to provide a new home for this spirit, the farmers made a corn dolly from the very last stalks of the crop. The dolly would spend her time indoors over the winter, waiting to be plowed back into the ground at the start of the new season. In places where the corn dolly custom was not established, the last few stalks of corn were violently beaten into the ground, thus driving the spirit back into the earth.

The dolly was made into the shape of an old woman, representing the Crone aspect of the Harvest Goddess. She was drenched in water as a further propitiation to the gods and to ensure that plenty of rain would feed the harvest to come. Different areas had different styles of corn dollies.

However, the custom of preserving the spirit of the harvest was not always carried out in such a genteel way. The Phrygians, who lived in central Asia Minor and worshipped the mother of the gods, Cybele, carried out a different sort of ceremony. Their "corn dolly" was formed from thickly plaited sheaves of corn formed into a tall column. Any stranger found in the vicinity was captured in the belief that his presence there would mean that the spirit of the harvest had possessed his body and caused him to wander into the area. The hapless stranger was then trapped within this cage of corn and then beheaded in the belief that the blood that fell upon the ground contained the valuable "soul" of the crop.

CORNICELLO

An amulet designed to protect the wearer, the cornicello features the effigy of the horn, is made of horn, or is horn-shaped. "Cornicello" comes from an Italian word meaning "little horn."

CORNUCOPIA

Also called the horn of plenty, the cornucopia is often depicted in paintings and on friezes where it symbolizes the notion of boundless abundance, as flowers, fruits, sheaves of wheat, and other produce spill out of a hollow horn or a

twisting basket woven in the shape of the horn. The origin of the cornucopia is found in the Greek myth of Amalthea. Amalthea fed the infant Zeus a drink of goat's milk and was given the brimming goat's horn as a reward. Sometimes the infant Zeus is depicted being fed the milk from the horn itself. The cornucopia, as a symbol of a bounteous harvest, is also associated with Ceres, the goddess of corn, and also with Fortuna, goddess of good fortune.

The idea of a bottomless, bounteous container has similarities to the symbol of the cauldron.

COSMIC EGG

See Egg.

COSMOGRAM

This is a flat graphic symbol that represents the cosmos, and is often used as a meditative focus. The mandala is a cosmogram, as are the

elaborate depictions of tortoises holding up the planet.

Cosmograms commonly feature the most basic shapes of the circle (representing the planet, and unity) and the square (the earth and the directions).

COWRIE SHELL

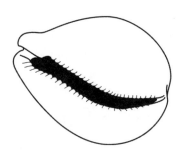

More than any other shell, the cowrie has a marked resemblance to the female genitalia or yoni. Because of the ancient idea of the Doctrine of Signatures, the shell is therefore endowed with magical powers of fertility, good luck, and wealth. Originating from the Malaysian area,

cowrie shells were used as currency for some time. Their use in decorative masks, headdresses, and other items was widespread, where it had the new addition of being a status symbol because of its use as small change.

The cowrie also represents another body part: the eye. Therefore, along with other objects from the natural world that have a similar appearance, the cowrie is considered to protect against evil.

CRESCENT MOON AND STAR

The crescent moon is possibly the most distinctive moon symbol; it shows the changing shape of the moon and also the return to the same shape. Like the moon, it is connected to the female principle and the element of water. It is also linked to virginity. Goddesses with a strong moon connection—such as Diana, or Artemis—are often depicted with the unmistakable crescent moon shape close by. In Christian iconography, Mary the Virgin, also known by the lyrical epithet Star of the Sea, appears standing on a crescent moon with stars in the background, hinting at her goddess nature. She generally wears the color blue, symbolic of spirituality and chastity. The crescent moon that rests on its "back" looks like a chalice.

The crescent moon with the star is one of the most iconographic symbols of Islam, although the symbol is believed to predate the faith by thousands of years as the symbol of another of the great moon goddesses, Tanit Astarte, the Queen of Heaven. There are several stories that explain why the symbol was adopted. One is that the founder of the Ottoman Empire, Osman, had a dream in which the crescent moon stretched across the earth. Because of this, he kept the existing moon goddess symbol and made it the emblem of his empire.

Incidentally, the croissant—virtually a national symbol of France—is said to have been invented when the Turks were besieging Budapest in 1686 (another account gives the city as Vienna three years earlier). They dug underground passages with the idea of reaching the center of town without attracting attention. However, a baker, working through the night, heard the noise and raised the alarm. As a reward for saving the city, the baker was given the right to bake a special pastry in the form of the crescent moon that was featured on the Ottoman flag.

CROSS

See First signs: Cross.

CROSS AND CROWN

A Christian symbol, the Cross and Crown is a reminder of the rewards that come in heaven (the crown) after the tribulations of life (the cross) are over. Some latter-day Knights Templar organizations use this symbol.

CROSS LORRAINE

Essentially a heraldic device used by the Dukes of Lorraine, the Cross Lorraine is a vertical bar with two horizontal bars, originally equally spaced at either end. However, this cross is used elsewhere too. In the Catholic Church the cross signifies the rank of cardinal, and in renaissance alchemy it was used as a symbol of spirit and matter.

Additionally the Cross Lorraine is used to denote one of the degrees within Freemasonry. During World War II it was adopted by the French Resistance as their secret symbol, an emblem to stand in opposition to the swastika, which had been rendered sinister by the Nazis, and lost for a time its meaning as a positive sun symbol.

CROSSROADS

In fairy stories and myths, it is often at the crossroads where mischief awaits, usually in the form of otherworldly spirits. Effectively, the crossroads symbolizes the intersection of two paths, making four potential routes, and a place where a decision must be made, not only practically, but metaphorically too. The X of the crossroads marks a spot where two worlds meet.

One of the more recent tales about an encounter at a crossroads concerns the renowned blues guitarist and musician Robert Johnson. Johnson is alleged to have met the devil at a crossroads, and to have exchanged his soul for his remarkable talent as a musician and songwriter. Johnson exacerbated this devilish reputation when he recorded a track called "Cross Road Blues," based on a myth from the Deep South. This legend tells that a daring person who fancied striking a deal with Satan should wait for him at a crossroads late at night. The origins of this story go back to African folklore, where a deity called Esu was the guardian of the crossroads. When Christianity took over, these old gods were, quite literally, demonized, and Esu was transformed into the devil. Hecate, too, personified as the Queen of the Witches, was called the Goddess of the Crossroads.

In Celtic mythology, corpses belonging to those considered "unholy" were buried at crossroads in order to prevent them coming back to life and because the crossroads was a gate to the otherworld. Gibbets were placed at crossroads for the same reason.

CROW'S FOOT

The crow's foot is also known as the Witch's Foot, and was feared as an indicator of death, used in casting spells against enemies. Crows, like ravens, were associated with the witches and warlocks who were believed to be able to transform themselves into these black birds so that they could travel unnoticed to their sabbats.

The name "crow's feet" is also given to the lines that radiate around the outer corners of the

eyes with the coming of age and the inevitable approach of death.

CRUCIFIX

A Latin cross with a model of the body of the Christ fixed to it. It is used in the Christian tradition as a reminder of the sacrifice that Christ made for humankind.

CRUX DISSIMULATA

In third-century Rome, early Christians were persecuted to such a degree that their lives were threatened and the symbols of their faith had to be disguised. One of the ways they recognized one another was by the sign of the fish or ichthus; another way was to disguise the cross cleverly as something else. The meaning of Crux Dissimulata is "disguised" or "dissimilar" cross.

One of the more ingenious forms of this secret symbol,

shown here, was the anchor. The top of the anchor is formed like a cross and, in addition, the anchor is plainly a symbol of stability. Because anchors are associated with the sea, too, the fish symbol could easily be incorporated into it. The Crux Dissimulata was used as a secret symbol and a rallying call for adherents to the new and dangerous faith.

CRYSTAL BALL

Combining the sphere's perfection and totality with the clarity and brilliance of crystal, the crystal ball is a part of the toolkit of the professional clairvoyant or seer. The clarity of the crystal matches the "clear sight" of the psychic. When used for scrying, the crystal ball acts as a focus for meditation, enabling the adept to access a place that is out of time in order to be able to see into the future.

This practice of scrying is carried out in various ways. Instead of an expensive crystal, cheaper methods are apparently just as effective for the talented psychic. A bowl of water, a mirror, a drop of blood, or a pool of ink can be used. However, the glamour of the genuine crystal ball is hard to beat.

CUBE

The cube carries all the symbolism of the square (at its most basic, the material world and the elements) except that it is, of course, three-dimensional. The cube is solid, stable, reliable, and often forms the basis of other buildings. It is also a symbol of moral perfection. The cube is a symbol of material eternity. One of the most famous cubes is the Ka'aba that stands at the center of the Grand Mosque at Mecca, and which is a symbol of power and eternity.

If the cube is unfolded, it turns into a cross; this cross gives us the standard floor plan of Christian churches and further reinforces the idea of stability and eternity.

One of the five Platonic solids and one of the Tattvas, the cube represents the element of earth.

DARUMA

This is a small doll intended to resemble the founder of Zen Buddhism, the Bodhidharma Daruma. Daruma brought the teachings from India to China in the sixth century. The dolls are ubiquitous in Japan as a good-luck symbol par excellence as well as a reminder of the need for patience.

The dolls are rounded and chunky, reflecting the story that the Bodhidharma spent such a long time (reputedly nine years) meditating motionless in a cave that his limbs atrophied. A weight inside the base of the rotund little figure means that it may wobble but it never falls over, and this feature symbolizes Daruma's persistence in his meditative process as well as illustrating the Buddhist tenet that you can fall over seven times but still get up again on the eighth. He was so zealous that he is even reputed to have cut off his eyelids so that he could not fall asleep, and this is why the dolls also have wide, staring eyes. Coincidentally, the gift of tea was given to Daruma by God to help him keep awake.

Given as a gift at the New Year, each of the eyes of the Daruma doll are colored with a marker when certain goals are achieved. When both eyes are colored the little doll is burned on a shrine as an offering.

DEARINTH

A relatively new sign, the dearinth was invented by Oberon Zell as the symbol for his Church of All Worlds. Zell is credited with inventing the term "Neo-Pagan." The symbol represents a labyrinth but also cleverly includes the figure of the god and goddess. The nine concentric circles of the dearinth relate to the nine levels of initiation within the church.

* * *

DEGREES OF WITCHCRAFT

Witches and wizards might write their names, followed by a symbol that denotes the level of his or her initiation into the craft.

FIRST DEGREE [INVERTED TRIANGLE]

This shows the neophyte that has been introduced to the most basic teachings and traditions. The shape of this inverted triangle is also drawn in the air as the "threefold salute," and is drawn in the sequence of breast, breast, genitals, breast.

SECOND DEGREE [1]

The second stage of witchcraft, and a deeper level of knowledge is also represented by a gesture that emulates the shape of the upright triangle: mouth, breast, breast, mouth.

SECOND DEGREE [2]

The Fivefold Salute describes the shape of an inverted pentagram by tracing a line from genitals to right breast, then left hip to right hip, right hip to left breast and back to genitals.

THIRD DEGREE

This is the sign used by fully fledged witches and wizards. Formed of a pentagram surmounted by an upright triangle, it is traced in the air from mouth to breast, then back to the mouth, genitals, right foot, left knee, right knee, left foot and back to the genitals.

DHARMA WHEEL

The Dharma wheel or Dharmachakra is used as a symbol in both Hinduism and Buddhism. It is an eight-spoked wheel, sometimes rendered quite decoratively. Each spoke of the wheel represents one of the pillars of belief that applies to these Dharmic religions.

1. Right faith
2. Right intention
3. Right speech

4. Right action
5. Right livelihood
6. Right effort
7. Right thought
8. Right meditation

The wheel symbol in general is complex and is covered elsewhere; this particular wheel represents the notion of overcoming obstacles, difficulties, and challenges.

DJED

An ancient Egyptian symbol of stability, the djed is an image of a pillar with four platforms piled on top of it. As with other pillar-like symbols the world over, the djed also signifies the World Axis, the World Tree, and the phallus.

DOORWAY

The simple doorway—an everyday object that goes unnoticed most of the time—is symbolic of a tran-

sition between one world and the next. Such a doorway may take different forms, as a dolmen, a torii, a gateway, but the meaning remains the same. In C. S. Lewis's Narnia novels, the wardrobe into which the children step to enter the magical world of Narnia is a good example of this symbol. Both heaven and hell lie beyond gates or doorways, and the threshold of such a place is seen as the place where two worlds meet and sometimes collide. Many rituals involve the initiate stepping through a doorway of some kind. The vesica piscis represents a doorway where the world of spirit enters the world of matter.

DORJE

See Vajra.

DOT

See First signs: Dot.

DOUBLE HAPPINESS

This good-luck symbol, ubiquitous in China or in places where there is a strong undercurrent of Chinese culture, comprises the character meaning happiness, written twice, hence the name Double Happiness. The meaning of the sign is inferred in its name, and it is a popular symbol for practitioners of Feng Shui. The sign is effective if placed in the sector of the home that relates to relationships. It is also said to be particularly lucky for newlyweds.

DREAMCATCHER

The forerunner of the dreamcatcher was a Native American spiderweb of feathers and beads, a simple little charm made from a small hoop of flexible wood, such as willow, with an interlacement of plant fibers designed to look like a cobweb.

This little amulet was used particularly as a protection for babies and small children. Hung over their cradles and beds, it was thought to entrap any negative spirits that came in the form of nightmares. These malevolent entities, entangled in the web, were sizzled in the heat from the rising sun. The spiderweb shape gave homage to Asibikaasi, the mythical spider woman, whose magical webs could catch anything.

The elaborate dreamcatchers of today, an essential part of the kit for any self-respecting New Ager, were invented in the 1960s and '70s as part of the resurgence in Native American culture and belief.

DREIDEL

During the Jewish holiday of Chanukah, the usually strict rules forbidding any kind of gambling are relaxed slightly. The dreidel is a wooden spinning top, its four sides

inscribed with letters. These letters form an acronym that reminds the players of the meaning of the holiday. The initial letters, *nun, gimel, heh,* and *shin,* stand for a phrase which, when translated, means "A great miracle happened there," and the top is spun to win small treats such as sweets and chocolate coins. The dreidel is symbolic of fun and of the holiday period but carries a serious message at the same time.

DRILBU

The Drilbu is the bell-like object that appears sometimes in the right hand of Buddhist statues, and is the female counterpart of the male Vajra or Dorje. Its Sanskrit counterpart is called the Ghanta.

The Drilbu symbolizes knowledge, emptiness, and wisdom, and the notes of its bell are a reminder of the transient nature of everything. The actual object is made of an amalgamation of seven different metals, each of which is associated with the planets and is a magical symbol in its own right. The Drilbu is a musical instrument as well as a ritual object. It is chimed three times to focus the attention of the people attending any ceremony. Its sweet-sounding resonant note also welcomes in good spirits and drives away any evil ones.

The Drilbu has the same feminine symbolism as the chalice in the Western tradition. It is called the Ghanta in the Hindu faith.

DRUZE STAR

This five-pointed upright star, comprised of five distinct diamond shapes, is the emblem of the Druze faith, an offshoot of Islam. Each segment is often colored according to its meaning.

The five points of the star remind followers of the religion of the five universal principles of the faith:

1. The masculine element, the sun and the mind. This segment is often colored green.
2. The feminine element and the moon, colored red.
3. The Word, considered the mediator between the divine and humankind, colored yellow.
4. Will and the realms of possibility, colored blue.
5. Finally, the white segment of the star represents actualization, the manifestation of the Word and the will.

Egg

The egg is as powerful in its symbolism as it is potent as a life-force. The World Egg is a ubiquitous symbol for the egg from which the universe is said to have hatched, an idea that appears in creation myths from all parts of the world. The Celts, Hindus, Egyptians, Greeks, Phoenicians, and many more all agree about this idea.

The form this cosmic hatching takes is variable though. Often, the egg rises from primeval waters and is incubated by a bird; in Hindu belief, this is the Hamsa, a goose. When the egg hatches, the yolk and the white become heaven and earth.

The Shinto tradition says that the universe resembled a giant hen's egg that broke open, with the heavier parts becoming the earth and the lighter, the heavens. There is also a theory that the entire universe is contained in a huge egg that stands upright.

The egg is a symbol of new life, and this idea is borne out with chocolate eggs at Easter, which in itself is a celebration of the pre-Christian fertility goddess, Eostre, who also gives her name to the hormone estrogen. The subsequent celebration of Christ's death and resurrection meant that the egg kept its significance as a symbol of new life and hope. Archaeologists have found clay eggs in Russian burial sites, reinforcing the belief in the egg as a symbol of immortality and of rebirth.

In alchemy, the Philosopher's Egg symbolizes the seed of spiritual life, and depicts the place wherein a great transformation takes place.

The ancient riddle of what came first, chicken or egg, was deftly if disappointingly answered by Angelus Silesius, who said:

The chicken was in the egg and the egg was in the chicken.

ELVEN STAR

This seven-pointed star has several different names and occurs in many different magical traditions, including Sacred Geometry. Most prosaically, it is known as the septagram. For wiccans and pagans it is also called the faerie star, for others it might be referred to as the star of the Seven Sisters since it is associated with the cluster of seven astronomical stars called the Pleiades (or Flock of Doves). These celestial sisters were believed to guard the Axis Mundi as depicted by the Pole star.

Wherever it occurs and by whatever name it is known, the Elven star is a reminder of the sacred significance of the number seven; the seven days of the week, the seven planets of the ancient tradition, the seven magical metals, and the seven pillars of wisdom. For the Egyptians this star represented the seven spheres of the afterlife and the seven wise people that the soul would meet on the journey.

The septagram is also an important symbol in the Kabbalah where it corresponds to the sphere of Netzach or Victory. Here, too, it acts as an aide memoire for all the things that come in groups of seven.

Like the pentagram, the Elven star can be drawn without the pen leaving the paper, a tell-tale quality of a protective symbol. Specifically, the Elven star is said to defend secrets from the outside world.

Aleister Crowley adopted a seven-pointed star as the seal for his Astrum Argentum (Silver Star) Order.

EMERALD TABLET

See Smaragdina Tablet.

Endless Knot

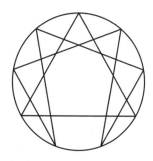

Different interpretations of the Endless Knot occur in different cultures, including Celtic, Chinese, and in Tibetan Buddhism where it is one of the Eight Auspicious Symbols, or Ashtamangala. The knot can be drawn without the pen leaving the paper—this is generally a clue that the symbol is one of protection.

Philosophically, the knot is constructed of "something" (the rope, representative of matter) and "nothing" (the spaces in between), symbolic of spirit. These two elements represent the co-dependence of wisdom and compassion, male and female, night and day.

Since the knot has no beginning and no end, there are also comparisons to be drawn with the circle.

described as "the essence of being." It was revived by G. I. Gurdjieff, the mystic/teacher whose teachings have had a far-reaching effect on the last few generations of esotericists. Gurdjieff used this deceptively simple shape to demonstrate his theories about certain cosmic laws. The primary law that the Enneagram demonstrates is the natural "highs" and "lows" of any aspect of life, whether emotional, mechanical, or commercial. Those who have studied the Enneagram in depth believe that it helps them to accept these fluctuations as part of the natural order.

The Enneagram of Personality sees the symbol used as a way to define the nine different personality types identified by Gurdjieff.

Enneagram

This nine-pointed geometric figure, with an open side, is an ancient sign that, in Kabbalistic mysticism, is

Enso

Belonging to Zen Buddhism, the Enso is a circle, drawn quickly and simply with a brush stroke,

although years of practice in the art of calligraphy are likely to have preceded the ease with which the symbol can be drawn. The Enso symbolizes eternity, the perfect meditative state, the "no thing," and enlightenment.

EVANGELISTS' SYMBOLS

The four evangelists—Disciples of Christ who witnessed and wrote about the events in the life of the Messiah, which comprise the four main books of the New Testament—are often represented not as men but as hybrid creatures. Not only that, but the four men—Matthew, Mark, Luke, and John—are each associated with the four points of the compass, the elements, the winds, and with the four rivers purported to run through Eden. Each evangelist is also ascribed a sign of the zodiac. Collectively, they

symbolize stability and the four pillars of the faith.

The angel is the symbol of Matthew. Mark is the lion, whose symbol in stone proliferates around St. Mark's Square in Venice. The bull is the symbol of Luke, and the eagle represents John. Wherever they are represented, these creatures have wings, as a sign of their divine nature as messengers from God. These hybrid animals are also called the Tetramorphs.

EVIL EYE

This is a gaze or stare which is believed to cause actual harm. There are numerous talismans, amulets, and charms intended to counteract the affect of such a deadly gaze. *See* Eye (Part 8).

FALUN GONG SYMBOL

The symbol for the philosophy or spiritual practice of Falun Gong is an amalgam of two ancient Eastern signs. Two concentric circles encompass a central swastika, while four yin-yang signs and four further swastikas are evenly spaced around it.

Falun Gong itself is a relatively new movement—it was founded as recently as 1992 by Li Hongzhi—although its practices are based on the ancient art of Qi Gong. Falun Gong relies on certain physical movements and meditation techniques to promote health, harmony, and the balance of mind, body, and spirit although the Chinese government denounced Falun Gong as a cult.

"Falun" means "Wheel of Law/ Dharma" in Chinese Buddhism, and the wheel symbol itself (the "Falon") replicates the energy wheel that adherents of the practice say is located in the center of the body, akin to a chakra. This wheel, once "installed" or awakened, turns continuously, when clockwise absorbing energy from the cosmos, or when counterclockwise, getting rid of waste matter from the physical body. Adepts say that meditation and repetition of the set exercises of the Falun Gong discipline result in them actually being able to see the Falun. The Falun Gong emblem also acts as a mandala or also as a cosmogram, a miniature schematic of the universe.

FAROHAR

A version of the winged solar disc, the Farohar is a Zoroastrian symbol whose name means "to choose." The symbol represents some of the philosophical facets of the religion.

The three layers of feathers on the wings represent the three main tenets of the faith: good thoughts, good words, good deeds. The disc itself symbolizes the sun, and the notion of eternity. The two banners are a reminder of duality (good and evil, black and white, spirit and matter, male and female) and the need for balance between opposing elements.

The man seeming to sit on the top of the disc represents Zoroaster himself, and serves as a reminder for his followers to live a morally upright life.

FASCES

A symbol of Roman Imperial power, the Fasces was originally an axe or an arrow with a bundle of birch sticks tied around the handle with red cords. The numerous sticks represented unity and strength in numbers, but as a symbol of authority, it also implied punishment for those who failed to adhere to the rules. The birch rod itself is synonymous with the idea of punishment, its wood used for the schoolroom canes that were inflicted on children in less enlightened times.

The symbol of the Fasces carried great resonance for the Italian people and was revived by Mussolini as the emblem of his political party in the 1930s. Hence, the Latin word for "bundle" became the origin of the word "Fascist," which carries far more sinister connotations than a simple collection of sticks.

FEATHER

The Egyptian goddess of truth, Ma'at, has the ostrich feather as her attribute. There is a very specific reason for this. Because the ostrich is a flightless bird, the design of its feathers is different to those of other birds where one side is larger than the other. The ostrich feather, however, is perfectly balanced and symmetrical, and so is a fitting emblem of justice.

The symbolism of feathers is closely aligned to that of wings and birds. They stand for ascendance, flight, communication with the spirit realms and the element of air. Shamanistic use of feathers is for all these reasons; the feathers enable the soul to become as light as the feather and transcend the boundaries of gravity, time, and space. Shamans of all nationalities wear feathers as a part of their ritual apparel.

The eagle feather is the most valuable of all feathers. In some parts of the world, this feather, synonymous with all the power of the bird, is considered so sacred that only card-carrying Native American tribal members may own them. Eagle feathers that are found in the wrong hands are the cause of heavy fines.

The swan's feather appears in the cloaks of Druids; because the swan is the bird of poetry, its feathers magically confer these powers on the bard.

Used at the end of the arrow as a "flight," feathers have a practical as well as symbolic use. Additionally, feathers are a symbol of sacrifice. This is because, when chickens and other birds were ritually slaughtered, all they left behind was a few feathers, fluttering to the ground.

The other major symbolic meaning of the feather associates it with vegetation and with hair, primarily because of a similarity in appearance.

FETISH

Although, recently, the fetish has erotic connotations, the origins of the word are from the French *fétiche* and the Portuguese *feitiço*, meaning charm. In sorcery, a fetish is something that is believed to have a spirit of its own, used for magical purposes. It is likely that the first fetish objects were stones of some kind, not necessarily small ones. The Black Stone at Mecca and the Stone of Destiny are good examples of fetish objects whose power, as such, has accumulated over the centuries that people have revered them. "Lucky" or "unlucky" numbers are fetishes, as are "lucky" or "unlucky" days of the week.

Bodily fluids or parts such as fingernails and teeth are fetish objects, considered to contain the energy of the creature of origin. Smaller fetish objects were carried in pouches or bags, a practice that continues today in many forms. These fetish or medicine bags should never touch the ground. The reason for this is that contact with the earth is sacrilegious in some way for these empowered objects. It is for exactly the same reason that flags, symbols of national identity, also never touch the ground.

FIRE WHEEL

See Tomoe.

*   *   *

Five Pillars of Wisdom

Islam is conceptualized as a building, which is raised on five "pillars." These are: the tenets of the faith, prayer, almsgiving, fasting during the month of Ramadan, and the pilgrimage (or Hajj) to Mecca (which each adherent of the faith must carry out at least once in his or her lifetime.)

Fleur de Lys

Seen regularly as a heraldic symbol, the stylized flower-inspired Fleur de Lys is much older than many people may realize, appearing in Mesopotamian art, on ancient Egyptian reliefs, and even on Dogon objects. The literal translation is the "flower of the lily" and it is a symbol of purity, being associated with the dove and the Virgin Mary. At Rennes-le-Château, the Fleur de Lys is a prominent symbol, too, in the Church of Mary Magdalene.

Flower of Life

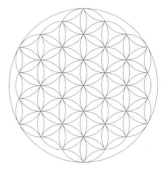

The ubiquity of this beautifully satisfying geometric symbol is astonishing. It appears at the Golden Temple in Amritsar, in a Buddhist temple at Ajanta, India, in the Louvre and at Ephesus. It has been embroidered onto the robes of sultans. It can be seen in Cordoba, Marrakech, Beijing, Lebanon, Egypt, and Japan. It is chiseled into wood in Holland and carved into stone in Scotland and Austria. The oldest example of the Flower of Life is believed to be 2,500 years old.

The Flower of Life design is deceptively simple. It consists of a series of evenly spaced interlinking circles. As more circles are added, the pattern emerges. The design has been favored by religions, architects, and scientists alike.

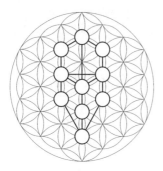

Flower of Life showing Kabbalistic tree of life

Despite the seeming simplicity of the design, hidden within it are subtle complexities that have such a profound meaning for some that they believe the Flower of Life depicts the fundamental forms of time and space.

The most obvious symbols inherent within the Flower of Life are the circle, the hexagon or six-pointed star, and the vesica piscis. Furthermore, three intersecting circles alone form a Borromean Ring which is also known as the Tripod of Life symbol.

Some important symbolic sequences can be derived from many-circled versions of the design, for example Metatron's Cube can be derived from the Flower of Life, and the five Platonic solids can then be "extracted" from Metatron's Cube. As if these fundamental principles of sacred geometry were not

enough, the Kabbalistic Tree of Life can be discerned within the Flower of Life, as can the Seed of Life.

For many, the Flower of Life is an object of mystery which may well unlock the secrets of the universe, since they believe that it contains a record of information about all living things. The Flower of Life is used as a focus both for study and meditation.

FORKED CROSS

See Y of Pythagoras.

FRUIT OF LIFE

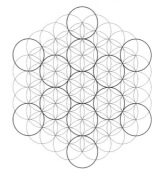

The Flower of Life pattern, if constructed of at least five circles down and across, holds another symbol within it. This is the Fruit of Life, formed from a six-rayed star of five circles in all directions. There are 13 circles in total. This star shape then gives the foundation for the construction of Metatron's Cube, from which, in turn, the five Platonic solids can be made.

Fu

In China, the Fu is an ancient symbol of good luck, and is still popularly used in talismans and charms. The word "Fu" sounds like the word for bat; so, by association, bats are auspicious, too, especially if they are five in number. The actual ideogram of Fu shows a god blessing a farm, which is an analogy for the earth; the farm is split into four parts, the four parts resembling the four directions and the four elements.

Furka

See Y of Pythagoras.

Gammadion

The gammadion is a form of swastika, but with shorter arms, and is so called because it is constructed from four Greek "gamma" letters. This sign was widespread, appearing across Europe and through to India. Like the swastika, it is a solar symbol, and the four arms of the symbol represent all the universal objects and concepts that come in groups of four: the directions, the seasons, the elements, the solstices, and the equinoxes.

Gar

See Gungnir.

* ✳ *

FOOD MAGIC

Every week of the year, on most continents around this planet, millions of people participate in a profoundly magical ritual whereby two very basic everyday food-stuffs, which are available in supermarkets or on stalls pretty much anywhere you care to mention around the world, have a spell cast over them by means of a sacred incantation. The person officiating over this ceremony makes symbolic gestures with his or her hands and arms. This spellbinding usually takes place in a language very few fully comprehend, a language full of secrets, and as a result these mundane objects are transformed into something as mystical, sacred, and awe-inspiring as anything you could ever imagine.

In addition, this ritual generally takes place in a building whose architecture and design has been informed by knowledge of the directions, shapes, and patterns that link the heavens with the earth in an arrangement of the sacred symbols which some say were dictated to humans by the very angels themselves.

When the Holy Communion of the Roman Catholic Church takes place, the simple ingredients of bread and wine are transformed, many believe, into the actual body and blood of the Christ. This is not just a symbolic representation, some say, but a very real and profound belief that underpins the foundations of the religion. By eating this holy, sacred food, imbued with magical intent, the recipient voluntarily absorbs the spirit of the Messiah.

The ritual and perceived reality of this act are inseparable, but bread and wine are not the only sacred foods we absorb as part of our everyday lives. We need food to live, so it comes as no surprise that we have accorded many ingredients with magical powers. Indeed, some of the things we eat every day carry both constituent elements and meanings which go far beyond mere nutrition. Many other foods—nuts, apples, and other fruits and vegetables—are covered in other sections of this book, and this is by no means an exhaustive inventory, but a look at some of the foods, real and mythical, which have become symbols in themselves.

AMBROSIA

For the Greeks, ambrosia was the food of the gods. Given that it conferred immortality, the deities on Mount Olympus guarded it jealously. As well as ensuring eternal life, ambrosia could be used as an ointment that could heal any wound. However, for a mortal, eating ambrosia was a big mistake. Take the story of Tantalus, for example. He was invited to eat with the gods, and so, presuming that he was accepted as one of them, he ate ambrosia. In the tradition of all good dinner party guests, he decided to return the favor and invited the gods to his place. Deciding somewhat sycophantically that they should feast upon all the good things that they had given him, he served up the flesh of his own children, and was banished to Hades.

CHOCOLATE

Long before the Western discovery of the Americas, the natives of Brazil, Mexico, the West Indies, and South America used the seeds of the chocolatl tree to make a stimulating drink. These bean-like seeds were cacahuatl, or cocoa. Primarily symbolic of love, chocolate is a sensual food with aphrodisiac properties that are due, in part, to association. However, its melting point is the same temperature as blood, a very satisfying sensation.

The botanical name of the plant gives a clue as to its sacred status. *Theobroma cacao* means "food of the gods," from the Greek "theo," meaning god and "broma," meaning food.

The beans were so highly valued that the Mayans used them as currency. Possibly the world's first chocoholic, their ruler Montezuma was completely addicted to the beans. He drank them infused in cold water with no seasoning. He served this sacred drink in goblets of beaten gold, and at the coronation of Montezuma II in 1502 a concoction of chocolate and psilocybin mushrooms was served to the guests. This must have been a heady mixture.

Cortés cultivated the plant primarily because of its reputation as an aphrodisiac; this secret was divulged by one of the nineteen young women given to him by Montezuma as a tribute. Perhaps the 2,000 chocolatl trees that he consequently planted were testimony to the efficacy of the beans in keeping the ladies satisfied.

By 1550, chocolate factories were operating in Lisbon, Genoa, Marseilles, and other European cities. The recipes became more and more refined. Catherine de Medici slowed down the progress of chocolate for a while because it was so good that she wanted it all to herself. However, although the Church tried to ban many of the foodstuffs that had been discovered in the New World, especially those that were considered as stimulants, their advice was largely ignored and it is possible that this disapproval increased the popularity of this illicit substance. Neither Catherine nor all the forces of the Church could stop the world from becoming chocolate-coated.

Today, the form of chocolate has changed so much that Montezuma would probably find it unrecognizable, both in taste and form. However, it is still unrivaled as a token and symbol of love.

HONEY

Legislation decrees that all packaged food carry a "best before" date, but this seems to be particularly unnecessary in the case of honey, since jars of the stuff found in the tombs of Egyptian kings of several thousand years ago has proved to be perfectly edible even now. It could well be because honey is so long lasting, and because it is used as a preservative, that it is a symbol of immortality and is used in funerary rites. The bees that make the honey have their place in the realms of magical creatures accorded with supernatural powers, but more of that in the Fauna section. The Promised Land is said to "flow with milk and honey" as being the very best that the gods can offer.

The sweetness of honey is believed to confer gifts of learning and poetry. We'll never know if the story that Pythagoras existed on honey alone is true, but the fact that the rumor exists is in accord with his god-like status. As well as being edible and fermentable, honey has healing and antiseptic qualities, and a dollop of honey smeared onto a wound will soon draw out any impurities and speed the healing process.

Honey is said to be an aphrodisiac and to encourage fertility and virility, wealth and abundance, and is a symbol of the sun, partly because of the flowers from which it is made but also because of its color.

MANNA

When the children of Israel were struggling to survive in the wilderness, manna appeared, miraculously, overnight, and so they could eat. Precisely what manna was—or is—is debatable. Some believe it might be a kind of fungus, others believe that it might be sap or resin exuded from the tamarisk tree. The symbolic meaning of manna is of something provided freely by the universe or by God and is the ultimate reminder that we have everything we need. Manna is also associated with the Bread of Life or the Eucharist.

MEAD

Like honey, mead also carries the gift of immortality. The Celts believed it was the favored drink of the gods in the otherworld. Mead is a sacred drink in Africa, too, where it is believed that drinking the stuff will make you more knowledgeable. Worth a try! Mead is very simple to make—it's simply honey mixed with water and allowed to ferment—and this process of

fermentation is akin to a magical process in itself, which is akin to transmutation in alchemy.

MILK

Given that milk is the first food, it's not surprising that it is associated with many stories of the Creation, and is a symbol of divinity. Amrita, or soma, the absolute nectar of life for Hindus and the equivalent of ambrosia, was created as a cosmic sea of milk was churned. The curds that were created by this epic stirring formed the earth, the universe, and the stars. Along with honey, there is an abundance of milk in the Promised Land, and Indian myths tell of a magical milk tree in heaven. Because of its color and its association with the feminine, milk is a symbol of the moon.

The main food source for milk for us human beings (once we're weaned) is the cow. The cow is sacred in India because during times of famine it made far more sense to keep the animal alive for its milk rather than slaughter and eat it purely for its meat, so all parts of the cow are accorded sacred status and are ruled over by one or other of the gods or goddesses.

In the hidden symbolic language of alchemy, the Philosopher's Stone is sometimes called the Virgin's Milk.

NECTAR

Nectar is often referred to as ambrosia, but has secrets of its own to tell. Flowers create it, and its scent attracts the bees, which then transform the nectar into honey. Seemingly insignificant, nectar is nevertheless a very magical ingredient, created from flowers, sunshine, and bees working together in a collective consciousness known as the "hive mind" in an environment which itself is constructed from one of the key shapes in sacred geometry, the hexagon.

SOMA

Like the Greek Olympians, the Indian deities had a type of food, like ambrosia, that ensured their immortality. This was soma, or amrita. Whereas dire consequences befell any mortal that dared to partake of ambrosia, the Indian gods were more generous with their soma, and any mortal that ate it was immediately given immortality and access to heaven. The ancient Indian Vedic scriptures, the Ramayana, tell the story of Rama, an epic hero, the perfect man. Rama was born after his father was visited by an angel. This angel brought with him some magical food. Eating this soma meant that Rama's father was able to sire offspring that were the human incarnations of the god Vishnu.

WINE

The symbolic meanings of wine are generally attached to the red variety; it seems that a nice dry white or a sweet rosé carries no hidden mystery. Here are some things to think about next time you open a nice bottle of claret.

The red color means that wine is often linked to blood, particularly since the wine is the "blood" of the grape. Because it looks like blood, wine is often used in rituals where blood would otherwise be called for, and because ceremonial wine is often drunk from a shared chalice, it is seen, like bread, as a unifying principle. Wine is male, and bread is female. As a partner to bread in the ritual of the Eucharist, the consecrated wine is transformed into the blood of the Christ, a reminder of both sacrifice and immortal life, and it's this transformative power that accords wine with much of its mystique. When the water is turned into wine in the story of the marriage at Cana, what is really being shown here is the transformation of the mundane into the magical, the earthly into the heavenly. It is this magical process of fermentation at work that explains why wine is associated with Bacchus/Dionysus, and the intoxicating power of wine is symbolic of divine possession.

The phrase "In vino veritas" links wine to the truth and is a reminder that those intoxicated by perhaps a little too much of that nice claret will be more likely to speak the truth than most, which can be good or bad, depending on the circumstances.

GLOBUS CRUCIGER

This is the globe surmounted by a cross, which is one of the Christian symbols of authority, and its symbolism is obvious. The orb represents the earth, and the cross, that major symbol of the faith, is Christ's supremacy over it.

The Globus Cruciger is often depicted as an actual object but was also used purely as a symbol on Roman coins from the time when Christianity became the prominent religion, around the fifth century AD. Prior to this, the lone orb had been used in the same way, to imply authority. The addition of the cross brought the well-known emblem into the Christian domain. In Britain, the Globus Cruciger appears as a physical object that is used during the coronation of the monarch. It is called the Orb and is part of the Royal Jewels.

GOAT OF MENDES

Also called the Sigil of Baphomet or the Sabbatic Goat, this sinister-looking symbol features an inverted pentagram containing the head of a goat, the upward V of the star framing the horns. This symbol has become an icon of modern occultism, believed to be the very representation of the devil himself, which was exacerbated when Anton La Vey adopted it in the 1960s for his Church of Satan.

Sometimes the symbol is encircled with a double ring, containing the Hebrew letters spelling "Leviathan," the mythical sea monster that features in the Old Testament.

GOPURA

The ornately elaborate gateway into the Hindu temples, the Gopura carry the same significance as the Japanese Torii, marking a transition between the world of matter and the world of spirit.

GRAY WOLF

Otherwise known as Lupus Met-talorum, in alchemy antimony is disguised as the gray wolf. This gray wolf is the penultimate stage in the making of the Philosopher's Stone, so in terms of the spiritual and psychological development of humans, it symbolizes the condition that brings someone very close to the enlightenment; however, both physically and metaphorically speaking, the final stage of making lead into gold is yet to come, so the gray wolf can symbolize either success or failure.

GREAT SEAL OF THE UNITED STATES OF AMERICA

See United States dollar bill.

GREEN MAN

The symbol of the Green Man could be said to lurk in the subconscious minds of anyone with an affinity for leafy, wooded, and bosky places, although the term was not coined in the UK until the 1930s. Such a character—latterly interpreted as being the raw spirit of Nature—exists not only in the British Isles but in India, Asia, and Arabic countries too.

With a head seemingly constructed of leaves and vines, the Green Man is sometimes depicted as human, and sometimes as an animal. Despite his popularity as a garden ornament and its proliferation in garden centers, one of the oldest Green Man symbols discovered thus far is a piece of stonework on an Irish obelisk that dates back to 300 BC. Irish myth features a character called a Derg Corra, meaning "man in the tree," and it may well be the case that he and the Green Man are one and the same. See Part 5, "Sacred Geometry and Places of Pilgrimage," for an example of the Green Man made into a living maze.

Signs and symbols of Freemasonry

Although many of the entries in this encyclopedia have an association with Freemasonry, many secret signs and sacred symbols belong specifically to this discipline, hence the need for a separate entry dedicated to the craft.

The Catholic Encyclopedia describes Freemasonry as

a system of morality veiled in allegory and illustrated with symbols.

Many of the signs and symbols associated with this ancient brotherhood are necessarily to do with building and architecture, and the instruments of these disciplines are used to carry analogies. One of the central tenets of Freemasonry, however, is that there should be as little dogma as possible, and so the meanings of many of the associated symbols are deliberately oblique and can remain open to personal interpretation.

1. ACACIA

Represents the idea of initiation, and is also used in Masonic fu-nerals as a symbol of rebirth. The martyred master mason who designed the Temple of Solomon at Jerusalem, Hiram Abiff, had his burial place marked with an acacia branch. See Acacia in Part 4.

2. BLAZING STAR

Freemasons give this name to the pentagram. Freemasons, like Pythagoras, regard the number five as sacred.

3. COLUMN

Many of the symbols within Freemasonry take their inspiration from the Temple of Solomon, the first temple in Jerusalem.

The structure of the Masonic Hall generally has two columns at either side of its main door that relate to the original columns set by the architect, Hiram, in the porch of the temple. These original columns were made of brass or bronze. The pillars are known by their Hebrew names and are also referred to in the

Kabbalah; on the right is Jachin (meaning stability) and the left is Boaz (meaning strength). The columns also have a male/female polarity, Jachin often painted red to symbolize the sun and fiery qualities of the active male principle, and the female Boaz painted white for the moon and the passive feminine virtues. In rites, the columns are used to denote the grade of mason. Apprentices stand before the red column, Masons stand in front of the white column, and the Master Masons in the central space between the two.

4. COMPASSES

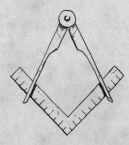

One of the foremost symbols within Freemasonry, the compasses combine with the Masons' Square. The letter G might be incorporated into the design, especially in older representations, and other elements might be added; a sun and moon, for example.

Although Freemasons prefer to leave many of their associated symbols open to interpretation, we can make some assumptions about this particular emblem simply by looking at its form and by bearing in mind how the tools are used.

Both the compass and the square are mathematical tools, used for precise measurements in disciplines that can leave no room for error: building, construction, and architecture. There is a natural symbiosis between these tools, since the circle is used to form the square, and the square can be used to give form to the circle; this is called squaring the circle and is a fundamental rule applied to geometry, sacred or otherwise. Any instruments used for measuring must, ergo, be symbols of judgment and definition.

Further, in this Masonic pairing, the feminine circle (which it is the sacred task of the compasses to create) forms a perfect union with the masculine square; therefore the spiritual combines with the material, earth with heaven. Another aspect of the compasses and the square delves even further into the symbolism of the circle and the square, with the former representing space and the latter, time. The mason, as "architect," rules over all these aspects and dimensions.

Because they are used to draw a perfect circle, the compasses themselves have significance as a tool used by God as the "architect" of the universe. This idea is represented perfectly in the William Blake painting *The Ancient of Days Measuring Time* in which God stretches toward earth, compasses in hand, with the golden disc of the sun behind him.

Compasses work by turning on a central axle or pivot. This means that they are also a symbol of the Axis Mundi, of the circular nature of time, and of the ouroboros, the serpent which continually swallows its own tail.

4a. THE SQUARE

There's a common phrase, "on the square" or "on the level." This means to be open, honest, proper, and above board, and springs directly from Masonic practice and ritual.

All the symbolism of the square and of the number four is applicable to this tool; it stands for solidity, respect, security.

4b. THE ANGLE OF THE COMPASS

Accounts differ as to whether the angle of the compass carries any special significance. The Masonic Compass is certainly drawn in different degrees. Some say that this represents the different degrees within Masonry, but again this is a matter for the inner sanctum of Masons.

4c. THE TRIANGLE

Both the square and the compasses form a triangle, a symbol both of stability and of the spirit world.

4d. THE SIX-POINTED STAR

Hidden within the square and compasses symbol is another magical sign, the Seal of Solomon, the hexagram or six-pointed star. This can be made if a line is drawn across the open point of the square and compasses. The seal is formed of two interlocking triangles and is one of the most ancient and universal magical symbols, also used in alchemy. Among other meanings, this star can be interpreted to mean "as above, so below."

4e. THE LETTER G

This does not always feature in the symbol of the compass and the square, and when it does there is ambivalence as to its meaning. Some say that it stands for God, others argue Geometry. Other interpretations including the notion that the G stands for Generation or possibly Government or even the Great Bear, the star that signifies the celestial pole or center, not only a physical center but a philosophical one. However, Masons agree that there is no definitive answer.

5. HIRAM ABIFF

The legend of Hiram Abiff is the central core and inspiration for Freemasons. Hiram was a Master Mason who specialized in metalwork, and was one of the prime designers of the Temple of Solomon in Jerusalem. Here is the legend.

After the temple was completed, three of the other workers decided that they wanted to extract the secrets from Hiram that would qualify them to be Master Masons. They positioned themselves at the doors of the temple and individually demanded to know these secrets. Hiram refused each one in turn, telling them that the knowledge they desired could be gained only by experience. The three turned on Hiram and killed him; one struck a blow to his throat with a rule, the next hit him on the chest with an iron measuring square, and the third finished the job by hitting him on the forehead with a hammer. Full of remorse for the crime that they quickly realized was a fruitless murder, the "three ruffians," as they came to be called, buried Hiram and placed an acacia tree over his grave.

However, although Hiram was effectively dead, his memory lives on and so effectively he is reborn. The initiation of the grade of Master Mason reenacts the ritual of the death of Hiram. As there are any hard and fast rules which apply to the symbolism inherent within Freemasonry, the three blows symbolize three different kinds of death: the death of the body (the blow to the throat), the death of the feelings (the strike on the chest), and the death of the mind (the blow to the forehead). Thus, the would-be Master Mason leaves his old self behind, the initiatory process symbolizing his rebirth into the higher moral values that were held by Hiram, of integrity, knowledge, and detachment. In other words, the mason is reborn as a better individual, having risen above the ignorance, hypocrisy, and envy personalized by his murderers.

6. HAMMER AND CHISEL

The hammer, in use at Masonic meetings, is not used simply to gain the attention of the gathering. Effectively, it represents the powers of the intellect that drive the thoughts and the will of the individual. At lodge meetings, the hammer is the symbol of the authority of the Worshipful Master who presides over the meeting.

The chisel is only useful if it is directed by the will of the hammer, and so represents the intellect and finer discernment.

7. LEVEL AND PLUMBLINE

Again, the level and the plumbline attached to it are inseparable items of practical building equipment that serve a deeper symbolic meaning within Freemasonry. The level comprises a set square, from the center of which hangs the plumbline. The plumbline is used to define both the vertical and horizontal lines, so it takes on the symbolism of the cross, too. The vertical level symbolizes the apprentice, and the horizontal, the degree of Fellowcraft.

It is also worth bearing in mind the philosophical meanings of the word "level," meaning steady and honest, as well as its practical application as a tool. These two meanings are inextricably linked from the actual symbol of the tool itself.

8. RULE

Correct measurements, defined by the rule, are essential to the physical construction of a building, and ensure that the design concept will work in the real world. Also of significance are the degrees of measurement that are depicted on the actual ruler itself; in the imperial measurements, these degrees of 12 and 24 correspond to the daily cycle of the sun. In this sense, the rule represents the macrocosm. The rule also keeps everything in order, and acts as a guide.

9. TRIANGLE

To Freemasons, the triangle symbolizes the Greek capital D, which they call the "shining Delta." The triangle also indicates the meanings of things in triplicate, such as "right thinking, right speaking, and right doing." On a microcosmic scale, the base of the triangle represents duration, and the two sides symbolize the qualities of light and darkness, male and female, etc. Possibly the most famous symbolic use of the Masonic triangle—which traditionally has an angle of 36 degrees at the apex and two angles of 72 degrees at the base—is the one that includes a blazing star

and also a pentagram as seen on the Seal of the United States and on the United States dollar.

10. TRACING BOARD OR TRESTLE BOARD

As with many of the symbols inherent within Freemasonry, the tracing board itself is a symbolic representation of an important piece of practical equipment used in masonry.

The tracing, or trestle, board has its origins in the flat piece of wood or cloth that was used as a drawing board by the Master Mason, on which he sketched the diagrams, schemes, and measurements needed for the building work in question. Initially represented as a piece of cloth which was rolled out on the floor at the beginning of a Masonic meeting, the tracing board is now a piece of wood that contains the signs and symbols relevant to the Brothers within their degrees of Masonic hierarchy. The boards are elaborate works of art, with the symbols woven into the whole in a pictorial, allegorical way. The symbols that are already mentioned in this section all take their place. The seemingly simple builders' tools serve to remind the initiate of their more esoteric spiritual meanings that amount to the betterment of the person and personal enlightenment.

There are hundreds, if not thousands, of different sorts of tracing boards, all usually the work of individual artists. Different tracing boards show the different degrees of the craft.

As well as showing pictures of the tools involved with practical masonry, tracing boards might tell the story of Hiram Abiff's murder or perhaps show pictures of the ritual reenactment of this crime as part of initiation ceremonies. Tracing boards also represent features of the actual temple: the pillars, the checkerboard floor, the porch with its two columns.

11. MASONIC APRON

The humble apron of the working Mason is elevated to almost religious status by the Freemasons. Generally made of leather, the way the apron is worn symbolizes the status of its wearer, with the bib worn up for the apprentice, or down by superior grades. Wearing the apron is representative of work and the necessity to be busy and industrious, and also of the fig leaves worn by Adam and Eve; as such the apron preserves the modesty of the wearer. Like the tracing board, the Masonic apron has the signs and symbols of the craft embroidered on it.

One of the most famous of the many Masonic aprons is that which belonged to George Washington. Given to him in 1784 by the Marquis de Lafeyette, whose wife embroidered the apron, it displays many Masonic symbols. Nothing is left to chance; the border colors of red, white, and blue are not only the national colors of France but also of the United States. Other symbols on this historic apron include:

- the All Seeing Eye—watchfulness, the Supreme Being;
- rays—show the power of the Supreme Being to reach inside the hearts of men;
- rainbow—symbolic of the arch of Solomon's Temple that is supported by the two pillars, Jachim and Boaz;
- moon—the female principle;
- globes on top of pillars—peace and plenty;
- the three tapers—symbolize the three stages of the sun; rising in the east, in the southern sky at noon, and setting in the west;

- trowel—symbolic of spreading love and affection, the "cement" that binds the Brothers of Freemasonry;
- five-pointed star—represents friendship;
- checkered pavement—often a feature of temples and again is based on the floor of Solomon's original temple and represents the duality of opposites, male and female, and so on;
- steps—represent the degrees of masonry;
- coffin—represents death and therefore rebirth and is a recurrent motif in Freemasonry;
- skull and crossbones—symbols of mortality but also of rebirth;
- acacia;
- compasses;
- the square and level;
- the ark—safety and refuge;
- tassel and knot—the ties that bind the Brothers;
- the sun—the Light of God, the male principle;
- sword and heart—symbolic of justice being done; nothing can be hidden from the eyes of the Great Architect;
- seven six-pointed stars—here, seven stands for the seven liberal arts and sciences;
- beehive—a symbol of industry

and a reminder that humans should be rational and industrious at the same time.

12. 47th PROBLEM OF EUCLID, ALSO KNOWN AS THE BRIDE'S CHAIR

This mathematical theorem has been called one of the foundations of Freemasonry. It is called the 47th Problem for no more esoteric reason than Euclid published a book of theorems, of which this was number 47.

Its significance within Freemasonry is somewhat nebulous. However, the beginnings of the Fellowship in architecture and construction, and the usefulness of the 47th Problem as a measuring device, might give us the answer. The design features in Masonic regalia including lodge decorations and Masonic "jewels."

The 47th Problem is also called the Egyptian string trick, and a practical demonstration in making of the shape illustrates its efficacy perfectly. Take a piece of string and tie 12 knots at exact intervals along the string. Then join the ends of the string, again making sure that the knots are evenly spaced. Hammer a stick into the ground. Put one of the knots over the stick. Stretch three divisions of knots and sink another stick into the ground at the point of the third knot. Then take a third stick and skewer it into the ground at the point where a fourth knot falls. This gives a triangle in the proportions of three, four and five, and further, the lines of the string can be extrapolated to make three squares of 9 parts, 16 parts, and 25 parts.

This simple device enabled the Egyptians to remeasure their fields after the Nile flooded every few years, washing away the boundary markers. The Egyptian string trick results in a perfect right angle, an essential device in the construction of a building, and as essential today as it was thousands of years ago, although methods of constructing the angle may have changed. Pythagoras traveled to Egypt and may have discovered it there, or he may have discovered it alone. Whatever the case, it is this geometrical solution that caused him to shout "Eureka." In addition, it is said that 100 bulls were sacrificed in honor of the importance of this seemingly simple discovery, indubitably one of the secrets that was part of the hidden knowledge of the Master Mason; it may well have been one of the pieces of information for which Hiram Abiff was murdered.

13. ASHLAR

In material terms, ashlar is the rough stone that comes straight from the quarry. In philosophical terms, to the Freemason, ashlar symbolizes the rough and imperfect state of man before he is rendered smooth and perfect in his ideally realized state. It relates to the alchemical idea of base matter that can be perfected through intellectual and spiritual realization.

14. POINT WITHIN THE CIRCLE

A seemingly simple symbol, the circle with a dot at its very center is a sign of birth and resurrection dating back to Egyptian times when it was used as an emblem of the sun god, Ra. The symbol is associated particularly with the days of St. John the Baptist and St. John the Evangelist, which fall on the summer and winter solstices respectively.

15. THE TEMPLE FLOOR

Although it is stated time and time again that the symbols inherent within Freemasonry are nondogmatic and are as such open to interpretation, it is safe to say that the features of the actual temple form an important part of the secret signs of the craft. The floor of the temple is no exception.

It is constructed of checkered tiles of black and white. These colors represent the duality of opposites; night and day, dark and light, male and female, fire and water, earth and air, and all the other manifestations of this concept. In ancient Egypt, the colors were used as a reminder of the need to unify spirit and matter.

16. GAOTU

Abbreviated words, initials, and acronyms form a large part of Masonic ritual, since the pronunciation of certain words is believed to dilute their power and abbreviations are used instead. The abbreviation of GAOTU stands for Great Architect of the Universe, which in turn refers to God. Here there is a parallel to the nature of God as the builder or designer of the macrocosm, and the role of the Freemason as the designer of the microcosm.

* ** *

GUNGNIR

This is the magical weapon known as Odin's Spear or Javelin. Like Mjolnir, the magical hammer belonging to Odin, Gungnir—whose name means "The Unwavering One"—has two very practical qualities that render it an essential tool in the arsenal of the powerful thunder god; it always hit its mark, and it always returns, like a boomerang, back to the thrower. As well as being a sacred object, there is a runic symbol, Gar, that also represents the Gungnir.

HALO

The halo, aureole, or aura all refer to an emanation of light, generally depicted appearing around the head. The halo is a symbol of spiritual sanctity or of divine grace, used in Christian iconography, for example, in pictures of saints. Although the halo is the sign that a person is blessed by the divine, some people claim that they can actually see this phenomenon, and that the many colors of the aura that surrounds the entire body can be used as a diagnostic tool.

HAND OF FATIMA

Also known as the Khamsa, the Hand of Fatima is named for Fatima Zahra, the daughter of Mohammed. It is a very ancient symbol, often used as a talisman, and in the Middle East it is ubiquitous, appearing in houses, shops, taxis, and hotels. The hand is not really shaped like a normal human hand, but has two balanced thumbs and no little finger. The eye in its palm wards off the evil eye, so the Hand of Fatima is a double symbol of protection since the palm, held up, is a forbidding gesture. Khamsa actually means "five" and has relevance for both Muslims and Jews.

Peace activists have adopted the Hand of Fatima in recent years; a reminder that the two faiths have many commonly shared beliefs.

HAND OF GLORY

If magical charms have more efficacy the harder they are to construct or come by, then the Hand of Glory must be powerful indeed. Noticeably absent from New Age emporia, the Hand of Glory was popular with thieves during the sixteenth century. It was a light, or candle, made from the severed hand of a hanged convict. After this grisly relic was mummified by being embalmed in oils and special herbs, it was turned into a candle using tallow also made from a hanged corpse.

The Hand of Glory was the favored tool of thieves because, once alight, it was said to render household members unconscious. Therefore the thief could go about his nefarious activities undisturbed.

HEX SYMBOLS

In the southeastern part of Pennsylvania lives a population of European settlers, primarily from the Rhine area. These people come from different religious communities including Lutheran, Moravian, Quakers, Mennonites, and others. Some of these groups, despite their deeply held religious beliefs, are united by one thing: a thriving belief in witchcraft, also known as Hexerie, from the German, *Hexe*, meaning "witch."

Despite their godliness, these are a very superstitious people. One of the popularly held beliefs is that a cross, drawn on the doorlatch, will prevent the devil from entering the house.

HERALDRY

The symbols and signs of heraldry act as a sort of historical shorthand, encoding the attributes of the families to whom the heraldic crests belong. The various coats of arms, still in use today, originated in the need to be able to identify opposing armies and single combatants. This necessity dates back to the time of hand-to-hand combat, almost 1,000 years ago, although soldiers of much earlier times painted images on their shields that held significance for them, personally, as well as being a sign of identity. Although the blazes, escutcheons, badges, mottos, and crests may at first appear to be a dense forest of impenetrable symbols, their secrets can be interpreted easily. This entry does not pretend to be an exhaustive analysis of the elaborate heraldic codes, but gives a general overview of some of the most commonly used emblems.

THE GREAT SEAL OF THE UNITED STATES OF AMERICA

The Great Seal that is featured on the United States dollar bill contains many heraldic attributes. Here are some features to look out for.

1. *Shape—the shield versus the lozenge*

Since women didn't go to war, women's heraldic designs are depicted on a lozenge-shaped framework (which looks like a diamond tipped onto one point), as opposed to the shield of the male. The lozenge itself, suggestive of the vesica piscis, is a feminine symbol. Although the shield shapes vary, the difference between the two shapes is easily recognizable. Similarly, members of the noncombative clergy use the lozenge or oval shape.

2. Color

The colors used within heraldry are called tinctures. There are also fields of patterns known as furs, the most common of which is called "ermine," and resembles the fur of the ermine stoat; the other is called "vair" and comes from a variegated gray-blue colored squirrel. The names of the colors are different, too, retaining their archaic (primarily French) origins.

Gold = Or
Silver = Argent
Red = Gules
Blue = Azure
Purple = Purpure
Green = Vert
Black = Sable

In order that they may remain as clear and visible as possible, a color is rarely laid on top of another color, and the same rule applies to the metallics.

3. Divisions

The shield, or lozenge, can be divided in a number of ways. Split in half horizontally it is called "party per fess." Vertically, it becomes "party per pale." When it is divided diagonally from left to right, it is "party per bend." The opposite direction gives "party per sinister." The "field" of the lozenge or shield can also be split with a saltire cross, or a "normal" one. It can be divided by a chevron, or into three with a Y-shape. There are other variations; lines can also be wavy or curved.

4. Charges

A charge is, effectively, a picture. It can be any object, a symbol, an animal, a plant. Exotic creatures have a large part to play in heraldry; unicorns and dragons join their more realistic counterparts, boars, lions, eagles. The symbolism of these creatures is explored elsewhere in this book, but there may also be a specific link belonging to a family coat of arms, which will have passed into the annals of the family history. The Fleur de Lys has its place as the symbol of the French ruling classes, for example.

5. Crest

This is the element that rests on top of the emblem, effectively crowning it. It tends to appear above the shield, and is the symbolic counterpart of the plume of feathers that knights once wore on their helmets as a sign of distinction and recognition. Because women did not have any occasion to wear a helmet, the lozenge generally has no crest.

6. *Mottoes*

This is a phrase that describes the bearer of the heraldic emblem. It acts as a sort of historic mission statement; the name of the family might be used in the motto as a pun or play on words. The motto can be in any language although Latin and French are possibly the most popular.

7. *Supporters*

The shield or lozenge is sometimes supported, generally by animals that stand upright and appear to hold the shield. Again, these creatures bear a relevance to the owner of the heraldic device.

OTHER HERALDIC SYMBOLS

Symbols used within heraldic devices generally are concise shorthand for the qualities of its owner, and the individual meaning can be found in other parts of this book. The lion, for example, signifies valor; the fox, a wily intelligence.

Heraldic devices have meanings of their own; the "mullet," for example, is not a fish, but a star that denotes the third son. Other curiosities include the Bezant, or gold coin, meaning that the owner can be entrusted with treasure; the escutcheon, a small shield that shows a claim to, or descent from, royalty; a talbot is a hunting hound. A martlet is a symbol of a small bird with no feet, the mark of the fourth son who will have to rely on his own resources since he will not be able to rely on an inheritance. The stirrup signifies action.

There is a whole series of magical protective symbols that the community paint or carve onto the sides of their barns or houses. Called Hex Signs or Barn Signs, these magic symbols are used for a variety of reasons, including averting evil, bringing fertility and prosperity, promoting health, and control of the weather. Many of these signs, which are individually designed, become closely interlinked with a specific family, akin to a coat of arms, and are even tooled into the leather covers of the family Bibles.

These hex symbols are beautifully decorative and use universally familiar symbols in their design, including hearts for love, stars for good luck, oak leaves and acorns for strength and growth. They also use the image of a bird called a distelfink, a type of finch that lines its nest with thistledown. This bird is particularly associated with good fortune. The "double distelfink" brings double the luck.

HEXAGRAM

See Seal of Solomon *and* I Ching.

* ✳ *

HOLY GRAIL

To say that something is like searching for the Holy Grail implies that the search is for a highly treasured and elusive object that might never be found. If there is a genuine Holy Grail, like the Philosopher's Stone, it has retained its hard-to-get status.

The Holy Grail legend has direct links with two mystical pre-Christian items; the magical cauldron of the Celtic gods that never emptied and kept everyone satisfied, and the magical chalice that represents spiritual authority and kingship. However, received information about an actual physical Holy Grail says that it is either the cup that Christ drank from at the Last Supper or the vessel that caught his blood during his crucifixion. The sacred vessel subsequently went missing.

There is a rumor that a fragment of the true Holy Grail, known as the Nanteos Cup, is secreted somewhere in the United Kingdom, specifically in Wales. The cup, made of olivewood, is reputed to have been brought to Glastonbury by Joseph of Arimethea, where it was looked after by the monks who lived at the abbey. The Dissolution of the Monasteries in the sixteenth century, in which monasteries were abolished and their valuable property seized by the Crown, meant that the sacred relic had to be removed. It allegedly ended up at Nanteos Mansion near Aberystwyth. Although it is now just a small fragment of wood, water drunk from it is claimed to have healing powers. Sadly, this marvelous story currently has no forensic evidence to support it and so the Holy Grail remains true to its symbolic meaning, tantalizingly beyond our grasp, for the time being at least.

The Grail legends of the Arthurian tales also symbolize the quest for something beyond reach. The knights, galvanized into action to find this object of desire, soon realize that they are seeking something much more than a cup; given that the shape of the grail is a feminine symbol and a powerful emblem of the spirit, according to Jung it symbolizes "the inner wholeness for which men have always been searching." As such, the Holy Grail has marked parallels with the Philosopher's Stone of the alchemists, and an equally elusive nature.

HORIZONTAL LINE

See First signs: Horizontal line.

HORNED SHAMAN

This symbol has a deep resonance for many, and was first discovered in the cave paintings of Ariège in France. These paintings date back to 10,000 BC. The figure may be the precursor to Cernunnos and other antlered deities. The horned shaman is also called the Dancing Sorcerer, said to represent a shaman performing a ritual ceremony. However, this theory cannot be proven conclusively.

* ** *

Horns of Odin   Horseshoe

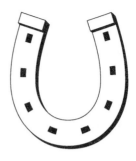

Norse legends tell of a magical mead that was brewed from the blood of a wise god, Kvasir; to drink this mead would be to benefit from the wisdom of the god. Odin managed to find this drink, and the triple horns represent the three draughts that he drank.

The horn itself is both a masculine and phallic symbol, but because it can be used as a container, it encompasses the female aspect, too. The triple horn appears in stone carvings, over the heads of warriors, implying rewards in Valhalla, the Hall of Slain Warriors that is the home of Odin.

Today, the symbol is used as a sign of identity by followers of the Asatru faith. Asatru is a relatively modern religion that acknowledges the much more ancient pre-Christian Norse beliefs.

The horseshoe has acquired symbolic significance not because of its function, but because of its shape and the metal used to make it. It is shaped like the arc, one of the first sacred symbols that represents the vault of the heavens. When it is "upside down" it is also shaped like the last letter of the Greek alphabet, omega.

Flip the horseshoe the other way up, however, and it resembles the crescent moon, therefore invoking the protection of the moon goddess. The iron that the horseshoe is made from further enhances this protective quality. Iron is a protective metal, which evil entities will go out of their way to avoid. The horseshoe also looks like the yoni, further strengthening its links with the goddess.

The horseshoe is a well-known good-luck symbol and appears on greetings cards, wedding souvenirs, and the like. People nail them up over doorways for the same reason, although there is some controversy as to which way up the horseshoe should go. One school of thought says that it should rest on its curved end to hold in the luck, which, if the horseshoe were reversed, would pour away. However, pre-Christian superstition says that the horseshoe should be positioned so that it looks like the sky, and also like the yoni.

HOURGLASS

The function of the hourglass is to mark the passing of time, as sand trickles through the narrow waist in the middle of the transparent glass container that is the same shape as a figure of eight. Therefore, the hourglass is often used as a motif to show the inevitability of death.

However, the shape of the hour-glass, as well as being a visual sym-bol and a word used to describe the figure of a shapely woman, is

a lemniscate, or infinity sign. This indicates eternity. That the hour-glass can be turned upside down to start the cycle all over again makes it an optimistic symbol of rebirth.

I CHING

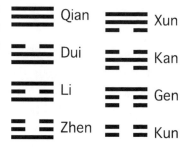

The I Ching is an ancient Chinese system of philosophical divination, possibly dating back to the eighth century BC, which is still in use today.

The I Ching, or Book of Changes, was the only book that escaped destruction when all the Chinese philosophical works were burned in the third century BC. Either dried yarrow stalks or special coins, usually with square holes in the center, plus knowledge and a fair sprinkling of intuition, are the tools of the I Ching.

The basis of the system is just two simple lines, one continuous, one broken. The most profound symbols are usually the simplest, and these two lines encompass the universal source of all things, also known as the Tao (as in Taoism).

The unbroken line represents all aspects of the positive; male, sun, fire, heat, action, odd numbers, yang. The broken line represents the opposites.

These lines combine to make 64 possible combinations.

The lines also form a set of eight trigrams that represent the elements of air, water, fire, and earth, with the four sub-elements of breath, sea, thunderbolt, and mountain.

The interpretations of the I Ching are beautifully oblique; the philosophy behind this system is about finding balance. Both the flags of Vietman and of South Korea feature trigrams from the I Ching.

The purposes of the symbols tell the story of the lifestyles and concerns of the people down the passage of the years; the importance of a good catch for fishermen, protection against thieves and ghosts, how to frighten away enemies.

The intentions of these ancient symbols are extremely varied and there seems to be one for almost every conceivable occasion. The lists read a little bit like a magical book of household management. There are staves included to help ensure the quality of butter, for lock breaking, and even for raising the dead.

Popularly referred to as Magical Staves, these signs are sometimes comprised of several runic symbols merged together (a bind rune), while others stand alone.

ICELANDIC STAVE SYMBOLS

Early Icelandic grimoires (magical texts full of spells and occult information) contain long lists of curious, angular-looking symbols, all intended for a specific purpose. Their origins go back to the ancient rune system, with a sprinkling of later medieval and Renaissance magic thrown in for good measure.

AEGISHJALMUR

One of these stave symbols is called the Helm of Awe or Aegishjalmur. It looks like a snowflake, except it has eight arms radiating from the central point instead of six.

Its purpose, as the name suggests, was to instill fear in the hearts of enemies and to guard the wearer against abuse of his own power. To work properly it needs to be engraved onto lead and then pressed into the forehead.

Latterly, followers of the Asatru belief adopted the Helm of Awe as one of their cornerstone symbols.

HULINHJALMUR: TO MAKE YOURSELF INVISIBLE

Although invisibility is likely to be an incredibly useful asset, the construction of this stave is particularly tricky. It might not seem too difficult to engrave it on a piece of lignite using magnetic steel that has been hardened by soaking in human blood, but the instructions for blending of the ink could be a real nuisance. The recipe calls

for three drops of blood from the index finger of the left hand, and three from the ring finger of the right hand; two drops of blood from the right nipple and one from the left. To this is added six drops of blood from the heart of a living raven. All this blood needs to be melted down with the raven's brain and parts of a human stomach. *Voilà.* Now you see me …

DISCLAIMER

Hulinhjalmur, it will be noted, has no counter stave to restore visibility. Neither the author nor the publishers of this book accept any responsibility for misuse of rune staves.

ICHTHYS WHEEL

At first glance, this looks like a simple eight-spoked wheel. However, the name of Christ is cleverly hidden within it, and like the vesica piscis, was a way for early, persecuted Christians to recognize one another.

The Greek letters I X O Y E can be laid over the circle.

I H S

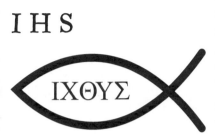

These initials form a symbolic monogram for Christ. The monogram comprises the letters *iota*, *ete*, and *sigma*, which are the first three letters of the name of Jesus in Greek, *Iesous*. The letters also stand for the Latin phrase, *Iesous Hominum Salvator*, meaning Jesus, Savior of Man.

Later, the symbol became a sign of peace.

The IHS symbol is generally embossed onto the communion wafer, and the initials surrounded by the rays of the sun.

INCENSE

Its origins in *incendere*, the Latin word for fire, the importance of incense as a magical symbol lies in the resins and spices that it is made from, its perfume, and the action of its smoke that rises up toward the sky. This smoke is believed to conduct prayers, messages, and devotions toward the deities. The scent is said to please the gods as well as lifting the spirits of worshippers, and the fact that frankincense was one of the three gifts given by the Wise Men to the infant Christ is a reminder of its significance. In Christianity, incense was first used in burials as a symbol of purity that would drive away demons and to carry the soul up to heaven. However, its use soon expanded, and today, incense has a prominent part to play in rites of all kinds, especially within the Roman Catholic Church and the High Church of England. Neopagan groups, too, use incense for the same reasons.

Burning of incense transcends faiths and cultural boundaries. For Native Americans, the fragrant smoke given off by tobacco and other herbs when they share the calumet or pipe carries exactly the same significance as the incense that is burned in churches and the "dhupa" (or dhoop sticks) of Hindu ritual. For Hindus, incense represents the element of air and the perception of consciousness.

The tower of smoke that rises up from the incense is symbolic of the Axis Mundi.

Practitioners of ceremonial magic might use incense so that disembodied entities, such as elementals or other spirits, might use the smoke to make themselves manifest.

bow providing a bridge between heaven and earth. This sign, which looks like a child's drawing, serves as a reminder of the complex belief of man as the microcosm and the universe as the macrocosm.

The Indalo figure has become a logo for the village of Mojacar in particular and for the whole area in general. Sometimes he is called Mojacar Man.

INDALO

This is a prehistoric symbol of magical significance, found in caves in the Almeira region of Spain and known to have been created about 5,000 years ago.

The symbol is very simple, showing a stick man holding an arch above his head. The arch represents either a rainbow or the vault of the heavens. Indalo was perceived to be a go-between between man and God, the rain-

INFINITY

Often the simplest symbols are the ones with the richest meanings. The infinity sign, the figure of eight, and the lemniscate all refer to the same shape that contains a wealth of complex meaning within its fluid lines. This mysterious symbol is found on an everyday object, the camera, where it appears as the infinity lens focus.

To get a sense of what the infinity sign is and how it feels, find something circular and flexible— an elastic band will do. Then twist it once. That is the lemniscate. The flat, one-dimensional circle is suddenly lent a new dimension by this simple twist.

As a mathematical device, the infinity sign was first "discovered" in 1655 by John Wallis, but its significance as a religious symbol is much older.

The infinity sign has its origins in the Arabic numerals that actually came from India in the first place. The sign can be drawn in one continuous movement, making a seesaw movement of clockwise and counterclockwise loops. These loops reflect the balance of opposites; male and female, day and night, dark and light. Because the circles of the lemniscate sit side by side, the sign implies equality between these opposing forces, with the connecting point in the center the convergent point. The sign epitomizes the idea of sexual union and of "two becoming one." The infinity sign stands for wholeness and completion.

The lemniscate appears in the elaborate curlicues in Arabic calligraphic renderings of the Name of God, the elegant loops providing a decorative device as well as pointing toward the idea of eternity.

The symbol appears in the tarot, as part of the Magician card. In the Pamela Colman/Rider-Waite

version, the magician has the lemniscate floating boldly above his head; in other decks, the brim of his hat conceals the shape. Disguising the symbol in this way is a suitable device for such a mysterious character.

INVERTED CROSS

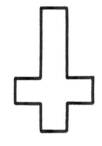

The "upside down" crucifix, or Cross of St. Peter, has become a sinister symbol purportedly belonging to Satanists, whose penchant for reversing certain aspects of the Christian faith (such as the Mass and the Lord's Prayer) is well documented. In horror movies the inverted cross represents the devil. However, the inverted cross originated as the type of cross upon which St. Peter chose to be executed since, like St. Andrew, he felt unworthy of being crucified on the same type of cross as Christ. Devout Catholics view this particular cross as a sign of deep humility and unworthiness in the sight of the Messiah. The pope is said to be the successor of St. Peter and so, logically, has been photographed with this type of cross in the background, giving rise to hysterical conspiracy theories about satanic influences within the Catholic Church.

IRMINSUL

This early Anglo-Saxon symbol has been adopted as one of the cornerstone signs of the Asatru religion. It takes the form of a single pillar, with an ornamented cross bar or a sun wheel surmounting it.

The word itself means "great pillar" and it is connected to the Nordic World Tree, or Yggdrasil, that connects the earth with the heavens. The root of its name is shared not only by Yggdrasil but also by the god Odin, and is a clue

to the close connection between the three.

JAIN SYMBOL

Also called the Parasparopgraho Jivanam, this sacred symbol of the ancient Jain faith (an offshoot of Hinduism) is constructed from several other signs and symbols.

First, the outline of the symbol is called the Lok and is representative of the universe. The lower part reminds Jains of the concept of seven hells. The central part represents the earthly plane, and the upper portion represents the heavens. Then, working from the top down, the curved arc represents not only the moon, but is called the Siddhasila, the final resting-place of souls that have been liberated from the karmic wheel of death and rebirth. These souls are called Siddhas.

The dot or bindhu within the arc is indicative of the zero, the every thing and the nothing combined. It is also representative of the Siddha.

Below the arc are three further bindhu. These represent the Three Jewels of Jainism, namely, the rules for attaining the desired liberation of the soul. These rules are:

- Right Faith (Samyak Darshan)
- Right Knowledge (Samyak Jnan)
- Right Conduct (Samyak Charitra)

Below these three sacred dots is the swastika, the very ancient solar symbol. Here, the four arms of the swastika symbolize the four realms into which a soul may be reborn; a soul can become a heavenly being, a human being, an animal being, or a hellish being.

Underneath the swastika is the upraised hand, a universal symbol meaning "Stop!" Inside the hand is the word "Ahimsa," one of the tenets of Hinduism and Jainism, which is an offshoot of this faith. Ahimsa means "nonviolence" and the word itself is contained within a wheel. The combination of the hand and the word within the wheel are a reminder to stop and think before acting, to do nothing which could harm any creature, otherwise the wheel of birth and rebirth will keep on turning and the soul will never be liberated.

JAPA MALA

See Rudraksha.

JERUSALEM CROSS

This is one large cross with smaller crosses in between the arms. Originally used by the Crusaders, hence its name, the five crosses symbolize the five wounds of Christ.

JEWELRY

The precious metals and beautiful gems that make up jewelry spring from the womb of the earth. Legends tell us that these gems are mined by dwarves and that jewelry is constructed by elves and goblins.

Metals and gems are themselves full of hidden meanings. Gems symbolize not only material wealth but also wisdom and the riches of the mind and spirit. Buddhist doctrines are called "jewels." And, as the song says, diamonds really are forever! Not only the stones, but also the precious materials that go into the design of jewelry, are eternal and incorruptible. Ancient jewelry often looks as new as the day it was made, and was worn by royalty as well as commoners.

There is evidence that people adorned themselves with jewelry as long ago as 40,000 years, and the very earliest kind was made of shells, animal bones and teeth. The importance of this jewelry was such that people were even buried with it.

Jewelry is not only decorative: it can be functional, too, for instance, to hold clothing together (buckles, brooches, pins, and clips). It stores wealth (think of the archetypal gypsy, dripping gold—this jewelry is the same as money in the bank). Jewelry can take the form of protective amulets and talismans, with countless designs intended specifically to avert the evil eye. It also denotes status or membership of a group or tribe, or can give information about the wearer, for example,

the wedding ring as a symbol of binding, or the jet mourning jewelry worn by bereaved Victorians. In Rome, the Sumptuary Laws gave instructions as to who had the right to wear specific sorts of jewelry.

The wearing of religious symbols, like the crucifix or Star of David, may sometimes be the cause of contention because of a lack of understanding of religious and cultural values. For example, a woman working at a major airport in the UK was told that her crucifix could be offensive. In addition, there have been instances where the facial jewelry of some Hindus has been looked at askance by people who do not understand the reasons for this adornment. A deeper understanding of the reasons that people choose to wear certain jewelry can only help to bring more harmony between diverse cultures. The nose ring, for example, is a practice copied from Indian cultures where piercing is believed to enhance fertility.

RING

Wearing a ring indicates a link or bond; the wedding ring is the perfect example of this. In J. R. R. Tolkein's *The Lord of the Rings*, the mystical ring bears the inscription "one ring to bind them." The Fisherman's Ring, which is exclusive to the pope, is used as his personal seal, being broken when he dies.

The ring, of course, is a circle, and so it carries all the symbolic significance of the shape; eternity and unity. The signet ring has a personal seal or other hieroglyphic device engraved on it used as a sign of identity.

Solomon had a particularly magical ring, the possible source of all his wisdom. He used it to conjure up the demons that then became his slaves, but when he lost the ring all his wisdom disappeared too, until the ring was returned to him.

Plato describes a ring that belonged to the shepherd Gyges. His ring had a rotating bezel that, if turned inward, made him invisible.

The fingers on which rings are worn also have significance. The fourth finger of the left hand that is traditionally designated for the wedding or engagement ring has a direct link to the heart. Archers in China and Persia wore rings to protect their thumbs, so the thumb ring indicated military rank. A ring worn on the index or "pointing" finger indicates authority.

In India, toe rings, or bichiya, also denote status. Worn on the second toes of both feet, they are a sign of marriage. Hindus traditionally consider it disrespectful to wear gold below the waist so these rings are usually, but not always, made of silver.

NECKLACE

A necklace is a sign of identity, more visible and more immediately obvious than the ring. For example, it can signify a chain of office (as in the ornate mayoral necklace) or a chain of bondage, like the collars worn by slaves. The goddess Kali is immediately identifiable by her necklace of human skulls, and witches traditionally wear a necklace of acorns. Amulets and talismans often appear as pendants, and lockets of all kinds store hidden information.

JIZO

This is a Japanese Buddha symbol. Almost cartoonlike, Jizo is depicted as an innocent, childlike character, venerated as a protector of the souls of children and unborn babies.

Jizo is ubiquitous in Japan, often appearing as a statuette dressed in robes. People also surround the Jizo statuette with offerings of food, sweets, incense, and pebbles.

KABBALAH

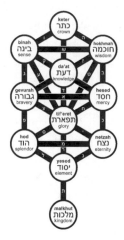

YAH, the Lord of Hosts, the living Elohim, King of the Universe, Omnipotent, the Merciful and Gracious God, Supreme and Extolled, Dweller in the Height whose habitation is Eternity, who is Sublime and Most Holy, engraved His name and ordained the Universe in thirty-two mysterious paths of wisdom, by the three Sephariam, namely, Numbers, Letters and Sounds, which are in Him and one and the Same

(from the Sefer Yetzirah)

A VERY SHORT HISTORY

Most systems of faith have an exo-teric, or external, level of under-standing that is aimed at the masses, and an esoteric, or inner, level of meaning that is the preserve of the priests and initiates. The deeply mystical Kabbalah is the enigmatic aspect of the Jewish doctrine. The word has its root in Hebrew, QBL, meaning "to receive" or alternately "mouth to ear," or "the unwritten law," and like most mystery trad-itions its secrets were originally communicated orally. It shares the same root as the word "Cabal," meaning "secret intrigue."

These secrets, so the story goes, were given directly from God to the archangels, who then passed the information on to Adam after his expulsion from the Garden of Eden, in order that he might regain his former favor in the eyes of God. The secrets passed through Noah to Abraham, who shared the mysteries with the Egyptians. From here the Kabbalah spread to other parts of the world. Moses, too, had kabbalistic instruction directly from God. According to Jewish mystics, the third time he climbed Mount Siani he spent forty days learning its secret doctrine from the angels while he was wandering in the desert. Thereafter, Moses concealed the teachings that appeared for the first time in written form in the first four books of the Old Testament.

In the first century, Rabbi Simeon Ben Jochai had to hide in a cave with his son for twelve years, avoiding execution because of his criticism of the Roman Empire. During this time, the Rabbi taught the secrets of the Kabbalah to his son, and these teachings appeared as a book, published in thirteenth-century Spain, called the Zohar. It is this book which is the cornerstone of the Kabbalistic doctrines.

The universality of the ideas within the Kabbalah means that it has been adopted by numerous different religions. Not surprising, since the beauty and logic of its construction is awe-inspiring and all-encompassing. There was a general upsurge of interest in eso-terica in the Middle Ages and this era saw the development of a Her-metic Kabbalah, a combination of Kabbalistic teachings and Greek hermeticism. In turn, alchemy and Rosicrucianism were influenced by its secrets, as was Freemasonry. The tarot takes its influence from the Kabbalah. The Golden Dawn based its symbolic language on that of the Kabbalah. Its influence

has been all-pervasive, thousands of years after the angels imparted its intricacies to the First Man.

The doctrines encompass the Four Worlds and the Tree of Life, while the latter, in turn, encompasses the Ten Numbers and the Twenty-two Letters.

THE FOUR WORLDS

The Greatest Name, Jehovah, or IHVH, has an element attached to each letter. Further, the letters also represent the Four Worlds. These are Atziluth (emanation), the world of pure spirit, an archetypal world where there is no separation or division. This is the world of the gods. Atziluth is associated with the element of fire and the letter I, and from it the other three worlds are "born."

Briah, "cosmos" or "creation," is the next world, represented by the letter H and the water element. This is the world where separation begins, where one idea might separate from others, although this world is still formless.

Yetzirah, represented by the V and the element of air, is the next world born from Briah. This is the domain of imagination and thought, corresponding to the astral world, a level of consciousness that immedi-ately precedes the physical.

The fourth world is Assiah, which means "to do." Assiah is the material world, represented by the final letter H and the earth element. It is the here and now, our physical reality, the world of separation that is constructed from the finer elements that precede it.

THE TREE OF LIFE

This is the most famous graphic representation of the Kabbalah's diverse unfolding of ideas. All of nature is enclosed within its relatively simple form, which has multilayered dimensions of significance that belie a straightforward graphic representation. Its ten spheres or sephiroth represent the ten numbers, and are connected by twenty-two paths or branches that also represent the twenty-two letters of the Hebrew alphabet. The letters and numbers comprise the thirty-two paths of wisdom that are written about in the Sefer Yetzirah, the very early kabbalistic text said to have been written by Abraham.

The three columns of the tree are symbols in themselves. The central one represents balance or equilibrium. The one on the right is called Jachin, male energy; on the left is Boaz, female energy. These are the pillars that were represented in the Great Temple in Jerusalem and which also influence the design of Masonic temples. They also appear in the tarot. Here are the component elements of the tree.

The Ten Numbers

Behold! From the Ten Ineffable Sephiroth do proceed the One Spirit of the Gods of the Living; Air, Water, Fire, and also Height, Deoth, East, West, South and North
[from the Sefer Yetzirah]

In the diagram, these are represented by the spheres or sephira.

ONE

The uppermost sephira of the tree is one, the Crown (Keter). It is the start of manifestation, positive, but undefinable because it as yet bears no relation to anything else.

TWO

To the right of Keter, just below it, is the sephira of Hokhmah or Wisdom, the number two. It enables a line to be made between it and the number one.

THREE

To the left of Hokhmah is Binah, meaning "understanding." It makes a triangle and all three numbers give definition to one another.

These first three sephiroth represent Atziluth, the element of fire and the first of the four worlds described above.

FOUR

Next, moving down the tree, beneath Hokhmah, is Hesed, or Mercy. Now the universe contained within the tree can have four elements and four directions, and can form a square.

FIVE

To the left of Hesed is Gevurah, meaning strength. This implies the idea of time, without which nothing can happen in the universe as we experience it.

SIX

With Tif'eret, meaning beauty, another dimension is added; as well as the four elements and "above" and "below." The number six contributes the notions of past and future and consciousness of the self.

SEVEN

Netzah, or victory, is the next of the sephira. It sits below Hesed. It represents the notion of the emotional nature and the pure joy of existence. Despite the possibility of suffering, the soul is happy to be made manifest in human form.

EIGHT

Hod, or Splendor, symbolizes the intellectual nature, or thought.

NINE

Yesod, the Foundation, brings the notion of Sense of Being, adding to the emotional and intellectual natures of Tiphareth and Netzach to give man a sense of reality.

TEN

The final sephira, sitting at the bottom of the tree, is called Malkhut, or the Kingdom. Here, the void represented by the zero has become manifest, and self-consciousness is fully developed within a physical world. It is appropriately sited at the base of the tree since it is the sphere of all life on earth.

The Triple Veils of the Negative: the threefold nature of zero

In the Kabbalah, the concept of nothing, or zero, is called Ain, the void. This concept embraces two further ideas: firstly Infinite Space, called Ain Soph (without limit). This concept is represented by the dot, or bindhu, which contains the seed of everything within it. There is also the concept of a time–space continuum, Ain Soph Aur, the Limitless Light. These abstract ideas are the Triple Veils of the Negative.

The twenty-two letters

Like other magical alphabets from different traditions, the characters of Hebrew are thought to be the magical symbols with which God created the physical world by means of the sounds they represent.

These letters are generally split into three groups. There are three "mother" letters that correspond to the elements of air, water, and fire. The seven "double" letters correspond to the seven traditional planets, and the twelve remaining "simple" letters are linked to the signs of the zodiac. Again in common with other alphabets, the letters also correspond to numbers and so have a double meaning. The letters are represented in the tree diagram by the twenty-two paths that link the spheres that contain the numbers.

Kabbalists also link the five parts of the human soul to the four elements, plus the fifth element, ether, or the quintessence. Earth is the "animal soul" named Nephesch. This is the domain of the instincts and the senses. Air symbolizes the

intelligence and is called Ruach. It corresponds to the breath, too, and has the same meaning as Prana in Sanskrit philosophy. Water is called Neshamah, and in common with other traditions this element corresponds to the intuition. The fiery part of the soul is called Chiah, and has the same meaning as Chi, the essence of life. Finally, Yechidah encompasses the whole, the Highest Self, symbolizing spirit.

These further intricacies and connections within this fascinating system are far too elaborate to explain within the confines of this book, in the vigorous depth that they deserve. Hopefully this brief description of the concepts used within the Kabbalah will provide a fundamental grasp of its mysteries.

KAPALA

The kapala, or Thod Pa, is one of the "charnel ground" implements used in sacred rites in Tibetan Buddhism. It is a bowl or chalice made from a human skull, highly decorated and extremely valuable.

It is thought that the use of the skull may originate from much earlier times, from the practice of human sacrifice. The kapala is a symbol of the triumph of good over evil. Each skull is carefully selected, washed, and sanctified before use.

A kapala made from the skull of a child that died prior to puberty is particularly desirable, because of its purity. The object is usually held with the left hand.

KERUB

The original Kerubim are very different from the chubby-cheeked little creatures that seem to pop up everywhere these days, which are in fact completely different creatures known as putti. The "true" Kerubim are imposing, winged creatures who guard the thrones of gods and kings as well as the Mesopotamian Tree of Life. The Book of Ezekiel in the Old Testament of the Bible describes the four Kerubim, each of which have a different head; the lion, the bull, the eagle, and the human head. These were later absorbed into the symbols of the four evangelists, Matthew, Mark, Luke, and John, of the New Testament.

These mighty Kerubim are also the embodiment of the energy in the Tetragrammaton, the Name of God in symbolic form.

KEY

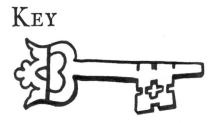

The key, or clavicle, is symbolic of access to something that has been hitherto kept hidden or which is a secret. However, keys are used for locking as well as for unlocking, and deities that are depicted holding keys, for example, may symbolize the need to keep something private or occluded. A key need not be a physical object, and the act of unlocking is not restricted to mundane artifacts. A code, for example, may hold the key to understanding a secret language or cipher. Holy and sacred words were considered such powerful locking/unlocking mechanisms that they were rarely used; for example, the words "Open Sesame" were a key that unlocked the door into the treasure cave.

Our ancestors used the physical key as a magical charm or talisman, an example of sympathetic magic, when something needed to be unlocked in some way. For example, Jewish midwives put the key to the synagogue into the hand of a woman who was about to give birth, in the hopes that the association would help the baby "unlock" the door of the womb. Keys were buried with people in order that the gates to the Uunderworld would open easily.

St. Peter, one of the apostles of Christ, holds the keys to the "pearly gates" of heaven. These crossed keys have become a papal symbol and represent the powers given by Christ; one key is gold (the sun, and male energy) and the other is silver (feminine energy, the moon). The golden key signifies the power to bind or release in heaven, and the silver represents the same powers on earth. Prior to their adoption by the pope, these gold and silver keys were the attribute of the Roman god Janus, whose two faces mean that he can look in two directions at the same time. These keys symbolically unlocked the gates of the solstices.

Initiation, too, provides a key that unlocks secret knowledge or information. The key is a symbol of power, a visible sign of this initiation. Being given the keys to a town or city is a great honor, with implications of power and ownership and has parallels with the medieval custom of handing over keys as a way of granting power. The "key of the door" that is given on the 21st birthday signifies the coming of age into adulthood, and the tarot card that is numbered 21 is the card of the World.

KHANDA

A symbol belonging to the Sikh religion, the Khanda symbolizes the four aspects of the Sikh faith as well as encompassing the four sacred weapons within its shape.

The double-edged sword that gives the Khanda its name is in the center of the symbol. It stands for the creative power of God and the knowledge of divinity.

The circle around the edge of the Khanda dagger is called the chakkar, or wheel, and the word shares the same root as chakra. This is also a medieval weapon, and like all circular symbols, it represents eternity and unity.

The daggers at either side of the symbol, which cross over at the bottom of the symbol, are called Kirpans. These knives belonged to the guru Hargobind and symbolize the balance of spirit and matter.

KNOT

Knots, because they symbolize the act of binding, hold powerful symbolic and magical significance. The notion of binding extends to the spirit, as well as material things. In some pagan wedding rites the hands of the bride and groom are bound together, physically, as a symbol of the vows that bind them together, body and soul. For Buddhists, the untying of a knot sig-nifies an unbinding from material things, to become liberated from them, and is therefore symbolic of death.

Knots hold a great significance for fishermen, not a surprise considering that fishing nets are constructed from knots. Any person who risks his life by putting themselves at the mercy of the elements tends to have an understandably superstitious approach to life. Some fishermen still carry a piece of rope with three knots in it, although they may have forgotten what these knots symbolize. The first knot, if untied, brings fair winds; the second, storms; and the third keeps these storms in check. Arabic men believe that the knot is a powerful talisman against the evil eye, so they tie a knot into their beards. However, it is forbidden for pilgrims to Mecca to wear any knots in their clothing.

The Qu'ran mentions a specific charm for the making and using of knots. It reads:

Say thou: "I take refuge with the Lord of Daybreak
From the evil of all He hath made
And from the evil of the dark night when it spreads

And from the evil of those who blow upon knots
And the evil of the envious when he envies."

This refers to the magical practice of using the breath to charge an item with magical powers.

Because weaving and knitting are female crafts that involve a complicated series of knots, and because women "knot" their hair, knots and knot magic are closely associated with witches. In the Qu'ran, for example, there is a warning against "those who breathe on knots." This refers to the witches that were supposed to cast spells in this way. The Three Fates of Greek mythology weave and knot the threads of existence. Midwives ensured that birthing mothers had no knots about their person that might hinder the birth of the baby.

Egyptians believed that the knot symbolized eternal life. They tied their sandals in such a way that the knot made an imprint on the ground, a reminder of the Knot of Isis.

KNOT OF ISIS

See Tyet.

KOKOPELI

Kokopeli, in Hopi Indian, means "wooden backed." It is the name of a symbol that first appears in pre-historic rock carvings, a hunch-backed little figure with antlers on his head, playing a flute. Although the true age, provenance, and explanation for this curious symbol are indeterminate, Kokopeli is believed to be a fertility symbol, hence the antlers and the small bag (possibly containing seeds) which he sometimes carries. Koko-peli represents the essence of the creative force, in whatever form it might take.

There is a Hopi legend which says that Kokopeli traveled from village to village playing his flute. Wherever he went, he was wel-comed with a huge party, the vil-lagers singing and dancing all night. In the morning, presumably through the haze of a terrible hangover, Kokopeli had evidently shared his magical powers of fecundity since all the fields were full of healthy crops and all the girls would shortly find that they were pregnant. Kokopeli also symbolizes the end of winter and the coming of spring, hope, and new life.

KUNDALINI SERPENT

This is the symbol used to describe the vast reserve of physical and spiritual energy that lives, half-dormant, at the base of the spine. Derived from a Sanskrit word meaning "spiral" or "coil," the Kundalini Serpent is coiled into three circles, with its tail in its mouth, similar to the ouroboros. Kundalini energy is female, and when awakened systematically by techniques such as yoga and meditation, she spirals up the spine via the chakras toward the top of the head, where she joins the male energy that comes down to meet her from above. This descending masculine energy symbolizes the consciousness of the unity of the universe.

LABARUM

The earliest Christian symbol, prior to the adoption of the Latin Cross, was the Labarum. This symbol has a very early provenance, since it is believed to have been an adaptation of the Egyptian ankh and was also a symbol of the sun god, Mithras. In this case, it appears enclosed in a wheel. The Labarum proved a handy device for bridging the gap between Mithraism (the favored religion of the Roman soldiers) and Christianity.

Not only does the symbol contain the first two Greek letters of Christ's name (hence it is also known as the "Chi Roh" or the "Monogram of Christ") but it was given immediate prominence when Emperor Constantine saw the symbol in a dream.

Constantine was a major figure in the spread of Christianity, the first Imperial Emperor to adopt the new religion. Some accounts of his vision of the Labarum say that his entire army saw the symbol hanging in the sky. This anecdote, incidentally, has parallels to the story of the crescent moon and star symbol, also seen in a dream by Osman, founder of the Ottoman Empire.

Like Osman, Constantine's dream told him that the sign would bring victory, and so he had it painted onto his soldiers' shields.

It may have been coincidence that shortly afterwards Constantine's forces won the Battle of the Milvian Bridge, but nevertheless the Labarum's place as a hugely important symbol was determined, adopted as the emblem of the Empire in AD 324, 12 years after the decisive victory.

LABRYS

Although the word *labrys* is Greek and refers to the double-headed axe or hatchet, the symbol exists all over the world, in India, Af-

rica, and England as well as in the European countries.

The single-headed axe is symbolic of the power of light (because it sometimes makes sparks) and of thunder and lightning. It is often seen as the favored weapon of various gods, such as Thor.

The double-headed axe is more complex. The first instrument of its kind is believed to have been made 8,000 years ago, and it was the favored tool of the Amazonians who lived in central Asia, specifically in the Kazakhstan area. Because of its shape, it carries much of the significance of the tau cross. Its name suggests that it is connected to the labyrinth; both were powerful symbols in the Minoan culture of ancient Crete, as was the bull. The labyrinth at Knossos used the image of the Labrys as a decorative device. The double-headed axe is sometimes seen over the head of the bull or ox, whose horns it resembles. In addition, the bull was ritually slaughtered using the Labrys.

The Minoan culture was predominantly matriarchal and because of this, and because the Labrys has strong links to the female Amazonian warriors, the term "battleaxe" has come to mean a ferocious woman. Various lesbian groups adopted the symbol sometime in the 1970s, and some women wear it as a piece of jewelry to indicate their sexuality.

LABYRINTH

The earliest recorded instance of the word "labyrinth" is in descriptions of the labyrinth that housed the minotaur in Greek myth. The name means "house of the double axe," a reference to the Labrys that was a powerful emblem of Minoan culture. Although the labyrinth and the maze are often referred to as the same thing, a maze has lots of different paths, including branches that lead to dead ends, whereas a labyrinth has only one winding path that leads ineffably to the center and offers no possibility of choice. The space available within the labyrinth is used ingeniously to ensure that the path is as long as possible.

The most significant symbolism of the labyrinth is that of the journey of the soul to its center and then back toward the outside once more, the cycle of death and rebirth, a metaphysical pilgrimage of the spirit. The center of the labyrinth represents the womb, and to reach the center of the "labyrinth of life" is initiation and enlightenment. In this sense the labyrinth has parallels with the mandala as well as with the spiral patterns of the Celts, a good example of which can be seen on the massive stones in front of the entrance at Newgrange in Ireland.

Labyrinth patterns are universal, and earlier than the mythical labyrinth. They appear on fragments of amulets from ancient Egypt, on Mycenean seals, and on Etruscan vases.

Labyrinth patterns were adopted by Christian churches, the earliest of which is in Algeria, at the Reparatus Basillica, dating back to the year 324. There is generally held to be significance in the number of concentric shapes or layers of the path, and also its length; the famous labyrinth at Chartres Cathedral, for example, has 11 concentric circles and is exactly 666 feet long. Because the number 666 is usually misconstrued as having evil origins, this has led to some wild conspiracy theories about the designer of the labyrinth, but 666 is a sacred number, the number of humankind. In the center of this particular labyrinth is a six-petaled flower that conceals the hexagram or Seal of Solomon within it, a reminder that labyrinths are sometimes called Solomon's Maze.

Because the winding trail of the labyrinth moves both in a clockwise (deosil) and a counterclockwise (widdershins) direction, it symbolizes the course of the sun and the waxing and waning of the moon.

LADDER

An everyday object, the ladder nevertheless has esoteric meaning as an aspect of the relationship between heaven and earth. At its most basic, the ladder is symbolic of ascension, transcendence, and the fulfillment of potential; the

Greek word for ladder is "climax." A ladder is also synonymous with the idea of communication between the worlds. The notion that the material and spiritual worlds used to be connected by a ladder, that was either removed or broken, is a common symbolic thread running through many cultures, although the Shinto faith says that the goddess Ameratasu, who borrowed the magical ladder, kept the connection. The ladder sometimes depicted on the tracing boards of Freemasonry signifies initiation and a penetration of the higher levels of the cosmos. A rainbow also serves as a ladder, or bridge, between the celestial realms and the ones below.

The number of rungs on this symbolic ladder is important, too, The Buddha has a ladder of seven colors, and in the Mithraic religion there was a ceremonial ladder of seven rungs, each made from a different metal that corresponded to each of the known seven planets, from lead, the base metal, to gold, considered to be the most sublime. Climbing this ladder was a physical representation of the ascent through the Seven Heavens.

The ladder is also one of the many vertical items that signify the Axis Mundi.

LATIN CROSS

The Latin Cross (or Christian Cross) is the typical cross shape that is the major symbol of Christianity, no matter what form the faith takes. When the body of Christ appears on the cross, it then becomes a crucifix. Such has been the impact of this symbol on the religion that its major places of worship are built in the shape of a cross as seen from above.

The Latin Cross is symbolic of the victory of life over death, and in a happy coincidence, the benediction made when the sign of the cross is drawn in the air not only indicates the "Father, Son, and Holy Ghost," but coincides with a much earlier use of the cross; as a symbol of protection.

The Christian Cross as we know it today was not always the symbol of the Church, and it may not even be the case that Christ was crucified on this sort of cross. Accounts vary, but a tau cross, a simple straight beam, or perhaps even a living tree might have been used. Logic dictates that,

because it was used as a particularly gruesome torture implement, this kind of cross would not have been an encouraging symbol for what was then a new religion. The Chi-Roh or Labarum was used instead, but by the third century the cross had been accepted.

The form of the cross itself holds an intriguing hidden secret. If its measurements are drawn correctly, that is, four square parts in the vertical to three square parts in the horizontal (making six parts in total since the square that links the upright and the cross part can be shared by both) then this shape can be folded into a neat cube. Furthermore, other geometric shapes can be made from this versatile cross if diagonal folds are included.

The Freemasons have explored some of these shapes.

LEMNISCATE

See Infinity.

LEVIATHAN CROSS

The Leviathan Cross is also sometimes referred to as the Crux Satana, since it was adopted by Anton La

Vey as a symbol for his Church of Satan. However, there is no record of this particular cross having any other satanic connections prior to this. The cross was used by both the Knights Templar and the Cathars.

In alchemy, the Leviathan Cross is the symbol for sulfur, which is one of the three essential elements of nature along with salt and mercury (quicksilver). The symbol itself is quite elaborate. There are two bars on the upright part of the cross, symbolizing double protection and a balance between male and female. At the bottom of the cross is the infinity sign or lemniscate, which also becomes the double ouroboros. The cross also carries phallic connotations.

LINGAM

In the Hindu faith, the lingam is a ubiquitous symbol whose name also means "sign." This Sanskrit word shares its root, however, with the words for both "plough" and "phallus." The lingam is symbolic of the phallus and procreation, but with the emphasis on creative energy and the spirit of life, rather than eroticism. The lingam is the symbol of the great Hindu deity Shiva.

In yoga, the lingam is envisaged as a tower of light that rises up from the base of the spine. The Kundalini Serpent of energy rises up this tower of light, which represents the power of knowledge.

Lingam symbols occur naturally in the landscape as certain standing stones and rocks, but the linga that are a fundamental feature in temples are man-made, carved from stone. The base of the object is square, symbolic of the earth, stability and security, and the upper part is cylindrical.

The lingam, on its own, effectively belongs to the world of theory, of untried and untested things. In conjunction with the yoni, however, the lingam becomes empowered. The yoni is symbolic of the womb, female energy and creativity. The pair are inextricably linked, the yoni symbolized as the shallow basin that surrounds the lingam.

The temple lingam is anointed with oil and water and decorated with flowers. It is one of the many objects that represent the Axis Mundi.

LION OF JUDAH

This is not only the symbol but also the honorary title of the Ras Tafari, the Emperor Haile Selassie. According to followers of the Rastafarian faith, Haile Selassie was the Messiah.

Legend says that the emperor was descended from the tribe of Judah, whose emblem was the lion.

The Rastafarian Lion of Judah carries the flag of Ethiopia in his mouth and the crown of the emperor on his head.

MAGEN DAVID

See Seal of Solomon.

* * *

MAGIC CIRCLE

The circle is a powerful symbol, standing for strength, union, protection, and eternity. A magic circle signifies all these things, and has the added benefit of being "charged" by various rituals. A magic circle is generally inscribed on the floor or ground as a way of delineating the area in which magical activity will take place.

Prior to occult activity, the circle is "cast." Different practitioners of magic have different methods of doing this. However, salt is popular in constructing the circle because of its protective qualities. Candles and incense are used too. Due respect is given to this magic circle as a sacred space, symbolic of the microcosm.

Practitioners of the occult arts set great store by the correct construction of a magic circle. Aleister Crowley, for example, who liked to call up various otherworldly spirits, found at one time that the only thing standing between him and imminent demonic destruction was a circle of sand and some powerful magical intention.

MAGIC KNOT

Also called the Witch's Knot or the Witch's Charm, this symbol is comprised of four interlocking vesica piscis shapes, sometimes with the addition of a central circle. Because it can be drawn in one continuous line without the pen leaving the paper, it is a symbol of protection, and despite its name was often used in the Middle Ages as an anti-witchcraft symbol; however, it was also used by witches to control the weather or as a love charm, which indicates that the symbol was used homeopathically. There are lots of different magic knots.

MAGIC SEAL

This symbol uses numbers and shapes to make a magical symbol said to help the magician harness the powers and qualities of a planetary deity. Each planet has its own magic square and the size of this kamea and the order of the numbers in it are particularly significant. A shape is then overlaid on top of these numbers, connecting them together to make a sigil for the planet.

MAGICIAN, SIGNS OF

There is an ancient African belief in certain giveaway signs that describe a practitioner of the magical arts. The description is rather generalized, but here it is. The ideal sorcerer can be male or female, of average height, aged between 22 to 26 or, alternatively, between 30 and 55. Fair-haired magicians are allegedly more powerful than those with dark hair, and fuller lips are better.

MALTESE CROSS

See Templar Cross.

Man in the maze

A symbol belonging to the Native Americans, found both in basketry and in Hopi Indian silver work.

The symbol shows a maze, with the figure of a man about to either leave or enter it. The symbol represents the choices and decisions that a person has to make during the journey of their life. The center of the maze is dark, signifying the unknown world and the mysteries of initiation, and the outer area is light, the known world, and familiar things.

Manaia

For Maoris, the Manaia was a mythical bird-like creature, a protecting spirit and a messenger from the gods, hence the resemblance to the bird. This stylized symbol is frequently seen as an amulet, made

from a type of Maori jade called greenstone.

Mandala

The word "mandala" is Sanskrit, and means "circle." The mandala itself may be enclosed in a square or might contain squares and other shapes, such as the triangle, within it. They can also contain animals, flowers, and plants. Despite its name, it is not always necessary for the mandala to be circular in shape. An important symbol within the Hindu tradition, the mandala is now recognized everywhere for its beautiful colors and pleasing patterns even where its significance as a piece of religious design may not be understood.

The mandala can be as simple or as complex as the designer wishes it to be. Monks created the original mandalas, at least 2,500 years ago, as a part of their traditional spiritual training. The mandala is a mystical and magical map of the universe, constructed in such a way that the focus of attention is drawn continuously to the center and then back to the outer frame.

As a focus for meditation, the shapes and patterns of the mandala can be open to interpretation by each individual. However, every individual element, including the colors that are used, has significance.

The image of the unfolding petals of the lotus flower, in the center of which yogis envisage themselves sitting, is a mandala. A perfect physical representation of the shape is found at the Temple of Borobudur, in Java. The entire temple, viewed from above, forms the traditional circular mandala, sitting in a square framework with gates at each quarter. Walking around this three-dimensional mandala, in the correct sequence, is a meditative process.

Carl Jung recognized the usefulness of creating mandalas as part of his psychological explorations, and described them as "a representation of the unconscious self."

MANDORLA

See Vesica piscis.

MANEKI NEKO

See Beckoning cat.

MANIKIN

Also known as the poppet (hence the word "puppet") or sometimes the voodoo doll, the manikin, in magical symbolism, is a model of a human being, a representation of a real person, and not a child's toy. Constructed by a practitioner of magic, the idea is that whatever happens to the doll also happens to its human counterpart. The doll only "works," though, if its constituent parts include some physical substance from the person it is supposed to be: hair, blood, or spittle, for example. The doll is "dressed" in a scrap of the intended person's clothing.

The uses of such dolls generally have a sinister twist, malevolent rather than benevolent. The common perception is of the manikin used as a sort of psychic pincushion, each pin believed to inflict a similar wound in the unfortunate person that it represents. They are also used to attract love, in which case the manikin is made to represent the person that is the object of the maker's desire, with emphasis placed on the sexual parts. Then the doll has to be blessed, buried, and dug up again, when a pin is used to pierce the heart in much the same way as Cupid's arrow.

However, possibly the most sinister kind comes from the Amoy region of China. Peach wood—itself a magical substance—is collected, in secret, in the dead of night. This raw wood is hidden somewhere close to a pregnant woman, but it is important that she should not know of its presence. As soon as possible after the baby is born the wood is retrieved and carved into a doll that resembles the baby in gender and in any other possible way. Various spells follow, so that the doll becomes animated with a part of the unfortunate infant's spirit. Allegedly, this can damage the soul of the baby in such a way that it may be impaired or even killed.

The manikin is a fine example of sympathetic magic, the idea that a part of something extrapolates to encompass the whole.

MANJI

The meaning of this word is simple; it means the "Chinese symbol for eternality." It is essentially a swastika, the ancient solar symbol. However, in the Buddhist belief system it signifies the balance of opposing forces, harmony, and dharma (proper conduct, doing the right thing).

The Manji can face either way, and like the swastika (despite some superstitious beliefs about it) both directions have positive connotations. Facing to the left and turning clockwise, it signifies love and mercy. Facing to the right and turning counterclockwise, the Manji stands for intelligence and strength.

Mankolam

See Paisley.

Mark of the Beast

Created by infamous ritual magician Aleister Crowley, the self-styled Great Beast, the Mark of the Beast became, effectively, his own personal sign. It cleverly combines the ancient sun sign (the circle with the dot) with the emblem of the crescent moon, all comprised of three overlapping circles. It does not need an expert in hidden signs to be able to discern the overall image created, which reveals Crowley's overarching fascination with sex magick.

Mark of the Bustard

This is a three-branched symbol that appears on the cloaks of shamans. It represents communication between

the world of death and the world of resurrection. The same symbol, if seen in the dust around the bed of a recently deceased person, says that the soul of the person has left the body and taken wing.

The bustard itself, although it seldom flies, symbolizes the union between earth and heaven.

Mask

A mask covers the face of the individual, effectively blocking out his or her own identity and replacing it with the spirit or personality represented by the mask. Many people who have worn masks describe the ease with which their own personality dissolves when the face is hidden or disguised. There are three main categories for the use of masks: in theater, in carnival, in funerals. In addition, shamans use masks to help them take on the spirit of an animal or a deity.

In ancient Greece and Rome, the chorus was the name given to the actors who described the events taking place. They wore masks that represented archetypal human emotions; the classical "comedy" and "tragedy" masks come from this tradition. Similarly, the masks of the Japanese No Theater convey universal archetypes: old man, young girl, mother, father, for example.

There was a Persian sect called the Maskhara, who wore animal masks or else blackened their faces, making themselves unrecognizable during their henbane-fueled rituals. This anonymity probably meant that they felt more able to give in to the effects of the drug, sublimating their human personalities.

The very real possibility that a seemingly inanimate object such as a mask can sublimate the ego means that the ritual use of a mask is a dangerous practice. Wearing a mask that symbolizes the "dark" side or the base tendencies can cause those qualities to manifest in the person. Additionally, because the skin or head of an animal is believed to retain the essence of the creature, it is a distinct possibility

that the spirit could possess the wearer of such a mask, the human body possessed by this spirit.

The Konoga masks of the Dogon, an African tribe from Mali, are worn during the masked dances that replicate the actions of God when the universe was made. These dances possibly started out as a way of encouraging the spirits to bless the hunt, but have evolved into something with a wider breadth of meaning that is described in the actual name of the mask; Konoga means "hand of God."

The Kachina masks of the Hopi Indians are worn to welcome back the benevolent spirits that spend time with these people for six months in every year.

MAYPOLE

The maypole used to be a very common sight in many northern European countries, where it was a symbol of the phallus of the May King as well as a representation of the World Axis or World Tree. Although we tend to think of the maypole as a rural phenomenon, they were erected in cities, too. Traditionally, the pole was decked with flowers, with several long ribbons attached to the top. During

a useful focus for other sociable activities, too. During the Restoration in 1660, there was a general resurgence in the popularity of the maypole, which became a symbol of defiance. At this time there were over a hundred maypoles freshly erected in London, hard to believe for a modern-day dweller in the city.

The pagan origins of the maypole were effectively forgotten, as the pole became a quaint symbol of rural pursuits and an archaic relic of a "Merrie England" that has become a thing of the past.

pre-Christian Beltane ceremonies, the girls would each take one of the ribbons and dance in a counterclockwise direction, while the boys took the other set and danced clockwise. This deosil/widdershins dance represented the male/solar powers interweaving with the female/lunar qualities, a celebration of the harmony inherent within the universe that was also a powerful fertility ritual.

However, evangelical Protestants considered the maypole an anti-Christian object that could lead to lewd behavior and even, God forbid, merrymaking on a Sunday. The consequence of this change in attitude was a general maypole ban; many were chopped up and burned. However, there were pockets of insurrection where people refused to remove the maypole, since it provided

MAZE

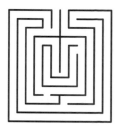

The maze carries similar symbolism to the labyrinth in that it represents a metaphorical journey. However, whereas a labyrinth consists of one long path that maximizes the use of the space available and is as long as possible, the maze generally has meandering twists and turns and many deadends. See Part 5, Sacred Geometry and Places of Pilgrimage, for an unusual example of a living maze constructed in the image of the Green Man.

MEDICINE WHEEL

The "genuine" medicine wheel is a Native American construction, a three-dimensional, physical object that is made from stone, laid out in a circular pattern, generally in North America. They are investigated in depth in Part 5. However, the medicine wheel is also drawn as a form of meditation. The medicine wheel is a symbol of Native American spiritual belief, the circle representing the ideas of infinity, rebirth, motion. Ultimately the circle is the symbol of the Zero Chiefs, the notion that the zero is not "no thing," but "every thing."

The individual elements within the wheel vary according to the preferences of the designer; feathers, sun wheel symbols, animal totem

MEHENDI

This is the ancient art of adorning the hands and feet with henna paste. It is carried out as a ritual in any part of the world where the henna-producing *Hawsonia inermis* plant grows, although it is safe to say that India is most closely associated with this symbolic art form. Formerly the paste was made at home in quite an elaborate process, but these days the paste can be bought in tubes that make it easier to apply.

Its most popular use is in decorating the bride for her wedding. Less wealthy brides use the mehendi as a substitute for expensive gold jewelry.

The style of the designs and the use of the symbols vary from country to country and from region to region, and many of the meanings of the traditional patterns that are still in use have been lost over the years. Unsurprisingly, most of the patterns bring wishes for fertility, prosperity, and a happy life. Sometimes the names of the bride and the groom are secreted in the curlicues of the design. Traditionally, the bride is not allowed to do any housework until her wedding mehendi designs have faded away.

seven archangels of the celestial spheres that relate to these planets.

The menorah has become an instantly recognizable emblem of the Jewish faith, and appears on the coat of arms of Israel, among other places.

MERKABAH

MENORAH

This is the seven-branched candelabra of the Jewish tradition. The Bible is very specific as to the construction of the golden menorah that was made for the Holy Temple in Jerusalem, and it is described as three branches that come out from either side of a candlestick. The seven lights are significant since they number the seven days of creation and were originally lit, one day at a time, until all seven lights were glowing at the end of the week. The lights also signify the seven planets, and accordingly the

In the Kabbalistic tradition, all ten of the qualities of the Tree of Life are collectively referred to as the Merkabah, or Chariot of God. This mystical chariot gives God the power to descend from heaven to enter the souls of men. The symbol shown here is used as a meditative focus, to attain the state of mind and spirit necessary to achieve union with the elements of the Tree of Life and so become part of the collective spirit of the cosmos.

* ✳ *

MESOPOTAMIAN TREE OF LIFE

Believed by some to be the "original" Tree of Life, the symbol which is universal, appearing in all cultures, the Mesopotamian one was said to be a colossal tree which grew in the center of the world, and from whose roots flowed the Apsu, the primordial water from which all life emanated.

MESSIANIC SEAL

Comprised of a string of three symbols, starting with the vesica piscis, then the Star of David, and topped by a menorah, this seal is the insignia of the Messianic Christian Movement, a group that has adopted some Jewish practices into their rituals, possibly in an attempt to persuade Jewish people to convert to Christianity.

The symbol is believed to have been used by very early followers of Christ, and is found carved onto stone that dates back to the first century AD.

METATRON'S CUBE

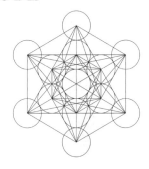

In Christianity, Judaism, and Islam, Metatron is said to be one of the most powerful angels in heaven. It is testimony to this power that Metatron was allowed to be seated in heaven, a privilege that was reserved only for God. However, Metatron was seated because it was his role, as scribe, to record the history and deeds of humankind.

Metatron's Cube can be formed from the Fruit of Life symbol, by using the points of intersection to make the shape geometrically correct. The power of this complex geometric symbol lies in the shapes of the five Platonic solids hidden within it.

Early Kabbalistic documents say that Metatron formed this "cube" from his soul.

Apart from its geometric significance, the cube is a powerful symbol of protection, able to keep away demons and other unwanted influences.

MEZUZAH

In Hebrew, Mezuzah means "doorpost," but the word refers, in this case, to the small container that is attached to the doorposts of any Jewish buildings, be they homes, government offices, shops, etc. This small case contains a piece of paper or parchment with two verses from the Bible, from the Book of Deuteronomy. Jewish religious law requires that a Mezuzah is attached to every doorpost.

Written on the reverse side of the paper is the word "Shaddai," which is one of the names of God believed to be a notarikon for a phrase which, in translation, means "Guardian of the Doors of Israel."

Since the doorway is symbolic of a move between two states of being or between this world and the next, it makes sense that they should need to be protected. The Mezuzah, when it is constructed properly and affixed with due reverence, is a powerful tool of protection. It is customary for Jewish people to touch or kiss the Mezuzah when they pass by.

MIRACULOUS MEDAL

This is one of the many symbols, called Marian Symbols, adopted by followers of the Virgin Mary within the Catholic Church. This particular symbol is said to have come in a vision to St. Catherine Laboure in 1830. In the vision, Mary herself directed the design of it. It is intended as an emblem of charity.

The symbol consists of an intertwined M and a cross, and 12 stars that represent the Twelve Tribes of Israel. The hearts signify the Sacred Heart of Jesus and the Immaculate Heart of Mary.

MIRROR

The belief that a reflection can somehow be an actual part of the soul may be a primitive one, but it reaches far into our collective conscious. The mirror is somehow regarded as a mystical gateway into another world. Lewis Carroll plays with this idea to great effect in *Through the Looking Glass.* Here, the mirror is a window to a parallel universe of opposites, a sort of negative image of reality. The mirror is used as a magical object, again, in the fairy tale of Snow White, where the mirror of the evil Queen has a spirit of its own that can see what is going on elsewhere in the world. The mirror can tell the Queen "who is the fairest in the land." Like the mirror in this fairy tale, the mirror always reflects the impartial truth, and so is symbolic of honesty and purity.

The Buddhist Mirror of Dharma reveals the causes of past actions, so here the mirror symbolizes not only truth but also enlightenment. For Tibetan Buddhists, the "Wisdom of the Great Mirror" teaches a secret similar to that of Plato's Cave of Shadows: that the things reflected in the mirror are just another aspect of the Void. In Japanese mythology, the mirror that belongs to the goddess Ameratasu draws light from the darkness of a cavern and beams that light back out into the world.

The ancient Celts believed, too, that the mirror could capture souls, and their women were buried with a mirror to keep the soul safe.

Mirrors appear repeatedly in myths and legends from all over the world. A broken mirror is a symbol of doom, the archetypal bad omen, and popular superstitious belief says that the person breaking the glass will suffer seven years' bad luck, although there are certain unusual measures that can be taken to minimize this. These include burying the mirror in a piece of thick cloth deep in the ground, presumably so that the reflection of the "bad luck" is hidden in the dark.

A black bowl filled with water makes a reflective surface; the water is associated with the moon, itself a mirror of the sun, and for those with the talent to move outside the confines of linear time this scrying bowl provides a magical mirror that can be used as a divinatory tool. The use of reflective surfaces is one of the most ancient forms of divination. Pythagoras had a magical mirror, which he placed in moonlight in order to "charge" it with lunar, occult powers. He then used the mirror to divine the future.

The reflective surface of the witch ball, hanging in a window, wards off evil spirits by reflecting their malevolence right back at them. In this sense, it has a similar use to the hexagonal mirror used by practitioners of Feng Shui. This mirror is fixed above the doorway of the home, the eight sides of the frame repelling bad influences from all directions, a protective symbol.

There is a primitive idea among some people that a photograph somehow captures part of their soul. Effectively, a photograph is a reflection created by the mirror reflexes inside the camera. If the mirror reflects the soul, then the well-polished mirror is symbolic of the purity of the soul as well as of knowledge, consciousness, and self-awareness. The eye, itself a reflective surface, is called the Mirror of the Soul and is believed to be able to convey what is hidden inside the conscience of its owner.

The ancient Celts believed, too, that the mirror could capture the soul, and their women were buried with a mirror to keep the soul safe. Everyone knows from horror movies and gothic tales that vampires have no souls; sometimes this is indicated by their lack of reflection in a mirror. In Bram Stoker's *Dracula*, the evil count throws Jonathan Harker's shaving mirror out of the window in case his secret is revealed.

Mjolnir

Also known as the Hammer of the Gods or Thor's Hammer, the Mjolnir symbol owes its significance to its long history as a supernaturally powerful object.

The word carries with it connotations of crushing and grinding, both in the agricultural sense (it shares its root with the word "meal") and in the destructive sense. Both the hammer and the axe are associated with lightning because, like lightning, they strike fast and hard. Thor, as the god of thunder, found lightning to be a useful and appropriate weapon.

The origins of this particular hammer are steeped in myth. One of the legends describes it as having fallen to earth as a meteor; other sources state that the trickster god, Loki, manufactured it. Its power was legendary, too. Mjolnir was able to destroy mountains or topple giants with a single strike. A particular feature of the hammer, which made it especially useful as a weapon of war, was its boomerang-like quality of returning to whoever threw it.

As an amulet, the Mjolnir offers protection, and despite origins that are squarely placed within the pagan realms, it has managed to slip the wide net cast by Christianity. It continues to be popular today as a major symbol of the Asatru faith.

advisor to Queen Elizabeth I. He devised a magical sign that he called the Monad, which is illustrated here. Published in 1583, the Monad of Dr. John Dee is an amalgam of the four symbols that represent the sun, the moon, the elements, and fire (since this related to Aries, the first sign of the zodiac). This Monad carried such logical symbolic meaning that it was adopted by the alchemists and the Rosicrucians. Dee also pointed out that his Monad contained the constituent symbols of all the planets too.

MONAD

The Monad, in essence, refers to the upright symbol of a vertical line, but is also taken to mean the one, the godhead, the intellect. The root of the word is Greek and it shares its origins with the word "monastery" as well as "mono."

Dr. John Dee was an occultist and astrologer and most famously was

NAVAJO SAND PAINTING

Bearing some relation to the rangoli patterns of India, sand painting is not restricted to the Navajo people but is also practiced by Australian Aborigines and Tibetan monks. The Indian and Tibetan drawings serve to remind of the impermanence of life.

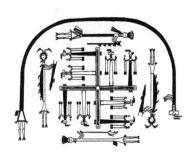

NAZAR

However, the Navajo version of this very ancient art is carried out specifically for healing purposes. There are numerous different traditional designs, created painstakingly like the rangoli, by letting the fine sand run through the fingers, accompanied by prayers and chanting. The symbols in the picture include representations of the gods to whom the appeal is made.

Once the painting is finished, the "patient" destroys the image by sitting in the middle of it where he not only absorbs the energy of the symbols but also releases his "illness" into the sand. This sand is disposed of with care, as it is considered toxic after it has been used in this way.

The authentic ritual sand paintings are a closely guarded secret. Any paintings likely to be seen by the outside world will have been created in a different way, using incorrect colors or sequences of shapes to ensure these sacred symbols retain their potency.

This is an amulet designed specifically to repel the evil eye. Originating in Turkey, the Nazar is found in shops frequented by tourists. It is a pretty piece of circular blue glass, with additional dollops of glass set in a concentric circle of blue and white to represent the eye. Traditionally, the nazar is hung in windows or doorways to repel undesirable influences.

NER TAMID

The Ner Tamid is the Hebrew name for the sanctuary lamp, which burns constantly in both synagogues and Roman Catholic churches and chapels. Other names include the Altar Lamp or Eternal Flame.

The lamp is a sacred symbol of the omnipresence of God (in the Tabernacle) or Jesus (in the

means "blessed protector." The charms are generally made of paper or fabric that is made into small packets or pouches and then consecrated in a temple ritual. They usually have the name of their temple of origin on the front and a symbol of good luck or prosperity on the other side. Sometimes, Omamori are made with more permanent materials, such as wood or metal.

Church), and the flame itself equates the spirit of God or Jesus to the power of light and the sun, which also burns constantly. The lamp is made from red glass to differentiate it from other candles. Keeping such an important symbolic flame alight is an important task; however, this is much easier now, since electric versions are available.

OMAMORI

These amulets are given to devotees of the Shinto religion when they make an offering or donation to a shrine. Omamori, in Japanese,

OMPHALOS

Omphalos is a Greek word meaning "navel," although the concept is not restricted to Greece but is an archetypal symbol found all over the world. Because the navel, in the human being, is the point of contact with the life-force generated by the mother, the omphalos, similarly, connects the earth with the life-force generated by the godhead.

Usually symbolized by a great stone, the omphalos is representative of both the physical navel and spiritual navel that is the center of the world. The idea also equates to other symbols including the lingam, the World Tree, and the Axis Mundi.

The most famous omphalos stone in the world is the one at Delphi in Greece. Ancient Greeks considered this omphalos to be the center of the earth; not only that, but this particular omphalos stone was a channel of communication between three worlds: the mortals living on the earth, the deities in heaven, and the dead in the underworld. Legend has it that Zeus sent out two eagles from opposite ends of the earth to determine the exact position of this auspicious spot. The omphalos was situated at the point where the birds crossed in flight.

There are many other omphalos symbols scattered around the globe. The stone that the Ark of the Covenant rested on, in the Inner Sanctum of the Temple at Jerusalem, is an omphalos. For Buddhists, it is symbolized by the tree that the Buddha sat under when he achieved enlightenment. The Celts have several single standing stones, called menhirs, that are phallic symbols as well as omphalos symbols.

* ❋ *

ONNIONT

For the Iriquois an Onniont is a particularly potent form of Aaskouandy, which itself is a magical charm believed to have a mind of its own. The Aaskouandy generally comes in the form of a stone or similar object that is found unexpectedly.

The Onniont comes in the shape of a fish or serpent, and gives its owner the power to pierce anything in his way, such as trees, rocks, or wild animals, in order to reach the object of desire.

ORPHIC EGG

This is the symbol of an egg encircled by a coiled snake, and depicts the Greek myth that the world was hatched from a silver egg; this silver egg sat in the darkness, an image that is closely associated with the moon. It is sometimes called the Cosmic Egg.

ORTHODOX CROSS

This is a Latin Cross with two additional crossbars at the top and a slanting bar at the bottom that

resembles the footrest that, some people argue, was a feature of the cross upon which Christ was crucified. The additional bar at the top of the cross represents the initials I.N.R.I., meaning "Jesus of Nazareth, King of the Jews," a phrase designed to taunt Jesus.

Because the lower footrest slants diagonally, it symbolizes two directions, heaven and hell. The thieves who were executed at either side of Christ have their destinies symbolized by this slant. The repentant thief takes the upward path toward heaven, while the other, not at all repentant, goes to hell.

Ouroboros

The circle and the serpent are both symbols that are potent with mystical meaning, and they come together in the ouroboros.

The serpent that constantly revolves, swallowing the end of its own tail, most commonly forms the circular or oval shape of the ouroboros. However, sometimes the symbol is constructed of a dragon rather than a serpent, or a pair of snakes that swallow one another's tails. The dragon and the serpent are closely connected; both creatures often guard treasure of some kind.

The ouroboros is a primal symbol of great antiquity. Although it makes its first appearance in ancient Egypt around 1600 BC, it is likely to be even older than this. The ouroboros was named by the Greeks, and means "self-devourer." The ouroboros speaks of motion, continuity, and self-fertilization.

Although the name is Greek the ouroboros as a concept appears elsewhere; for example, in Norse myth the great serpent Jormungandr is so large that he can hug the planet and still be able to grasp the end of his tail in his teeth. It also appears in Hindu myth as the serpent goddess Nahusha, who creates the world. It also hints at the image of the Cosmic Egg that is encircled by the spiraling snake.

The most obvious explanation for the ouroboros is that it symbolizes not only the cyclical nature of time and the seasons, but also the eternal cycle of rebirth. This idea makes sense because the serpent's habit of shedding its skin makes it an ideal symbol of rebirth and renewal. For the Gnostics, the ouroboros symbolizes eternity. At the same time, it serves as a reminder of the confines of the material world, and yet of aspiration to a higher state of being.

The serpent is a creature of the earth, close to the ground. The circle is a symbol of completion and spiritual perfection, and in this sense, the ouroboros demonstrates a union of opposites, heaven and earth working in harmony.

There is also a double ouroboros, where the serpent twists into the infinity symbol.

In alchemy, the symbol speaks of purity, wholeness, and infinity.

PA KUA

This is a hexagonal shape formed by the eight trigrams of the I Ching. These trigrams are sometimes carved onto wood and used to frame the mirror of the same name that is said to be an effective tool belonging to the ancient discipline of Feng Shui.

PAISLEY

The name "paisley" might seem incongruous for a design motif which is of Eastern origin. The original pattern, known as the "buta" in Persia and as the "mankolam" in India, made its way across the continents in the form of shawls and fabrics brought back by Scottish soldiers returning from the colonies in the nineteenth century. The weavers in the small Renfrewshire town of Paisley, already known for its woven and printed fabrics, copied the designs; hence the name.

There are several theories as to the inspiration for the familiar, curving teardrop design but it is generally believed to have been inspired by plant or fruit forms. The mango that inspired the man-kolam is an emblem of fertility and good luck. It may also be a derivation of the shape of the leaf of the sacred Bodhi tree that the Buddha was sitting underneath when he gained enlightenment.

PALAD KHIK

The Palad Khik is a very specific kind of amulet that originates in Thailand. The phrase means "Honorable Surrogate Penis" and this accurately describes the form of the charm. The Honorable Sur-rogate Penis is secreted underneath the clothes of Thai males, offset from the real thing, in the hopes that it will absorb any evil spells that might be directed by malicious people against the genuine penis.

The Palad Khik originated in India and was brought to Thailand 1,200 years ago. These ancient amulets once featured inscriptions to Shiva, then to Buddha. The idea

of protecting the sexual parts nat-urally transcends any religious boundaries. However, modern Palad Khik amulets bear inscrip-tions written in an ancient style of script that is impenetrable to most latter-day Thais, but which no doubt lends an enticing antique appeal to the tourist market.

PALM CROSS

The Palm Cross is traditionally made and given to Christian churchgoers on Palm Sunday, just before Easter, to commemorate the victorious entry of Christ into Jerusalem not long before he was crucified. Palm leaves—a symbol of victory—were strewn on the ground along the route taken by Christ, hence their use in the man-ufacture of the crosses.

PAPAL SYMBOLS

The regalia, insignia, symbols, and emblems belonging to the pope, the Roman Catholic Church, and the Vatican are so numerous that they merit a separate entry. These symbols tend to be occluded in mystery, often subject to conjec-ture and confusion. However, any mysteries can be clarified with a little analysis.

Most importantly, the pope himself is a living, breathing symbol, the human representation of God on earth.

TRIREGNUM

Also called the tiara or Triple Crown, the Triregnum has not been in use since the early 1960s, but prior to this time was used in the coronation of the pope and subsequently in important processions. In appearance, it looks similar to some of the headgear depicted in ancient Egyptian reliefs and statuary and it fulfills many of the functions associated with ritual headgear and crowns; it enhances the status of the wearer, making him taller and more noticeable. The Triregnum brings the wearer closer to heaven; the shape can emulate the halo or a similar sign of sanctity. There have been several of these "crowns," and 22 are still in existence today. Since 1342, when the third part was added, the symbolic aspects of these tiaras have been the cone shape, the rich encrustation of jewels, and of course the three levels that give the Triregnum its name. When Pope Paul VI decided to simply lay the crown

on the altar in St. Peter's Basilica after the Second Vatican Council, the very act itself symbolized an acknowledgement of a new time for the Vatican, a time of humility and, effectively, a new start cognizant with changing times.

There are numerous theories about the symbolic meanings of the three parts of the crown: moral, temporal, and spiritual authority; the Holy Trinity; the acknowledgement of the wearer as being Father of Princes, Ruler of the World, and Jesus Christ on earth; also, the heavenly, earthly, and human aspects of the universe.

The Triregnum, although currently not in use as a physical object, appears on the flag of Vatican City.

THE FISHERMAN'S RING

This is a gold ring with a depiction of St. Peter casting his nets from a boat, also known as the Pescatorio. A new ring is cast for each pope, including his name around the edge of the picture, and the ring that belonged to the old pope is smashed. This means that there is only ever one of these rings in existence. The destruction of the ring had a practical purpose as well as a symbolic meaning (signifying the end of the old reign). The ring was used by the pope to seal private correspondence, so destroying it ensured that no one could use it in the interregnum, the period where there was no pope. The image on the ring is now represented as a stamp, although the kissing of the ring is still a mark of respect for the pope.

THE CROSSED KEYS

Another of the symbols of the Vatican flag and other papal insignia is that of the crossed keys of St. Peter, to whom Christ gave the keys to the Kingdom of Heaven. One key is silver and one key is gold, the two bound together by a red cord. The silver represents the authority of the pope on earth and the gold, his authority in heaven. The keys are crossed in a saltire cross.

THE UMBRACULUM

Traditionally, the pope was always shaded in some way, and the Umbraculum, or Umbrella, which appears on papal insignia, signifies not only this idea but also the notion of protection. At one time a man would walk along with the actual object ensuring that the pope was shaded and protected at all times. This practice no longer continues but the emblem remains. It has parallels to the parasol that is one of the eight sacred symbols of Tibetan Buddhism.

PAPAL CROSS

This cross has three cross bars, of graduated lengths. Like the Triregnum, the symbolism of these three bars is open to conjecture, but it is generally held that they represent both the Holy Trinity and the three aspects of the power of the pope. This cross also looks rather like a ladder, and so it represents a symbolic stairway to heaven.

PARASPAROPGRAHO JIVANAM

See Jain symbol.

PAX CULTURA

The symbol of the International Banner of Peace, or Pax Cultura, was designed with the intention that it would act as a kind of cultural Red Cross symbol, to protect sites or areas of universal cultural heritage or importance during time of war. This symbol comprises three circles (representing art, science, and religion) formed into a triangle shape, surrounded by a further circle, representing the idea of unity.

* ✳ *

PEACE SIGN

This circular sign, with its upside-down forked cross shape, is ubiquitous as a peace sign and, specifically, as the symbol for the Campaign for Nuclear Disarmament. Although the sign is not strictly secret or particularly sacred, it is a good example of how a sign is designed and how the elements of symbols can be misinterpreted.

Some Evangelical Christians have supposed that the cross-type symbol inside the circle is a nod to the cross that was used for upside-down crucifixion at the hands of the emperor Nero, called the Cross of Nero or the Cross of St. Peter. This particular cross has unfortunate connotations of satanism because of their reported penchant for turning Christian symbols or prayers back to front or upside down. The cross shape also resembles a particular runic symbol that is used by some neo-Nazi groups, although here again there is a gross misunderstanding. The symbol actually means "elk," a creature that has no shady symbolic meaning whatsoever. However, this was misinterpreted as meaning "life." Therefore, if inverted it should, in theory, mean "death." All the neo-Nazis got for their pains was an inverted elk, which is more comic than sinister.

The actual invention of the symbol has a simple story. Gerald Holtom, instrumental in the Campaign for Nuclear Disarmament, created it. A Christian, Gerald originally used the Christian Cross within the circle, but there were objections from parties who felt that this could be misinterpreted or might alienate some parties. So Holtom thought about the shape of a human being in despair, with arms outstretched downwards in a pleading gesture, and the sign was born. Although it started out as being the emblem of the CND movement, the symbol is now universally accepted as a sign of peace.

PENTACLE

Sometimes there is confusion between the pentacle and the pentagram. For the record, the pentagram is the five-pointed star symbol, whereas the pentacle is a more generic term for a mystical or magical symbol.

It is likely that the word "pentacle" originates from the Latin root, "pend," to hang; hence "pendant." A pentacle is often designed to hang around the neck.

The pentacle can be made of any material, although Trithemius (a fifteenth-century abbot with a great knowledge of the occult) recommended "virgin parchment" or a square plate of silver. Various symbols and signs that are appropriate for its intended use are then drawn or engraved on the pentacle, including the signs belonging to the forces or spirits that the magician decides to invoke. Sometimes the reverse of the pentacle features the Seal of Solomon, adding even more magical kudos to the object.

For more complex magical endeavors, such as raising spirits, a series of powerful pentacles are designed, which the adept reveals one at a time to the spirits in question until the object of the exercise is accomplished, at which point the pentacles are all covered up again.

PENTAGRAM

It is possible that the pentagram was discovered by very early astronomical research, in the Tigris–Euphrates area, some 6,000 years

ago. Archaeologists have found fragments of pottery with the symbol, dating back to 4,000 years ago, but it was Pythagoras who really brought the five-pointed star to the prominent position it holds today.

If an apple is cut in half across its "equator" then the pattern of the seeds is revealed, a perfect five-pointed star or pentagram. The repercussions of this hidden magical symbol are far-reaching. Five, comprised of the feminine number two and the masculine number three, is the number of harmony, of the union of opposites (for example in sexual congress), and of marriage. It is also the number of humankind because of the five points of extremity of the human body. When Eve gave Adam the Apple of Knowledge in the Garden of Eden, therefore, it was not just a piece of fruit she was offering him, but a potent symbol of wisdom.

Eating the fruit that contains the pentagram resulted in a profound awakening for Adam and Eve. They became not only aware of their own sexual natures, but they realized that they could make their own choices.

Not only is the pentagram a symbol of power, but it is imbued with actual power and is used in spell casting and the revelation of secrets.

The pentagram is either pentagonal or star-shaped. The earliest representations of it appear scratched on the walls of caves, and it is understandable that ancient humans would have a natural and automatic reverence for the stars; this is as relevant today as it was then.

The ubiquity of this sign can't be stressed enough. It is associated not only with pagan practice but also with Christian mysticism, Druidry, magic, sacred geometry, alchemy, and the Kabbalah; it appears in the tarot where it can represent the suit of coins, and it is an important symbol in Freemasonry, where it is called the "Blazing Star."

One instance of its use was as a secret symbol whereby followers of Pythagoras could recognize each other since, as Adam had discovered, it was the key to higher knowledge.

Pythagoras held that five was the number of man, because of both the division of the soul and of the body into five parts each. Further, the five points of the pentagram represented the elements: earth, air, fire, water, and psyche, or ether in the Eastern tradition. The followers would describe the sign of the pentagram upon themselves in exactly the same way as do pagan people, who use it as a sign of protection, in much the same way that Christians use the Latin Cross.

If you want to try it, here's how. The sign starts at the left breast, and then goes to the forehead, then to the right breast, then the left shoulder followed by the right shoulder, and back again to the left breast. Pythagoreans would accompany this with a greeting of "good health," because another hidden meaning within the pentagram is that the initials of the five elements which each of the points represented were an anagram for the name of the goddess of healing, Hygiea.

In the Kabbalah, the pentagram represents the upper five sephiroth on the Tree of Life, whose qualities are justice, mercy, wisdom, understanding, and transcendent splendor.

Freemasonry draws upon much of the Pythagorean symbolism of the pentagram, although it is also seen as a reminder that Christ was spirit descended into matter, and as such represents the Star of Bethlehem.

The inverted pentagram has been accorded a more sinister interpretation than was ever intended; up until relatively recently it didn't seem to matter which way up the star landed: after all, this symbol is like the circle in that it has no beginning and no end. However, the symbol of Baphomet makes use of the upside-down pentagram.

The pentagram is the sign of Venus, both the planet known as the morning star, and the Goddess. Over the course of four years and one day, the planet describes the shape of a pentagram in the sky. Uniquely, Venus is the only planet whose movements trace such a graphically recognizable symbol, a secret sign written in the sky.

PERSIAN RUGS

If you have a Persian rug in your house, then every day you unwittingly walk over an ancient series of elaborate secret symbols whose colorful intricacies hide a wealth of information.

No two Persian rugs are ever the same. Despite the fact that some of the patterns may have been copied for centuries, the makers weave in a deliberate "mistake" so that the pattern is never perfect; this is an acknowledgment that only Allah is perfect.

The rugs themselves divide into two general categories; those with curving, floral patterns, and those with a more geometric design.

Some of the inspirations for these patterns include the architecture of mosques, flowers, trees, and other vegetation, animals, spirals, and the curious paisley design. Some patterns were drawn by the original designer without his hand ever leaving the page.

The patterns of the rugs also tell of their provenance and the tribes that designed them, each tribe having its own unique patterns.

Some of the hidden patterns within Persian rugs have specific meanings. These include the parrot (love), the pomegranate (abundance), the Tree of Life (eternity), the carnation (happiness), and the camel (wealth).

PHILOSOPHER'S STONE

There are few symbols so crammed full of esoteric meaning or arcane mystery as the Philosopher's Stone. It is so elusive that it has no actual pictorial emblem, but is hidden within a series of cleverly veiled clues and linguistic ambiguities from the realms of alchemy.

The process of making the Philosopher's Stone reputedly requires just seven steps, and oblique instructions for these steps are described in the Emerald Tablet. However, like the Holy Grail, the Philosopher's Stone exists on a metaphysical level as well as any supposed physical level, so analysis of these instructions has to be carried out on many levels. This is the stone of the philosophers for a very good reason.

Essentially, to the alchemists, the Philosopher's Stone was a substance that could effect the transmutation not only of lead into gold, but could turn any substance into something else, seemingly having the same power as a magic wand. The stone was also able to restore youth and so had the power of eternal life.

Reputedly, the ingredients needed to make this stone would not necessarily come about by hard work, but would be revealed to a very few "chosen ones" by the angels; angelic intervention itself is often a synonym for a stroke of inspiration or intuition that goes beyond logic.

There have been a few characters throughout history who have claimed to have discovered the Philosopher's Stone, including Paracelsus. In the sixteenth century, he put forward the theory that the Philosopher's Stone was an undiscovered element, which all the other elements were made from. Sir Isaac Newton was intrigued by alchemical processes and delved deeply into the mysteries of the Philosopher's Stone. Perhaps the bruising stroke of inspiration he received when the apple fell on his head and he "discovered" the universal law of gravity was his own personal Philosopher's Stone, won not by hard work but by deductive reasoning and a timely knock on the head.

PHURBA

This is a sacred knife, used only in ritual practices by Tibetan Buddhists. Like the Athame of the Western tradition, it is employed to create the sacred spaces that are used for rites and ceremonies. Its design is based on a stake used in ancient times to tether sacrificial animals, and it is used to describe a magic circle in the same way as a compass. The phurba can only be owned or handled by initiates.

PRAYER FLAG

Belonging to the Tibetan Buddhist tradition, these are lengths of colorful flags that bear images and mantras or prayers. The flags take two forms, either horizontal strings of many flags, or single, vertical flags. Both kinds traditionally punctuate the sacred landscape, fluttering in the breeze among the mountains, temples, stupas, and monasteries of Nepal and Tibet, although they are now seen in other places.

Typical prayer flags come in a series of five differently colored cloths with woodblock designs that represent the five elements. The order and significance of the colors is blue (space), white (water), red (fire), green (air), and yellow (earth). The designs include mantras and depictions of auspicious symbols such as the Triratna.

Tibetans believe that the prayers printed on the flags are carried to the gods, hence their appearance in high places. As the colors fade, so the prayers become a permanent part of the universe. Pristine strings of new flags join the faded and tattered older ones, symbolic of the continual renewal of life. In common with other sacred items, prayer flags should not touch the ground.

PRAYER STICK

A fetish object belonging to the Native American tradition, prayer sticks vary in size and materials but all of them share the same intention, that of carrying prayers to the gods by means of the feathers that are attached to the stick in such a way that they flutter in the breeze.

PRAYER STRING

Effectively a string of beads of a number that is significant to individual belief systems: despite their different names or different num-

bers of beads, prayer strings all fulfill the same functions, as an aid to meditation or prayer and a reminder of the tenets of the faith.

For Catholics, the prayer string is called the rosary, from the Latin, rosarium, so called because of its association with the Virgin Mary, for whom the rose is an attribute. Today's rosaries most frequently contain fifty beads grouped in sets of ten with a larger bead between each set and a cross at the very end. Each group of ten is called a decade. The beads are "told," that is, they are passed through the fingers with each repetition of a selected group of prayers.

For Buddhists and Hindus, the prayer strings are called Mala, and have 108 beads. One hundred and eight is a sacred number in the Dharmic religions, corresponding to the stages of development of the world, the number of manifestation. The goddess Sarasvati holds a Mala with 50 beads; as goddess of learning, she is also goddess of the alphabet, and each of these beads corresponds to the 50 letters of the Sanskrit alphabet.

For Muslims, the prayer string is called the Tasbih, and has 99 beads that correspond to the 99 names of Allah.

Sikhs use a piece of woolen string as a Mala, with 99 knots rather than beads.

LESTOVKA

This is an unusual Russian form of prayer string, generally made of leather and belonging to "old" believers such as the Russian Orthodox Old Ritualists. The 99 "steps" are made by looping the leather strip around twigs or sticks of wood and the whole is completed with four flaps—generally triangular in shape, which represent the four Gospels.

KOMBOLOI

Not strictly a rosary, the Komboloi is the string of worry beads that are often seen in the hands of Greek men. The Komboloi looks similar to the rosary but has no religious significance.

PRAYER WHEEL

Also known as Hkhorlo, or Mani Wheels, prayer wheels are an inherent and essential part of Tibetan Buddhism.

The actual prayer wheel itself comes in many different sizes. Some are small enough to be held in the hand, others are large enough to be placed in streams where the action of the flowing water keeps the wheel turning. Wheels a meter or more high can be seen at temples. Whatever the size, the basic construction of the prayer wheel is the same. A central axle has a long strip of paper wound around it. On this paper is written, over and over, the words of the mantra "Om Mani Padme Hum." The paper is encased in a drum, and in the smaller hand-held wheels, the protruding axle acts as a handle so that the wheel can be turned.

Sometimes prayer wheels are constructed with a piece of human skull bone secreted in the handle.

Symbolically, the wheel itself used to be so sacred in Tibet that it was never used for such a mundane purpose as transport; and any carts or vehicles there were usually not of Tibetan origin.

Prayer wheels are always turned in a clockwise direction, following the path of the sun and to ensure that the words written on the paper are traveling in the right direction.

Symbolically, it is believed that the combination of the elements of the prayer wheel and its turning action produce a powerful energizing spell, which connects the microcosm (the person doing the turning) with the macrocosm (the gods and the universe). Both the written and spoken forms of the syllables of the mantra carry a sacred power that is further enhanced by motion.

It seems that the symbolic purpose of the prayer wheel is far more powerful than its physical form, however, and it is now possible to get electronic prayer wheels (called Thardo Khorla) or digital prayer wheels, which will download onto a computer.

Q

See Quintessence.

QUESTION MARK

This sign is used every day, isn't it? Therefore, it may not be thought of as a symbol of mystery, but that is just what it is. It also resembles the sacred staff of augurs, the lituus that ended with a spiral. Its component elements are the wave, turned on its side. The wave is emblematic of the area between the spiritual and material worlds, that is, between what is a possibility and what exists in actual reality. The dot, or bindhu, below, is synonymous with either the seed of potential, or actual reality.

The question mark is used to describe uncertainty or apprehension, but the element of the dot means that the symbol acts as a reminder that the person asking the question has the possible answer within himself.

QUINTESSENCE

Quite literally, the quintessence stands for the "fifth essence" (from the Latin "quintus," meaning five), and while not strictly speaking a symbol, it forms an important philosophical key to the understanding of many of our secret signs and sacred symbols. It is the element or feature that binds the different parts of a symbol into a harmonious whole, and can often be found in the center of a symbol, where it may be indicated with that most deceptively humble of symbols, the dot, or sometimes the letter Q.

RAELIAN STAR

If you should happen to see this particular symbol on the car bumper that is ahead of you, then you will know that you are likely to be following the vehicle of a Raelian cult member. The Raelians believe that the planet Earth was created by a people who came from the sky, but not from a god. These people are called the Elohim, and are extraterrestrials.

The symbol used to be comprised of a six-pointed star whose arms cleverly morphed into the ancient sun symbol, the swastika. However, the symbol was adapted and the swastika removed lest it should inadvertently cause offense. The Raelian star resembles a spiral galaxy.

RANGOLI

Rangoli patterns are known by various different names throughout India according to the region. The word describes both an ancient Hindu tradition and a form of folk art. Known as the Kolam in southern India, this is a beautiful, colorful, and elaborate design that is generally drawn on the floor or on the ground with dyed rice flour. Rangoli drawing is not restricted to high days and holidays but is a part of everyday ritual, even in the villages where, at the doorway of the house, the pattern welcomes not only visitors but is said to attract the goddess of abundance, Lakshmi.

Rangoli drawing started, it is said, when the son of a high priest died. All the priest's friends and relatives prayed to the Lord Brahma, who told the king to draw a picture of the boy on the floor. Brahma then brought the drawing to life, so restoring the priest's son.

The patterns are initially constructed with a series of geometrically placed dots, which help the artist to define the shape. The fine rice powder is held with the finger and thumb. The dots are then joined up by trickling the powder with the fingers, requiring concentration and a steady hand. Finally, the pattern is colored with dyed rice powder.

Despite the care and attention that goes into the drawing of the rangoli patterns, it is considered right and proper that footprints destroy them during the course of the day. This in itself symbolizes change and mortality, and is a reminder not to value material possessions, or the works of man, above the world of spirit and the gods.

The same conceptual celebration of the impermanence of life is celebrated in the finely wrought powder mandalas created by Tibetan monks.

REBIS

The Rebis, or Twofold Matter, is just one of the symbols used to denote the idea of the hermaphrodite. It is a perfection of being, comprised by a perfect balance of opposites. The yin-yang from the Chinese tradition and the yab yum from India are among the other symbols that reflect the same idea.

The Rebis illustrated here comes from the rich alchemical tradition. It is taken from Basil Valentine's *Theathrum Chemicum* (1613).

This particular rendering of it is crammed with symbols, as are many of the drawings of alchemy.

The oval shape of the frame suggests the egg, symbol of the cosmos and of new potential. Inside the egg is a human figure with one body and the two heads of a man and a woman. The figure stands on a winged, fire-breathing dragon that in turn is crouched on the orb of the planet. The dragon symbolizes manifestation, the fire that shoots from its mouth is symbolic of the spirit. The planet has wings, too, denoting the marriage of the earth with the heavens. Inside the planet, there is a cross, its four arms denoting the four directions and the four elements. In the center of the circle is the dot, indicating the fifth element or quintessence. There is also a square inside the circle, and a triangle.

Five stars surround the figures; five is the number of the union of the feminine two with the masculine three, the union of opposites and the number of marriage. Each star has six points; here, the number six stands for the male element of fire as depicted by the upward triangle, joining with the female element, water, the downward-pointing triangle. The star also alludes to the notion "as above, so below." Above the head of the man is the sun; above the head of the woman is the crescent moon.

RED STRING

You may spot someone wearing a piece of red thread or string around the left wrist. This symbol will tell you that you are looking at someone who follows the teachings of the Kabbalah, an esoteric form of Jewish mysticism. The red string itself is said to protect the wearer from the evil eye or from others' envy. The red string itself is an assuming item, and reminds the wearer of our humble origins and that to be human is to be fallible. It is worn on the left side of the body since this is the side that is believed to receive energy first.

Red string is tied around the tomb of Rachel, the great Jewish matriarch. This string is then cut up and given as amulets. Each string is tied with seven knots, and as each knot is tied, it is a reminder to the wearer to refrain from thinking negative thoughts about others. As a charm, it is full of positive intentions.

Although the piece of red string is as humble an object as its symbolic meaning, it is ironic that some people choose to pay a lot of money for one.

RINGSTONE SYMBOL

This is a sacred symbol of the Baha'i faith, and is so called because it frequently appears on rings or other jewelry, and is an identifying feature of followers of Baha'i.

Each part of the symbol has significance.

The upper line is the World of God; the central line is the world of manifestation of God's ideas, and the lower line stands for the World of Man.

The vertical line is the element that connects all three, and as such has the same significance as the World Tree.

The two five-pointed stars that stand at either side of the symbol represent the two messengers of God for this particular age, Bab, who called himself "the gate," and Baha'u'llah, a follower of Bab, who founded the Baha'i religion in the nineteenth century.

The official symbol of the Baha'i faith is an elongated five-pointed star, called the "Hakyal," meaning "temple." Baha'u'llah's writings sometimes appear in the shape of this star.

ROMA [ROMANY]
CHAKRA

A relatively new symbol, the Roma chakra was adopted as recently as 1971 at the first Romany Congress.

The symbol is a neat reminder not only of the origins of the Romany in India (hence its similarity to the chakra wheel), but it also points to the wandering nature of these nomadic people because it looks like the wheel of the Vardo, the special caravans which they have used for centuries. The wheel has sixteen spokes.

ROSY CROSS

The Rosy Cross or Rose Cross is believed to have been adopted by the Christian Church in its first century, and combines the masculine principle, the material world and the cycle of birth and death (the cross) with that of the feminine principle and spiritual unfolding (the rose). The rose also signifies the blood of Christ and the power of redemption, and represents Christ's mother, Mary—in her guise as the goddess—with whom the rose has always been closely associated.

However, the Rose Cross is known most famously as the symbol for the Rosicrucian Society, and the illustration shown here is based on the Rose Cross Lamen that belongs to the organization.

The Rosicrucian Order was founded by Christian Rosenkreuz, an alchemist traveling in the East in the fourteenth century who stumbled upon ancient teachings that he passed on to seven other men. They swore that the knowledge would remain hidden for one hundred years.

This legend was written about in two documents, the "Fama Fraternititis" and the "Confessio Fraternititis," published in 1614 and 1615 respectively. Like the alchemists, the Rosicrucians kept their knowledge veiled and clouded in riddles. However, the Rosy Cross symbol is said to hold the entire bundle of Rosicrucian philosophical secrets within it, providing it is correctly analyzed.

The Golden Dawn also made good use of the versatile Rose Cross, making it into a sort of one-stop dictionary of meanings and reminders. The zodiac and planets, the Hebrew alphabet, the Kabbalah, and a whole slew of other elements were heaped into this one intriguing symbol.

Ru

See Vesica piscis.

Rudraksha bead

The rudraksha tree, or *Eleacarpus ganitrus*, grows in the northern part of India and Pakistan, and the bead is actually its fruit, which shrivels to a hard, woodlike texture.

These beads are highly revered as sacred items, since they symbolize the tears that Shiva shed for humanity. Legend says that the first tear that dropped on the ground became the first rudraksha tree, the word itself meaning either "red eyed" or alternatively Rudra (Shiva) and Aksha (eye)—the Eye of Shiva.

The bead is a powerful symbol of protection against the evil eye, and symbolizes the eye of Shiva.

Rudraksha beads vary in price according to their perceived power, which is dictated in part by the number of "mukhtis," or facets, which comprise the bead. The most valuable and therefore the most efficacious, is the Ek Mukhti Rudraksha, or one-faceted bead, which is flat and generally has the oval eye shape, reinforcing its symbolic meaning.

Rudraksha beads are used as sacred ornamentation and there are numerous rules as to how, when, and by whom they should be worn. For example, it is considered bad form for a menstruating woman to wear her rudraksha beads. The beads are cleaned, blessed, and then charged with power before use.

These holy beads are also used in the japa mala or sacred prayer strings of the Hindu monks. These japa mala consist of 108 beads, since 108 is a sacred number in the Dharmic religions.

SACRED HEART

The Sacred Heart symbol was revealed in a vision to a nun, Mary Marguerite Alacoque, in seventeenth-century France. The heart

is encircled around the center with a crown of thorns, has flames shooting from the top, and the whole is surmounted by a cross. The actual elements of the symbol are self-explanatory, but the symbol rose to prominence when the Bishop of Marseilles consecrated his diocese to the Sacred Heart to try to avert the plague that was rampaging through the town. Somehow, the area remained immune from the disease and so the Sacred Heart gained a reputation as a symbol not only of good luck but also of divine intervention.

ST. ANDREW'S CROSS

See Saltire.

* * *

St. John's Cross

See Templar Cross.

St. Peter's Cross

See Inverted cross.

Saltire

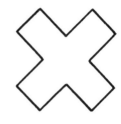

The saltire is also called the St. Andrew's Cross. Legend has it that when Andrew (one of Christ's disciples) was going to be crucified, he deemed himself unworthy to be executed in exactly the same way as his Messiah, so the diagonal cross was used.

How, then, did Andrew become the patron saint of Scotland and the saltire come to be adopted as the flag of the country, given that Andrew was born near Galilee more than 2,000 years ago? Apparently it was an accident. Legend has it that a Greek monk was warned that Andrew's remains were going to be moved from their burial place, and that he should take them "to the ends of the earth" for safekeeping. This determined monk (possibly St. Rule) managed to make it all the way to Scotland, where he was shipwrecked at a place that was later renamed St. Andrews. A chapel was constructed to contain the relics; later a cathedral would be built on the spot.

The Scottish flag, which shows the white saltire of St. Andrew on a blue background, is one of the oldest national flags in the world, and dates back to the ninth century.

Scales

Wherever scales or balances appear in mystical symbolism, they are generally used to denote a metaphorical kind of weighing rather than a physical one. Ma'at, the Egyptian goddess of truth, balances the heart (representing the conscience) on one side of the scales against justice (the ostrich feather) on the other. The ostrich feather is a useful analogy for justice since, unlike other feathers, its two sides are perfectly balanced. Other mythological and religious characters that hold the scales as a symbol of judgment and authority share the iconography of Ma'at. These figures include St. Michael, the archangel of the Day of Judgment. The astrological sign of Libra, too, is symbolized by the scales.

The notion of finding balance between opposing forces is a common thread running through esoteric beliefs including alchemy and the Kabbalah. The pivotal part in the center of the scales is itself symbolic of this point of perfection, a return to oneness between male and female, darkness and light, matter and spirit.

The scales and the sword together stand for truth and justice combined.

Compostela. To find out the reason for this, a little backtracking is necessary.

The scallop shell is home to a marine creature that, like all other animals that inhabit a watery environment, is associated with the moon and the eternal feminine. The personification of this idea is found in Botticelli's "The Birth of Venus," the painting of the goddess rising up from the ocean, standing on the shell, covering her modesty with her luxuriant tresses. The shell is shaped like the female sexual organ. Pearls also occasionally grow within these shells. Mary, the mother of Jesus, carried a "precious pearl" within her womb. Hence, the symbol of the shell on the cap of the pilgrim.

SCALLOP SHELL

The scallop shell used to be worn on the caps of pilgrims, particularly those that had completed the pilgrimage to Santiago de

SCEPTER

The scepter takes many forms, effectively a shorter and much more ornamental version of a staff. It is an emblem of authority and royalty, a phallic symbol. Breaking the

scepter indicates a symbolic castration, an abdication of power. In times of antiquity, the scepter was made of reeds, but it gradually became more permanent and decorative. The orb is the female counterpart to the scepter.

SCIENTOLOGY CROSS

Invented by L. Ron Hubbard, the founder of Scientology, this is a Latin Cross with four rays emanating diagonally from the intersection. Each of the eight directions of this a different feature of the faith; the self, creativity, community, survival of the species, life-forms in general, matter, spirit, and the Supreme Being.

SCIENTOLOGY SYMBOL

This symbol is composed of a letter S that links two triangles (which point in the same direction). The S stands for Scientology, and each of the triangles represent three tenets of the philosophy of Scientology; the upper triangle is called the KRC and stands for knowledge, responsibility, and control, and the lower ARC triangle represents affinity, reality, and communication.

The symbol was first used in 1952.

SCYTHE

One of the most common symbols of death, the scythe is the tool used by the Grim Reaper as he reaps his harvest of souls. This tool was also the attribute of the god Saturn, who also appears as Chronos, the god of time. The scythe of these ancient gods is not quite the doom-laden instrument that appears in the skeletal hands of the hooded Grim Reaper; it was more a reminder of the cycle of life.

SEAL OF SHAMASH

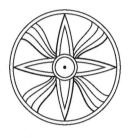

Shamash was the sun god in Mesopotamia. This symbol was used for a few centuries either side of 1000 BC in the Euphrates–Tigris region. Its foundation is the sun sign, the simple circle with a dot in the center, but here the foundation shape has the addition of four sets of three "rays," whose wavy lines look very like those used even today, by children, when they draw the sun. The vertical and horizontal beams were probably meant to represent the jurisdiction of Shamash over the four directions.

SEAL OF SOLOMON

Also known as the Star of David or the Magen David, the Seal of Solomon is a hexagram, a symbol whose outward simplicity hides a complex and layered inner meaning. There are several different versions of the Seal of Solomon, but in its most basic form it consists of two interlocking equilateral triangles, forming a six-pointed star.

The easiest way to understand many symbols is simply to look closely at their component parts and see what they appear to be. The upward-pointing triangle looks like a flame, and this is exactly what it represents. In its most basic form, this triangle is the elemental symbol for fire. The Western Tradition, the Eastern Tradition, the Kabbalah, alchemy; all are agreed. There is also agreement about the other triangle that balances on its point; it represents water.

Fire is the male element, and water is female. The inverted triangle is also the symbolic representation of the yoni. In India, the hexagram is called the Shatkona and represents the energies of Shiva and Kali locked in a constant embrace.

Imagine that the star is cut across the middle. On the left side is the element of air and on the right is earth. Further, the qualities of fire and water are represented: hot and dry, and moist and cold. Already this simple symbol is taking on a different dimension as the star becomes a map of opposing forces which combine to make all living things and is the symbolic epitome of the phrase "as above, so below." More prosaically, the Star of David has been used as the symbol for alcohol, quite literally, "fire water."

In alchemy, the Star of David is a reminder of the seven planets and the seven basic metals. At the top is silver (the Moon), then moving around the points of the star in a clockwise direction are copper (Venus), mercury (Mercury), lead (Saturn), tin (Jupiter), and iron (Mars). In the central space, also called the quintessence, is gold (the Sun). Sometimes the seal will acknowledge this central space with a dot or the tau symbol.

Alchemists are very fond of concealing their symbols in some way, and sometimes the star is disguised as a six-petaled flower. It is hidden in this way in the curious alchemical tome the Mutus Liber; as its name implies, this "Silent Book" has no words but consists of a series of pictures that describe the process of making the Philosopher's Stone, the primary ingredient in the Elixir of Life. Elsewhere, the star is concealed as a flower at the center of the maze at Chartres Cathedral and even in the U.S. dollar, itself a seething mass of hidden secret symbols.

This incredibly versatile symbol is called the Seal of Solomon because, so the story goes, it featured on a magical signet ring belonging to King Solomon. Supposedly, the ring gave him the power to understand the language of birds and animals, and to conjure up spirits to do his bidding.

The Star of David as a symbol of the Jewish faith—when it is also known as the Shield of David or the Magen David—only gained common use as recently as 1897. During the Nazi persecution of the Jewish people, stars made of yellow cloth were attached to their clothes. Although it had been intended to be a symbol of persecution, after the war this skewed meaning of the symbol was itself flipped over, and took on the opposite meaning, becoming a badge of honor and pride.

In Tibetan Buddhism, this universally important sign makes its appearance as the Dharmodaya of Vajrayogini. This is a three-dimensional hexagram with the Vajra at the center. The interior of the symbol is red, symbolizing bliss, and the exterior is white, signifying emptiness. The three angular corners of the triangle represent the "emptiness of cause, effect, and phenomena." The six smaller triangles stand for the six perfections: generosity, wisdom, concentration, effort, patience, and discipline. The smaller triangles at the top and bottom are empty, a reminder of the selflessness of all beings. Each of the four triangles at the sides has small "wheel of joy" symbols inside them. These four joys are joy, perfect joy, the joy of cessation, and innate joy.

SEAL OF THE KNIGHTS TEMPLAR

The Knights Templar were founded in 1118, with the mandate of protecting pilgrims on their way to Jerusalem. They were granted permission to quarter themselves on the Temple Mount itself. There are several seals associated with this venerable order, and the "traditional" seal is the one described here. The seal can be found engraved into stonework, particularly in churches and chapels, for example in Rosslyn Chapel in Scotland. The seal, wherever it is found, indicates the presence of the Templars.

The seal has images on both sides. On the front is depicted the image of two knights astride a single, galloping horse. This symbolizes several things. First, unity in action or a common purpose; the two men are on one horse, heading together in the same direction. Secondly, that fact that the two knights share one horse is a reminder of the vow of poverty taken by the knights. Thirdly, the symbol indicates the spirit of Christ, a reminder of the message in Matthew's gospel that says that wherever two or more believers are gathered together, then Christ will be there too.

The reverse of the seal shows the dome of the Church of the Holy Sepulchre in Jerusalem.

SECRET OF HERMES

See Smaragdina Tablet.

SEED OF LIFE

The seed of life forms a part of the construction of the larger Flower of Life geometric pattern. Its creation is simple but the hidden meanings within it are complex. Like the Flower of Life, it contains the circle, the vesica piscis, and the points of the hexagon or six-pointed star.

The seven circles that form the symbol signify the six days of creation plus the seventh day of rest as the central circle.

SEFER YETZIRAH SYMBOL

The Sefer Yetzirah is a Kabbalistic work known as the Book of Creation, the earliest Kabbalistic work, reputedly written by Abraham. The symbol associated with it essentially describes the order of Creation. Because the alphabet itself is a collection of secret symbols that contain the secrets of the universe within them, each component of the symbol also represents the 22 letters of the Hebrew alphabet.

The symbol consists of an upright equilateral triangle, surrounded by a seven-pointed star. This star is further surrounded by a large twelve-pointed star.

Inside the triangle are three letters, the "mother" letters that represent the elements of air, water, and fire. The seven-pointed star represents the seven "double" letters. The largest star symbolizes the twelve "simple" letters.

The Sefer Yetzirah also indicates the symbolic Tree of Life, or Otz Chiim, of the Kabbalah. The three "mother" letters are the three horizontal branches of the tree. The seven-pointed star symbolizes the seven vertical paths, and the twelve-pointed star indicates the twelve diagonal paths.

SERPENT CROSS

The tau cross or the Christian Cross with the serpent draped around it is an ancient symbol that has several meanings. It was adopted by the Christian faith to signify the triumph of the cross over the serpent, that is, the victory of good over evil, and as such, points toward the serpent that twined around the tree in the Garden of Eden. It also represents the transformation of the material into the spiritual as the serpent abandons its usual position on the ground and slithers upwards, toward enlightenment.

The Book of Numbers in the Old Testament of the Bible describes an incident when Moses is leading the children of Israel through the desert. Their numerous complaints and lack of faith led God to punish them with a plague of snakes. Moses counteracted this curse by following God's instructions to make a "brazen serpent," which he put on a pole, a charm against snakebites. This magical serpent was called Nehushtan, and worshipped as an idol.

The Serpent Cross also appears as an alchemical symbol, indicating the elixir of mercury, an effective healing substance once the toxin, represented by the snake, had been "killed."

SHATKONA

See Seal of Solomon.

SHIELD KNOT

The Shield Knot is a universal symbol of protection, seen in all cultures around the world. Although it takes different forms, the distinctive

features that make it a powerful protecting charm are the square shape and the interlacement pattern. One of the earliest known forms is from Mesopotamia and simply consists of a square with a loop at each corner. The same symbol appears in the Kabbalah as the "Shema," used to invoke the four archangels.

SHOFAR

This is a musical instrument that is made from the horn of a ram. It is based on the biblical horn that is reputed to have had such power and resonance that it blew down the walls of Jericho.

The Shofar is used ritually, sounded to signal the beginning of the Jewish New Year, Rosh Hashanah. The horn is blown one hundred times on this occasion. It is also used to signify the start of Yom Kippur, the Day of Atonement.

The use of the horn on this occasion follows an instruction in the Book of Leviticus, which directs a "blast" to be sounded "throughout the land."

SHOU

The Shou or Chou symbol is frequently seen but not often understood by anyone not able to understand Chinese. The symbol is an ancient ideogram meaning "long life."

Despite its antiquity it still appears in many places on furniture, woven into fabric and made into jewelry. The symbol looks a little like a peach stone. The peach was the symbol of the god Shou Hsing, who controlled events in the lives of human beings. The peach belonging to the god conferred the gift of immortality.

SIGIL OF AMETH SIGIL OF LUCIFER

Also called the Seal of the Truth of God (*ameth* means truth in Hebrew), the Sigil of Ameth is an elaborate symbol, containing an unusual six-pointed star. The hexagram is normally constructed of two triangles, one upright and one upside down. The star in this sigil is made using one line. This would imply powerful protection. In the center of the symbol is a five-pointed star, and written in various places are names of angels and of God. The sigil is connected to Enochian magic, since Dr. John Dee saw the sign in a vision, which he believed had been given to him by angels, although the symbol predates the time of Dee by about three centuries.

* ** *

Dating back to a sixteenth-century Italian grimoire called the Grimorium Verum or "Grimoire of Truth," this sigil is part of a "set" of secret signs which are said to help in invoking Lucifer. The origins of the sign have been lost in the mists of time although the pointed V shapes do represent the "horns," which are a telltale symbol of anything devilish.

SKULL AND CROSSBONES

A grinning skull sits above two bones which are crossed diagonally. At first this might seem almost like one of those everyday symbols we take for granted, but another look at the skull and crossbones makes it start to seem very peculiar.

We recognize it primarily in its form as the Jolly Roger, the wickedly grinning skull with the crossed bones underneath, which is the universal emblem of the pirate.

But where did this symbol originate?

As with many of these signs, the history of the skull and crossbones is shrouded in mystery. We know that it is very old (it has been used over the entrances to Spanish cemeteries and graveyards for centuries) and as a symbol of death it has no rival; indeed it has become the universally acknowledged symbol for poison.

It seems that the Knights Templar and the Freemasons may hold the key to the inner meaning of this symbol. The Jolly Roger started life as the "Jolie Rouge," the name given by the French branch of the Templars to the flag flown by their warrior ships, and which was later adopted by pirates.

In Freemasonry, the symbol is repeated six times on the Tracing Board which is spread on the floor of the temple prior to any rituals. Here, the skull and crossbones represents both death and life; by analyzing the symbol we see that the crossed bones form a saltire, a diagonal cross, which is symbolic of an evolutionary change.

So the symbol of death in the form of the skull is given another aspect, that of hope, progress, reincarnation, and of life after death.

It comes as no surprise, knowing this, that the Templars would bury their dead with the legs removed from the body and placed in the shape of the cross.

SMARAGDINA TABLET

A cornerstone of the tenets of alchemy, the Smaragdina Tablet (also known as the Emerald Tablet or the Secret of Hermes) is an ancient text, said to contain the teaching of Hermes Trismegistus, the founder of all things alchemical. The legend goes that Alexander the Great found the tablet in the tomb of Hermes. Inscribed on it, in Phoenician characters, were the instructions for making gold. The tomb is reputed to have been near Hebron, and the earliest translations of this mysterious recipe are in Arabic.

The use of emerald lends further exoticism to the story; however, at that time any green-colored stone was referred to as emerald and it is likely that the Smaragdina Tablet was made of green jasper. Whatever its material construction, the instructions on it have attracted the consideration of many illustrious characters over the centuries, including Roger Bacon, Albertus Magnus, Aleister Crowley, and C. G. Jung. Alchemy is full of hidden secrets and relies heavily on symbols, wordplay, and double meanings to hide its mysteries from all but the most perceptive and adept of interpreters. The words on the Emerald Tablet are no exception. There are several translations. Isaac Newton, who was an alchemist, provided the following interpretation that was found among his papers after his death in 1727.

'Tis true without lying, certain and most true

1. That which is below is like that which is above and that which is above is like that which is below to do the miracles of one only thing.

2. And as all things have been and arose from one by the meditation of one: so all things have their birth from this one thing by adaptation.

3. The sun is its father, the moon its mother.

4. The wind hath carried it in its belly, the earth its nurse.

5. The father of all perfection in the whole world is here.

6. Its force or power is entire if it be converted into earth.

7. Separate thou the earth from the fire, the subtle from the gross sweetly with great industry.

8. It ascends from the earth to the heaven and again it descends to the earth and receives the force of things superior and inferior.

9. By this means you shall have the glory of the whole world and thereby all obscurity shall fly from you.

10. Its force is above all force, for it vanquishes every subtle thing and penetrates every solid thing.

11. So was the world created.

12. From this are and do come admirable adaptations where of the means (or process) is here in this.

13. Hence I am called Hermes Trismegistus, having the three parts of the philosophy of the whole world.

14. That which I have said of the operation of the sun is accomplished and ended.

Solomon's Knot

This symbol looks like two links of a chain, set at right angles to one another. The sign is particularly ancient and does not belong to one particular people, although the Italian stonemasons called the Comacines, said to be the forerunners of the Freemasons, adopted it as their hallmark and imbued it with mystical symbolism.

The designs of King Solomon's Temple remain a great influence on Freemasonry, so it may be that the Comacines named the symbol. It appears in the abstract patterns inside synagogues, so this may be the reason for the name.

Solomon's Knot, like many knot symbols, provides protection. It also resembles the ancient sun symbol, the swastika.

* * *

Spear of Destiny

As a possibly mythological artifact of Christ's last time on earth, the Spear of Destiny, or Holy Lance, shares some similarities with the Holy Grail, in that it is a mystical object said to confer marvelous, if dark, powers upon the owner. However, whereas the associations with the elusive grail are positive, the spear carries largely negative connotations, as befits the weapon used to ensure the physical death of Christ after the crucifixion. Effectively the spear is the counterpart to the grail, not only because of their respective feminine/masculine polarity.

The spear is mentioned only once in the Bible, in the Gospel of St. John. However, a fourth-century testament, the Gospel of Nicodemus, mentions the name of the soldier,

Longinus, who used the spear to pierce Christ. Therefore the spear is sometimes called the Lancea Longini, after this centurion.

Like the grail, the spear (or relics of it) has been the subject of a similar unprovable provenance wherever it has appeared in the millennia since its initial sinister use. It seems to have multiplied since its original appearance in Jerusalem, and among the cities that have laid claim to ownership of the spear are Rome, Paris, and Vienna. The Viennese Lance, known as the Hofburg Spear, was taken by Adolf Hitler although it was restored to Vienna after the war.

Hitler's brief ownership of the spear has added to its reputation as an object—and a symbol—of evil influence. As such, legends of the Spear of Destiny have influenced books, comics, and films.

SPIRAL

The spiral shown here comes from the Tibetan tradition, and is the symbol used to describe the origins of the universe. The spiral shown here turns in a clockwise direction, following the path of the sun, symbolizing the seed of potential energy; a good way to understand the power and movement contained within the spiral is to think of a coiled spring.

This particular emblem looks like a drawing of a snail shell; indeed, the spiral crops up in many places in the natural world, in both flora and fauna and in other phenomena, and has inspired not only artists but also mathematicians and philosophers. The unfurled fronds of the tree fern, in New Zealand, inspire the spiral motifs in Maori art. The tremendous energy of the whirlwind or twister is a physical example of the energy and power that can be contained within the spiral.

The spiral is rich in symbolic meaning. It radiates optimistically out from its center, ever expanding, full of endless possibilities. It has a three-dimensional quality that speaks of a journey in time, too, from past to future. The spiral represents the cyclical phases of evolution, and somehow inspires a curiosity about what is coming next.

Spiral motifs appear all over the world, from Neolithic cave complexes in Europe, on carvings of the goddess from the Paleolithic era, on Celtic stone carvings such as the ones at Newgrange, in the Hindu pantheon where it appears, for example, as the Kundalini Serpent, woken up from its tightly coiled state, spiraling up from the base of the spine. In Africa, the symbol for the sun shows a cooking pot surrounded by three red spirals. The Aztec feathered serpent god, Quetzalcoatl, shared the same symbol as the Tibetan seed of life; their warrior god, Huitzipotchli, has a coat of arms featuring five spirals contained within a circle.

The double spiral weaves in one direction and then in the next, a reminder of death and rebirth.

In Hindu temples, pilgrims walk in a circular path around the various shrines, taking an additional spiral around ritual objects such as the lingam/yoni. This clockwise journey is not only a meditative process but "charges" the energy of the place. There is also a (possibly apocryphal) story that Britain managed to repel a possible German invasion during World War II when a massed group of witches met together to protect the country by concentrating on creating a huge spiral-shaped pillar of energy. There are dances and movements, too, which re-create the energy of the spiral. Perhaps the most dramatic instance of this is the Turkish whirling dervish. A more sedate example is the folk dances that involve a spiral line of dancers circling in and out from a central point. The same idea is echoed in the spiral dances of Native Americans.

Spiraling back to the symbol on the snail shell, it is fascinating to note that, for the Mayans, the winter solstice was considered the start of the year, the time just before "real" time began. The symbol that represented this concept was the snail; the spiral on its shell inspired the Mayan sign for zero.

SQUARE

See First signs: Square.

STAFF

The staff is not only a weapon, but serves as a guide and as a support. It is a phallic symbol that also represents fire.

The staff takes many forms, as the Lituus of the augur, as the bishop's crozier that also looks like a shepherds' crook, and as the Khakkhara of the Buddhist monk that supports his steps and fulfills the same role as the staff of a pilgrim. The magic wand is another kind. The staff that Joseph of Arimethea pushed into the ground at Glastonbury, that sprouted into the mystical tree known as the Glastonbury Thorn, is a good example of the staff as a symbol of the World Tree and hence the Axis Mundi. The staff is a phallic symbol, connecting the heavens to the earth via the intermediary of the person that wields it and directs that power. Hence, it is also a symbol of authority.

STAR AND CRESCENT

See Crescent Moon.

STAR OF DAVID

See Seal of Solomon.

* ✳ *

STAR OF LAKSHMI

A Hindu symbol, this eight-pointed star, or Ashtalakshmi, is comprised of two interlocking squares. Each point of the star represents the eight kinds of wealth bestowed by the goddess.

STAR

The star is universally accepted as a symbol, and a part of our everyday language. To call someone a "star" is a great compliment. Our ancestors believed that each star had its own spirit, maybe that of the deity, an unborn soul, or the soul of a dead person that had a particularly notable life, an idea that is completely in accord with our use of the word to denote fame; however, there are always positive connotations surrounding the word. The light of a star is only visible in juxtaposition to the darkness surrounding it.

The appearance of a particularly unusual star in the sky heralds an important or auspicious event, for example, the Three Wise Men knew of an ancient prophecy, recorded in the Book of Numbers in the Old Testament that "there shall come a star out of Jacob." However, it was not only the birth of Christ that was heralded by a star. The Buddha shared this privilege as did the fire god, Agni, from the Hindu pantheon.

In terms of astronomical significance, the Pole Star provides a reliable aid to navigation and its unmoving position, static at the center of the great wheel of the heavens, makes it a symbol of the World Axis. This star is also, for many, a reminder of the constancy of God.

The Yakut tribes of Siberia believed that stars were the windows of the universe, alternately opened and closed to ventilate

the spheres of heaven. It's easy to imagine a black sky full of windows through which shines the powerful, illuminating light of heaven.

There are hundreds, if not thousands, of different star symbols. The number of points in the star is an important part of the design. The eight-pointed star might represent the idea of eternity and regeneration, in accordance with the number eight. The nine-pointed star might be a reminder of the nine muses, the Nine Worlds of Norse myth, or other aspects of the number nine. The pentagram, the hexagram, and the Elven star (or septagram) are explored under their own entries.

SUFI WINGED HEART

Similar to the Solar Winged Disc except with a heart in the place of the circle, the Winged Heart is the symbol of Sufism, the mystic branch of Islam.

Inside the heart is a pentagram with its point uppermost. Beneath the star is the crescent moon. Together these symbolize Islam, with the added dimension that the star itself symbolizes divine light and the shape of man, whereas the moon represents the reflection of this light and the notion of the responsiveness of the heart.

The heart represents the transition point between spirit and matter and is a reminder that man's heart can be attracted to material things, or it can be drawn toward matters of the spirit. Therefore, the wings symbolize the spirit and the notion of ascendance.

Sun Cross

See Celtic Cross.

Sun sign

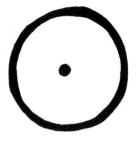

The sun is arguably the most prominent feature of our natural world— after all, without it nothing would

exist. Therefore it is natural that this bright star should be venerated as a deity and that its influence should be so universally pervasive.

The sun as a symbol takes many forms, but one of the simplest is the simple circle with a dot inside which is so simple and obvious as to require almost no explanation.

The sun is also represented as a wheel, turning in the sky from the eastern horizon to the western one. The most famous symbolic representation of this idea, and one of the most ancient, is the swastika. *See* Celtic Cross.

Swastika

For many people the swastika has been rendered sinister since it was adopted by Adolf Hitler's Nazi regime. They believed, mistakenly, that it was a symbol of a pure Aryan race. In fact, the swastika is a very old solar symbol, going back to Neolithic times, revered in many cultures, and found in many different forms, including being a sacred symbol in the sand paintings of the Navajo Indians. It is one of the few symbols that have almost universal meaning, significance, and distribution, and its spread extends throughout India and northern Europe to

Central America, and as far as eastern Asia. The name comes from the Sanskrit word *swasti*, meaning "well being" or "so be it," and there is a theory that it may have first been "invented" by basket weavers, since the swastika shape is produced during the weaving process.

In examining the component elements of the swastika, the first thing to notice is that the shape of the four arms resembles a wheel. Like a wheel, the swastika can rotate in either direction. Officially, if the arms are pointing in a clockwise (deosil) direction, then it symbolizes the sun, the male principle, the overt; if it is pointing counterclockwise (or widdershins) then it resembles the moon, the feminine principle, the covert. In this case, the swastika is sometimes called the "sauvastika." However, there is generally no differentiation in the direction of the swastika that can be discerned from its usage as a religious symbol, and it is certainly not the case—despite popular belief—that the left-oriented swastika is somehow "evil" or that this was the only swastika employed by the Nazis. For the Hopi Indians, the clockwise swastika stands for the earth, and the "reversed" one, the sun.

The wheel is a major symbol of the Dharmic religions, and so is the swastika. When used in Hindu temples, homes, and other places, the swastika is often decorated with a bindhu or dot in the center of the space between each arm. The swastika is one of the 108 sacred symbols of the Lord Vishnu.

The next thing to notice is that the swastika has four arms, which are jointed, giving further reinforcement to the significance of this number. The number four stands for solid, material objects, the constructed universe, order and discipline, and for the four corners of the world. It also indicates the four winds, the four cardinal directions, the seasons, and the elements, with the very center of the swastika representing the quintessence, also known as the fifth element. This central hub, the still center, points to the swastika as a symbol of the Axis Mundi.

In Freemasonry, the hub of the swastika resembles the Pole Star.

TALISMAN

Similar to an amulet, a talisman is more likely to be made specifically as part of a magic ritual designed with a particular intention in mind.

The aim of any good maker of talismans is to load the odds in favor of the desired result, by adhering to a strict set of rules when making the object. The complexities of these rules include making sure that the intention of the talisman is coordinated to the day of the week, its ruling angel, its ruling planet, and the hours that the influence of the planet is at its strongest.

MAKING YOUR OWN MAGICAL TALISMAN

The contents of this book should give enough guidance in providing the right symbols for your talisman. The chart below gives the correspondences between angels, days of the week, and the sigils and planetary symbols of those angels.

This "Talisman for Health" is taken from Sepharial's *Book of Charms and Talismans.* It was chosen because health is the best thing that anyone could wish for. The instructions below should give you the general idea for making talismans with other intentions. Here are the instructions.

Sunday	Monday	Tuesday	Wednesday	Thursday	Friday	Saturday
Michaël	Gabriel	Camael	Raphaël	Sachiel	Anaël	Caffiel
name of the 4 'Heaven	name of the 1 'Heaven	name of the 5 Heaven	name of the 8 Heaven	name of the 6 Heaven	name of the 3 Heaven	No Angels ruling above the 6 Heaven
Machen.	Shamain.	Machon.	Raquie.	Zebul.	Sagun.	

1. This particular talisman needs to be made on a Sunday. This is because the sun is the planet of fire, vitality, and the life-force. If you can make the talisman from gold, the metal of the sun, so much the better. If not, make it a golden color.

2. All talismans, no matter what their intention, should be made in the first, eighth, fifteenth or twenty-second hour of the day; these are the hours that the influence of the ruling star or planet is at its strongest.

3. All talismans need to be enclosed within a circle.

4. After making, the talisman can be worn or carried in a purse or bag.

THE TAROT: PICTORIAL KEY TO THE UNIVERSE?

Despite the opposition of Christian authorities to these cards, referred to by Scottish clergymen as the Devil's Picture Book, the tarot is an evocative and intriguing set of symbols that are supposed to be linked to various mystery traditions such as the Kabbalah, witchcraft, paganism, and alchemy, and have always retained their mystical charisma as a form of divination. The tarot is connected to the zodiac and the planets, and Jung expounded the notion that the images held within the cards indicate archetypal personalities and symbols. "Normal" playing cards have their origins in the 78 cards of the tarot, after the removal of the 22 cards of the Major Arcana and the knights of each of the four suits. The two "spare" jokers in the pack are the only remnant of the profoundly important tarot card called the Fool.

"Arcana" means a mystery or a hidden secret, so it is apt that the origin of the cards, as befits any symbolic system of such significance, is also cloaked in mystery. That the cards act as an oblique way of disseminating occult teaching is agreed, though. The tarot's origins have been variously attributed to Hermes Trismegistus, the founding father of alchemy, also to the Egyptians, to the Indians, to the Arabs, and to the Chinese.

It is possible that the Knights Templar were responsible for introducing the cards to Europe, using the images to conceal the magical lore of the Saracens from a suspicious Church that was eager to persecute the demonic influences of the heathen East. It is also possible that "normal" playing cards had the knight removed to disguise the Templar involvement with them. Nevertheless, the medieval Church still viewed the cards with great alarm and believed that the heretical sect, the Cathars, were using them to disseminate their wicked Gnostic ideas. Between 1378 and 1450 the cards were banned in Regensburg in Germany, Marseilles, Paris, Siena, Venice, and northern Italy. Later, however, the Church would try to adapt the cards to suit the Christian doctrines in the same way that they tried to absorb the mythology of the zodiac.

There's another theory that the tarot cards were spread by the nomadic Gypsy people. Count de Gebelin, renowned for his analysis of, and research into, the tarot, said that the word had Egyptian origins, *tar* ("road") and *ro* ("royal"). Therefore, he posited that the name signified the "royal road to wisdom." Another interesting theory as to the provenance of the name is found in the curious palindrome, ROTA TARO ORAT (TORA) ATOR, which translates as the "Wheel of the taro speaks of (the law of) Hathor."

Whatever their origins, these cards are an evocative embodiment of many of the most significant symbols; they carry a language of their own, which transcends the many words that are used to describe them. The tarot reaches deep into our subconscious mind. The opulence and prolific imagery of these cards, in particular the Major Arcana, makes their use as a mere divinatory tool seem somehow irrelevant. Although there are thousands of different tarot sets that are all as diverse as the interests of their designers, each card has fundamental elements that contribute to its archetypal meaning. Every tiny element within a card is significant, from the colors used to its number and its relationship to the card that falls before or after. Which way do the figures face? How do they hold themselves and what is their appearance? Are they young or old? Sallie Nichols, in *Jung and Tarot*, describes the system as "an effective bridge to the ancestral wisdom of our innermost selves." This is a bridge of symbols; what follows is a brief analysis of some of those symbols.

THE MINOR ARCANA

The "lesser secrets" are split into four suits of 14 cards, making 56 cards in total. The first thing to notice is that each group corresponds to the elements and the male/female energies. The Wands are fire, and Swords are air, both male elements. The suits of Coins and Cups represent earth and water respectively, female elements. These cards run in a sequence from ace to ten followed by four picture cards, the jack, the knight, the queen, and then the king. Barbara Walker draws an interesting parallel between these cards and four stages of life as outlined by the Tantric philosophies.

1. Sambhoga, the Life of Pleasure, the beginning of life and the time when the child has its every need fulfilled by its parents, represented by the Cup of Life, which begins to fill with experience.
2. Nirmana, the building process, is the period of young adulthood, represented by the wand, scepter, or Vajra as a symbol of the assertion of power.
3. Artha, or earth, stands for the gathering of material possessions, the fruition of efforts, the suit of Coins or Pentacles that represents riches of all kinds.
4. Moksha means liberation, effectively the "art of dying." The air element represents the soul or breath that leaves the

body. This is depicted by the sword, symbol of release. This suit generally has a feeling of danger or calamity about it.

Until Pamela Colman, working with A. E. Waite, revolutionized the Minor Arcana by giving each one an individual pictorial representation, they were simple sets listing the number of appropriate emblems.

THE MAJOR ARCANA

These 22 cards form the suit that was abandoned to create the deck of regular playing cards. This short sequence of pictures has been called the "quintessence of occultism," and parallels are drawn between their symbols and the letters of the Hebrew alphabet. Twenty-two is the same as the number of paths between the Sephiroth in the Tree of Life diagram, each one an aspect of the Creator. Ten of the cards also seem to match the aspect of the Sephiroth, too, from the Fool that represents the formless void of the Ain Soph, to the Wheel of Fortune that represents the Kingdom, the final Sephiroth.

The symbols used in the Major Arcana also correspond to certain aspects of the zodiac. For example, the Lover card equates to Gemini.

The card of the Moon also shows a crab or a lobster, emblem of Cancer. The card for Strength shows the lion, Leo. In short, there are as many interpretations of the tarot as there are people to interpret them.

In a sense, the cards are a sort of mystical mirror, reflecting back whatever the individual wants to see. Having said that, the decks used here in the descriptions of the cards include the Marseilles Deck, the first pack of tarot cards to gain prominence. It first appeared in 1748 and is still widely used today. The A. E. Waite/Pamela Colman deck is also examined. The following descriptions are only a suggestion of the hundreds of different interpretations of the signs that are secreted in the cards.

The 21 numbered cards are often put together in three groups of seven; the first seven cards of the sequence signify the realm of spirit; cards eight to fourteen represent the soul, and the last seven are the material realms. The Fool has no number.

THE FOOL: ZERO

The Fool is commonly depicted as a young man in motley clothing, striding along without a care in the world, a bundle over his shoulder, staff of the traveler in hand. A dog jumps up at him and rips his clothes, exposing his buttocks. The Fool appears to be dangerously close to the edge of a cliff. The numberless nature of the card indicates that the Fool is somehow outside of society, and to the observer, the Fool appears to be aptly named.

The Fool

However, there are other aspects to this character. The limp bundle he carries is generally white, the color of initiation and secrets. His cap has a feather, symbolic of transcendence and truth. The motley of his clothes is the same color worn by kings and priests as well as the jester, and the Fool ignores the animal, material world (the dog) in favor of his spiritual quest, no need for a companion on this particular journey. The staff he carries is not only a useful tool, but is similar to the wand that connects the earth with the heavens.

The image on the card suggests someone at the start of a journey. His bag is empty, ready to be filled with the wisdom he will acquire. This lack of possessions indicates the philosophical ascetic in many religious traditions, who trusts the universe to provide him with whatever he needs.

The Fool is striding forward into the unknown; the zero speaks of potential as well as of completion. The Fool is the only character from the Major Arcana that retains a place in the more mundane playing cards, appearing as the card that can replace any other (his multi-hued clothing gives him a chameleon aspect) or else upset the balance. He is a reminder of the spiritual nature of life's journey, and his story unfolds throughout the rest of the tarot cards.

THE MAGICIAN: NUMBER 1

The first numbered card of the Major Arcana, the Magician, or Juggler, shows a man standing in front of a table. The table has four legs firmly upon the ground, representing the reality of the mate-

The Magician

rial world, a stable base. On top of the table are the symbols that constitute the suits of the Minor Arcana as well as the elements; the cup, the sword, the wand and the coin or pentacle. These, however, do not symbolize reality; the trickster nature of the magician means that they are illusory. The Magician, like the Fool, wears the motley clothing of the priest or adept.

Somewhere in this card appears the lemniscate, the figure-of-eight or infinity symbol. In some cards it is concealed in the swirl of his hat; in the Pamela Colman/A. E. Waite tarot, it floats above his head and no attempt is made to disguise it. In this interpretation, the magician points with one hand to the heavens and with the other, to the earth; this posture says "as above, so below," the physical form of the meaning of the Seal of Solomon.

Whereas the Fool has a happy-go-lucky approach to life, the Magician is far more serious, full of intention. He holds a wand in one hand and a coin in the other. Because magicians traditionally use tricks to direct our attention elsewhere, it could be that he intends the coin (the world of matter) to be the focus of our attention, or he could be distracting us from it, alluding to the illusory nature of our interpretation of reality. The Magician effectively opens the game of life.

THE HIGH PRIESTESS: NUMBER 2

The High Priestess

As the Magician has the male number, the Priestess has the number of the female. She's sometimes called the Popess. The Pamela Colman card shows her sitting between the two columns, Boaz (female) and Jachin (male), that are not only the columns of the kabbalistic Tree of Life but also the pillars that were used at the Temple of Solomon and which still influenced the design of Masonic temples. Other elements to note in this card are the book or scroll, symbolic of wisdom and the secrets of the universe that she holds. There is a veil, indicating secrets that are revealed only to the initiate; the crown showing heavenly authority, and a throne, symbolic of earthly power. The seated posture of the High Priestess is reserved for those who hold a position of great power. Apart from Hermes, the Scribe of the Heavens, the only character in heaven who is seated is God.

There may also be a representation of the phases of the moon. Anything with three parts, symbolizing the triple aspect of the moon, can serve this purpose. The crown of the Priestess sometimes has three layers, or in some decks the symbol may be more obvious. In the Pamela Colman interpretation, the Priestess not only has a crescent moon at her feet but her crown is in the shape of the Akhet, the Egyptian symbol for the sun coming over the horizon that also looks like the "balancing scales" glyph of Libra. The Priestess symbolizes balance between two opposing forces. A cross is also part of the imagery of this card, generally appearing on the breast of the Priestess, indicating her sacred status.

THE EMPRESS: NUMBER 3

The Empress

Like the Priestess, the Empress is also a seated, powerful female figure. Many of the clues on this card shout "authority," from her posture to the items that she holds or that surround her. She wears a crown, and holds a scepter and a shield that has an eagle on it. Whereas the Priestess has an air of mystery about her, the Empress holds much more worldly authority while retaining a feminine softness

that is denied the Priestess. Her clothing is less rigid, and she is generally depicted in a setting of daytime and openness, rather than in the dark. The scepter she holds looks like the Globus Cruciger. The globe is the material earth and the cross is the spirit. This spirit symbolism is further underlined in some instances where the Empress is given a pair of wings.

Whereas the Priestess's arms are closed, the Empress's arms are open, indicating a maternal or outgoing nature. The Priestess guards something whereas the Empress reveals something. The Empress is a figure of maternal love as well as authority; in the Colman interpretation her shield is heart-shaped and instead of the eagle, it shows the alchemical symbol for the female. This Empress has a field of wheat before her, symbolic of fertility, and a nod to the goddess Demeter.

THE EMPEROR: NUMBER 4

All the empirical qualities of the number four are represented here: strength, solidity, foundation. If the Empress is the archetypal mother, then the Emperor is the father. Sometimes this fourth card is called the Cube Stone. The

The Emperor

ally and he appears to be leaning against his seat, ready for action, in contrast to the Empress who sits firmly in her throne. His crown, too, is not the elaborate headgear of the Empress but is a helmet, a more appropriate piece of headgear for a man who rules actively rather than passively.

THE HIEROPHANT: NUMBER 5

The Pope

Emperor also has a shield that shows an eagle, but whereas the Empress and her bird face to the right and the conscious realms, the Emperor and his bird face the opposite direction, embracing the unconscious. Effectively, the cards face one another, opposite sides of a pair, balancing and reflecting. The fact that the Emperor shows his hidden side reveals his confidence. He also carries the scepter topped by the crossed orb, but whereas the Empress carries hers quite casually, the Emperor holds his firmly in an upright position, a phallic symbol of male authority. The Emperor holds his belt or girdle with one hand, another authoritarian, confident gesture, prepared for defense.

The practical nature of the Emperor is emphasized, too, by his posture. His legs are crossed casu-

Also called the Pope, the fifth card of the Major Arcana shows a male figure seated between two pillars, which carry the same symbolism as the ones in the Priestess/Pope card, namely the pillars of the Temple of Solomon that represent the pillars of the Kabbalah, Jachin and Boaz. Positioned in the center of these pillars, the Pope is the balancing factor between two opposing forces and an interpreter between the two worlds, not only the mouthpiece for God on earth but also the one who intercedes between man and God. The Pope wears the ancient triple crown, the Triregnum, and holds a scepter with a three-barred papal cross on the top of it. The hand that holds this scepter wears a white glove, a symbol of religious and papal authority and a sign of purity that has been adopted within Freemasonry. His right hand is raised in the traditional gesture of benediction, with two extended fingers. Before him, two people kneel to receive this blessing. They have shaven circles or tonsures indicating that they too are of a spiritual persuasion, likely to be monks. One points to the earth, the other toward heaven, symbolic gestures that define the way their blessings will be applied; one accepts the benediction as a spiritual boon, the other applies it in a practical way. Again, the "as above, so below" tenet is indicated by these arm positions.

The Lover

THE LOVER: NUMBER 6

This is the sixth card of the Major Arcana. The card is sometimes misinterpreted as the Lovers, plural, but the image depicts one lover, the man, who must choose between two ladies. This card is about choice, echoing the forked path of the Y of Pythagoras. It is interesting to note that the character portrayed on this card, for the first time, appears as an ordinary human being; he seems to have no mystical or magical attributes and is faced with a very human dilemma. Above the head of the lover and invisible to him is the winged figure of Cupid, bow and arrow poised to strike, indicating that in this case the choice may be made by external influences that are beyond the remit of the man himself; the powers of destiny at work.

The two ladies who seek his attentions represent two very different aspects of the feminine personality. One, wearing a headdress and seemingly more dignified, touches his shoulder, indicating a more spiritual relationship than the other, a loose-haired temptress whose hand hovers above his heart. The Lover is pulled between reason and the intellect (the head), and the passions of sexuality (the heart); his head is turned to the woman on his right, whereas the rest of his body swings to the left.

The number six is the number of sexual union, depicted perfectly in the six-pointed star, as the Shatkona, the union of opposites. It may be that the young man has to reconcile both aspects of the Divine Feminine within himself in order to become a fully rounded individual.

THE CHARIOT: NUMBER 7

Here, the Lover of the former card is crowned with gold, showing that he has resolved the conflict he was faced with. Here, the gold symbolizes the alchemical endgame of enlightenment and transcendence. The man appears to be driving the Chariot, symbolic of control. However, there's a twist that illustrates the need to examine every aspect of each card very closely. Significantly, the horses have no reins and the "driver" does not steer the Chariot but they appear to be as one. The

The Chariot

scepter is held in one hand and the other rests lightly on his waist, a casual but powerful gesture. He is secure, in the four-posted canopy, to enjoy the journey no matter where he is carried.

The card carries none of the ambiguity of destiny, but rather shows it as an unassailable force, depicted in the wheels of the vehicle. Nevertheless the figure is now master of his destiny. The Chariot is pulled by two horses, one white and one black, symbolizing harmony between opposing forces despite the fact that they seem as though they are pulling in opposite directions.

That the character now holds a scepter signifies a spiritual dimension as well as mastery of the material world. However, the name of the card is not the "charioteer" but the "Chariot," already giving a clue as to its emphasis. The Chariot is not only a physical vehicle but a spiritual one; the body is the "Chariot" of the soul that carries us where we need to be, directed by the conscious mind.

Seven itself is a sacred number of great significance that occurs time and again; the seven planets, the seven days of the week, the seven heavens.

JUSTICE: NUMBER 8

Justice

This is the eighth card of the Major Arcana, and the first of the second group of seven cards that represent the soul and the notion of equilibrium.

The image is of an authoritarian-looking female figure, powerful and assured as she sits in her throne. Her seated posture further underlines her authority. The significant symbols of this card are, first, the sword that she holds firmly in her right hand, almost using it in the same way as a scepter, a link between heaven and earth. This implies divine justice as well as the earthly kind. The second significant symbol is the scales that she grasps in her left hand. Together the sword and scales have become universal symbols for justice. The card is the eighth, implying symmetry, a reminder of the symmetrical lemniscate shape that is the infinity sign. The pillars of Jachin and Boaz appear once more, in the upright parts of the throne that Justice is seated upon. Sometimes the figure wears a blindfold, implying impartiality.

Finally, the figure wears a crown or helmet that depicts a solar emblem, signifying the light of truth.

Incidentally, A. E. Waite reversed the positions of the Justice card that appears traditionally in the eighth position, and the card for Strength, or force, that appears at number 11.

THE HERMIT: NUMBER 9

The ninth card of the numbered sequence of the Major Arcana shows an old man, his beard a sign of wisdom and experience,

The Hermit

that is not yet at an end despite his age and experience. When the god Wotan appears in human form it is often as a shabby old man wearing a battered hat; the Hermit signifies wisdom and the dedication of life to a higher authority.

THE WHEEL OF FORTUNE: NUMBER 10

The Wheel of Fortune

carrying a staff in his left hand and a lighted lantern in the other. That he is holding the lamp up as though lighting a path signifies darkness; however, the lantern carried by the Hermit, generally a person of spiritual persuasion, may refer to internal as well as external illumination. The figure is hooded and he faces left, looking back toward the cards that precede him almost as though he is lighting the way ahead for all the characters that precede him. The Lover that appeared in the sixth card reappears here, in the ninth position, effectively turned around by 180 degrees, no longer in a quandary about the choices he needs to make but assured in himself and happy to be alone, seeking the path of spiritual enlightenment. The staff he uses as a tool, signifying the journey

This is the tenth numbered card, indicating the closing of a circle. The wheel is a symbol of completion.

Whereas the Hermit indicates the solitary, unworldly life, the Wheel of Fortune is very much a card of the world, representing all its challenges and changes. There are two strange-looking creatures at either side of the wheel that is "crowned" with a sphinx-like figure bearing a sword. This figure, which has an alarming appearance, is completely disassociated from the travails of the creatures below.

All the symbolism of the wheel is contained in this card. It stands for the alternation of good luck and bad, dharma, the passing of time, and the need for life to have a balance of positive and negative experiences. The wheel is a solar symbol, representing the turning of the sun on its cartwheel journey through the heavens, a relentless life-force.

The two creatures can be interpreted as opposing forces and the dynamic of the wheel itself. The one on the right appears to be rising with the motion of the wheel, the one on the left is heading, at least temporarily, downwards. The A. E. Waite deck depicts this creature as a serpent. The opposing forces are also a reminder of the yin-yang symbol.

As the character in the Chariot does not need to steer his vehicle but is as one with it and the horses that pull it, the Wheel of Fortune is in some sense a representation of the continuation of that journey. The Wheel of Fortune is an impartial force of nature and a reminder that freedom of choice also means the freedom to rise to challenges, all a part of the rich breadth of experience that life has to offer.

STRENGTH: NUMBER 11

Strength

This card is sometimes called Necessity. In the picture, a fair-haired woman opens the jaws of a lion. However, she does not seem to be exerting any undue strength; she does not wrench open the mouth of the lion, but uses her fingertips, and the lion does not struggle. Her approach is gentle. The lion might be the more powerful creature physically, but he is no match for the human character. The card symbolizes the power of moral and spiritual strength versus pure brute force, or victory of the spirit over the flesh.

The hat of the woman, like the hat of the magician, has a lemniscate or figure-of-eight shaped brim. This implies magical or superhuman powers. Unlike the magician, however, she is not surrounded by elemental symbols and she carries no wand. All her powers are internal, a part of her being, not reliant on external forces. In the gentleness of the woman's approach toward the lion she uses a subtle power that is the premise of the female. Her strength is the strength of compassion, not physical muscle. The lion itself is a powerful symbol, of the Sun and the divine powers as well as an uncontrolled animal nature. This animal nature needs to be approached with gentle strength and understanding to become refined.

THE HANGED MAN: NUMBER 12

The Hanged Man

Although this card initially appears sinister, first appearances can be deceptive. The character is not hanging from his neck, but from his foot. In the Middle Ages the practice of hanging someone in this way was called "baffling," a punishment intended to humiliate. The word itself now means to "confuse" or "frustrate." The man does not appear to be unduly worried about his strange position. The hands behind his back might be tied together but could also be clasped. It is almost as though his dilemma is self-imposed, and the pose brings to mind the nine days and nights that the god Odin hung in the great World Tree, Yggdrasil, as part of an initiatory rite so that he might receive wisdom; the secrets of the runes were revealed to him during this time. Further, the casually crossed legs of the man make the shape of the figure four, the alchemical symbol for Hermes and for Jupiter.

In Yogic practice there are head-standing positions or asanas designed in part to provide another view of the world. The Hanged Man is symbolic of the initiate who puts himself through a difficult process in order to attain enlightenment, a purifying ritual. The character is not only suspended physically, but mentally and spiritually too. He has no way of releasing himself from his fate but must wait patiently for an intervening force to release him. The old name for this card was "Prudence."

DEATH: NUMBER 13

All the typical symbolism that we associate with death appears in this card. A skeletal figure, scythe in hand, strides across a field. Across the ground are scattered bones, a hand, a foot, the severed head of a crowned man. The skeleton's right foot rests on the head of a woman; he has no respect for those he strikes down. However, there are also new shoots appearing in the muddy field, signifying new hope and revitalization despite the apparent massacre all around. The number 13 is often seen as extraneous to the perfect number, 12, somehow outside of society. It makes sense, then, that the sum total of the 12 needs to be cut back to make way for what comes next.

Although the sight of this card in a tarot spread can be alarming, it does not signify a physical death but rather a change, an ending, or a new beginning. The Death character is a harvester, an essential process that signifies a gathering of sustenance for the winter months ahead, also a way of clearing the ground for the new crops to come. Death is an essential part of the cycle of life. The 13th card, therefore, symbolizes regrowth, reincarnation, and renewal, a continuance of the idea of initiation started by the Hanged Man. The skeleton itself symbolizes the inner part of ourselves that is rarely revealed. In order to make progress, sometimes that inner part needs to be examined closely to understand its mechanisms.

TEMPERANCE: NUMBER 14

Temperance is one of the cardinal virtues. It speaks of self-restraint, carefulness, and moderation. It also implies an easy-going nature, a sen-

XIIII

Temperance

The similarity to the imagery of this card to the astrological sign of Aquarius is quite striking. The sign is linked to the element of air and the circulation of the blood, the life-forces. The Temperance card may well be a reminder of rebirth and reincarnation; it is not just liquid that the woman pours with such care from one vessel into the other, but, symbolically, the soul.

THE DEVIL: NUMBER 15

The Devil card shows a winged figure, with distinct male genitalia as well as the breasts of a woman. His fingers and toes end in claws. His peculiar headgear includes a pair of antlers or horns.

His right hand is raised, and his left holds what appears to be

sible person that is wise enough not to be caught up in petty concerns, who can see the bigger picture.

The card shows a female figure, often winged, signifying a messenger from God. She wears a five-petaled flower in her hair that is often a hidden symbol for the five-pointed star or pentacle. The key feature, however, are the two jugs that she holds, pouring liquid from one to the other. One jug is blue and the other red; an alchemical process is at work here, because blue, a feminine color, mixing with the masculine red, produces violet, the color of the spirit. Knowing this, the flower is suddenly more than mere decoration, since five, representing the idea of marriage or the union of opposites, is the sum of the female number two wedded to the male number three.

XV

The Devil

a sword, although it has no hilt; this sword is all blade. The Devil stands on a small plinth that looks like an anvil. This is connected to a rope, and either end of the rope is knotted around the necks of a male figure to the right, and a female figure to the left. These characters are not straightforward, though. They wear hats with antlers, have the pointed ears of animals, long tails, and cloven feet.

The Devil is an archetypal figure of evil, of great antiquity, who existed long before the Christian Church "demonized" the old gods and spirits. The figure often appeared as a destructive spirit that was carried on the disease-ridden and pestilential winds of the deserts of Mesopotamia. It made sense for our ancestors to personify this natural phenomenon in order to control it somehow. Although we might think we know better, the Devil archetype still carries a powerful symbolic punch. The usual image of the Devil that resonates even today is of an androgynous, hybrid creature, whose animal nature is in conflict with the spirit, and this gives rise to the most basic interpretation of this card. It speaks of ill-gotten gains, giving in to the desires of the flesh, corruption.

At its most basic, this card is a reminder that man is effectively shackled to the material world, and can be corrupted (reverting back to a raw animal state) by these shackles.

THE TOWER: NUMBER 16

The Tower

This dramatic card shows a Tower, its crowned top falling toward the left as it is struck by a thunderbolt from the right. Two people are thrown toward the ground. In the sky are a number of circles that could be debris, hail, rain, or stones.

At first glance, this appears to represent some sort of divine retribution, following, as it does, the card of the Devil that warned against the temptations of materialism. The Tower should be the safest sort of fortified home. The card also brings to mind the collapse of the Tower of Babel, again an instance of godly punishment. However, the entire Tower is not decimated; the body remains intact, only the turret is damaged. The card represents the sudden turn in fortune that appears to be disastrous but which ends up being a positive force for change. It can also signify a sudden illumination (the lightning bolt that strikes suddenly and unexpectedly, illuminating all around) that presages a leap forward in consciousness. The pinnacle of the Tower represents the ego that sometimes has to be destroyed in the process of enlightenment.

This card symbolizes the unpredictable stroke of fate, the act of God or destiny, that shakes everything up, but that nevertheless carries benefits in its wake.

THE STAR: NUMBER 17

The Star depicts a young girl, naked, pouring water from two jugs into the river that she kneels at the edge of. One foot is in the water. Above her head is a large sixteen-pointed star made of two eight-pointed stars overlapping each other. Surrounding it are seven smaller symmetrically arranged eight-pointed

The Star

stars. This is the first appearance of stars on a card, but not the last. They represent the mingling of the earth with the sphere of the heavens. The surrounding landscape is fertile, and a bird sits on top of the tree on the left of the card, observing the scene. The bird is a symbol of the soul, as well as a messenger from the gods.

The jugs, like those in the Temperance card, are red and blue. They seem to pour endlessly, one splashing its contents onto the earth, the other adding to the water in the river. Therefore the girl nourishes the earth while replenishing the "waters of life" of the spirit, symbolized by the river.

Although this figure appears to have the same sort of angelic nature as Temperance, she has no wings, and one of the jugs is red, signifying earthly life. The giant fixed star—around which the others seem to orbit—signifies enlightenment, a further step in the progress of the human psyche. This tranquil, vulnerable and human figure stands firmly with one foot upon the earth that is the material world, the other in the water that is the domain of spirit, nourishing both with the divine power that is continually replenished, celestially, from above. This card represents hope and divine inspiration.

THE MOON: NUMBER 18

At the lower level of the three layers that comprise this image is a square-edged lake with a crayfish in it. Above, there are two dogs—or possibly a wolf and a dog—that look up to the moon, jaws open,

The Moon

possibly howling. To their left and right are the corners of two buildings, both slightly different; one has a roof, the other appears to be open to the sky and is reminiscent of the Tower that was struck by lightning in card 16. In the sky at the top of the card is the full moon, with a face that points to the left and with a halo of rays, like moonbeams, surrounding it. There are teardrop shapes surrounding it that seem to either emanate from the moon or, alternatively, are sucked into it.

The dogs are a reminder of the hounds that accompany the moon goddess. Dogs also act as psychopomps, guardians of souls in the spirit world. There is a nightmarish aspect to this card. The surrounding landscape is barren, only two small plants appear in it, a sort of no-man's land. This card represents the "dark night of the soul." However, the preceding card signifies hope, and the moon provides the light that is reflected from the sun, illuminating the way ahead, indicating that guidance will come from above.

THE SUN: NUMBER 19

Here, the sun beams directly over the heads of twin human figures of indeterminate sex, possibly children.

The Sun

children are symbols of the natural self, Adam and Eve, effectively, in their state of innocence before they ate the fruit of wisdom. This is the blessed state that all of us are born into. The Sun card signifies harmony, happiness, a promise fulfilled, and the moment of completion that defines enlightenment.

JUDGEMENT: NUMBER 20

Judgement

Whereas in the card of the moon the droplets were absorbed by the planet, in the Sun card the droplets are generously falling to earth. Behind the twins is a wall constructed from four levels of bricks. The twins remind us of the astrological sign of Gemini and it has been said that one represents the soul, the female, lunar element, and one the spirit, signifying the sun, and male energy. Again, a tarot card indicates the union of opposing forces. The hope of the star that had to be held close to the heart during the tribulations of the lunar landscape in card 18 comes to fruition in this card; the Sun heralds the dawning of a new and better day, nightmares dissolved in the heat of its rays. The children play innocently in the full light of day, bounded by the solidity of the material world (the wall) and bathed in heavenly blessings. The

Here, the dominant figure is the winged trumpet-blowing angel that appears in a framework of clouds and beams of light, a truly apocalyptic vision. Below, in front of a mountainous landscape, two figures face a third that is climbing out of a trench in the ground. The third figure has its back to us but the tonsured hair is the same as

The Encyclopedia of Secret Signs and Symbols

that of the character that appeared before the Pope in card 5. The other two figures are a woman and an old man; they are praying.

This card represents Judgement Day, the resurrection or awakening of the dead. The figures are naked, stripped of all worldly goods, reborn. The trumpet symbolizes the voice of God that wakes them, but this symbolism is not a straightforward biblical revelation; it can also be the trumpet of enlightenment as we are reborn as fully integrated human individuals. Self-awareness and the ability, as adults, to throw off earthly concerns, mean that we can become as innocent and alive as the two children in the preceding card. The Judgement card is a call for truth, and a promise to the self to maintain and look after this born-again consciousness. The idea of a "call" from the trumpet also indicates another kind of call, the call toward a vocation or an external driving force that causes us to place the material world in second place.

THE WORLD: NUMBER 21

This is the last of the cards of the Major Arcana. The number itself signifies the coming of age when the "world" is given symbolically

by the key when a person reaches his or her 21st birthday.

The card shows a young woman, whose sex is concealed by an artfully placed scarf. Her legs make the 4 figure, in common with the Hanging Man's posture. She looks to the left, wands in both hands.

The girl is enclosed in a laurel wreath in the shape of the vesica piscis, and surrounding her are the four Tetramorphs; human/hybrid figures that rule over the elements and the four corners of the earth. These figures are winged. Working clockwise from the upper left-hand corner they are the man, the eagle, the lion, and the ox.

This is the card of victory and rebirth. The vesica piscis that the girl emerges from is a magical doorway from the spiritual world to the material world. Here, the wreath seems to be comprised of two halves that are joined together at the top and bottom, and it also represents the egg that itself is a symbol of creation. The laurel leaves are symbolic of victory, given to great heroes. The presence of the tetramorphs not only witnesses this victory but signifies the four corners of the world that now belong to the girl. The two wands imply a perfect balance of opposites, conscious and unconscious, matter and spirit, the harmony of the universe.

Tattvas

The Tattvas are a series of basic shapes, which contribute to the Hindu system of classifying the elements by giving them a recognizable form. The shapes themselves have influenced holy buildings, particularly the Stupa. The Tattvas are described as the building blocks of the universe and compare in many ways to the Platonic solids. In Sanskrit, the meaning of the word equates to "thatness" or "essential nature of."

The shapes, then, and their associations, are as follows:

1. The crescent moon, or "apas," defines the element of water. It is colored silver or white.

2. The circle, "vayu," is represented by a blue circle.
3. The upright triangle, or "tejas," symbolizes fire, in common with other systems for symbolizing the elements.
4. Prithvi is a yellow diamond that stands for earth.
5. The fifth element—the unifying factor, which in Greek is referred to as "ether"—is called Akasa and is symbolized by a black egg.

The names of the Tattvas also correspond to the names of the deities that rule the elements. In the same way that the elements have given rise to everything on our planet, all other colors can be made from the colors chosen for the shapes.

Tau cross

Instantly recognizable as a capital letter T, the tau cross forms the basis for another well-known symbol, the ankh.

The tau is a very ancient symbol indeed, being the sign of three major deities: the Sumerian sun god Tammuz, the Roman god Mithras, and the Greek god Attis.

The name comes from the word for the Greek letter T, and it is the last letter of the Hebrew alphabet.

There are similarities between all these deities. They all died and were resurrected, and so carry analogies with the sun that dies every night and is resurrected every morning. The T shape was daubed in ashes onto the foreheads of Tammuz followers; the symbol represents resurrection, reincarnation, life, blood sacrifice, symbolic death, and a gateway.

The tau is also known as the Robbers' Cross, because the thieves that were crucified at either side of Christ are believed to have been hanged on a cross of this shape and although it's commonly held that Christ went to his death on a cross with the upright post extending beyond the crossbar (the Latin Cross), it is likely that a tau cross was used.

St. Francis was particularly fond of the tau, and used it almost like a personal signature. In addition, the Egyptian hermit St. Antony put its power to good use when he used it to frighten away a hoard of demons. There are very few tau crosses left in the world, but there is still an intact one on Tory Island in Ireland dating back to the sixth century. This remainder provides a clue that early Egyptian Coptic Christians may have landed there.

TEMPLAR CROSS

This cross also goes by the name of the Cross of St. John, the Maltese Cross, the Campaign Cross, the Iron Cross, the Regeneration Cross, or the Fishtail Cross.

The sheer numbers of names that belong to this symbol give a hint as to its ubiquity, but what features set it aside from other crosses?

The Templar Cross has the distinctive curved or pointed ends (hence the "fishtail" epithet) drawing attention to these end bars and giving the cross eight points rather than the straightforward four of most other crosses. Eight is the infinity sign—standing for the cycle of life, death, and rebirth—seen in the lemniscate or figure-of-eight shape, hence the name "Regeneration Cross."

The cross is the emblem of the Knights of St. John, an ancient chivalrous order that originated during the time of the Crusaders. Also known as the Knights Hospitallers, the Knights set up a hospital in Jerusalem in 1080 to care for pilgrims. This is why the cross is still used as its emblem by the latter-day St. John's Ambulance Brigade.

TETRAKTYS

The Tetragrammaton—or the four-letter code word for the secret name of God—is sometimes drawn as a Tetraktys, which in Greek means "fourfold." This is a mystical Pythagorean symbol whose simplicity belies a complex meaning. It is comprised of ten dots which form a pyramid and this unassuming emblem actually symbolizes the universe. Pythagoras described it thus:

It is both a mathematical idea and a metaphysical symbol that embraces within itself the principles of the natural world, the harmony of the cosmos, the ascent to the divine, and the mysteries of the divine realm.

Starting from the base and working up, then, the four dots forming the foundation of the shape represent the four elements; the earth; the seasons; the cardinal directions north, south, east, and west. The next three dots above stand for earth, heaven, and hell, and also mind, body, and spirit. The next two dots are male and female, light and dark, yin and yang, and so on; and the final dot at the top of the triangle is the godhead.

Further, working down the pyramid this time, Pythagoras said that the first dot indicated the intellect; the second two, science; the third row, opinion; and the final, base row of four dots, sense.

In total the Tetraktys is comprised of ten dots; these ten simple dots symbolize the totality of the universe which exists in the now, and also the universe which is as yet uncreated.

TETRAMORPHS

Ezekiel had a vision in which he saw four figures that the Book of Revelation calls the Four Beasts.

These beasts are the bull, the lion, the eagle, and the man. There are several interpretations given to these four creatures that are collectively referred to as Tetramorphs.

Possibly the most common symbolism of the Tetramorphs is their relation to the four evangelists. St. Matthew is the man, the lion is St. Mark, the bull is St. Luke, and the eagle is St. John.

However, the animals also represent the four pillars of the Christian faith and the omnipotence of God.

The Tetramorphs are not restricted to the Christian tradition, though. The creatures that appeared to Ezekiel have universal resonance, shown by their depictions in prehistoric cave paintings. The man, the bull, the lion, and the eagle are universal symbols for the four points of the compass and the four elements. The eagle is air, representing all the aspects of the mind and intellectual activity; the lion is the element of fire, signifying action and strength; the bull is the earth element, representing labor and tenacity; and the figure of the man represents water and the idea of spiritual intuition.

THEOSOPHICAL SOCIETY

The emblem of this mystical society, founded by Helena Blavatsky in 1875, is an almost overwhelming smorgasbord of some of the most significant sacred symbols. Blavatsky had an overarching interest in, and an extensive knowledge of, the importance of sacred signs and symbols and so they were all chosen carefully as being significant to the organization, which has headquarters in countries all over the world.

Many of these symbols are themselves comprised of other

symbols, such as the Seal of Solomon that is made from two interlocking triangles. To examine the emblem closely is to unravel an extensive symbolic puzzle, and a more detailed explanation of its component elements are found under their separate entries.

The component elements of the society's symbol include the Seal of Solomon with the quintessence indicated at the center, the swastika, significant letters from the Hebrew alphabet, floral devices, the circle, the ouroboros, the crown, and various strategically placed bindhu or dots. Additionally, the symbol is said to contain within it all the possible numbers from one to ten; these numbers contain all possible numbers. There is a rectangle as part of the design of the base of the crown; however, the square does not appear as a symbol though it could be indicated in the many representations of the number four.

THREE-PRONGED CANDELABRUM

In Wicca, the three-pronged candelabrum is a part of the equipment needed for the ritual altar.

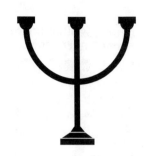

It holds three candles—white, red, and black—that symbolize the three aspects of the Triple Goddess, as maiden, mother, and crone.

THYRSUS

The thyrsus was a sacred implement used in rituals and festivals during the time of the ancient Greeks. It was a staff, standing about as high as its owner, made from a giant fennel stalk topped with a pine cone and wrapped with vine leaves.

As a phallic symbol, it was combined with a goblet or chalice, symbolic of female energy and used to counterbalance the staff. As well as being a symbol of male energy, though, staffs or long poles of some description have a universal use as a sacred instrument to connect the heavens to the earth, a conductor for the divine spirit.

TILAKA

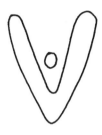

"Tilaka" is a Sanskrit word, meaning "red," and is the name for the symbols worn on the head, face, and other parts of the body by Hindus. The Tilaka is a sign indicating affiliation to various Hindu deities, each god or goddess having its own Tilaka.

Tilakas are drawn onto the body, and the forehead in particular, with colored pastes made from ashes (vibhuti), sandalwood paste, clay, or other substances such as kumkum or sindhoor.

Perhaps the most basic form of the Tilaka is the red dot, or bindhu, worn on the forehead. This indicates the third eye and the rising sun.

Generally, men wear the largest Tilakas.

A man sporting a Tilaka made of three horizontal lines that are made from gray or white ashes is a sign that the person is a Shivaite, or follower of Shiva. The three lines are called the tripundra. Followers of Vishnu wear a Tilaka in the form of a yellow paste that is made from the clay of a holy river, such as the Ganges, melded with sandalwood paste. The symbol is two vertical lines that are sometimes joined at the bottom.

Women also wear Tilakas as a sign of beauty, or to indicate their marital status; in this case, they are marked with a yellow line just below the hairline.

Babies also wear Tilakas, but in this case, the black dots dabbed onto the face of the baby are put there to make the baby ugly, and therefore of no interest to any passing evil spirit.

TIRATANA

A Buddhist symbol, the Tiratana is also known as the Three Jewels of Buddhism. These concepts are depicted as a flame that holds three

circles protected within it. The flame is symbolic of eternity, and the three circles are the Buddha, his teachings or Dharma, and the Sangha, his followers.

TOMOE

This word means "turning" or "circle" and the symbol shows two, three, or four comma-like shapes making a spiral. These shapes are emblematic of flames; hence, the symbol is sometimes called the fire wheel. It belongs to both Shinto and Buddhist faiths and can be seen in temples of both denominations. It was also used in Japanese Samurai heraldry.

The tomoe with two flames looks very like the yin-yang emblem and symbolizes the same concepts. When it is drawn with three flames, the tomoe represents the earth, heavens, and humankind, which are the three foundations of the Shinto philosophy.

TORAH

This is the Book of the Law of the Jewish faith, comprising the first five books of the Old Testament. It appears as a sacred scroll in synagogues, where it is called the Sefer Torah. The power of the sacred words on this scroll means that it is used as a magical amulet, believed in particular to heal children or pregnant women.

TORII

In Japan, the Torii is a gate, but this is not a common or garden Western-style opening. The Torii is a Shinto symbol that marks a liminal place, the threshold between this world and the next, between the sacred and the profane, between the material world and the spiritual realms. The Torii tells the pilgrim that he or she is entering a sacred place, and ritual washing of the hands and rinsing of the mouth takes place before stepping through this holy doorway. Buddhist temples sometimes have these sacred gates too.

Torii are now found everywhere and have even found their way into modern architectural use, where they may be rendered in various metals rather than the traditional wood or stone. However, its origin as the entrance to the Shinto shrine is where the torii is seen at its most meaningful.

The word "torii" is believed to come from the Shinto words for "bird" and "place," and the kanji (Chinese pictorial character) for torii is the same as that for "bird." Birds are universally accepted as being able to carry messages between man and his gods and so

this theory fits with the idea of the torii marking a boundary between two worlds.

TOTEM

The idea of a totem as a sort of spiritual mascot that protects and guides a single individual or an entire clan has transcended its origins as an ancient shamanistic concept. Originally an Algonquin term, a totem is an animal or plant whose attributes are shared by the person to whom it belongs. A totem belonging to a tribe provides a vital part of its identity as well as a means of understanding the workings of the physical world.

Although we generally think of totems as belonging to Native American spirituality, they are found in different cultures all over the world.

The revelation of the totem is generally part of an initiatory ritual. For some this takes the form of a shamanic ceremony forming part of the rite of passage at puberty.

A shared totem is a strong bond of kinship or brotherhood; the word itself carries this meaning.

Totem poles are the physical manifestation of a spiritual idea, tall trees carved with birds, animals, fantastical creatures, and other symbols that tell the story of the people they belong to. Because the poles are made of wood, they rot easily and so it has proven difficult to pinpoint their origins precisely.

TRIANGLE

See First signs: Triangle.

TRIDENT

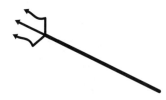

The trident, or trisula, is a long staff or pole topped by three prongs. Whoever wields a trident wields great power, although this power might take different forms.

The trident is the symbol of the Hindu god Shiva, whose followers wear a trident-like Tilaka symbol on their faces. In the hands of Shiva, the trident represents the three phases of time, past, present, and future, or possibly heaven, earth, and hell. The trident has its own hand gesture or mudra, too, called the trishulahastra.

In the hands of Poseidon or Neptune, the trident has a practical use, since it emulates the shape of one of the earliest fishing implements. Poseidon uses it to control the seas, so it is a symbol of authority. Because of its association with water, the trident is the alchemical symbol for this element.

Where a trident has three prongs of even length, it is a secret symbol of the cross of Christianity. However, Satan is often seen harrying the souls in hell with a trident. It is likely that he is depicted with it in order to associate him with the pre-Christian gods who also used it.

This versatile three-pronged tool is also a fire symbol—the prongs look like flames—and it is therefore a symbol of thunderbolts and lightning. As such, many of the sky gods carry a trident, too. These include Thor or Wotan of Norse mythology.

Triple Goddess Tripod of Life

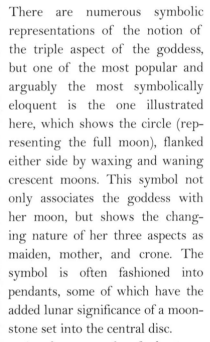 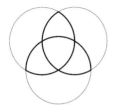

There are numerous symbolic representations of the notion of the triple aspect of the goddess, but one of the most popular and arguably the most symbolically eloquent is the one illustrated here, which shows the circle (representing the full moon), flanked either side by waxing and waning crescent moons. This symbol not only associates the goddess with her moon, but shows the changing nature of her three aspects as maiden, mother, and crone. The symbol is often fashioned into pendants, some of which have the added lunar significance of a moonstone set into the central disc.

Another example of the symbol also uses the moon, solely in its crescent form. The triquetra is made of three of these crescents.

Also known as the Borromean Rings, this is a simply constructed symbol that consists of three rings which intersect evenly. An extension of a smaller design called the vesica piscis, and part of a larger design of great symbolic importance called the Flower of Life, the Tripod of Life symbolizes the many aspects of the number three. It also acts as a reminder of all the qualities that come in triplicate, such as the body, mind, and spirit, as well as the Father, the Son, and the Holy Ghost, i.e. the Holy Trinity of the Christian faith.

Triquetra

A very ancient symbol which in Latin means "three cornered," the triquetra (or triqueta) is comprised of three interlocking vesica piscis shapes, sometimes linked together with a circle. It is similar to the Nordic valknut in its construction and although the sign predates Chris-

tianity it has been used as a symbol of the Holy Trinity; in fact, it has been adopted anywhere a symbol for three connected items or concepts needs to be indicated.

A clue as to the magical, protective nature of the triquetra is that it can be drawn without the pen leaving the paper.

TRIREGNUM

See Papal symbols.

TRISKELE

The triskele or triskelion belongs to both Buddhist and Celtic traditions, and appears in various forms in many artworks and carvings. It is comprised of one shape repeated three times to produce a wheel-like pattern. Traditionally the triskele can appear as three teardrops, three fishes, three interlocking spirals, or the three legs that gives it its Greek meaning (as in the symbols for both the Isle of Man and Sicily). There is also an intriguing version called the Three Hares Triskelion, which again features in both Buddhist and Celtic belief. The hare triskelion in particular is the source of much conjecture. Given that the hare is a nocturnal animal and a lunar symbol (the shape of the animal can be picked out from the craters and ridges of the surface of the moon), it also stands as an emblem of the goddess.

The triskele is a symbolic representation of the importance of the number three, and a sun symbol similar to the swastika.

TRISULA

See Trident.

TROLL CROSS

An early amulet, said to give protection against trolls, this cross was made of iron, a metal that further reinforced the aspect of safety since it is generally avoided by mis-

although they are only considered to be sacred objects after they have been empowered by being blessed.

TYET

chievous entities. The sign is not really a cross as we know it, rather a circle with a C-shaped base.

TSA TSA

In Tibetan Buddhism, the tsa tsa is a small votive statuette of the Buddha, or of other deities, or meaningful objects such as the stupa. They are formed in a mold, or stamped out from clay or plaster. Making tsa tsas is both a meditative process and a vocational task that brings favor from the gods, and making them is an obligatory skill taught to monks. Tsa tsas can be worn, or carried as an amulet, in which case they are carried about in a little portable shrine called a gau.

Tsa tsa figurines have special ingredients added that further empower the figure. These additions include herbs, flowers, or even the funerary ash of lamas or other holy people.

These little statuettes can be seen everywhere, in homes, temples, in caves, or beside mountains,

The tyet is a symbol from ancient Egypt, also known as the Knot of Isis or the Blood of Isis.

The tyet is reminiscent of the ankh (except with the crossbars brought down to the sides) and so carries some of its symbolism as a sign of eternal life. However, the tyet also resembles the knotted piece of cloth that was used during menstruation. The knot in itself is of significance, since the Egyptians, in accord with other peoples around the world, believed that knots could both bind magic or let it loose.

The tyet was used as a funerary symbol, when it was made from a blood-red stone such as carnelian or red jasper. It was tied around the neck of the corpse, as a symbol of protection for the spirit in the life to come. The Blood of Isis was a powerful substance, containing

The Encyclopedia of Secret Signs and Symbols

blood from the womb of the great goddess.

Unicursal Hexagram

Any sign, symbol, or shape that can be drawn in one continuous line without the pen leaving the paper can be described as unicursal. The five-pointed star or pentagram is a good example. Generally, the six-pointed star is drawn as a separate pair of interlinked opposing triangles, but the unicursal variety was adopted by Aleister Crowley who perceived it to be important as a personal symbol. It was likely that he knew that unicursality is frequently an important feature of any magical symbol that has protective properties, because the unbroken line of construction means that there are no openings that an unwanted entity might be able to use to gain access to the safe place in the center. It is also sometimes called the Magic Hexagram.

Crowley further added to the power of this symbol by adding the five-petaled rose, itself symbolic of a hidden secret that conceals the pentagram within it, if the central point on the outer edge of each petal is joined together. The pentagram is the emblem of the Divine Feminine. In this instance the star secreted within the rose balances on its point, becoming an inverted pentagram that can imply the superiority of matter over spirit or, the need (according to the renowned witch Gerald Gardner, who was a contemporary of Crowley's) to be able to face the darkness in order to understand it.

The points of the hexagram and the pentagram add up to 11, which signifies divine union.

Unification Church Symbol

Members of the Unification Church are popularly known as Moonies, after the organization's founder, the Korean Sun Myung Moon (born Mun Myong Mong). When Moon founded the church in 1954, he called it the "Holy

Spirit Association for the Unification of World Christianity." Although Moon's original vision was that the church should unite all the disparate Christian denominations (these tenets are outlined in a book called *The Divine Principle*, which amalgamates the Bible with various Asian spiritual traditions), the more established churches opposed Moon's vision, with the result that the Unification Church became a separate religion.

Some of the practices and beliefs of the Unification Church mean that it is viewed with suspicion as a cult, its members seemingly held in the thrall of its charismatic, and possibly eccentric, leader. Included among the more unusual practices of the church are the mass weddings of partners that are chosen apparently at random.

Disregarding any outside opinions about the teachings of the church, its symbol is distinctive and was invented by Moon himself. This is one of the relatively rare occasions where the meaning of a symbol is described by its living inventor.

The central circle is God, truth, life, and light, and is believed to be based on an ancient Japanese symbol called the Kuruma, a "mon" symbol, that is, a Japanese heraldic device enclosed within a circle. The Kuruma represents a carriage wheel and carries all the symbolism of the wheel in general.

Four main arms radiate from this central circle. These represent the four ideals of the central circle reaching all four directions. The circle is further divided to make twelve segments that symbolize the twelve parts of the human character, the twelve disciples of Christ, etc.

The outer circle represents the harmony of the universe and giving/receiving. The arrowhead notches in either side of this outer circle give a feeling of movement.

UNITED STATES DOLLAR BILL

If you ever find yourself hanging around in an airport, say, at a loose end, then get hold of a dollar bill and have a close look. It's so crammed full of arcane imagery that a close scrutiny of it will pass

the time as effectively as the most gripping novel.

It is a wonderful example of symbolism in action and shows just how powerfully these ancient magical symbols still resonate in the modern world. Although the design of the dollar has changed several times, some elements have remained constant. Here, then, are those magical symbols.

On the reverse of the dollar, the most noticeable emblem is that of the Great Seal of the United States. This takes the form of a pyramid with its cap severed and replaced by a triangle with an eye inside; this is the All Seeing Eye.

This symbol has been associated with the Illuminati and with Freemasonry and its appearance on the dollar has given rise to all sorts of conspiracy theories. The phrase "Annuit Coeptus," which is written around the top of the seal, translates as "(we) favor the things which have begun" and indicates that there is work yet to be done.

The banner around the bottom of the seal reads "Novus Ordo Seclorum," which means, roughly, "A new order of the Ages."

Although Latin is not actually understood by many people and is officially designated a "dead" language, the use of Latin is a secret sign in itself and lends gravity to the statement, belying the youth of the American nation whose Declaration of Independence was signed in 1776.

Also featured on the dollar is the bald eagle, which is the official bird symbol of the United States. The eagle holds the olive branch of peace in its right talon, but it is prepared to fight, too, as indicated by the arrows in its claws. There are 13 fruits in the olive branch, perfectly balanced by the 13 arrows. It is worth noting here that the covert bird symbol of America is the dove—aptly, the Latin name for the dove is Columba. The dove is the bird of peace and conciliation and so provides a nice counterbalance to the eagle, although it does not actually appear on the dollar.

Another bird appears on the dollar, too, but it is hard to find. An owl—symbol of wisdom—is supposed to appear on the note.

Above the eagle is a crown of stars, again, 13 in total. This represents the number of states that first joined the Union. The stars can be joined to create Solomon's seal, one of the most powerful of all symbols. That the stars combine to create another symbol is a clever nod to the phrase, which streams along on a banner underneath: "E Pluribus Unum" means "Out of many comes one" and refers to the many states that make one Union.

URAEUS

This is the Egyptian symbol of an upright cobra, head reared in readiness for attack. The Uraeus was the guardian of the sun god, Ra, permanently ready to spit poison at his enemies.

The Uraeus was the definitive symbol of royalty, sovereignty, and divinity. Horus and Set are depicted wearing the Uraeus, and it was the only symbol worn by the pharaoh that actually legitimized his status as ruler. Worn as a headband, with the rearing cobra sitting at the point of the third eye, the Uraeus has parallels with the Kundalini Serpent.

The Uraeus was initially the symbol for the divine goddess in all her aspects, in particular Wadjet, a very early deity that was the protector of Lower Egypt. The protector of Upper Egypt was Nehkbet, the mother goddess whose symbol was the vulture; together, these goddesses were called the Two Mistresses.

The rearing cobra is also a hieroglyphic sign, meaning "goddess" or "priestess."

URIM AND THUMMIM

So charged with mystery and secrecy are the Urim and Thummim that there is debate as to what exactly they were. What is known for sure is that they were connected to the breastplate of the high priest of the ancient Hebrews.

The Urim and Thummim were contained in a secret pocket behind the "essen," or breastplate, of the priest. It is possible that they were knucklebones or small stones which had been brought out of Egypt by the Israelites; another theory asserts that they were sacred names written on plates of gold to act as talismans. It has also been posited that the Urim and Thummim were not objects at all, but the name for a process of divination whereby God could be contacted, enabling decisions to be made; a form of augury. What is agreed is that the names translate as "light and perfection" or "light and truth."

When a slip of paper with the Tetragrammaton (the name of God) written on it was slipped underneath the Urim and Thummim, then the 12 jewels of the breastplate apparently started to glow. This glowing meant that the breastplate was turned on and tuned in, acting as a sort of radio transmitter for messages from God to his people.

The last priest that was able to access these divine messages from God was Eleazar, who allowed Moses to communicate with God directly. After that time, it seems as though the ability to talk to God in this way was somehow lost, and the Urim and Thummim were used purely as a divination tool, a more indirect form of higher communication.

* * *

VAJRA

Some Buddhist statues are seen holding an object that looks like a double-headed scepter in one hand, and a bell in the other. These objects are the Vajra and the Ghanta, respectively, male and female.

"Vajra" is a Sanskrit word, literally meaning "diamond-like" and "the hard and mighty one," although the meaning goes deeper than this, carrying metaphysical significance. It is also known as the "thunderbolt," because it is the destroyer of ignorance. The Vajra is an important symbol, and carries complex meanings within its shape.

The central space inside the Vajra indicates the dot or bindhu, that apparently most insignificant of symbols that is also possibly the most important. The bindhu represents the sphere of actual reality.

On either side of the bindhu are lotus flowers, symmetrically balanced, representing the material world and the spiritual world. The flowers each have eight petals.

The lotus flower itself symbolizes the plight of the human being, born into the mud or mire of the material world, but attaining spiritual realization by striving beyond these origins.

From the lotus flowers spring flames or prongs, generally five in number. This number might vary, but both sides are always symmetrical. The number five in this instance represents the five Buddhas and their wives, and their collected energies and qualities. It is also symbolic of the five wisdoms, which are:

- the wisdom of individuality
- mirror-like wisdom
- reality wisdom
- wisdom of equanimity
- all-encompassing wisdom

Collectively, the ten prongs are a reminder of the ten perfections, which are:

- Generosity
- Proper conduct
- Renunciation
- Insight
- Diligence
- Tolerance
- Truthfulness
- Determination
- Kindness
- Serenity

The prongs are also a reminder of the steps on the journey to enlightenment and of the ten directions: north, south, east, west, northeast, northwest, southeast, southwest, and finally, above and below.

These prongs either curve together to form a point, representing the holy mountain, Mount Meru. The closed ends of the Vajra make it a symbol of peace; however, sometimes the Vajra has open ends. This is a sign of the wrath of the deity who holds it. This is the type of wrath, though, that can destroy all illusions or negativities. The open-ended Vajra sometimes has the addition of flames shooting out of the ends.

Incidentally, the Tibetan name for the Vajra is the "dorje."

The Indian city of Darjeeling, famous for the tea that grows in the area, is named after this concept. The name is corrupted from the original Dorje Lingam.

VALKNUT

The valknut consists of three interlocking triangles and has some similarity to the triquetra or the triskele. The Valknut is of Viking origin and is seen on rune stones and in carvings, and is con-

nected with the god Odin. The name means, roughly, the Knot of Death or the Knot of the Slain.

The knot is likely to have been a protective device, a quality shared by other knot symbols. It carried a promise that Odin would protect the spirit of the warrior who died in his name, and a reassurance that the warrior would soon be reincarnated.

VERTICAL LINE

See First signs: Vertical line.

VESICA PISCIS

Sometimes, a clue to the meaning of a symbol is given in its name. The vesica piscis translates as the vessel of the fish and this information, in combination with its shape, means it takes just a short leap of deductive reasoning to suppose that it refers to the vagina. The shape is constructed from the shape made by the intersection of two circles and Pythagoreans believed it represented a similar intersection of the spiritual and material worlds, a sacred doorway between two states of being. The vesica piscis is one of the most important shapes in sacred geometry.

The Egyptian representation of the vesica piscis, the Egyptian Ru symbol, which similarly represents the vagina as a doorway through which a spirit entered the material world, is an apt metaphor that supports the Pythagorean theory.

The vesica piscis is also known as the mandorla, referring to its almond shape. The symbol is often used to frame figures in religious iconography. It also appears in the 21st card of the Major Arcana of the tarot, which depicts the World.

Also any place where the goddess is worshipped will generally have a representation of the vesica piscis; for example, it is seen on the cover of the well at Glastonbury.

V.I.T.R.I.O.L.

To call someone "vitriolic" means that they are cruel or that they have a caustic turn of phrase. However, the word has its origins in alchemy.

Vitriol itself used to be called Oil of Vitriol and refers to sulfuric acid; this name was given by the eighth-century alchemist Jabir Ibn Hayan. Sulfuric acid was considered a prime constituent in the making of the Philosopher's Stone, and further, a clue to the manufacture of this elusive substance—which was reputed to give the gift of immortality—is held in the initials of the word. The initials of the word, then, for alchemists means:

Visita Interiorem Terrae Rectifando Invenies Operae Lapidem.

Translated, this means:

"Go down into the bowels of the earth; by distillation you will find the stone for the work."

As with all things alchemical, there can be more than one meaning to this hidden phrase. Not only does it refer to the manufacture of the Philosopher's Stone, but it also has a philosophical and metaphys-ical meaning regarding man's own enlightenment and how to attain it.

VOUDON VEVES

Voudon is an intriguing religion. Brought by African slaves to the Caribbean toward the end of the seventeenth century, the primary tenet of Voudon is that the spirit that animates the physical body during life continues to survive after the death of that body. The spirit develops and grows until it takes on the status of a divinity, or loa.

Catholic missionaries were keen to stamp out any traces of the native religion, but Voudon is a powerful force and its followers gradually started to morph some of their own deities with the Catholic saints. The syncretism was almost perfect; any Catholic priest visiting a home of the Voudon was pleased to see a household shrine full of the "correct" statuary of the Catholic faith; the householder, however, saw his preferred spirits and deities

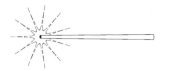

in a slightly different form. Even elements of the liturgy appear in Voudon ceremonies.

An important feature of the Voudon faith is communication with the loas. To accomplish this, the loa is encouraged to possess the body of a living human being, and much ritual and ceremony is designed with this aim in mind.

Each deity has its own symbol, or veve. The mambo, or priestess, draws the symbol onto the ground in fine cornmeal. The veve is effectively a welcome call to the spirit in question and it is essential that the mambo render the symbol correctly, despite the fact that many of them are very elaborate.

As well as veves for deities, there are veves that call for specific requests. There is a huge range of these symbols that cover all eventualities from debt collection to increasing potency and all things in between. The veve shown on the previous page is dedicated to Erzulie Freda Dahomey, the loa of dreams and love.

WAND

It's likely that the wand belonging to the fairy at the top of the Christmas tree will only work in the correct hands, but if not, what an enviable tool it would be. But it's not only fairies who carry wands or similar objects.

The wand is an essential tool for anyone who aspires to a position of authority and power: witches and wizards, druids, bishops, the monarchy. If it sounds strange to think of a bishop holding a wand, think of his crozier, the highly decorated staff with a bend in the end like a shepherds' crook; the crozier is his wand. Similarly, the scepter of the monarch fills the same role. Essentially, the wand connects the user to the spirit world or to magical powers.

The wand itself is a thin stick or rod, held in the hand, and signifies both the power of the person holding it and the extension of that power. The baton of the conductor concentrates the attention of the orchestra to where it's needed; the stage magician uses his wand to direct our attention away from something else.

Wandlike tools have a long history. Wands were found in Egyptian tombs where they would have enabled the soul of the deceased to use the other items laid out for use in the afterlife. Moses carried a wand of hazel, and hazel or willow is also the preferred wood for the construction of dowsing rods, another kind of wand. Indeed, the material from which a "magical" wand is made will have great significance, too; druids, for example, use a staff made of yew wood to divine the future.

Aesclepius, the son of Apollo, carried a wand around which two serpents were entwined; this is a wand which carries healing powers, called a Caduceus.

In the tarot, the suit of Wands is related to the element of fire.

WHEEL

The influence of the wheel in symbolism is profound and far-reaching, and nowhere in the world is untouched by its influence. The Tibetans, for example, considered the wheel so sacred that it was never used for simple means of transport. Native Americans built medicine wheels, a representation of the cosmos, in their deserts.

The number of spokes of sacred wheels is significant. The Buddhist Wheel of Dharma, for example, has eight spokes, because eight is the number of the Noble Eightfold Path. The Wheel of Life, however, has six spokes that represent the six states of being.

The wheel carries much of the same symbolism as the circle, however, the primary difference is the turning action of the wheel that rotates continuously, reflecting the cycles of the sun and the moon, the planets, the seasons, the highs and lows of man's existence, and time itself. The wheel, naturally, symbolizes death and rebirth. Our ancestors saw the universe as a vast wheel that turned relentlessly, encompassing everything within it. The zodiac, too, is the celestial "wheel of animals."

The Wheel of Fortune is named for an Etruscan goddess, Vortumna, meaning "she who turns the year." The Romans renamed her Fortuna. This wheel holds the idea that the destiny of man is symbolized by a wheel, sometimes bringing good fortune, sometimes bad, but always balancing in the end since the eight segments of this wheel carried a balance of opposing situations or ideas. Traditionally, these are passion and patience, riches and poverty, glory and humility, war and peace. This wheel reappears in the tarot, depicted in the aptly named Wheel of Fortune card.

Unsurprisingly, the wheel is a powerful solar and lunar symbol. During the time of the winter solstice, blazing wheels of fire were rolled from the tops of hillsides to symbolize the turning of the seasons, the planetary sun symbolically represented as it rolled down the "hill" of time and into the darkness of the winter season. The symbol of the wheeled chariot is ubiquitous, and represents the idea of the cycling of the planets. The sun god frequently appears in a golden chariot pulled by lions.

The still point at the center of the wheel gives another symbol, that of the Axis Mundi or omphalos, the center of the universe.

Hindu and Celtic beliefs about the wheel coincide, both sharing a notion that a mystical person was in charge of the turning of the wheel. In Hindu, he is called Chakravarti, meaning the Lord of the Wheel, the same name given to the Druid Mag Ruith. The wheel of the Mag Ruith is made of yew wood, appropriate because the yew is the tree of death

and rebirth. Legend says that if this wheel ever appears on earth it will signify the end of the world.

The wheel symbol is disguised in the so-called rose windows that appear in cathedrals, such as the one at Chartres. In the Middle Ages, they were called "rota," which means wheel. Effectively a form of mandala, Jung called them "representations of the Self of Man transposed onto the cosmic plane."

In alchemy, the wheel represents the time needed for the alchemical matter to be decocted or brewed. The fire that had to keep the potion at a constant temperature both day and night was called the "fire of the wheel."

WINGED DISC

This is a very ancient symbol, seen in varying forms around the world. It is a solar symbol, resembling a winged sun. Ancient Assyrians saw it as the symbol of their sun god, Shamash; the combination of the wings and the disc indicate eternity, the sun, and the communication between man and gods.

WINGS

WISDOM EYES OF BUDDHA

Naturally, wings are symbolic of flying, weightlessness, and release. Wings signify an ability to rise above the constraints of gravity, and by association, the limitations of the material world. Wings are an expression of the sublime, the desire to transcend everyday reality.

In symbolism, any creature that is given wings as an attribute has some connection with the spirit world, either as a deity or as a messenger between earth and heaven. Birds are the supreme manifestation of this idea in the natural world as are angels in the idealized world. The Taoist Immortals, who had wings so that they could fly to the Isles of the Immortals, had other birdlike qualities too, including a special diet that made downy feathers grow on their bodies.

Wings also symbolize knowledge, enlightenment, and the freedom that these can bring. There is a saying in the Rig Veda, "He who understands has wings." Inspiration also appears in the form of wings.

This symbol, of the watchful eyes of the Buddha, is to be found on stupas, in the position where the actual eyes of the Buddha would be if the building were a statue of the god himself. These eyes are painted on every side of the building, a reminder that the Buddha is able to watch over all four corners of the earth in his omnipotence.

The Wisdom Eyes have a bindhu above and between them at the point of the third eye, signifying enlightenment. Underneath the eyes is a squiggle that looks a little like a question mark. This is the Sanskrit character for the number one, and symbolizes the unity of all things.

The Wisdom Eyes of Buddha are so prevalent in Nepal that they have by default become a symbol of the country itself.

WITCH BALL

The witch ball is a large, hollow glass ball, often with mirrored or

otherwise reflective surfaces. The first recorded use of a witch ball comes in 1690 and they gained in popularity during the eighteenth century, hung in windows to repel witches and other malevolent forces, who would presumably be frightened off when they saw their own hideous faces staring back at them.

Some witch balls had strands of hair contained inside the hollow interior. These kinds were designed to absorb the evil spirit that would then be ensnared in the strands of hair and be unable to leave. In this sense, the witch ball fulfills the same purpose as the Native American dreamcatcher, with its net that entangles the nasties that come disguised as nightmares.

The witch ball is probably the precursor to the brightly colored reflective balls that are hung on Christmas trees.

World Axis

The notion of an axis that runs through the center of the world and connects the earth with the heavens and the underworld is common among many peoples. This concept is symbolized in various ways, for example as the column or pole, as the mountain, as the World Tree, and even as columns of smoke rising into the air. The spinal column, too, is symbolic of the World Axis as are obelisks, towers, menhirs, staffs, standards, and similar objects and symbols.

The omphalos, or navel, also represents the same concept.

Wreath

This is a garland of flowers and leaves, too large to wear on the head, but often used to denote victory or triumph in games, in war, in competitions of all kinds. Laurel wreaths are a particular sign of distinction; the word "laureate" has the same root as the word "laurel." Wreaths are also used as a funerary tribute, since the solid outer layer of the object represents the material world, and the space in the center, the world of spirit. The circular shape symbolizes eternity.

Y OF PYTHAGORAS

Pythagoras his forked letter does
Of human life a scheme to us propose;
For virtue's path on the right hand doth lye
An hard ascent presenting to the eye;
But on the top with rest the wearied are
Refreshed; the broad way easier doth appear;
But from its summit the deluded fall;
And dashed among the rocks, find there a funerall ...

It was noticed by Pythagoras that the Greek letter Y, or upsilon, resembles a forked path. To the cognoscenti, therefore, such a simple symbol became laden with hidden meanings. Effectively, the two "paths" of the Y represent earthly wisdom to the left (vice), and divine wisdom to the right (virtue). The traveler must choose which path he shall take when he meets the point

of convergence, which symbolizes adulthood. An important concept in classical philosophy was that of free will to make choices, and the Y of Pythagoras symbolizes this concept perfectly.

In the Middle Ages, this type of cross—also called the Forked Cross or Furka—was the sign of a thief, because it resembles the forked tongue of the serpent.

YAB-YUM

In Buddhist and Hindu symbolism, yab-yum means "father mother" and consists of a male and female figure in an overtly sexual embrace. What might seem shocking to prudish sensibilities is a symbol of the unity of male and female, wisdom and compassion, spirit and matter, and is seen as a natural part of the cycle of life. The yab-yum symbol takes many different forms according to which deity/consort pairing is represented.

The yab-yum carries much of

the same symbolism as the yin-yang sign, or the Shatkona.

YANTRA

The yantra, in Hinduism and Buddhism, is a linear geometric figure that effectively embodies, in a symbol, the spoken chant or mantra. In essence, it is a symbol of the cosmos. The tradition of drawing and contemplating yantras goes back over 2,000 years and is the Hindu equivalent of the Buddhist mandala.

The yantra is used as a focus for concentration and meditation, and it contains some basic elements which are rich symbols in themselves.

The yantra usually contains a triangle, either upright (representing male energy) or inverted, representing female energy. Sometimes the yantra contains the interlocking triangles of the Shatkona. It will include a circle and a lotus flower, and the whole is encompassed within a square that has "gateway" points,

symbolic of the solidity of the earth.

Sometimes the yantra contains Sanskrit letters that not only give definition to the shape but also describe what it represents.

The most important of yantras is called the Sri Yantra, the "Mother of all yantras." The Sri Yantra consists of nine interlacing triangles; the space in the center implied as the dot or bindhu. Contemplation of the Sri Yantra is in itself a symbolic pilgrimage, with each step in the construction of this intriguing geometric shape taking us to the center, toward the spiritual goal of unity.

If sand is placed on a taut surface and the "aum" sound is chanted, then the resulting shape made by the vibrating sand is in the shape of the yantra illustrated here.

YIN-YANG

Also called the Ta Ki, the yin-yang symbol is Chinese in origin, from the Taoist tradition, although its meaning has extended throughout the world.

Two identical shapes fit snugly inside a circle. These shapes are formed by an S-shape that divides the circle. In the fatter part of each shape is a dot. Sometimes the shapes are drawn in opposing colors.

The shape of the yin-yang represent the interaction and interplay of opposing forces; yin represents the female, the moon, coldness, passivity; yang is the male element, the sun, heat, and action.

The bindhus or dots inside the fatter part of each shape borrow a color from its partner, and signifies balance and harmony despite seemingly opposing forces.

Zia Pueblo sun symbol

This is an ancient, magical symbol of the Pueblo Indians. It combines one of the most sacred signs, the circle, with four sets of four stripes. The whole is a symbol of the sun, which is the meaning of the word "Zia." Four is a sacred number for the Zia Pueblos, and here it serves as a reminder of the four seasons, the directions, the earth and its four corners, and the four elements, with the fifth element being contained within the whole. The symbol often features on pottery.

The Zia Pueblo symbol is used on the flag of New Mexico.

Zigzag

See First signs: Zigzag.

Zodiac

The true zodiac is a conceptual division of space into 12 equal segments, which radiate out from the ecliptic, that is, the apparent path of the sun.

However, the zodiac also refers to the 12 constellations of stars that nowadays symbolize different human personality types. The term "zodiac" has Greco-Roman origins and means "circle of animals," although these "signs" are not restricted to zoological beasts but encompass human forms, too. The Chinese zodiac bears no relationship to any constellations.

The zodiac is both a symbol in its own right as well as a collection of symbols. These symbols are totems for each of the 12 astrological signs. It is a circle of completion, a continually turning wheel, divided into a spiritually perfect number, 12. Each of the different segments expresses a phase of development in the cycle of the universe as well as in humankind collectively and for each individual, singularly.

If we assume the stars that form the constellations have always been there, then the actual origins of the zodiac are open to conjecture. Manly P. Hall states "one author . . . believed man's concept of the zodiac to be five million years old" although the identity of this author is not given. However, it is probably safe to say that the zodiac as we know it today has its origins in ancient Babylonia, although this antique zodiac consisted of 18 segments.

By 2000 BC, the Mesopotamians and the Egyptians were using four particular constellations as markers for the changing seasons. These four star clusters are the ones that we still call Taurus, Leo, Scorpio, and Sagittarius. These signs make logical signposts in the path of the year, falling as they do between the solstices (June 21 and December 21) and the equinoxes (March 21 and September 21).

A key character in the development of astrology was Ptolemy, a Greek mathematician, astrologer, and astronomer who lived in the second century AD. Ptolemy wrote a treatise called the Tetrabyblos, or Four Books. In this, he described the names of the entire set of 12 zodiacal constellations that we still use today. At this time, astrology and astronomy operated in tandem.

An Arabic mathematician, astronomer, and astrologer named Mohammed ibn Musa al Khwarizmi, also mentioned as having discovered algebra, expanded upon Ptolemy's ideas.

THE ZODIAC AND RELIGION

Given that the early Christian Church did its very best to smother anything that smacked of paganism or what they perceived as ungodliness, the fact that belief in the zodiac not only remained powerful but was allowed to develop seems unusual. Put simply, this is down to man's overwhelming desire to peek into the Book of Fate no matter the strength of his trust in the will of God or Allah.

Despite this, it is true that the early priesthood did try to destroy astrological theory. For them, the fatalistic nature of the zodiac ran counter to the idea of divine intervention and the teachings of Christ. However, the Arabic interest in the Tetrabyblos coincided with a period of intense study of the stars. They not only expanded on the Greek theories of astronomy and astrology but also developed equipment, such as the astrolabe, that could measure the altitude of the stars and their distance from one another.

In the meantime, Christianity was going through a difficult period and needed a shake-up. The second coming of Christ, predicted for the year 1000, never happened. Blind faith was all very well, but information was vital. Knowledge from the East was traveling toward the West because of the Crusades. The new centers of learning in Spain were real melting pots of ideas from Sufi mysticism to the Kabbalah, as well as mathematics and theology.

In the thirteenth century, Thomas Aquinas managed to fuse Christian mystery with some of the beliefs of Aristotle. He threw in a great deal of Sufi influence for good measure. These new teachings, and the new, open-minded attitudes that they portended, provided an open door for astrological ideas. They included the notion that the universe was akin to a ladder stretching between heaven and earth, with angelic beings governing the stars and the planets, which themselves influenced all the elements of the earth. There was a great deal of ambivalence about the zodiac; there still is. Then, as now, some Christians condemned it as the work of the devil, whereas others embraced it as part of the bigger picture ordained by God. Cathedral builders in the thirteenth and fourteenth centuries, excited by the "new" astrological ideas that were coming into Europe, used these ideas as inspiration for the design of several key buildings, including Chartres Cathedral. Symbols from the zodiac are not only beautiful to look at, but evocative, and lent themselves well to an overlay of Christian analogy, even if the veneer was particularly thin.

THE CELESTIAL MIRROR, THE HEAVENLY WHEEL

In the same way that early people believed that the body was a microcosm of the universe, made in the shape of God, then it was a logical conclusion that the zodiac, as a series of constellations with their own meanings and mythologies, was a celestial mirror that reflected the important events in the life of people down on earth. Therefore, it made sense that if the patterns made by the astrological conjunctions could be "decoded" then they could be used as a tool of divination for forecasting future events.

The fact that the positions of the zodiac signs have shifted in the 3,000 years since they were first discovered is often ignored, if it is realized at all. In her *Woman's Dictionary of Myths and Secrets*, Barbara G. Walker states that each sign is skewed by a month; that is, anyone born under a particular sign really belongs to the sign ahead of it, according to the original theory. In effect, this means that anyone currently born under the sign of Scorpio, for example, would have been closer to Capricorn when the zodiac signs were first "discovered" although there are some areas of overlap.

The Great Wheel (or Rsai Chakra in Hindu belief) of the zodiac has been interpreted in many different ways. For Egyptians it was the heavenly representation of the holy river, the Nile. For Zoroastrians the zodiac represented the 12 chiefs of the sun god, Ahura Mazda. The Akkadians, in 2000 BC, saw the zodiac as the furrow of the great bull god, El, as he plowed his way, slowly but surely, through the year.

THE CYCLE OF LIFE

Whatever people choose to believe or disbelieve about the zodiac, its influence is pervasive. Everyone recognizes what it stands for. It is likely that even the most hardened cynic will know his or her own astrological sign and what it means. Emperors, kings, presidents, and world leaders often have their personal astrologers; some are open about this, others are coy. During World War II, British Intelligence had their astrologer, Louis de Wohl, as did Hitler.

Each sign is linked to one of four elements and is ruled by a planet. In addition, each sign itself governs a wide variety of things including flowers, trees, herbs, cities, countries, metals, colors, and parts of the body. Every sign has a basic conceptual meaning that collectively tells the story of a series of developmental steps. Each individual zodiac symbol is investigated in greater depth below under its own entry.

Although the astrological signs generally start with Aries, the circular, wheel-like nature of the zodiac means that there is really no beginning or end to the signs.

DATES AND BASIC MEANINGS ASCRIBED TO THE SIGNS OF THE ZODIAC

SIGN	DATES	RULING ELEMENT	RULING PLANET	BASIC MEANING
Aries	Mar 21–Apr 20	Fire	Mars	Impulsion, the urge to act, will
Taurus	Apr 21–May 20	Earth	Venus	Perseverance, consolidation
Gemini	May 21–June 20	Air	Mercury	Polarity, adaptability
Cancer	June 21–July 22	Water	Moon	Passivity, attachment
Leo	July 23–Aug 22	Fire	Sun	Creation, life
Virgo	Aug 23–Sep 22	Earth	Mercury	Differentiation, diligence
Libra	Sep 23–Oct 22	Air	Venus	Balance, harmony
Scorpio	Oct 23–Nov 22	Water	Mars/Pluto	Passion, endurance
Sagittarius	Nov 23–Dec 21	Fire	Jupiter	Cultivation of spiritual side, expansion
Capricorn	Dec 22–Jan 20	Earth	Saturn	Elevation, conservation
Aquarius	Jan 21–Feb 19	Air	Saturn/Uranus	Transition to higher states, adaptability
Pisces	Feb 20–Mar 20	Water	Jupiter/Neptune	Intuition, self-sacrifice

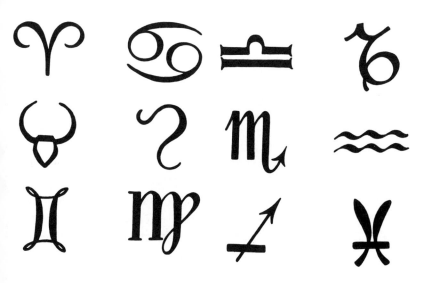

* ** *

The Encyclopedia of Secret Signs and Symbols

ARIES

Polarity:	Positive, male
Quality:	Cardinal
Ruling planet:	Mars
Element:	Fire
Body part:	Head and face
Color:	Red
Gemstone:	Diamond
Metal:	Iron
Flowers:	Honeysuckle, thistle
Trees:	One with thorns
Herbs and spices:	Mustard, cayenne pepper, capers
Food:	Onions, leeks, garlic
Animals:	Sheep and rams
Countries:	England, France, Germany
Cities:	Naples, Florence, Krakow, Birmingham (UK)

Although the zodiac is an unending wheel, Aries is often referred to as first in line in this herd of astrological creatures. This is because the sign is associated with the vernal equinox and the seasonal start of the year when everything begins to grow again. Aries represents the seed of life, potential, and possibility.

The ram

To the Greeks, Aries was a ram called Krios. Indians called it Mesha, the ram, or Aja, the goat. For the Persians, it was a lamb called Varak. To the Babylonians, however, it was either Zappu, meaning hair, or Hunga, the worker.

The glyph

This is the kind of shorthand symbol that belongs to each of the signs, used by astrologers, for example, when compiling astrological charts. These squiggles can be interpreted in a number of different ways. The glyph for Aries distinctly resembles the horns of the ram; horns themselves stand alone as a synonym for lust and sexuality. However, they could also represent an upward-shooting fountain of energy or even a flame. Because Aries rules over the face and the head, sometimes the glyph is superimposed over the face of a human figure to show Aries's influence. Again, because it governs the head and the mind, the horns are interpreted as reaching toward the spiritual world, another quality ascribed to Aries. It is interesting to see how the glyph, a simple sign, can start to qualify many different aspects of the sign itself.

Qualities

As we've seen, the stellar circle of animals as it exists today was slightly different and the sign that used to occupy the place now taken by Aries was Taurus, and there is a residue of the "bull in a china shop" notion about this position. The spring equinox is a time when new growth is prodigious, everything fighting to burst out of the ground after the barren winter months. The unharnessed energy and vitality of the ram or the bull is appropriate.

Ruled by the planet Mars which also rules the god of war, Aries's qualities include energy and vitality, determination, stubbornness, impulsiveness. Aries can also be quick-tempered and aggressively ambitious. The fire element of Aries is the fire of creation, burning erratically in all directions, an explosion of flame that can be creative or destructive, depending on how it is applied. The brute force and impulsion of the ram epitomizes this sign; as the first sign of the zodiac it has a childlike bluntness, and an honest, straightforward approach.

TAURUS

Polarity:	Negative, female
Quality:	Fixed
Ruling planet:	Venus
Element:	Earth
Body part:	Throat and neck
Color:	Pink
Gemstone:	Sapphire or emerald
Metal:	Copper
Flowers:	Rose, poppy, foxglove
Trees:	Ash, apple, cypress
Herbs and spices:	Cloves, sorrel, spearmint
Food:	Wheat, berries, apples, grapes
Animals:	Cattle
Countries:	Ireland, Switzerland, Iran
Cities:	Dublin, Lucerne, Mantua, Leipzig

The bull

Second in line in the parade of zodiacal creatures, Taurus symbolizes the bull and has changed in form very little over the millennia. Sometimes he looks ahead, toward Gemini, sometimes he looks backwards to the animals in his wake. Astrologers from Persia,

Greece, India, and Babylonia all agreed that the Taurus constellation was a bull. Aldebaran, the brightest star in the Taurus constellation, was called the heart of the bull. Persians referred to the constellation as the Bull of Light. Taurus comes over the horizon at a time between the vernal equinox and the summer solstice, a time in the life of man that requires hard work, concentration, and consolidation in order to direct the seed of raw energy sown by Aries.

The glyph

The glyph for Taurus resembles the head and horns of the bull; whereas the horns of Aries signify the brute force of the ram, the horns of Taurus point toward the bull as a beast of burden, and even look a little like a yoke. The planet Venus and the element of earth rule Taurus, and the bull moves the earth as he plows its furrows. Despite being the epitome of male power, the bull is aligned to female energies and represents Earth Mother qualities. Taurus rules over the throat and so is closely linked to sounds and music, and the glyph is interpreted as the larynx, situated in the throat, with the Eustachian tubes running from it.

Qualities

All the archetypal bull-like qualities are given to people that are born under the sign of Taurus: an immense capacity for hard work, resilience and stubbornness, stability, reliability, and domesticity. Added to this is an acute sensitivity to all the sights, sounds and scents of the material world, which leads to a great pleasure in sensual delights. The bull rules over the neck and throat, indicating a love of music and the spoken word. When this is added to the other sensory qualities then the bull's sensitivity to beauty is highlighted. The earthiness of the bull is reflected in a lust for all the pleasures of life, and also means that the bull is warm-hearted, generous, and energetic.

GEMINI

Polarity:	Positive, male
Quality:	Mutable
Ruling planet:	Mercury
Element:	Air
Body part:	Arms and hands, shoulders, collarbone, and lungs
Color:	Yellow
Gemstone:	Agate
Metal:	Mercury
Flowers:	Lily of the valley
Trees:	Nut-bearing ones
Herbs and spices:	Aniseed, marjoram, caraway
Food:	Nuts, vegetables that grow above the ground
Animals:	Small birds, butterflies, monkeys
Countries:	Wales, Belgium, United States
Cities:	London, Cardiff, Plymouth (UK), San Francisco, Melbourne

The twins

There is agreement among the various astrological disciplines that the constellation representing Gemini is two people generally embracing or holding hands, but the sex and the relationship of the pair are debatable. For Egyptians, the pair was a man and a woman. Romans thought that the sign represented Apollo and his twin sister Diana. The Persians and Greeks had them as twins called Dopatkar and Didumoi. Babylonians thought that they were twins but did not define the gender; and in India, they were called the Lovers, or Mithuna. Gemini could be physical twins, or lovers, or simply androgynous; it doesn't really matter. Whatever their gender, the sign represents duality both in outward appearance and identity, the concept of soul mates. Early representations of Gemini show a couple making love, signifying the union of opposites in harmony that is also indicated by the yin-yang or yab-yum symbols.

The glyph

The glyph for Gemini, appropriately, looks like the Roman numeral for two. The two upright figures are effectively joined both at the head (the world of spirit, communication and ideas) and at their feet (the world of matter, quite literally, common ground).

Qualities

Gemini arrives just before the summer solstice, the halfway point of the year. The symbolic twins speak of the need for contact with another person, the importance of establishing and maintaining a relationship and the idea that two can make a perfect whole while each struggles to retain its own identity as a single person. Gemini is representative of opposing forces, material and spiritual; sometimes one of the twins is mortal (indicated by a scythe) and the other is immortal (holding a lyre).

Belonging to the air element and ruled by Mercury, Gemini is communicative, idealistic, inquisitive, versatile, and inventive.

Gemini is frequently associated with mythological twins such as the founders of Rome, Romulus and Remus, or the heavenly twins, Castor and Pollux. They also appear in the tarot as the Lovers. People born under the sign of Gemini are supposed to be dualistic in their interests and lifestyles, restless, impatient, and easily bored. It is

their life's quest to reconcile the opposing forces within and to bring about internal harmony.

CANCER

Polarity:	Negative, female
Quality:	Cardinal
Ruling planet:	Moon
Element:	Water
Body part:	Heart, lungs, and stomach
Color:	Silver gray
Gemstone:	Pearl
Metal:	Silver
Flowers:	White flowers in general
Trees:	Ones that are rich in sap: birch, maple, pine
Herbs and spices:	Saxifrage, verbena, caraway
Food:	Milk, fish, and fruit and vegetables that have high water content
Animals:	Creatures with shells
Countries:	Holland, Scotland
Cities:	Manchester (UK), Amsterdam, Tokyo

The crab

The constellation known as Cancer was not always depicted as a crab, but whatever its form the shell has always been consistent.

Early European astrologers depicted Cancer as a crayfish. For the Egyptians it was the scarab beetle, a sacred creature representing death and rebirth that was also the sign of the god Khepera. However, the Persian, Greek, Sanskrit, and Babylonian words for the constellation all mean the same as "crab." The constellation itself was possibly the most important one in the zodiac, since it contains more fixed stars within the arc of its influence than any other sign. It was not only the Mayans who predicted the world would end when these planets aligned within the constellation. The Romans, too, believed that Cancer had been placed in the sky by Juno to signal the end of all things whenever she decided this should happen.

The glyph

The distinctive "69" glyph that is the astrological shorthand for Cancer can be interpreted in a number of ways. The symbol is constructed from two separate parts that are identical, but polarized by their position. For some this "see-saw" symbol shows the up-and-down nature that is commonly held to be a Cancerian trait. Because the constellation appears just after the summer solstice when the seasons are changing, the two spirals could represent this shift. Some see it as two spermatozoa, coming together to make one seed, and again, conception and birth are linked to the sign. Following the theme of nurturing and fertility, the sign might be a pair of breasts. Others see it as representing some of the fixed stars within the constellation itself, one pointing up, and one down, demonstrating the concept "as above, so below."

Qualities

This constellation appears just as the seasons begin to change, and the Sun's movement teeters from ascent to descent. A lunar symbol, Cancer belongs to the water element and is known to be passive, domesticated, imaginative, romantic, and sometimes self-absorbed. The influence of the Moon points to a vivid imagination and inner depth, both qualities consistent with the sign. All the creatures that have been identified with this constellation share one common feature: the shell. This symbolizes self-protection and points to the withdrawn nature of some Cancerians. Cancer rules over the parts protected by this shell: the heart, the lungs and the stomach.

LEO

Polarity:	Positive, male
Quality:	Fixed
Ruling planet:	Sun
Element:	Fire
Body part:	Heart and back
Color:	Gold
Gemstone:	Ruby
Metal:	Gold
Flowers:	Sunflowers, marigolds
Trees:	Bay, palm, citrus, laurel
Herbs and spices:	Saffron, peppermint, rosemary
Food:	Rice, honey, grapes
Animals:	Cat family
Countries:	Italy, Romania, Sicily
Cities:	Bath, Rome, Prague, Bristol, Los Angeles

The lion

The constellation known as Leo has always been represented by the lion; the Babylonians sexed the lion as female, and named her Urgula, the lioness. The Romans called this star Regulus, meaning "Heart of the Lion"; the word also means "little king" or "paw of the lion." One of the first names for Leo was Babylonian and means "Great Light" and indeed the sign's first name was the Great Light, a reference to its ruler, the Sun.

Leo is the only sign in the zodiac that is ruled by the Sun, a star, in contrast to the other zodiac signs that are all ruled by planets.

The glyph

The sigil for Leo could be the tail of the lion. Alternatively, the circle can be seen as the heart (ruled by the lion) with the scooped curve symbolizing the excitement and the uplift in emotions that the Leo feels when something particularly beautiful or inspiring is experienced. The downward slope, however, signifies the unfinished projects that so often litter the life of the Leo personality. The glyph may also signify the lion's mane.

Qualities

Leo appears over the horizon at the height of summer, and like the Sun, the Leo has a passionate and extrovert nature. Generosity and nobility are said to be major attributes of the sign along with dominant powers of leadership.

The fire element of the Leo makes it theatrical, flamboyant, creative, and hospitable, with regal or noble tendencies that can come across as condescension. The fire is the controlled heat of the Sun, though, as opposed to the untamed flames belonging to Aries. The lion is the symbol of power, royalty, and pride, the symbol of emperors, which can be used to good or bad effect. The mane of the lion symbolizes the rays of the Sun, and an attribute of the Leo person is said to be manelike hair. The Egyptian zodiac, the Dendera, shows an image similar to the card called Strength in the tarot. A woman tames a lion, holding open its jaws with apparent ease.

Leo rules over the spine and the heart. St. Mark is represented by the winged Leo, which is seen carved in stone, striding majestically around St. Mark's Square in Venice.

VIRGO

Polarity:	Negative, female
Quality:	Mutable
Ruling planet:	Mercury
Element:	Earth
Body parts:	Solar plexus and bowels
Color:	Dark brown, green
Gemstone:	Sardonyx
Metal:	Mercury or nickel
Flowers:	Brightly colored small flowers
Trees:	Nut-bearing trees (like Gemini)
Herbs and spices:	Turmeric, saffron and all others with a strong yellow color
Food:	Vegetables that grow in the ground
Animals:	Domestic pets
Countries:	New Zealand, the West Indies, Turkey, Greece, Brazil
Cities:	Paris, Athens, Heidelberg, Boston

The virgin

Despite her name, over the course of the millennia since the signs of the zodiac were first defined, Virgo has been portrayed as the prudish virgin, the wanton temptress, and all other aspects of the feminine in between these two extremes. She has been identified as many different goddesses. For the Romans she was Ceres, holding a sheaf of corn, symbol of fertility and the harvest; Virgo also appears at the time that the crops are being gathered together. Egyptians linked her with Isis and with Ma'at, the goddess of truth. All of the names for Virgo refer to her as the Virgin or the Maiden.

A Greek legend links Virgo to Astraea, the goddess of truth and virtue who lived with the other immortals among human beings on earth. However, when Pandora opened the box and released all manner of nasties into the world, the earth became unbearable. Astraea stayed for as long as she could bear it, although she eventually left the earth, the last of the deities to do so, her finer sensibilities offended by the behavior of humans. It is said that Astraea will return to earth when humankind is ready for her.

For Christians, she is personified as Mary, the virgin mother of Christ, sometimes portrayed with a five-petaled Marian flower that conceals the five-pointed star or pentagram. Early depictions of Virgo show her as a winged angel.

The glyph

The glyph for Virgo links it with the signs for Scorpio and Libra, and has also been proposed to stand for MV, Maria Virgo, referring back to the Virgin Mary. Sometimes the final loop of the triple arches is depicted as the fish or vesica piscis shape, that symbolizes the world of spirit entering the world of matter and further underlines the connection with the Christian virgin.

Qualities

The qualities of Virgo, ruled by the element of earth, are tranquility, discrimination, efficiency, grace, and intelligence. Self-control and self-discipline add to the equation, as well as methodical diligence and tidiness. Virgo is a spiritual sign, and this has been shown by depicting her with the wings that signify ascension of the soul. Appearing during the time of the harvest, Virgo is maternal, fertile, nurturing, and prepared for whatever might come her way.

LIBRA

Polarity:	Positive, male
Quality:	Cardinal
Ruling planet:	Venus
Element:	Air
Body part:	Back, kidneys, and ovaries
Color:	All shades of blue
Gemstone:	Sapphire, jade
Metal:	Copper or bronze
Flowers:	Blue-colored flowers, roses, hydrangeas
Trees:	Ash, poplar
Herbs and spices:	Mint, arrack, cayenne
Food:	Pear, tomato, asparagus, beans
Animals:	Lizards and other small reptiles
Countries:	Austria, Burma, Japan, Argentina, Canada, Upper Egypt
Cities:	Copenhagen, Johannesburg, Lisbon, Vienna, Frankfurt

The scales

The distinctive symbol that represents Libra, the seventh sign of the zodiac, is the set of scales, the only inanimate object that represents a zodiac sign (although they are often shown in the hands of a human figure). Some schools of thought say that Libra was the last zodiac sign to be officially recognized, and was formerly a part of the preceding sign, Scorpio. Others contest this notion, however.

The idea of balance or equilibrium is confirmed by the many ancient astrological disciplines that give Libra this quality. The Indians, Persians, Greeks, and Babylonians all agreed about this. The Greeks called the sign Zugos, meaning "yoke." Unsurprisingly, Libra was associated with Ma'at, the Egyptian goddess of justice; the figure of a woman with scales of balance and the sword of justice still carries a powerful symbolic punch as the representative of the law.

The glyph

The astrological shorthand for Libra does indeed look like the yoke that the Greeks thought the constellation represented. However, it also bears more than a passing resemblance to an Egyptian symbol called the Akhet. This sign shows the sun rising between two hills and the Egyptians called the constellation Ta Akhet, meaning "place of the sunrise." The Akhet also speaks of balance between male and female or the Sun and the Earth, with the space between them being the mediator or balancing factor.

Qualities

Libra was an important sign for Romans since they believed that Italy fell under its jurisdiction, partly because Rome was founded on October 4 when the Sun is in this part of the zodiac. Latterly, it is agreed that the country belongs to Leo.

Libra belongs to the element of air, and has a gentle temperament, peaceful, affectionate, orderly, and elegant but also changeable and prone to mood swings when the balance is disturbed. Because Libra appears at a mellow time of year when there is a lull in activity after the harvest is gathered in, it is possibly more relaxed and dispassionate than other zodiac signs. Not surprisingly, Libra is the sign of the diplomat, a person who can see both sides of a story and make an impartial judgment. This quality fits with the fact that Libra is the only inanimate object in the zodiac.

♏ SCORPIO

Polarity:	Negative, female
Quality:	Fixed
Ruling planet:	Mars/Pluto
Element:	Water
Body parts:	Reproductive organs
Color:	Deep red
Gemstone:	Opal
Metal:	Steel or iron
Flowers:	Rhododendron, geranium
Trees:	Blackthorn and other bushy trees
Herbs and spices:	Witch-hazel, aloes, catmint
Food:	Strong-tasting foods
Animals:	Crustaceans, insects
Countries:	Morocco, the Transvaal, Algeria, Norway
Cities:	Fez, Liverpool, Hull, New Orleans, Milwaukee

* ** *

The scorpion

Of all the astrological shapes that are superimposed over their constellations, the stars that group together for the sign of Scorpio really do resemble a scorpion and so it comes as no surprise that ancient astrologers were in complete agreement that this was what the stars represented. Antares, the red star that is included in the shape, was known as the Heart of the Scorpion, dedicated to the god Mars because of its fiery color.

The glyph

The modern shorthand symbol for Scorpio has a very different appearance from ones that are seen in medieval manuscripts. Then, it looked far more like an actual scorpion. Egyptians use the symbol of an upright serpent to represent the sign (both are poisonous creatures). The modern sigil—which looks like an M with a curved, arrow-headed uplift continuing on from the last upright—could be the severed tail of a scorpion or the male sexual parts. The arrow at the end of the "tail" also looks like the tail of a dragon.

Qualities

Scorpio appears midway through the fall, a time of decay but also a time of fermentation, when Samhain or Halloween is on the horizon. Scorpio rules over this festival, dedicated to the dead. Ancient Egyptians believed that their god Osiris was sent to the otherworld while Scorpio was in the heavens. However, because Scorpio rules over the reproductive organs, the idea of rebirth is never far behind; a child conceived during the reign of the scorpion is generally born into the sign of Leo. A strong sex drive is an attribute of this sign.

Many astrologers say that Scorpio people may have to face more adversity in their lives than other signs; however, this would assume that they are karmically prepared for this and are more than able to cope. The sting in the tail of the scorpion implies quick-wittedness and a sharp intelligence as well as a sharp tongue. Traits also include a deep, passionate nature and a magnetic, shrewd, creative, and intense personality. This intensity is due in part to the influence of Pluto, although prior to the discovery of this planet, Mars was assigned to the scorpion.

SAGITTARIUS

Polarity:	Positive, male
Quality:	Mutable
Ruling planet:	Jupiter
Element:	Fire
Body part:	Thighs and hips
Color:	Dark blue, purple
Gemstone:	Topaz
Metal:	Tin
Flowers:	Carnations and pinks
Trees:	Lime, oak, birch, mulberry
Herbs and spices:	Aniseed, balsam, sage
Food:	Grapefruit, bulb vegetables, dried grapes
Animals:	Horses, also any animals that are hunted
Countries:	South Africa, Spain, Australia, Hungary
Cities:	Budapest, Toledo, Stuttgart, Cologne, Sheffield, Washington, DC

The centaur/bowman

All ancient astrologers are agreed that the constellation called Sagittarius is conceptually personified by hunting. In India, the bow alone represented the sign. The centaur himself appears in the Persian zodiac, drawing back the bow. In Rome, it was the goddess of the hunt, Diana, who wielded the bow and arrow.

The centaur itself is half-human; the other half symbolizes a leaning toward a bestial side. This duality can also be interpreted as the spiritual side of man (depicted by the arrow that is just about to be released into the heavens) being "weighed down" or somehow impeded by the physical world.

The glyph

The sigil for Sagittarius is one of the most obvious in the zodiac. It shows the arrow, symbolic of spiritual transcendence. Significantly, there is a bar at the base of the arrow, which carries all the connotations of the cross, the four elements, and the material world. This points, again, toward the duality within the sign, a struggle to balance the world of matter with the world of spirit. Sagittarius is hunting for more than mere game, and symbolizes the notion of a spiritual quest, too.

Qualities

Sagittarius comes into the sky at winter, a time when there is a natural pause in the circle of the seasons, a time for hunting. Therefore, the qualities assigned to Sagittarius include a certain nomadic nature and a love of wide-open spaces. The fire that rules the sign has passed from the dangerous explosion belonging to Aries and the steady flame belonging to Leo, and appears in Sagittarius as the flame of spiritual enlightenment, the same flame that appears over the heads of certain saints and other enlightened characters. Sagittarians may spend their lives attempting to unify the material with the spiritual. A very practical sign, Sagittarius is elevated, by the torso of the horse, to be able to see the bigger picture and the wider horizon beyond the trees. The four hooves, standing squarely on the earth, echo the four directions of the cross at the base of the arrow; above all else, the Sagittarian aims high while having his feet firmly on the ground.

CAPRICORN

Polarity:	Negative, female
Quality:	Cardinal
Ruling planet:	Saturn
Element:	Earth
Body part:	Knees, joints and bones
Color:	Black, dark gray, brown
Gemstone:	Turquoise, amethyst
Metal:	Lead
Flowers:	Ivy, hearts-ease, hemlock
Trees:	Yew, elm, pine
Herbs and spices:	Knapweed, comfrey, hemp
Food:	Potato, spinach, barley, beet, malt
Animals:	Goats and other cloven-hoofed animals
Countries:	India, Mexico, Afghanistan
Cities:	Oxford (UK), Mexico City, Delhi

The goat

The Capricorn constellation, so the ancients agreed, was definitely a goat; however, it generally appeared as a goat/fish hybrid. For the Persians it was called the Sea Goat, Vahik; for the Babylonians it was the Goat-Fish; for the Greeks it was called the Goat-Horned One. Mahara, meaning Sea Monster, was the Sanskrit name. The only exception was the Romans, who saw the goddess Vesta in the constellation. Modern images of Capricorn often tend to lose the sea-monster aspect, but older interpretations show it with four legs and the tail of a fish, or an entire rear end comprised of a serpent-like tail.

The glyph

The Capricorn sigil is an unusual squiggle, which could be a sketch of the horns of the goat. However, the glyph appears in various forms. The sign is a combination of straight lines and curves that point to the dual nature of the Capricorn, the material side on the earth and the spiritual side in the water. There was an old saying that time ended with Capricorn. Again, this was because of the time of year that the constellation loomed over the horizon, and its intimate association with Saturn, also known as Chronos, the god of time.

Qualities

Capricorn comes into the sky at the time of the winter solstice, the "gateway of the gods." In the Far East, this time heralds the New Year. Saturn, the ruler of the sign, denotes patience, perseverance, and industry. The hybrid nature of the symbol points toward an inherent duality. On the one hand is the sure-footed mountain goat, closely in touch with its earth element and aspiring to the heights, worldly and intellectual. On the other is the aspect of the sign that relates to water: unconscious and psychic powers, depth, intuition. Capricorn is hardworking and ambitious but with a mystical aspect to its nature. The Saturnine aspect of the sign is reflected in the dignity and self-discipline common to those born under it, who can be withdrawn and contemplative.

It is the quest for people born under this sign to reconcile the two very distinct aspects of their nature: the worldly with the spiritual, the ambitious with the contemplative.

AQUARIUS

Polarity:	Positive, male
Quality:	Fixed
Ruling planet:	Saturn/Uranus
Element:	Air
Body part:	Circulation, ankles
Color:	Turquoise
Gemstone:	Aquamarine
Metal:	Aluminum
Flowers:	Orchid
Trees:	Fruit trees
Herbs and spices:	Those that have a sharp or unusual flavor
Food:	Any foods that preserve well: dried fruits, preserves, pickles
Animals:	Large birds that can fly for a long time; the condor
Countries:	Sweden, Russia
Cities:	Salzburg, Moscow, Leningrad, Hamburg

The water carrier

The Greeks and Persians called the constellation the Water Pot. However, for the Babylonians this star cluster was a goddess and to the Romans, it was Juno.

For the Akkadians, the sign was called "Ku ur Ku" meaning "Seat of the Flowing Waters," or alternatively Rammanu, god of the storm. The sign is often depicted as a human figure pouring water from some kind of a vessel. This figure can be of either gender. In the tarot, the Aquarius archetype appears in two possible places: as the card called Temperance, featuring a winged woman circulating water by pouring it between two jugs, or as the Star, which features a young girl, naked, pouring water from two jugs onto the earth. These dual streams of water echo back to the Egyptian concept of the sign, depicting a god who also pours the same two streams of water.

The glyph

The sigil for Aquarius is self-explanatory. It shows wavy lines, representing water. The zig-zag shape of the lines, though, portrays the idea of water as an active principle, a life-force akin to electricity. The girl in the portrayal of Aquarius seen in the tarot card called the Star actually stands in the water she is pouring, again indicating it as something more than just a liquid. The two streams of water in the sigil point to this same notion, of water as one of the elements but with another quality. Homeopathy relies on the power of water to be able to dilute and yet strengthen the essence of the remedy; this magical power may provide a clue about the meaning of the two lines.

Qualities

Before the discovery of Uranus, Saturn, the planet that confers gravity and a certain weight, ruled Aquarius. Uranus, however, adds another element to the Aquarian psyche, that of innovation and a reputation for eccentricity. For example, Aquarius is the sign typified by the mad professor archetype. The Aquarian, ruled by air but with a mystical attachment to water, has little regard for material objects and is more concerned with the mind and the spirit, primarily concerned with quenching the thirst of the soul before that of the body. This makes for a certain emotional detachment. The air element makes the sign intuitive and given to leaps of deductive reasoning.

The Age of Aquarius

Much has been written about the Age of Aquarius, but what exactly does this mean? The "ages" of the zodiac work backwards, i.e. the age that we are now leaving is the age of Pisces, which actually comes after Aquarius in the zodiacal wheel.

The exact date of our entering this new age is difficult to determine, although each age lasts for 2,160 years. Some pinpoint the transition to 1962, others say it will start in 2377. It is interesting to note that the preceding age, which for many was associated with Christianity, was the age of Pisces, whose symbol is the fish. This is still a symbol of the faith 2,000 years after Christ stepped on this earth.

The Aquarian age is said to be the dawning of a time of change. These changes will include freedom in all senses of the word, humanitarianism, and a raising of consciousness and awareness.

The glyph for Aquarius carries within it a clue about at least one of the things that will be a planetary concern with the coming of the new age—the element of water.

PISCES

Polarity:	Negative, female
Quality:	Mutable
Ruling planet:	Jupiter/Neptune
Element:	Water
Body part:	Feet and immune system
Color:	Sea green
Gemstone:	Moonstone or bloodstone
Metal:	Platinum or tin
Flowers:	Water lily
Trees:	Willow, alder, trees that like to grow near water
Herbs and spices:	Lime, succory
Food:	Cucumber, pumpkin, melon, lettuce, turnip
Animals:	Otters, beavers, and other water-loving mammals; fish
Countries:	Portugal; deserts in general
Cities:	Jerusalem, Warsaw, Seville, Bournemouth, Santiago de Compostela

The fish

The Greeks and the Persians both called this constellation "Fish." For the Babylonians it was Two Tails. They divided the star cluster into two separate shapes, Simmah, the swallow, and Anunitum, the goddess. The symbol for Pisces is traditionally the two fishes, swimming in opposite directions, their mouths nevertheless joined by a cord. This cord is faint within the actual constellation, but still visible. The Babylonians called it Riksu, the Arabs Al Risha. This cord is a vital part of the sign and has been given esoteric significance.

The glyph

The sigil for the fish comes from Egyptian sources and has hardly changed since this time, unlike glyphs belonging to other constellations. The original Egyptian sign showed the two opposing curves, but they were separate; the connecting line was added in the fourteenth or fifteenth century, making the sign into its current H shape.

Qualities

Although some modern interpretations of Pisces omit the cord, the fact that the fish are joined rather than being separate is very significant, a good demonstration of how a seemingly simple line within a symbol can mean so much. The duality of the fish is well known although it can signify different things, such as the soul that desires the stimulus of the material world, and the spirit that wants to leave these things behind. However, one cannot survive without the other. Pisces carries with it this spirit/soul significance in seventeenth-century alchemical writings.

Because of their association with water, fish are symbols of the goddess, the feminine aspect, and some say that the fishes swimming in opposite directions indicate the supposed female trait of not being able to make a decision, or of a trait belonging to both sexes, of being pulled in opposite directions.

Because the fish symbol is closely aligned to the Christian faith, the Pisces symbol is sometimes found in churches where no other astrological symbolism is displayed. Christ was born at the start of the Age of Pisces. Pisces people are said to be dreamy, impractical, deep thinkers and interested in psychic matters.

The sign comes into the sky just before the vernal equinox, just before spring; it is the "last" sign of the zodiac, and as such represents the idea of rebirth. It is appropriate that fish come from that great womb of rebirth, the sea.

ZOSO AND THE FOUR SYMBOLS

"Zoso" is a very good example of a modern sequence of symbols that perhaps gives an indication of how other magical emblematic amalgams are formed.

Although the symbol was never intended to have a name, it is commonly called the Zoso because the first of the four symbols appears to spell this word. It was chosen by the guitarist Jimmy Page of Led Zeppelin. The band decided that they should use symbols instead of names for their fourth album (which is usually referred to as *Led Zep 4*).

Page, renowned for his interest in occult matters in general and Crowleyana in particular, has never spoken publicly about the component elements of his own symbol, but it is believed to have originated in an old alchemical grimoire dating back to the sixteenth century. The sigil itself points to the link between the planet Saturn and Page's zodiac sign, Capricorn. The "Z" is a commonly used symbol for the planet, and the "oso" stands for the element of mercury, also associated with Saturn.

The symbols of the other band members are the triquetra (chosen by John Paul Jones, bass and keyboards). Drummer John Bonham chose the Tripod of Life or Borromean Rings, and singer Robert Plant chose a feather enclosed within a circle. The feather bears a similarity to the feather of justice used by the goddess of truth, Ma'at, to balance against the souls of men, and is also likely to signify transcendence. The circle stands for completion and wholeness.

Part Two

FAUNA

THE SECRET SYMBOLS
OF THE ANIMAL REALM

This section not only encompasses real animals, insects, and birds, but also takes a look at some of the more fantastical creatures that occupy a significant space in our collective psyche.

The attributes of all our animals, real or otherwise, give us an incredibly rich and diverse catalog of symbols. Sometimes, the reasons behind these symbolic meanings are due to historical misconceptions about the habits of certain creatures, and probably date back to a time when we were less well informed than we are now. These curiosities—such as the beaver being a symbol of chastity because of the notion that it would rather eat its own testicles than be captured—give us a delightful insight into the minds of our ancestors.

APE

See Monkey.

BAT

For fans of horror movies, the bat has become an animal to be feared; the vampire bat is a satanic agent that sucks the soul from the body along with its lifeblood. However, there is more to the bat than purely negative symbolism.

In China, the ideogram for good luck, "fu," sounds the same as the word for "bat" and so the animal is a lucky charm. Some bat caves in the East have remained unchanged for thousands of years; the bats that live there are revered as sacred animals.

The nocturnal nature of the bat has given it some negative associations. It is symbolic of the night devouring the day; the bat is said to swallow the light because it wakes at dusk, the time between day and night. Christian belief, too, regards the bat with suspicion because it is seen as an incarnation of Satan.

However, the nocturnal nature of the bat makes it, like the owl, a creature that has access to hidden knowledge and secret information, able to detect things in the hours of darkness that are not accessible to diurnal creatures. Before echolocation was recognized and understood, the bat's ability to find its way about was a source of great intrigue, adding to the mystique of the animal.

BEAR

For the Celts, "bear" was synonymous with "warrior." The name of the greatest Celtic king, Arthur, shares the same root as the name for bear—"artos"—meaning "bear-like." This warrior-bear attribute was not restricted to the male; in the kingdom of the Gauls, there was a ferocious warrior-queen called Artio. The Greek goddess of the hunt, Artemis, also shares the bear's name.

The bear is an earthy creature, and in northern European pre-Christian society, it represented worldly power and authority, the equivalent of the lion in other societies.

The bear is associated with the moon. As the moon disappears for a time, so does the bear, when he hibernates during the winter months. Diana/Artemis, the goddess of the hunt (who also has close links to the moon), is often depicted with a bear, and can shape-shift into the form of a bear. The constellations Ursa Major and Ursa Minor—the Great Bear and the Little Bear—are the stellar incarnation of this goddess. These constellations are always visible in the northern hemisphere, and so are effective markers for the seasons.

The Finno-Ugric people made graveyards for bears until relatively recently. They laid out the bones of the bears very carefully, so that the animal could return from the dead. The power of the bear is borne out by the fact that the actual word for the animal was seldom used, replaced with other terms such as "the brown one" or "bruin," "the old fellow" or "honey eater." This is because the power inherent in names was such that to say the name of the animal was equivalent to invoking its spirit.

Native Americans have a specific kind of witch doctor called a bear doctor, able to take on the form of a grizzly to vanquish the tribal enemies.

BEAVER

Typically, the beaver is a symbol of industry, renowned for its building skills and often used as a logo for these reasons. We say that a busy person works like a beaver.

However, there are other aspects to the animal. It has godlike status for some Native American tribes, and its bones were taken special care of, kept in a secret place for a year and then buried with due ceremony to bring good fortune to the hunt. Because the beaver carries with it a strong sense of home, family, and domesticity, for Native Americans it has all the instinctive qualities of the female.

There is a curious legend about a beaver hunted for the valuable medicine allegedly contained in its testicles. Rather than be captured, the beaver bit off his own testicles and threw them in front of the hunter, thus rendering himself valueless to the predator who was, nevertheless, free to take the object he desired. This peculiar anecdote gave early Christians the imagery they needed to make the beaver a symbol of chastity and purity, willing to cast off all impurities in the face of a devil who then departed, thwarted.

BEE

The importance of the bee is reflected in its appearance on coins from Ephesus dating back to the fifth century BC, and in Minoan symbolism where the goddess appears as half woman, half bee. In Egypt, the bee was the symbol of the Lower Kingdom.

The bee itself is symbolic of industry and mutual cooperation; however, there is also a spiritual side to this insect. One of the symbols of Aphrodite was a golden honeycomb, and it was believed that the souls of her priestesses inhabited the bodies of bees. These priestesses were called "Melissae," a word that has the same root as that of honey and bees. Male counterparts equating to drones, called "Essenes," accompanied the Melissae. Essenes were eunuchs.

Because bees produce wax, they are frequently linked to places of Christian worship such as abbeys, since the monks and nuns used the wax to make candles for the church.

As with many winged creatures, the bee is able to communicate in ways alien to human beings. The bee performs an elaborate dance to indicate the whereabouts of a particularly rich crop of flowers. Bees are believed to have magical powers to foresee the future, and are considered by many to be deities in their own right. It is perhaps for this reason it has been customary, for hundreds of years, for the beekeeper to tell the bees all the news of the household, particularly of births or deaths; a swarm of bees was regarded as carrying the soul of the deceased away with it.

Because bees feed on the nectar of flowers, and therefore fundamentally on sunlight, they are agents of transmutation, making something from nothing. They construct their honeycomb from thousands of perfectly symmetrical hexagons, and in turn, this structure contains the many secrets of the Flower of Life and of the six-pointed star or hexagram.

BEETLE

See Scarab.

BISON

See Buffalo.

* * *

BUFFALO

The marshy wetlands that the buffalo inhabits are universally acknowledged to be "transitional" places, territory that sits somewhere between the seen and unseen worlds. Therefore, the buffalo carries with it a significant amount of symbolism as a creature that has two hooves in the material world of man, and the other two in the spirit world of the gods and the ancestors.

The white buffalo comes with huge significance attached to it for Native Americans, due no doubt because the appearance of such an animal is an incredibly rare occurrence; odds of one in a million have been quoted. To them, the appearance of such an animal is on a par with the reappearance of Christ. The place where a white buffalo is born is liable to become a focus of pilgrimage. People come to give gifts to the animal because of its sacred significance as a harbinger of peace, plenty, and good fortune.

BULL

The sacred stature of the bull dates back to at least 3000 BC, when early Hebrews carved the effigy of a god, called El, who appeared in the shape of a bull, at the end of their ritual staffs.

The bull is the archetype of brute masculinity, fecundity, tyranny, and ferocity. The bull also has its part to play in the story of Hercules and his monumental labors. A bull that is wreaking havoc on Crete tests Hercules's huge strength. He strangles the bull into submission, and it is shipped away to Athens.

Bull sacrifice is such an ancient rite that any definitive origins are uncertain, and although in the Ellora Caves there is a painting of the goddess Kali slaying a bull, its ritual slaughter is far older than the purported age of the painting (*c.* AD 500–1000) suggests. To ancient people, the bull was such a supremely powerful animal that being splashed in its blood conferred immortality. In Rome, a bull cult introduced from Asia Minor in the second century BC inspired a ritual called the *taurobolium.* The initiate stood in a trench, immediately below a board with holes pierced in it. A bull, standing on top of the trench, had its throat slit, and the hot blood gushed down through the slats, drenching the devotee. This gory ritual was the reenactment of a Mithraic legend

about the bull's blood as the origins of all life, and so rejuvenated the body and soul.

A remnant of the earlier bull sacrifice still takes place today, in the Spanish bullfights that have become synonymous with the country and its people. This particular ritual is a throwback to the same Mithraic legend as the *taurobolium.* This legend says the bull was the first creature on Earth. Mithras killed the bull and all other living things sprang from the blood that was spilled on the ground. Many of the oldest bullrings in Spain are on the sites of former Mithraic temples or at least are very close to them. Spain is not the only country to have bullrings; they also exist in South America and France.

The bull is immortalized in the night sky, being one of the symbols of the astrological zodiac in the form of the constellation Taurus.

BUTTERFLY

Unlike the bee that goes from flower to flower with a great sense of purpose and intention, the butterfly seems to flutter about quite aimlessly, no great ambition lurking behind its beauty.

In view of the fact that the Greek word for butterfly, *psyche*, is the same as that for soul, it is interesting to note that winged creatures are universally thought to be able to communicate with other worlds and higher powers. There was a belief that human souls incarnated into butterflies between lifetimes. The connection between the spirit and the butterfly reaches across the world—from the Celts, who believed that the butterfly was a human soul in search of a mother, to the Aztecs, who believed that the last breath exhaled by a dying person took the form of a butterfly.

The life cycle of the butterfly is highly visible at every stage, making it a symbol of transformation. Some Native Americans—particularly the Blackfoot—believe that the butterfly brings dreams. If a Blackfoot Indian paints a butterfly onto the wall of a tribal lodge, it is an indicator that any other patterns painted or drawn there were not simply the work of a man alone, but were inspired by the Great Spirit, for whom the painter acted merely as a conduit.

CAMEL

The camel has a disdainful expression that some might see as a sign of a bad temper. Despite its truculent demeanor and stubborn reputation, the camel is invaluable to people, the only creature that can carry them across a desert. A symbol of sobriety and temperance and commonly known as "the ship of the desert," the camel can survive for long periods without drinking and has been used by people for thousands of years to help them travel to otherwise inaccessible places.

Since the camel protects people on perilous journeys across parched land, the allusion of it as a guardian is implied in the Persian holy scriptures. In the Avesta, winged camels watch over the earthly paradise.

St. John the Baptist, among other ascetics, chose another aspect of the camel as inspiration for his unworldly lifestyle. The creature's austerity meant that the coarse material made from its hair provided a suitable cloth for robes.

CAT

Even the most common household moggie has a mystique about it and the potential for the supernatural powers that people have ascribed to cats for thousands of years.

Typically, in Western civilizations, the cat (particularly if it is black) belongs to the witch; it is her familiar, her companion, and her alter ego. As such, the cat shares magical secrets and arcane knowledge which, of course, she cannot explain to mere mortals, since they don't speak her language. There is an unspoken communication between the witch and her grimalkin that transcends any language used by other creatures.

The ancient Egyptians regarded the cat so highly that they revered it as a deity. Bast was the cat goddess, and mortal cats whose fur was of three different colors, or who had eyes of different shades, were honored in particular for their Bast-like appearance; it is not just the black cat that holds power. Egyptian priests believed that cats carried the magnetic forces of nature and so close proximity to the creatures enabled them to access these powers. If a cat died a natural death in the home, the Egyptians would shave their eyebrows as a sign of mourning.

However, the cat does not have such an honorable reputation everywhere, for example in the Buddhist tradition. Because it was absent at the physical death and spiritual liberation of the Buddha, it is viewed with suspicion as a base, earthly creature, lacking respect. The only other creature that was not there was the serpent. The link between the cat and the serpent comes in the Kabbalah, too, and also in Christianity; in pictures where the cat appears at the feet of Christ it carries the same negative imagery as the snake.

Although black cats are the archetypal good-luck symbol in the West, in Islam the opposite is true. Cats are regarded favorably unless they are black, in which case they are viewed with great suspicion since djinn can transform themselves into black cats. In the Western tradition of cat lore, the animal has nine lives, whereas its Eastern cousin has to manage with only seven.

CICADA

The first literary mention of the cicada is in the *Iliad*, reputedly written in the seventh or eighth century BC, where Homer calls them "sage chiefs exempt from war." This is likely to refer to the peaceful and melodious sound that they make.

The sound of cicadas chirruping in the warm evening air is very beautiful, and it is not surprising that the insect has musical links, some of which explain the provenance of the cicada. There is an Italian myth that the cicada was created by the gods after the death of a mortal woman who was an exceptional singer, since when she died the entire world seemed empty and bereft without her music.

Like other winged creatures, cicadas represent disembodied souls, and are thus a symbol of immortality. In China it represents the spirit as it disengages itself from the body at the moment of death, and so a carving of the insect was placed on the mouth of the dying person to hasten the process. For the same reason the cicada is depicted on funerary items. However, because the insect seems to respond to the calls of the farmers in the paddy fields, it is a fortunate omen, an emblem of wishes and dreams that come true.

COUGAR

See Jaguar.

COW

Because of its milk that is a staple food for many human beings, the cow is arguably one of the most useful animals in the world. It was one of the first animals domesticated by humans, and its symbolic importance is rich. It is emblematic of fertility, abundance, wealth, the universal mother, and of rebirth. The cow is also a gentle and compliant creature.

It is not surprising that the cow is universally thought of as a mother figure. In Egypt the cow was personified as Ahet, the mother of the sun itself. To make themselves fertile, Egyptian women wore amulets of the goddess Hathor, with the head of a cow, in her guise as Creatrix. In Europe, too, the cow was the mother-ancestor of all living things, called Audumla, the milch-cow. In Greek myth, one of the names for the Great Cow was Europa, which means "full moon." The stars were said to be the children of Europa.

Curiously, the cow was also considered a psychopomp, a creature able to conduct the souls of the dead to the underworld. The psychopomp aspect of the cow is still celebrated in the Nepali festival called the Gai Jatra, or cow festival. In a boisterous celebration, every family that has lost a member during the course of the year has to take part in a procession, leading a cow, or, if no animal is available, then a child dressed in a cow costume is considered to be a fair substitute. The cow is believed to guide the soul on its final journey, including a voyage through the Milky Way, the constellations of stars said to be the milk splashed by the Great Cow that was the mother of the universe.

The cow as a sacred animal is a fundamental part of Hindu iconography. In India the cow is so revered, and treated so gently, that it often causes a traffic hazard as it ambles along busy city roads. There are several reasons for the sacred status given to the creature. Not only does the Hindu faith have respect for all animals (vegetarianism is a tenet of the faith), but the god Krishna was a cowherd for a time, and one of his names is Bala Gopala, "the child who protects the cows." Hindu deities rule over each and every part of the cow. During times of famine, the cow is far more useful as a creature that can produce limitless amounts of milk, than as a dead beast that would provide meat for a limited period only.

COYOTE

The coyote shares many of the characteristics of the fox; it is the trickster god, the miracle-worker, the shape-shifter, and as such plays an important part in Native American belief. Because coyotes can be heard howling at night, they are often associated with the moon. The coyote is one of the sacred animals that can open the door to the other world and it acts as a messenger between this world and the next. The coyote is sometimes held responsible for all the evils of the world, and in the countries where it makes its home it is generally a symbol of bad luck.

CRAB

When Isis tried to reconstruct the body of her murdered husband Osiris, there was one part missing. The Nile crab, named the Oxyrhynchid, had devoured his penis. So in Egypt the crab was a cursed creature. Elsewhere, the crab is closely associated with the moon; their growth is affected by the lunar cycles and it is possible that their appearance at the edge of the sea as the tides turned would have promulgated the link.

The crab appears as the zodiacal sign of Cancer, looming over the horizon at the time of the summer solstice and another reminder of the turning of the tides of the seasons as the sun starts its descending path.

CRICKET

See Cicada.

DOG

One of the traditional pet names for the dog, Fido, comes from the same Latin root as the word "fidelity," and the trust and faith that a dog and its owner invest in one another is a defining feature of their relationship. For thousands of years humans and dogs have been close companions, living together, working together, and forming a close bond of mutual understanding. Every society has its dog mythology, its deities, and its symbols. The dog is often the companion of a god, too, in addition to being a psychopomp, guiding the souls of the dead to the next world. On a more earthly level the animal can be a guide dog or a guard dog, directing and protecting, one of the greatest allies known to humankind; man's best friend, indeed.

The dog's keen sense of smell takes on almost supernatural connotations, a skill denied humans and something that cannot be seen or detected by us. This is part of the reason why the dog acts as mediator between the seen and unseen worlds, seemingly gifted the powers of second sight and psychic abilities. The Egyptians were very keen that their corpses would smell as sweet as possible so as not to offend the sensitive nose of the jackal-headed god Anubis, who shepherded these souls through to their next dwelling place.

While some witches have cats as familiars, others have their dogs, in honor of the goddesses of death and their hounds. Hecate, the goddess of the underworld and the queen of witches, had her dogs; like the devil, she haunted crossroads, her pack of hounds at her feet. Latterly Sirius Black, Harry Potter's shape-shifting godfather, keeps a close eye on his charge by changing into a great black dog. Sirius, of course, is named after the Dog Star.

It is a telling sign among humans that often the animals with the greatest cultural and symbolic significance are the ones that it is considered wrong to eat. The majority of the world sees the eating of dog flesh as a great taboo.

Dolphin

The dolphin has become ubiquitous as a symbol of the so-called New Age, due in part to its benevolently smiling appearance, its intelligence, its ability to communicate verbally with others of its kind, and the fact that it's a mammal that is comfortable in an environment normally reserved for fishes.

The name comes from the Greek *delphinos*, meaning "womb." The name of the Delphic Oracle where the priestesses gave their prophecies holds the same root; the temple was dedicated to Apollo, who arrived at Delphi in the shape of a dolphin.

For thousands of years the dolphin has been considered a helpful friend to humankind. It also acts as a psychopomp or guide to the other world. This is a fitting role for the dolphin given its ability to exist in a dimension alien to humans and because it has been seen to save those who might otherwise have drowned. The dolphin is symbolic of metamorphosis. There is a Greek legend about some pirates who, after capturing Dionysus and tying him up, fell overboard and turned into dolphins.

In its role as the saver of souls, the dolphin is compared to Christ and also to the Roman sun god Mithras, whose worship was superseded by that of the new god of Christianity.

Donkey

To call someone a "silly ass" is a derogatory term which implies that the ass is unintelligent; it is fair to say that the donkey does have a reputation of being obstinately stupid and, fair or not, this overarching quality forms a significant part of its symbolic meaning. Stupidity is a dangerous characteristic and this may well be why the donkey's reputation is that of a dangerous, almost demonic creature.

The ass is also a symbol of lewdness, carnality, and the lower sexual urges. There is a Greek myth in which Apollo turns the ears of King Midas into those of an ass because he eschewed the formal temple music in favor of Pan's pipes, inferring that the king would rather enjoy sensual pleasures than take a more enlightened delight in the harmony of the spirit and the higher mind. The donkey has long been seen as the poor man's horse and so it symbolizes poverty and humility; Christ rode on the back of an ass when he entered Jerusalem, and his parents Mary and Joseph traveled in the same way.

FISH

FOX

The fish lives in the depths that are synonymous with the underworld, and it has access to secret places that are forbidden to humankind. Water is closely linked to the womb, and the idea of birth and rebirth, and so the fish takes on this meaning too. Because it quite literally has access to hidden depths, the fish is party to secret and sacred information—the Vedas, which are said to contain all arcane knowledge, were delivered by a fish acting as the avatar of Vishnu. Similarly for the Celts, the salmon was a fish associated with wisdom and hidden knowledge. Christ chose from fishermen for his disciples, and early Christians, who had to keep their religion a secret, identified one another by a piscine symbol called the Ichthys.

Fish can lay vast numbers of eggs and therefore are symbolic of fertility and life. In the East, a pair of fish is used as a lucky charm in wedding ceremonies. There is an astrological sign that features two fish swimming in opposite directions—Pisces—and in Buddhism, a pair of golden fish is one of the Eight Auspicious Symbols.

Wiliness, slyness and cunning, craftiness, trickery and guile, and yet wisdom too: these are all the qualities that are generally accepted throughout the world as belonging to the fox. An intelligent animal, Reynard, the famous fox that appears in fairy tales, has human characteristics and often converses with men and women in their own language.

The first recorded instance of hunting the fox with hounds is from the sixteenth century, but the tradition is supposed to be much older. Although the animal was hunted for its beautiful pelt, the actual chase often turned into an escapade that resulted in a slaughter so bloody that the fur itself was rendered completely useless. The reason for the persecution of this creature, beyond mere straightforward culling, remains a mystery, although it may stem from early Christian belief that made the fox synonymous with that most cunning of tricksters, the devil.

Because foxes live in holes and tunnels in the ground, they are attached to the earth element and accordingly are the totem animals of several earth deities. The fox is also the symbol of the seducer or, most dangerously, the seductress; the "foxy lady" is aptly described.

The fox is the totem animal of Dionysus, whose seductively foxy priestesses wore fox skins.

FROG

In fairy tales, all it takes for an ugly frog to transform into a handsome prince is a single kiss from a beautiful princess. In this story, the frog is a symbol of transformation. The frog is a transformational creature in real life, too, and because the life cycle of this amphibious creature is carried out in so visible a manner it is a reminder of resurrection and the cycle of life, of birth, death, and rebirth. Egyptian mummies were wrapped with amulets depicting the image of the frog as a charm to help the person's soul to be reborn.

The frog's links with water are obvious, and it often appears on rain charms. In ancient China, the frog's image appeared on the drums that were played to summon thunder, the herald of much-needed rain. In Egypt, the frog symbolized fertility (because of its enthusiastic mating habits and abundant spawn) and so they were sacred to Hekit, the midwife of the gods.

"Frog" has become the English-speakers' nickname for the French, who notoriously eat frogs' legs as a delicacy. Indeed, before the French ruling classes adopted the fleur de lys as their emblem, the frog was France's national symbol.

GOAT

Horny in all senses of the word, the goat is arguably most infamous as a symbol of lust and procreation, a reputation gained in no small part from the influence of the so-called Goat of Mendes (sometimes called Baphomet) in ancient Egypt. This powerful deity was worshipped in a way that involved slaves copulating with goats in a ritual intended to honor the procreative power of nature. This Egyptian god was identified by the Greeks as Pan, the god of nature, who sometimes wore goatskins. Later, for Christians who were keen to demonize any trace of the old pagan religions, the goat became the personification of the devil.

Romans, too, saw the goat as a symbol of lasciviousness and fertility. Barren women were advised to have sexual congress with goats or, alternatively, to have their backs whipped with the skin of a sacrificed goat, cut into strips. This ritual was believed to purify the women and may even have inspired the name of the festival during which it was performed—"Lupercalia"—possibly from *luere per caprum*, meaning "to purify by means of the goat."

Finally, what of the scapegoat? The first mention of it occurs in the Old Testament. A ritual involved two goats. One was set free and the other sacrificed. The liberated goat, however, was laden with the sins of the people and sent out into the desert to perish, its death often hastened by its being pushed over a cliff; the name of this cliff, Azazel—"the goat that departs"—was also the name of a demon. The concept of the scapegoat exists today as a term for someone who takes on the blame for the wrongdoings of others.

HARE

Because the hare is a nocturnal creature, it carries all the symbolism of the moon; light in the darkness, concealed wisdom, arcane information, intuition, and the goddess. The moon is symbolic of rebirth and resurrection, because of its visible phases, and the hare shares these qualities, too. Significantly, in some parts of the world the shape of the hare is visible in the face of the moon, further reinforcing the mystical connection between the two.

The hare is renowned for its fertility, and it is in this guise that it is simplified as the Easter bunny. The springtime goddess, Eostre, governed the cycles of fertility and so her symbol was the egg; hence the chocolate eggs given to children at Easter, a remnant of a pagan tradition that has never been satisfactorily explained away by its Christian adoptees.

Some Native American tribes that have adopted Christianity link the hare with Jesus Christ, since the previous savior of these people was a great spirit hare called Menebuch who had Christ-like qualities. Menebuch came down from the heavens to educate humankind in all his ways, and to protect them from monsters and evil spirits.

Three hares joined at the ears and running in a circle in the form of a triskele is a mysterious ancient symbol that seems to have transcended cultural boundaries and geographical borders. At the center of the circle, the ears of the hares form an equilateral triangle. This motif appears in Buddhist caves 2,500 years old; in Muslim artwork and designs; in synagogues and in several places of Christian worship throughout Europe. There is no definitive interpretation of the symbol although it may represent the attributes of the Triple Goddess, an age-old concept that transcends religious dogma.

HORSE

For millennia the horse has enjoyed a spiritual, symbolic, and mythical significance that arguably surpasses that of any other living creature. Accordingly, its symbolic significance is massive and varied. That the horse has long enjoyed a vital link with humankind as a hunting companion, a beast of burden, as a means of travel, and as an agricultural asset is demonstrated by its image being seen in Paleolithic cave drawings, such as at Lascaux, dating back approximately 30,000 years.

The horse belongs to the sun and the element of fire. Horses proudly draw the chariot of the sun god. At the same time, the horse also belongs to the moon and the element of water, since it carries on its back the god of the oceans, too. It was believed that where a horse stamped, a spring appeared, and so the animal becomes a life-giver. In Greece there is a sacred well, called Hippocrene (the Horse's Well), which is shaped like a horse-shoe and is dedicated to the Muses. Pegasus, the winged horse, was held to have created this particular sacred well.

The horse symbolizes life and death, darkness and light, good and evil, depending on the context in which it is seen. As well as being a bringer of life, it is also a psycho-pomp, a creature that guides dead souls on the journey to the next life. As well as having spiritual significance, like the dog with which it shares many characteristics, the horse is valuable in purely practical terms, too. It represents power and wealth, since having a horse—or many horses—confers superiority on the owner, not only in terms of monetary value but in the distances he is able to cover and the speeds at which he can travel. This leads to another aspect of the horse—it is a symbol of freedom. Horses were used by warriors and so are linked with Mars, the god of war, and with all the associated male attributes: virility, sexuality, and strength. Wotan/Odin's horse, Sleipnir, had supernatural powers, possessing eight legs as well as being able to gallop over water as though it were solid land. Horse goddesses include Epona, the mother-goddess of the ancient Britons, and Rhiannon. The sacred status of horses meant that the sacrifice of such a creature was a rare and profound event, and even today, there is repugnance among many people at the thought of eating horseflesh; not eating an animal is a sure sign that it is regarded as sacred.

HYENA

A carrion eater that exists purely on the earthly plane, the hyena carries none of the symbolism of the raven, which also eats waste, but is considered divine because it operates in the element of air. It is impossible for the hyena to transcend either the coarseness of its surroundings or the degrading acts it has to commit in order to survive.

Despite all this, the hyena is considered to have magical powers, and is considered something of a magician. Allegedly, it could hypnotize any animal by walking

around it three times, it could imitate the human voice so accurately that it could cause people to leave their homes, and it was believed to have a jewel in its eye that enabled it to see into the future.

JAGUAR/PANTHER

To Native Americans, the name of the jaguar is synonymous with a creature that "kills with one blow," while the word "panther" comes from the Greek *panthera*, meaning "all beast," showing just how important our ancestors considered this animal to be.

The Mayans believed that, since the dawn of time, four jaguars guarded the entrance to their valuable corn fields. Since these people followed a lunar calendar, the jaguar, a nocturnal creature, connected to their goddess of the moon, who is sometimes depicted with the claws of this great cat. Its association with the night and therefore occult knowledge gave the jaguar the gift of second sight and prophecy, which explains why it sometimes appears depicted with four eyes, two for normal sight and two for supernatural vision. The jaguar was one of the major deities of the Mayans, appearing on their calendars, and venerated in the form of the jaguar priests who officiated at only the most important and sacred rites and rituals. The Incas, too, revered this big cat and built temples in its honor.

While the jaws of the jaguar were emblematic of the gates of heaven, it was also considered to be the lord of the underworld, no doubt because of its ability to kill swiftly and surely, and was therefore one of the many creatures with the sacred responsibility of guiding souls to the world beyond. In the same way that the lion and the eagle are juxtaposed in many cultures, the jaguar was similarly aligned with this bird, which was called the "jaguar of the skies." Gods and kings wore the skins and feathers of sacred animals as status symbols, and the Aztec emperor sat on a throne of eagle feathers and jaguar skin. The animal carries the same powers of creation and destruction as the fire that, legend says, it brought to humankind.

LAMB

It might seem odd that the adult version of the lamb—the sheep—carries quite negative symbolism, as a creature that blindly runs with the flock, unable to think as an individual.

However, the lamb is a much more positive symbol. It stands for innocence and purity, the spiritual, the compliant, and gentleness. Further, the lamb is a symbol of spring, of new hope, and of triumph over adversity. The first lamb of the season, as the most potent personification of these qualities, was usually sacrificed to the gods.

The sacrificial nature of the lamb carries resonance through the Christian, Jewish, and Muslim faiths. Hence, the symbolism of Christ as the Lamb of God, sacrificed for all mankind but resurrected by a beneficent God. There is a specific symbol, the Paschal Lamb, which perfectly embodies this notion; the lamb appears with a halo and a banner, symbolizing both sanctity and victory.

The lamb is also a symbol of peace, and where it appears with the dove, this aspect is compounded. Sometimes the lamb and the lion appear together, a universal symbol of concord and harmony and the balancing of opposites.

LION

One of the most powerful animals and appropriately laden with rich symbolic meaning, the lion is synonymous with the sun, and as such is best personified as Leo, the zodiac sign that has the great golden star as its ruler. The lion even looks like the sun, with its tawny coat and shaggy golden mane.

The lion is the totem animal of kings and emperors, of Apollo, of Mithras, of Christ, of Krishna, of the Buddha. Its counterpart, the eagle, is called the Lion of the Skies.

Christ is known as the Lion of Judah, and Mohammed's son-in-law, Ali, who acted as mediator between the Prophet and the people, was called the Lion of Allah. Krishna is known as the "Lion among Wild Creatures" and the Buddha is the "Lion of the Shakyas."

The lion, with its shaggy halo of a mane, might seem to be the ultimate personification of male energy. However, there are female deities who share the attributes of the lion, and the lioness is a ferociously protective mother. Hathor, the Egyptian goddess, has the head of a lion when she appears in the aspect of destroyer. Cybele, the Phrygian earth mother, rides in a chariot pulled by lions, and the lion, as well as the bee, was sacred to her.

There is a negative side, however, to the great power of the lion. It is no accident that the collective noun for a group of lions

is a "pride," and the sin of pride is said to be the negative aspect of the zodiac sign of Leo. Further, power can lead to corruption unless there is an awareness of moral and ethical values. The male lion can also be a symbol of laziness, and it is a well-known fact that the lioness is the one who does the majority of the hunting and cub-care.

MONKEY

Many animals simply symbolize aspects of their own personality. The monkey is mischievous and agile, and has a wily intelligence. It is also a good mimic, although it is not always certain that the animal understands precisely what it is imitating; in this sense the monkey is a symbol of randomness. A recurrent theme of the monkey is as an emblem of chaotic, unguided, unconscious action.

In the Ramayana, it is a monkey called Hanuman who helps Vishnu rescue his bride from a demon, and is deified as a reward. The monkey is a sexually active, fertile creature, and in India women are known to strip off their clothes and hug the effigy of Hanuman in the belief that this will help them to conceive.

Monkeys also have a propensity

for anger, and the Egyptians, recognizing this, used the hieroglyphic symbol of the monkey to mean "angry."

In the Mayan calendar, too, the monkey held prominence, regarded as hard working, a gifted orator, and talented at artistic pursuits in general. To call someone a monkey was considered to be a great compliment. The monkey appears in the Chinese zodiac, too, and people born under its sign are said to be intelligent, agile, decisive, and entertaining.

MOOSE

A sacred animal for Native Americans, the moose is closely linked with the raven, considered a gift from this godlike bird. The animal is symbolic of male energy in that it is a good and persistent hunter; conversely it is also a female symbol, partly because of its unpredictable nature.

The moose is often happy standing neck-high in water, where it grazes on aquatic plants such as water lilies, and this link with water and the earth further underlines its feminine traits. Another characteristic of the moose is its solitary nature. It does not travel in herds,

preferring to live singly. The calf is weaned at six months and its mother drives it away prior to the birth of a new baby. Therefore, the moose is symbolic of detachment and independence.

MOTH

A nocturnal creature, the moth is considered the butterfly of the night although it carries rather more sinister symbolism than its frivolous sister.

One of the archetypal images of the moth is of it dancing around a flame. This nocturnal creature craves light so much that it will immolate itself in pursuit of it. There is a dichotomy about this image. On the one hand, it symbolizes the sublimation of the ego as death makes the soul a part of the collective unconscious. On the other, it is an emblem of stupidity, vanity, and hubris.

Like the butterfly, the moth symbolizes the disembodied soul. However, the moth is also seen as a destructive force since, unlike the butterfly, it can do damage and is sometimes seen as a pest. Although the clothes-eating moth is something of a rarity, moths in general have suffered a bad reputation.

MOUSE

PIG

The mouse, such a small, seemingly insignificant creature, is one of the forms taken by the great god Apollo. There is a dichotomy with this symbolism, representing the idea of the god in both his aspects—as destroyer and as protector. Apollo, like the mouse, destroys by spreading plague, whereas in his guise as the harvest god it falls to Apollo to save the crop from the attentions of the little creature.

In Europe, the mouse was symbolic of the soul leaving the body, an idea shared by other tiny creatures. It was believed that the soul/mouse escaped through the mouth as the dying person breathed their last breath. This supposition was so well founded that it even has witness reports.

The mouse also appears with the great elephant-headed Indian god Ganesh. Curiously, the huge Ganesh is described as "riding" this tiny animal. The physical improbability of such an arrangement does not matter, however, since this is a symbol of Ganesh's humility.

Calling someone a pig is a pejorative term, implying that the person is dirty, greedy, and generally uncouth.

The pig is regarded as ignorant, gluttonous, and selfish, an animal that wallows in its own filth (notwithstanding the fact that the animal is actually extremely clean and scrupulous), one of the animals considered "unclean" by both Hebrews and Muslims and which is forbidden as food to followers of these faiths. To throw "pearls before swine" is to offer something to someone who is unable to appreciate it.

In Tibetan Buddhism, the pig represents worldly desire in all its forms—lust, material possessions, food. It sits at the center of the Wheel of Dharma as a symbol of things that tie us to the cycle of materialism, holding us back from spiritual enlightenment.

However, there's another side to the coin. All animals that were considered holy or sacred were also forbidden to be eaten, and the pig, too, despite its negative connotations, held sacred status, linked to the mother goddess in lots of different faith systems. The sow is a prolific mother, giving birth to many piglets. The fecundity of this creature means that she is associated with Demeter/Ceres, the earth goddess and mother of the harvest. To Hindus, as Varahi, she is the boar-faced goddess who protects holy buildings. Durga, also, takes on the form of the pig as Vajrabarahi. The Egyptian goddess of the night, Nut, was depicted on amulets as a sow being suckled by her piglets. The Celtic mother goddess, Ceridwen, was called the Old White Sow, and both the deity and the pig were associated with the moon. Only the gods were considered worthy to eat the meat of the pig.

In China, the pig is one of the auspicious animal signs of the Chinese zodiac, where it symbolizes hard work, love of family, and a caring nature. However, it seems that pigs might fly before they manage to shake off some of their more unfortunate associations.

PORPOISE

See Dolphin.

*   *   *

RABBIT

Incredibly fecund, the rabbit is a symbol not only of fertility, but also of sexuality and lust, personified by the "bunny girl." "Bun" is an old English word and refers to the distinctive circular shape of the animal's tail. Although the rabbit didn't make its appearance in the British Isles until the twelfth century, its prolific breeding habits meant that it was soon prevalent everywhere and it adopted a little of the same symbolic meaning as the hare, minus the mystery accorded the hare as the more elusive nocturnal creature.

Because of its fecundity and gregarious nature, the rabbit is a symbol of love and peace for some Native Americans. There is a courtship ritual called the Rabbit Dance.

The rabbit's foot is still seen by some as a particularly potent good-luck charm. While having its foot severed is presumably not very lucky for the rabbit itself, as a totem object the foot is believed to bless its owner with the same fertility and swift-footedness as the animal. The efficacy of the piece of rabbit worn as a charm did not escape the Lakota warriors, who believed that an armband of its skin would enable them to run as fast as the rabbit itself.

Rat

For some superstitious people in Britain, especially those that have links to the sea, it is taboo to call the rat by its name, so it's called the "longtail" instead. This is because rats traditionally leave a sinking ship, and this ancient idea runs so deep that rats are still viewed as harbingers of doom. This points toward the power of the rat, since to mention a name is to call on the power of its owner.

In the West, much of the symbolism of the rat carries negative connotations. To call someone a "rat" means that they are immoral, despicable, dishonest, and greedy. Rats are considered unclean, scavenging animals, associated with bubonic plague and other diseases.

However, the rat is also a resilient creature and its intelligence and ability to survive almost anything is universally acknowledged. Even these seemingly positive traits are given a negative twist, however, when it is described as "cunning." The intelligence of the creature is seen to be purely self-serving and somehow immoral.

In the Hindu belief system, in contrast, the rat is the creature of foresight and prudence. In addition, in China the rat is one of the rulers of the years of the zodiac, where it symbolizes imagination, creativity, adaptability, and ambition.

Salmon

One of the most sacred creatures of the Celts, the salmon is a symbol of wisdom and esoteric knowledge. In fact, in this culture, the salmon is arguably the epitome of the fish symbol in general. To eat the flesh of the salmon was once akin to a shamanistic act, a means of attaining its wisdom as well as its reputed powers of second sight. Celtic folklore teems with anecdotes about the powers conferred by this sacred fish, which is generally depicted living in holy wells and itself eating magical food, such as hazelnuts and rowanberries.

The salmon is synonymous with the idea of rebirth and of reincarnation since it traditionally returns to its breeding ground, leaping upwards against the current of the river to do so.

Despite the coming of Christianity, the salmon kept its prominent place as a sacred symbol; the use of the fish as an emblem of Christ no doubt helped.

SCARAB

The scarab is one of the most important symbols in ancient Egyptian belief, but why? What relevance, if any, does it have today? Modern Egyptians still believe that dried and powdered scarabs will help them to become fertile. However, it is as the sacred animal belonging to the god of the rising sun, Khepera, that the scarab is important.

The ancient Egyptians observed that the scarab beetle rolled its own ball of dung along the ground in the same way that the Khepera rolled the Sun across the sky. They also believed that the scarab hatched itself from this dung ball, symbolizing death and rebirth. As a god, the scarab was depicted with the wings, legs, and tail of a falcon.

The scarab was placed on top of the heart when a corpse was mummified. This was so that the heart, symbolizing the conscience, would not be able to speak because the scarab was in the way. Therefore, the soul could say nothing that might otherwise hinder its access to the afterlife. Such was the power of the scarab that its image appears everywhere in ancient Egyptian art and artifacts, on seals and amulets and on pieces of jewelry.

The prominence of the scarab for the Egyptians, however, seems to be a very recent trend when we realize that the beetle has been an important symbol since the Paleolithic period, between 10,000 and 20,000 years ago.

SCORPION

Because the scorpion is so dangerous—it has enough venom to kill a person—in the countries where it lives its name is often not mentioned in case the scorpion is somehow "invoked." Instead it is referred to euphemistically. Whenever this happens we know that an animal is particularly potent.

The scorpion is constantly prepared to attack, the sting in its tail always unsheathed. As such, the insect is the embodiment of brute aggression. This aggression is further promulgated by the fact that the female scorpion will only ever give birth once; her progeny have the grisly habit of destroying their mother by digging their way out of her belly.

The scorpion was a hieroglyph in ancient Egypt and was sacred to the goddess Selket, who had either the body of a scorpion and the head of a woman, or (more usually) the body of a woman with a scorpion sitting on her head. The power of this goddess resided in her ability to wield the power of the scorpion against her enemies; however, she could also use this power as protection from scorpions, too. Selket also had power over snakes and other poisonous reptiles, protecting pregnant women in particular.

SERPENT

Lying on its belly close to the earth, limbless, hairless, and cold-blooded, the snake represents the opposite end of the scale to the loftier spiritual heights to which humans aspire. The snake, or serpent, is arguably one of the most prominent animal symbols, and carries with it diverse and contradictory meanings.

Some of those contradictory messages include the serpent as a

symbol of evil but also of healing powers; of cunning and also of wisdom; as a life-form that is so base that it must be capable of reaching the greatest of spiritual heights. The serpent is considered, unsurprisingly, to be a phallic symbol, yet is also one of the oldest emblems of female power, seen, for example, held in the hands of the priestesses on Knossos as a symbol of their wisdom and power. This image brings to mind the latter-day snake handlers of certain charismatic churches in the United States, who believe that so long as they have faith then the snake will not bite them.

The dichotomy of the serpent symbol is embodied in the story of Adam and Eve. Demonized as an evil influence (the devil himself) that persuades Eve to offer the forbidden fruit of knowledge to Adam, this fruit nevertheless contains knowledge and in eating it, the pair open their eyes to a wider world. As a phallic symbol, the snake also makes Adam and Eve aware of their own sexuality, and the first thing they do after this realization is to cover their genitalia with fig leaves. The serpent is a symbol of regeneration, reincarnation, and of healing powers.

Evidence of the godlike status of the snake to the Native Americans, too, is evident in structures such as the 4,000-year-old Serpent Mound in Ohio. To Native Americans the snake was a dangerous creature, which deserved respect at the same time as suspicion. In fact, such was the reputation of the snake for telling lies and weaving deceit that the forked tongue of the creature was adopted as a description fitted to untrustworthy people, namely, the white man.

SNAIL

Since the snail carries its "house" with it, it is a symbol of self-sufficiency. The spiral shape of the snail's shell has significant meaning, since the spiral itself is a sacred shape, the golden mean. The Mayans took the snail shell as their inspiration to create a glyph for the concept of zero; thus, a humble little creature is immortalized in the symbolic rendering of a dis-covery that, quite literally, changed the world.

SPIDER

The motif of the spider as creator/creatrix is repeated all over the world. In many creation myths, it is the spider that weaves the fabric of the universe. However, the seeming fragility of the cobweb led to suppositions that what the spider made was, in fact, no more than the illusory veil of "reality" that the Vedic scriptures call Maya. The idea of spinning and weaving is also an attribute of the Fates, in both Greek mythology and in the Qu'ran.

Native Americans called the spider the "Thinking Woman," who has the power to both make the world and destroy it if it is not to her satisfaction. Because of its ability to move in different dimensions, the spider was used as a means of divination. The African bird-eating spider is particularly skilled in this art, apparently, and symbols are placed at the entrance to its home in such a way that the spider will disturb them as it enters and exits. These disturbances are interpreted as auguries.

Stag

The horns of the stag lend it a special significance as a magical and sacred animal, and as a masculine symbol; most horned animals carry this association, and because of these antlers, the stag is emblematic of fertility and male sexuality. Like the goat, it gives rise to the word "horny," meaning sexually charged. Not only are amulets representing the phallus often carved from stags' horns, but also in some branches of Chinese medicine, ground-up horn is used as an aphrodisiac. These same horns, because of their shape and the fact that they regularly drop off and then regrow, are also emblematic of the World Tree, thereby making the animal itself synonymous with the idea of rebirth, and therefore of the sun. It is no accident that the Hopi Indians cut their image of the sun god from a piece of deerskin.

The pre-Christian pagan god Pan has the cloven hooves and horned headdress of the stag. Wishing to render the old gods fearsome to their former worshippers in the hopes that they would turn to the One God of the new religion, the early Christians turned Pan into the devil, giving him the same characteristics, borrowed from the stag. The Celtic horned shaman Cernunnos bears a remarkable resemblance to Pan, too. Cernunnos was considered the ruler of the beasts and a god of plenty. Wherever a white stag appears in myths and folk tales and in dreams, it signifies the world of spirit. In the Arthurian legends, the appearance of this ethereal creature sends the knights off on spiritual quests. The stag is believed to have healing powers, too, and is sometimes depicted with an arrow piercing his side and herbs in his mouth. The stag has the reputation of knowing the uses of all the medicinal plants and herbs in the forest, so presumably he eats these plants in order to fix his wound.

Tiger

The very word "tiger" conjures up notions of fierceness, swiftness, and also great beauty. To fight like a tiger is to fight with great savagery.

In China, the tiger, rather than the lion, is the king of the beasts. Like the lion, it symbolizes nobility, power, ferocity, and authority. The tiger is also somehow seen as an angry animal; this is partly

explained by the legend of the first tiger, said to have been a young boy, whipped many times by his teacher—hence the stripes—who was pushed too far, escaped into the forest in a furious rage and transformed into the animal.

For any warrior, to eat tiger meat or to wear the skin of the tiger is said to give dominion over the beast. A remnant of this belief is borne out by the image of the old buffer in his pith helmet standing on the head of the tiger-skin rug, demonstrating the power of his "superior" male ego in the slaying of the beast. Women were forbidden to eat tiger meat in case it made them wayward or difficult to control.

There are parallels between the wolf and the tiger, too, as a symbol of raw sexuality. Chinese myth has a story very similar to the West's Little Red Riding Hood, which features a tiger in the place of the wolf, and there are stories of a fearsome creature called a were-tiger, a nocturnal monster that is driven to terrible acts by the appearance of the full moon. The tiger is believed to be a shape-shifter, and certain human beings have the power to transform themselves into the beast. The savage power of the tiger also makes it a symbol of protection; it would be a very great asset to have this animal on your side, especially since they are supposed to be able to consume evil spirits with no adverse effects. Because of this, effigies of tigers were placed on graves. The tiger is a very good mother and will defend her cub to the death. The dichotomy of the tiger symbolism—as a savage creature that also protects—is demonstrated perfectly by its place in Buddhist belief. Along with the monkey (symbolizing greed) and the deer (symbolizing love-sickness), the tiger, representing anger, is one of the Three Senseless Creatures of Chinese Buddhism.

TORTOISE

The tortoise may appear to be an innocuous and rather unresponsive slow-moving household pet, but to ancient humans it was a living

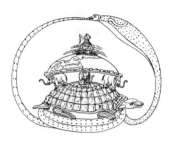

Confusa, the Confused Mass, the first stage in the transformation of matter to spirit.

TURTLE

See Tortoise.

collection of secret and sacred symbols, and as such, it was accorded the same kind of reverence as the greatest gods.

The four sturdy legs of the tortoise represent the four elements and the four directions. These legs support the flat underside of the creature, which represents the earth. The dome-shaped shell of the tortoise represents the vault of the heavens. Thus the tortoise carries the universe, a task shared by other sacred creatures such as the whale and the dragon. This is represented in the Hindu cosmogram or map of the universe, shown here.

The cosmos-supporting tortoise is linked in Hindu iconography to Vishnu, who is said to have emerged from the waters of creation carrying the earth on his back.

In Native American belief the World Tree grows out of the back of the tortoise.

In alchemy, the tortoise represents the Prima Materia or Massa

WHALE

The remarkable story of Jonah and the whale is really a story of initiation, a symbolic death, and rebirth. The whale in this story was originally referred to as a fish, as it was in many old stories. Jonah had been chosen by God as a prophet, but was quite understandably shy of telling the people of Nineveh that judgment would soon be upon them for their wicked ways, so he took to the sea to avoid this duty. When a violent storm arose, the sailors decided to throw Jonah into the sea in order to propitiate the gods. Instantly, the waters calmed, and there appeared a huge "fish" that swallowed Jonah. After three days and nights in the pitch-dark innards of this fish, Jonah decided that he had had enough, and that it would be easier to give the prophecy than spend any more time inside the whale. In a fortunate case of either serendipity or divine intervention, Jonah was regurgitated not far from where he needed to be.

Jonah is not the only character to have had the misfortune to spend time inside a whale. This particular form of initiation was the fate of several gods and mythic heroes, from Japan, Vietnam, and Polynesia through to Finland.

Jonah described the insides of the whales as *sheol*, meaning "the pit," so the gaping jaw of the whale is symbolic of the gates of hell. The stomach of the whale also becomes a symbolic womb that gives birth to Jonah. It is significant, too, that Christ spent the same amount of time inside the tomb before he, too, was reborn; therefore the legend of Jonah's whale was said to prophesy Christ's ordeal.

Whale hunting is a controversial subject. However, for the Inuit people who have been involved in this practice for thousands of years and so know the animal very well, the whale is the trickster. There is a myth that a beautiful woman, who occasionally entertains mariners, lives in a lavishly furnished apartment inside the belly of the whale, a story no doubt invented to comfort a drowning man.

WOLF

The wolf that disguises itself as the grandmother in the tale of Little Red Riding Hood shows the creature as a trickster, with malevolent intentions. However, the disguise isn't very good and the little girl recognizes the wolf by its easily identifiable features—huge teeth and massive eyes—and so makes good her escape. Here, the wolf is also a sexual predator, another emblem of the animal that has endured since ancient times; the "wolf whistle" is aptly named and the tendencies of the wolf itself are well known. Like the wolf in the fairy tale, its true nature is impossible to disguise for long, just like the proverbial "wolf in sheep's clothing."

The wolf also has a reputation of being a loner, hunting not in packs but singly. In Greece, it was associated with the gods Zeus and Apollo as a symbol of masculine power, energy, and sexuality. The Egyptians, too, worshipped the wolf, at the city of Lycopolis, which was even named for the creature. Here, the wolf also acted as a psychopomp, a creature that guided the souls of the dead into the afterlife. Anubis, the greatest of all the conductors of souls, had the head of a wolf or of a wild dog or jackal. The god of time, Chronos, has a wolf-like face, symbolizing the monster that devours human time.

It was a wolf that suckled Romulus and Remus, the legendary founders of Rome. Despite this maternal care, the word *lupa* meant "prostitute" as well as "she-wolf" and the Lupercal Temples were effectively brothels. Continuing with this theme, there's a saying in France that if a girl is a virgin she is said to *n'a jamais vu le loup*, i.e., to have never seen the wolf; the opposite is true for a girl who has lost her virginity.

The werewolf is arguably the most sinister aspect of this creature. Warlocks were believed to be able to transform into wolves in order to disguise themselves when they traveled to their unholy meetings, and the belief in a wolf/human hybrid is prevalent throughout much of the world.

Fantastical Animals

As though all the real animals in this world were not enough, we have invented a vast array of mythical animals, too, which fulfill a symbolic need not provided by the many wonders within the natural world.

Belief in imaginary creatures seems to last for a season, then fades away, to be replaced with the next "fashion." For example, it was once generally held that dragons really did exist; uncharted territory is marked on old maps with the legend "here be dragons." Winged, fire-breathing, serpent-like creatures seem to exist in a similar form all over the world although their names may vary. Fairies, too, were regularly spotted, and even photographed in the early part of the last century. Today, it seems that creatures from outer space—and infamous fantastic creatures like the yeti or the Big Cat or the Loch Ness Monster—fill the space that is somehow still not satisfied by all the world has to offer. These newer creatures, too, teasingly allow themselves to be seen but rarely in such a way that they give us incontrovertible evidence of their existence. And why should they? Ghosts and similar entities have never gone away, and if we believe the evidence of high street bookshops then it would seem that angels and cherubs hover above every corner.

Angel

The antiquity of angels is well established, their existence described long before the Old Testament was written, and certainly long before the coming of Christianity. The first creatures that resemble anything like the angels we know today are from the ancient Akkadian culture, dating back to 2350 BC. It is likely that the angel concept existed even earlier than this, though.

The history of angelic beings is difficult to pin down. The single most comprehensive and exhaustive writing on the subject is by a somewhat nebulous figure called Pseudo Dionysus the Aeropagite, who listed the groupings of angels that are still commonly accepted today, in a book written in the sixth century AD, called *The Celestial Hierarchy*. Both Pseudo Dionysus and the Bible agree that the multitude of angels is immense, this number being mentioned in the Bible as a mind-boggling "a thousand thousands (angels) ministered unto him, and ten thousand times ten thousand stood before him" (Daniel 7:10). The notion that each person has his own guardian angel is an ancient one. This is a comforting idea, especially for children. This is not, however, mentioned as such in the Bible, although it does claim that each one of the faithful is helped by an angel that will protect and guide him throughout his life. It appears that the angel archetype is such a potent symbol that they exist in our collective consciousness whether or not we believe in any kind of god.

CENTAUR

A horse/man hybrid, the centaur appears as the archer in the astrological sign of Sagittarius, and wherever he appears, he is a symbol of lust, the arrows signifying ejaculation as well as hunting prowess.

Centaurs are often depicted with sad faces, because they know that the brute force and lust that they represent needs to be balanced with spiritual power. Therefore, the centaur represents the constant struggle in human beings between spirit and matter, intuition and knowledge, conscious and unconscious.

DEMON

The idea of a creature that is the personification of evil forces is ancient. There are incantations designed to repel "demons" that date back as far as the first millennium BC although they are not referred to as such. Essentially, in a world that is comprised of opposing forces, there must be a balance of male/female, black/white, good/bad. It makes sense that we need there to be a shadow side to good forces.

Although the demon, as it is commonly accepted today, is seen to be a malicious and ungodly creature that is the epitome of evil, the word originally meant something rather different. The Greek "daemon" was a divine being with its own energies and powers; each person had such an aspect to their soul, which was connected to the Great Spirit and could be responsible for sudden flashes of inspiration or enlightenment; literally, their "genius." Places, too, had their "demons," represented, for example, in the spirits of the elements: the salamanders, sylphs, nymphs, and undines. Philip Pullman's *His Dark*

Materials trilogy uses the notion of this familiar spirit in a beautiful and memorable way.

Many of the pre-Christian deities of all nations had these creative, demon-like qualities. However, these ancient entities, if not absorbed and renamed as saints, were heavily discredited by the early Church and made into evil entities in the effort to replace the old pagan gods with the one patriarchal God of the Christian faith. To "demonize" something or someone is to "represent as a demon," i.e., to discredit or contaminate in some way.

Lilith, the first wife of Adam, is commonly described as an "arch demoness." Lilith already existed in a different form as the ancient goddess Astarte, who is connected to Venus/Aphrodite, but Lilith's refusal to adopt the missionary position, among other things, meant that she was cast out and replaced with the (seemingly) much more compliant Eve. Thereafter, Lilith was accused of all sorts of diabolic misdemeanors.

Psychologically speaking, the demon has come to symbolize the difficult part of the personality or psyche that a person has to come to terms with in order to achieve balance and peace of mind.

DOUBLE-HEADED EAGLE

This curious symbol is believed to have originated with the Hittites, a powerful culture from Asia Minor.

The double head of the eagle effectively doubles its strength and eagle-like qualities. It is also called the Eagle of Lagash. This was the ancient Sumerian city that used it first as their royal crest. The Turks then used the symbol. It represents omniscience, since it can look in two directions at once. As a symbol of absolute power, it appears on several national coats of arms including those of Imperial Austria and Russia. It is also used as a Masonic symbol.

DRAGON

Ancient maps, showing uncharted territory, are sometimes enscribed with the legend "Here Be Dragons." The word "dragon" comes from the Greek for "snake," a creature with whom it is associated, as well as sometimes being referred to as a "worm" from its Germanic name, *wurm*.

For an imaginary creature, the influence of the dragon is

a vision of a flaming dragon in the sky as a prophecy that Arthur would become king. This flaming red dragon later became the emblem of Wales. Over the border the Englishman George was given sainthood after he effectively killed a marauding dragon that was slowly but surely gobbling up all the young girls for miles around. Here, the dragon represents the devil, also personified as a dragon in the fight with the archangel Michael.

In the Chinese zodiac, the dragon is the fifth creature, and equates to Leo the lion.

FAIRY

The term "fairy" tends to be used as a catch-all to encompass all manner of "little people"—elves, pixies, banshees, and the like—all different aspects of a spirit of nature that is generally held to be invisible to human beings. It has been said that they represent the "paranormal powers of the spirit or the extraordinary capacity of the imagination," and as such can be said to symbolize an escapist aspect of the human mind that transcends the bounds of everyday normality as well as the laws of physics.

For generations, it seems that

far-reaching, existing in similar forms all over the world, an important archetypal emblem. The dragon can be symbolic of power, sovereignty, and spirituality, as well as of a variety of elements. The dragon can be an agent of good, to be encouraged, or an agent of evil, to be destroyed. Dragons have keen eyesight which often makes them guardians of treasure and keepers of secrets of some kind, a trait which gives them great wisdom as well as clairvoyant powers.

In both China and Japan the dragon symbolized royalty, and appeared on the garments of the emperor and the Mikado. The very word "dragon" was used instead of emperor: "the dragon's face" meant the face of the emperor, "the dragon's pace" his majestic walk.

In Britain, Uther Pendragon, father of King Arthur, was given

fairy-folk and human beings have rubbed along, side by side, sharing the same universe. It is possible that these creatures have their origins as the spirits of dead ancestors, which, prior to the coming of Christianity, were believed to take on a different form in order to guard and protect future generations. Features typical of the fairy are its supernatural powers, its ability to render itself invisible to human beings or to shape-shift, its spell-casting powers and its capability of flight. Fairies tend to appear as females but there are exceptions.

Fairies can be benign or malignant, and the natural world is crammed with plants, minerals, and the like which can either protect against them or which are their special domain or property. The hawthorn, for example, is a fairy tree and anyone cutting it down or taking parts of it would find it best to ask permission of the fairies first.

The word "fairy" shares roots with the word "fay," which in turn relates to the Fates of Greek myth, the personification of destiny. Morgan le Fay, also known as the Fata Morgana in the Arthurian tales, is a fairy, although very different from the tiny sort that little girls see flitting in and out of flowers, as are many of the most powerful fairy creatures throughout mythology. The Shakespearian queen of the fairies, Mab, represents the same kind of ambivalence as Morgan le Fay, with a propensity for malice that hints at a strong link between fairies and witches. Both fairies and witches often appear in groups of three, another link with the Fates.

The time of the fairies is said to be twilight, the transitional time between night and day. They can carry away the soul of a person who dies at this time and take it back to fairyland. The fairy could be said to symbolize the state of mind between childhood and adulthood, the conscious and the unconscious.

FATHER CHRISTMAS

Santa Claus, Old St. Nick, St. Nicolas, Sinterklaas, Papa Noel, Kris Kringle: whatever we choose to call him, for children, the concept of Father Christmas all boils down to the same idea; that of a magical, generous character who comes bearings gifts at Christmastime. The idea that good children will be rewarded with gifts while bad children will receive nothing has more than a semblance of the idea of rewards in heaven for the virtuous and is arguably one of the consequences of the Christianization of a much earlier, pagan figure.

These days, the popular image of Father Christmas is of a bearded, jovial old gentleman, of portly girth, wearing red. Clearly an expert in quantum physics and a past master in time bending, Santa apparently manages to visit every single household where children live, in one very exhausting night, traveling through the skies with a retinue of magical reindeer that have the powers of flight. In fact, his brightly colored garb is a relatively recent introduction, though not, as popularly supposed, wholly invented by the Coca-Cola Corporation but certainly popularized by them, inspired by an earlier cartoon that appeared in 1863, by one Thomas Nast whose work appeared in *Harper's Weekly* in the United States. Despite its comparatively recent age, this depiction of Santa as we recognize him today is now ubiquitous; it's an etching showing a smiling old man with holly tucked into the brim of his hat, clutching a pipe in one hand with a bundle of toys and gifts under his arm. Prior to Nast's interpretation, Father Christmas's appearance was much more subdued—a taller, slimmer figure dressed in a slubby brown or green color, as befitting his origins as a pagan spirit of nature.

One of the manifestations of this ancient nature spirit is in the guise of "Old Winter," personified in a Norse ritual whereby an old man went from door to door, fed and watered wherever he went. The idea was to propitiate the spirit of the winter. Santa, too, has food and drink left for him. Similarly, the god Odin (who also appears to humans as an old man with a beard) had a huge feast at Yule for the slain warriors in Valhalla. Children left their shoes stuffed with food for Odin's eight-legged horse, Sleipnir; in exchange, Sleipnir refilled these boots with gifts. These customs seem to have merged with the boisterous midwinter Saturnalia festival of the Romans. Later, in efforts to Christianize this pagan character, he was linked to St. Nicholas, a fourth-century Christian bishop born in Patara in Turkey who was known for his generosity. Indeed, in some parts of northern Europe, St. Nick still appears in the robes and hat of a bishop.

Santa's reindeer, it seems, are particularly appropriate animals to transport him through time and space. They carry much the same symbolism of the horse, able to conduct spirits between the world of the living and the dead. Lapps capture these wild animals in a very canny way. Reindeer are partial to the red and white fly agaric mushrooms, which contain psychoactive substances that induce hallucinations of flying. The Lapps scatter the mushrooms where the animals will find them, then simply wait until the reindeer are intoxicated, and lead them away.

GHOST

The idea that when a material being dies it leaves behind a shadowy imprint that will haunt the places it once inhabited is one that resonates around the world. The pervasiveness of the idea of the ghost indicates that it plays an important and deep-rooted part in the human psyche. Even the concept of a heaven or hell or other afterlife as a home for the disembodied spirit has not changed the fact that for many people, ghosts actually exist. Ghosts do not have to be human; animals, too, can haunt the places of the living.

Communication with ghosts used to be called necromancy and was considered by superstitious Christians to be one of the black arts. Today, this practice is called spiritualism, and the form of a spiritualist ritual includes a nod to a Christian God at the beginning and end of the ceremony. This is despite the fact that in Christian belief, the ghosts that still walked the earth were generally of those people who had not been buried under the auspices of the Church and were therefore to be avoided.

Ghosts represent the almost universal need for human beings to believe in a form of consciousness that exists after the physical death of the body.

GOBLIN

The goblin, like the gnome, is said to inhabit underground areas such as caves, tunnels, and mines, but unlike the gnome, they can live closer to the surface of the earth, lurking in among tree roots and under hedges. They generally have a more sinister aspect than gnomes, being even more prone to malicious behavior, which is particularly directed toward human beings who may have incurred their wrath.

Hopeful goblin-spotters can find the creatures in various places around the world that bear their name, such as Bryn y Ellyon, "the

Hill of the Goblins" in Somerset in the UK, or at the Gap of Goeblin, in France. In Tolkien's *The Lord of the Rings*, goblins equate to the fearsome creatures called orcs, who live underground and are the epitome of evil brute force.

GRIFFIN

The griffin has the body of a lion and the head of an eagle, sometimes with prominent tufted ears. It usually has wings, but not always. The griffin is sometimes confused with the wyvern, but has four legs unlike the wyvern with only two. These legs end in eagles' talons, too. As a composite of two particularly powerful creatures, which are themselves rich in symbolic meaning, the griffin is believed to be particularly important, possessing power equal to that of the gods whom it is often seen guarding. The griffin serves as an admirable symbol in heraldry, economically representing the attributes of the eagle and the lion in one single animal.

The griffin appears in many civilizations including Greek and Egyptian, and its key feature is to protect precious objects. In Crete, it was considered the guardian of throne rooms, and in central Asia, it guarded the valuable deposits of gold and precious gems that could be found there, descending upon anyone who appeared to be a threat and tearing them to pieces with their talons.

In medieval symbolism, the griffin represented knowledge, and later it came to signify the idea of a guardian; the ears represented attentiveness, the lion's body was for courage, the beak stood for tenacity.

The hippogriff, recently brought from mythological obscurity when it starred in the Harry Potter series of books by J. K. Rowling, is the product of a liaison between a griffin and a horse.

HARPY

In Greek myth, the harpies are

monstrous creatures comprised of the bodies of birds and the heads of women, with sharp talons, that emit a disgusting smell. The name "harpy" means "snatcher" or "plucker." The harpies eat carrion, and are three in number, called "Dark," "Squall," and "Swift Flyer." These names are suggestive of storm clouds, and it is interesting to note that this imagery is carried further by the fact that only Calais and Zetes, the sons of the North Wind, could get rid of the harpies by driving them away. Greedy and malicious, the harpies supplied the lords of the underworld with the souls of people who had died before their time.

MERMAID

Mermaids may be perceived nowadays as creatures that belong only within the realms of mythology and the imagination, but this was not always the case. Until the nineteenth century, there was still a law on the statute books, decreeing that any mermaid found in British waters was the property of the Crown. Indeed, Christopher Columbus reported seeing mermaids on his voyage to America, although what he actually saw might have been a

marine animal called a manatee that, notably, cradles its young in its arms in the same way as a human.

The mermaid symbol appears all over the world, and the consistency of her appearance leads many to suppose that they really do exist. With long streaming hair and the tail of a fish, the mermaid is the epitome of the goddess figure, naturally associated with the water element and living in the "womb" of the sea. There are also mermen and a whole population of merpeople hidden in the depths of the sea as well as in freshwater lakes. The very first mermaid stories are from the Assyrian culture and date back to 1000 BC. This first mermaid started her life as the goddess Atargatis, who loved a mortal man, a shepherd, but who inadvertently killed him. Distraught, she leaped into a lake, meaning to take on the form of a fish; instead, she became a human/fish hybrid, the mermaid.

Unlike the siren, whose intention toward people is generally malicious, the mermaid has a kinder attitude to human beings. For sailors, the sight of a mermaid is a warning of stormy weather to come.

Paradoxically, although the mermaid is a symbol of female sexuality and is an object of desire, the mermaid's tail precludes her having the sexual parts of a normal woman, and so she remains virginal, unobtainable, the object of frustrated dreams and desires and outside of the sphere of physical love; a goddess, indeed. There is another side to the mermaid's image that has a generally pejorative meaning. The symbol was used at Ephesus where there is a series of three signs, popularly supposed to be the world's first advertisement. These symbols are engraved onto a paving slab. They are a pointing finger, a coin, and a mermaid. Together, these indicated the local brothel, with the mermaid figure denoting the prostitute.

Mermaids in literature often fall in love with male humans but are thwarted by the inability of the object of their desires to be able to breathe in water, or to exist in the same element. Like the Little Mermaid in the Hans Christian Andersen story, they are prepared to go to great lengths for this love, and in this particular story, the mermaid exchanges her beautiful tail for human legs, although each footstep she takes is excruciatingly painful. The other typical attribute of a mermaid is her beautiful voice, and in the story of *The Little Mermaid*, her tongue is taken away so that she can neither sing nor explain what has happened to the handsome prince. Most importantly, love, not desire, drives her to exchange her immortality as a mermaid for the soul of a human, and in so doing she apparently leaves behind the animal part of herself and becomes a far superior creature.

NYMPH

In Greek, this word means either "bride" or "doll." Nymphs are spirits or deities that live close to water; waterfalls, streams, fountains, lakes, and wells all have their nymphs. Like the water that they are associated with, nymphs are notoriously ambivalent, changeable, and inconsistent. They preside equally over fertility and birth as well as death and decay. They are believed to steal children and to haunt the minds of the people who see them, sometimes driving them to madness. Reputedly, nymphs are at their most visible and dangerous during the time of the midday sun, so it is best to avoid the places where they are likely to be at this time.

In ancient Greece, temples at sacred springs were presided over by priestesses, all unmarried girls, also called "nymphs," and the temples themselves—called "Nymphaeae"—were used specifically for performing wedding ceremonies. Legend has it that these priestesses would give into orgiastic ceremonies at the time of the full moon, hence the term "nymphomania."

PHOENIX

The mythological bird called the phoenix exists under different guises: as the Garuda in India, as the Feng Huang in China, as the Ho-oo in Japan, and as the Benu Bird in Egypt. The main characteristic of this great bird, whose symbolic meaning resonates throughout myth, religion, and alchemy, is that it is reborn from its own ashes after combusting voluntarily. This unusual habit means different things to different people. To Christians, it is a reminder of the sacrifice made by Christ and his subsequent reward of resurrection and eternal life. For the Dharmic religions, it indicates the triumph of the soul over the body, and subsequent reincarnation. For others, the destruction by fire signifies the catharsis, or purification, of death.

The phoenix is also symbolic of the "dying" of the sun as it goes over the horizon in a welter of flames, and its "resurrection" the next day as it burns back over the horizon. This was the favored imagery of the Egyptians.

The phoenix is said to live primarily on aromatic smoke, not harming anything in order to eat. Therefore it is a popular symbol in Chinese and Indian Buddhist belief systems. In the same way, the bird has become popular in Christian literature and art as a symbol of resurrection and of life after death.

There can only exist one phoenix at a time, and its life span is reputedly anywhere between 500 and 1,461 years. Its habitat is also debated. Some accounts say that it spends its time in India, but there's also a tale that tells us that the bird's real home is in paradise. When the time comes for the phoenix to die, he has to fly into the mortal world, taking a journey across the jungles of Burma, across India, and on to Arabia. Here it collects the herbs and aromatic spices it needs, then it flies on to Phoenicia in Syria, finds a tall date palm tree, and then constructs its funeral pyre. As the next day dawns the bird rises again.

SATYR

A hybrid creature, the satyr consists of the body of a man with the legs, tail, and horns of a goat. The goat itself is considered to have a lascivious nature and the satyr takes on some of that symbolism. The great Greek nature god, Pan, was a satyr, possessed of a large and prominent penis as a symbol of the procreative force. However, because the early Christian authorities equated sex

with sin, it should come as no surprise that they connected the satyr to the devil. The Goat of Mendes, the goat/human figure worshipped by the ancient Egyptians, is still used as a pictorial representation of Satan. Satyrs attended Bacchus and Dionysus, who gave themselves to a life of wine, women, boys, song, and general debauchery.

SIREN

The beautiful appearance and seductive nature of the sirens disguise a monstrous intent. They have the heads and breasts of lovely and voluptuous women and the bodies and wings of birds, but it is the loveliness of their faces and the sweetness of their voices that they use, with devastating effect, to lure hapless sailors toward them, so that they can then kill and eat them. Famously, Odysseus had himself strapped to the mast of his ship after plugging the ears of his sailors with wax, so that he could hear the song of the sirens and yet be unable to succumb to it. The nature of the siren, essentially, is of an evil that is able to prey upon human weakness. Medieval texts describe them as "stout whores." Sometimes sirens are confused with mermaids, but in general mermaids are benevolent creatures whose domain is most definitely the sea. Sirens are more ambiguous, belonging on sea, land, and air.

The sirens symbolize the dangers of the sea, and death itself. Egyptians believed that they represented dead souls that had failed to achieve their destiny and spitefully decided to blight the lives of others, too. Essentially, the siren stands as a warning against the distractions of desire and of what can happen if a man succumbs to physical temptation. The mast that Odysseus made a conscious decision to strap himself to represents the axis of his soul, his backbone, and moral fiber.

Sphinx

The sphinx exists in slightly varying forms. It generally has the head of a woman and the body of a lion, although the most famous of the sphinxes, the Egyptian ones, do not

have wings, unlike the Assyrian and Greek versions.

The sphinx, as the epitome of mystery and hidden secrets, has endured for centuries. Her riddle—"what goes on four feet in the morning, on two feet at midday, and on three feet in the evening?"—may have been answered long ago, but mankind is still fascinated by her, and the true significance that lies behind her implacable expression can only be guessed at. She has a reputation as a devourer; the wings given to her by the Greek and Assyrians would suggest that she was of divine origin. Greek legends have the sphinx as an evil monster that ravaged the land of Thebes, asking riddles of anyone who came its way, and devouring those who either answered incorrectly or failed to answer at all.

Unicorn

This fantastical animal has a double meaning. On the one hand, it is synonymous with purity and chastity, yet on the other, the single horn on its head is clearly a phallic symbol. The positioning of the horn, though, in the center of the head and therefore at the symbolic seat of the mind, shows that the

horn, in this case, stands for sublimation of the sexual urge. Popular legend says that only a virgin who is pure in mind as well as body can touch the unicorn, and medieval tapestries of the creature with the Virgin Mary were a reminder of the virgin birth. However, even this innocuous imagery was prohibited by the Church in the late Middle Ages, regarded as too erotic.

The lion and the unicorn often appear as a pair, most notably on heraldic devices. Here, the lion represents the sun to the unicorn's moon.

VAMPIRE

The concept of an immortal creature, once human, that lives in a tomb and comes out at night to suck the blood of living creatures, which then become vampires themselves, is widespread throughout Europe, Russia, and many parts of Asia.

The fact that the vampire takes all its nourishment in this way is a reminder of blood's power as a sustaining life-force, and explains why ancient people daubed the dead in red ocher, in the hopes that the vitality of the color alone would restore life.

Vampires were once taken very seriously as a threat. In the Middle Ages, a Slav edict placed a heavy fine on any female vampire that was found guilty of taking blood from a man. The classic prophylactics against vampires have remained the same for centuries. These are the Christian Cross (since the vampire is the agent of the devil); the silver bullet (the metal encapsulates the essence of moonlight which is necessary to the vampire, and therefore effects a sort of homeopathic poison); garlic, a herb of protection that is hated by all demonic creatures; and finally, the wooden stake through the heart.

Today, there seem to be fewer blood-sucking vampires around than there used to be. However, the word is used to describe anyone who saps psychic energy from those around them. How to spot a vampire? The key feature is a lack of a reflection, since a reflection is a symbol of the soul the vampire doesn't have.

WEREWOLF

The idea that gods and goddesses could shape-shift into the form of animals or birds, and that shamans could absorb the spirit of an animal by wearing skins and feathers as part of ritual practice, is ancient. The werewolf is a part of this tradition. However, the reason why a wolf in particular should have been chosen to represent the evil side of human nature is worth examining.

The belief in lycanthropy (human/wolf shape-shifting transformation) was an ancient one that existed in classical times; even Virgil wrote about it. As any horror movie aficionado knows, werewolves change into wolves during the time of the full moon. Like vampires, they have no reflection, nor do they have a shadow. Since both reflection and shadow are symbolic of the soul, in taking on the form of a wolf, the human soul and conscience are left behind, the ferocious nature of the beast taking over entirely.

The belief in werewolves is evidenced by documentation that describes the trials—and punishments—of such creatures, although belief in them was starting to die out by the seventeenth century in Europe. For example, in 1615 a woman was burned alive, accused of lycanthropy. A man, traveling alone late at night, was attacked by a werewolf but managed to chop off its paw. The woman in question was missing a hand. Other werewolf trials, carried out under the jurisdiction of the Church, worked with the same kind of logic that was applied to witch trials, often using severe methods of torture until the accused either confessed or died.

ZOMBIE

The zombie is a Voudon term that has become the popular name for a revenant, or one that returns from the dead. Although this could be considered a handy skill, the unfortunate zombie has no soul, and will only survive if it has access to a sufficient quantity of meat from normal, soul-containing human bodies. In this, there is a parallel between the zombie and the vampire.

In Haitian myth, a corpse can be reanimated by a powerful sorcerer called a Bokor. The zombie is really nothing but a robot that must do the bidding of the Bokor, since it has no mind of its own; it is simply a ghastly mechanical creature. Although we may think of the zombie as nothing but a handy device for use in horror films, there are several reported eyewitness accounts, with names and dates mentioned, of people seen wandering around several years after their death, a reminder that folklore, no matter how bizarre, carries a powerful symbolic punch.

The term "zombie" has come to mean a person who carries out certain actions automatically, without seeming to apply any conscious thought or decision-making process.

BIRDS: DIVINE COMMUNICATORS

In the Qu'ran, the word for "bird" is synonymous with "fate" and in Greek, "bird" and "omen" have the same meaning. Orthomancy, a form of divination that involves watching birds, was common practice all over the world in ancient times. Birds' flight patterns were observed; the type of bird was considered; their calls and cries were pondered over, and sometimes this divination took the form of an analysis of bird entrails. Ancient Romans wouldn't make any important decisions without first consulting their augurs. Indeed, the Latin word *augury*, which is taken to mean an omen or portent, actually has its root in the meaning of the word "bird" and also gives us "inauguration." Bird augury wasn't exclusive to the Romans but was carried out by Tibetans, Indians, Native Americans, Mexicans, Egyptians, Mayans, and Celts. Sacred places around the world were defined by bird symbols and messages: Mexico City, Rome, and the site of the omphalos at Delphi were all founded in this way.

The idea, too, that birds somehow revealed the secrets of the alphabet to humankind is far-reaching. The best-known story is that Hermes, the messenger of the gods, "invented" the alphabet by watching the flight patterns of birds, cranes in particular. Robert Graves in *The White Goddess* tells us that the secret symbols of the alphabet were kept in a crane-skin bag, which makes perfect sense given also that the Alaskans used to use the skins of cranes, swans, and eagles as bags since these skins are the strongest.

In a beautiful, symbolic circle of completion, the feather or quill was a popular means of communicating the written word: the bird communicates in another way.

ALBATROSS

For sailors, this huge sea bird is said to be the reincarnated soul of a dead sailor that has come to help make a safe passage for the boat, or perhaps to give a warning of rough weather ahead. Therefore, killing or harming the albatross is the height of bad luck.

In the Pacific islands, the albatross is commonly believed to be a messenger from the gods, able to sleep on the wing. The bird is revered because of its close connection to the divine, and on Easter Island one of the statues has the beak of an albatross.

CRANE

There is evidence that the crane has been present on the planet for 10 million years and as well as this, the bird has a long life span—up to fifty years—so it is no surprise that, for many, the bird is a symbol of longevity.

The crane is a symbol of communication, too. A legend states that Mercury/Hermes invented the alphabet by watching the angular shapes of the birds' wings in flight. Thereafter the letters were carried in a bag made of crane skin. For ancient Greeks, the crane was a solar symbol and as such was dedicated to the sun god, Apollo, who disguised himself as the bird whenever he came to visit earth. In China and Japan, the crane similarly represents longevity and faithfulness, both traits that are true to the bird.

* ✳ *

DOVE

The dove carries a universal symbolism that is as ubiquitous as the bird itself. The world over, it is associated with the feminine aspect, love, and peace.

Pigeons and doves have carried messages for thousands of years and the notion of this particular bird as a messenger from the gods is perhaps more pronounced than for others. This is backed up by the story of the dove sent out by Noah to determine how far the ark was from land; the bird returned with a sprig of an olive branch, and the juxtaposition of the bird with the olive branch is a sign of redemption, peace, and resolution. Columba—the dove—is the "secret," covert bird symbol of the United States, its soft reasonable femininity counterbalancing the masculine glory of the more visible and overt eagle. The dove is also the symbolic bird of Israel.

DUCK

One of the more unlikely symbols of this seemingly innocuous bird is an association with the devil that was given to it by a thirteenth-century pope, Gregory IX. Gregory took it upon himself to preach a particularly impassioned sermon in which he denounced the bird as the personification of the demon Asmodeus, who apparently appeared to his followers in the unlikely guise of a duck and thereafter caused all sorts of unholy goings-on.

Like other migratory birds, the appearance of the duck was an indicator, to ancient people, of the changing of the seasons; therefore, it was believed to have the powers of prophecy. The duck is a useful ally, in general a benevolent creature, its links with anything remotely demonic an aberration. Because it is a water bird it is linked to Poseidon/Neptune, and in Egypt, where ducks were domesticated 5,000 years ago, it was associated with Isis and with the sun god Ra. The duck's take-off, as it skims across the surface of the water and into the air, effectively exchanging one element for another, symbolizes the journey of the soul into the next world.

EAGLE

One of the most important archetypal bird symbols, the prominence of the eagle is a worldwide phenomenon. The eagle is the "King of the Birds" and the "Lion of the Skies," and its use as a symbol is clear. It resembles power, authority, nobility, and truth; it is the ultimate solar symbol. In Greek the name of the eagle shares the same stem as *aigle*, meaning "ray of light."

Notably, the eagle is the symbol of one of the four evangelists of the New Testament, St. John. Here, the eagle represents divine inspiration. However, the saying "the enemy of my enemy is my friend" applies here, because the bird is reputedly the natural enemy of snakes, and the eagle has been regarded as on the "side" of God ever since the devil was symbolized as the serpent in the Garden of Eden, tempting Adam and Eve away from the straight and narrow path of good towards the twisting and corrupting path of evil. However, the eagle and the snake seen together symbolize the opposing concepts of matter and spirit, earth and heaven, instinct and intellect, the mundane and the sublime, and therefore the unity of the cosmos. In Norse mythology, the eagle sits in the great World Tree, Yggdrasil, counterbalanced by the serpent that twines about the tree's roots.

The eagle's reputation as a symbol of truth comes from its sharp-sightedness; the eyesight of the eagle is at least four times superior to that of human beings, and combined with its high-flying abilities it means that the bird can see the bigger picture, quite literally. Therefore, it is meant to be able to discern truth from falsehood. Because it flies so high, often appearing to be heading straight for the sun, people believed that the eagle was the only creature in the world able to gaze directly into the brightness of the sun without hurting its eyes. Therefore, the bird also symbolizes mental and spiritual enlightenment and the aspiration of a pure heart, able to look into the face of God with no fear.

Shamans believe that the eagle communicated its gifts directly from God, the bird acting as intermediary. They believe that the first shaman was conceived after an eagle impregnated a woman, another symbol of the bird as a divine spirit or winged messenger. This has parallels with another winged creature, the angel Gabriel, who told Mary of her impending condition. In both cases, the resulting child is a sort of spiritual hybrid, able to connect God and humankind.

The eagle has always been the emblem par excellence of emperors and empires, even prior to its presence on the imperial standard of the Caesars and its latter-day use as the symbol of the United States, where the altogether more humble dove balances its grandiose power. The death of an emperor was heralded by the release of eagles into the skies, symbolic of the soul ascending to the heavens. However, more sinisterly, the symbolic power and attributes of the eagle were appropriated by the Nazis to bolster their own image. This is an instance where a powerful symbol can be abused, something that also happened to another ancient solar symbol, the swastika, whose implicit benevolent meaning is unfortunately still tainted because of its use by the Nazis.

For Native Americans, the power of the eagle is such that possession of one of its feathers is the ultimate accolade, a sacred symbol of the mightiness of the bird and of its special place within the Native American pantheon. The eagle is the "father" of the people, a god, and illicit possession of a feather by anyone who does not have the right to have it is punishable by hefty fines. For the Aztecs, the eagle was not associated with the lion but with the jaguar, and the throne of the Aztec emperor was decorated with eagle feathers and jaguar skin to symbolize his association with these powerful creatures. The eagle "told" the people where Mexico City should be built, duly appearing perched on a cactus growing out of a rock, as decreed by an ancient legend.

HOOPOE

Hoopoes are appalling nest-keepers, rarely clearing out any debris. It's also a particularly bad-smelling bird. This could be why it's listed in Hebrew scripture as an "unclean" bird, which is not to be eaten. Despite this, images of the hoopoe feature on the walls of tombs in Crete and Egypt, and the bird has a long association with magic and the supernatural.

As a bird that can communicate between the world of spirit and matter, the hoopoe seems to be second to none. According to the Qu'ran, the hoopoe was the bird that told King Solomon about the queen of Sheba. Moreover, it was the only bird that could tell the king the whereabouts of essential underground springs.

The hoopoe is also one of the birds able to forecast the weather, particularly storms, and with good reason. A recent discovery confirms an ancient aspect of its symbolic and superstitious meaning. It seems that the bird is able to detect the minute piezoelectrical charges in the atmosphere that can herald either a storm or an earthquake up to ten hours before the event.

HUMMINGBIRD

On the Nazca Plains in Peru, artists living centuries ago carved out various shapes and patterns that are indecipherable from the ground, but when viewed from the air, come together in recognizable pictures. Among these images is a giant hummingbird that can only be seen when the viewer is about a thousand feet up. Ancient artists painstakingly created this secret symbol, hidden in the landscape, able to be seen properly only by the gods in their heavens or in a way they could never have envisaged, by modern humans centuries later, from the vantage point of an aircraft.

Given its origins in the Americas, it is from this area that the symbolic meaning of the hummingbird comes. In the Andes it is a symbol of death and res-urrection. It loses a significant amount of heat at night in order to conserve energy and seems to be dead if it is found at night. In the morning, however, the heat of the sunshine revives it.

One of the more epic myths about the hummingbird concerns a great warrior, Huitzil. His full name was Huitzilopochtli, which translates as "the hummingbird from the left." The "left" here refers to the otherworldly realms that run parallel to the known universe. The warrior's mother conceived him from a ball of brightly colored feathers, which fell from the sky.

The relevance of tobacco for Native Americans involves the symbolism of the smoke that it makes that rises to the heavens carrying messages to the gods. Given that birds do the same thing, there are many associa-tions between tobacco and birds, including the hummingbird. In a Cherokee myth, a shaman trans-forms himself into a humming-bird so that he can find the lost tobacco plant.

Aztec reverence for the hum-mingbird was profound. Shamans' cloaks and wands were decorated with the feathers of the bird.

KINGFISHER

The ancient name for the kingfi-sher is the "halcyon," and it carries with it a powerful legend that also explains some of the bird's sym-bolic significance. The Halcyon Days—an idyllic time of peace and tranquility—refers to the four-teen day period just before the end of the Greek winter when the weather is good and the seas are calm enough to facilitate the nest-ing of the legendary bird on the waves, although the real kingfisher does no such thing.

The kingfisher, as the halcyon bird, symbolizes the marriage of the sea and the sky, the earth and the air.

LAPWING

Because the nest of the lapwing, at the edge of a body of water, is so well disguised, the bird is symbolic of a hidden secret. And although some accounts of Solomon's introduction to the queen of Sheba have the hoopoe as the matchmaker, others give the lapwing this honor.

Lapwing chicks are able to be up and about very soon after they have hatched, and can run away immediately if there's danger; this precocious behavior gives rise to a phrase, "running about like a lap-wing with a shell upon their heads," coined by Ben Jonson, and taken to mean someone who behaves rashly.

The ethereal, sobbing cry of the lapwing means that the bird has sorrowful associations. "The Seven Whistlers" is an ancient folk tale found all over northern Europe. There's an old Gaelic name for the bird, the *Guilchaismeachd* or "Wail of Warning." In some parts of Britain, the legend says that the wailing is caused by six of the whistlers in search of the seventh; however, once the seventh whistler is found, the world will end.

In the Bible, the lapwing is mentioned as an unclean bird, a bird of taboo, which generally means that the bird was considered sacred and should not be eaten.

MAGPIE

The name of this bird not only tells us a lot about its nature, but also points toward the symbolism associated with it. "Mag" means "chatterer," and "pie" comes from "pied," meaning black and white.

Because the magpie is attracted to bright and shiny objects, it's a symbol not only of a hoarder, but also of a thief. Its clearly defined black and white markings have made it, in Christian belief at least, a symbol of the devil (because it refused to wear full mourning for the Crucifixion), and elsewhere it is viewed as a trickster, like other members of the highly intelligent corvid family. This ambivalence is reflected in the old counting rhyme about magpies whose verses are alternately positive and negative, like the coloring of the bird itself. The devilish symbolism is exacerbated because the bird can even imitate the human voice, an alarming talent to superstitious minds.

The predilection of the magpie for shiny objects means that is linked to mirrors and reflections. In Japan a woman would regard her husband's gift of a mirror with some suspicion. This is because of the belief that the mirror could turn into a magpie. This bird then spied on the wife on behalf of her husband. Even today, the backs of some mirrors in China are decorated with the magpie symbol.

In Greece, the magpie was the attribute of the wine god Dionysus. Wine loosens the tongue and causes people to chatter like the bird. This chattering gives us the name "gazette," a journal full of gossipy items, from the Italian for magpie, *gazza*.

Ostrich

The ostrich is a symbol of avoidance, or ignorance, because of its perceived habit of hiding its head in the sand. Although this characteristic is inaccurate, it is a reminder of just how certain symbolic meanings can be engendered in ignorance rather than in truth. The ostrich, in fact, protects its eggs by burying them in sand, and occasionally has need to disguise this place—the nest can contain a collection of up to thirty eggs from different birds—by lying on it. The ostrich is also considered stupid, because it eats sharp objects and stones; in fact these abrasive objects aid digestion.

It is ironic that the two best-known ostrich symbols concern misunderstandings, because as a symbol of truth, the ostrich feather is unrivaled. Such a feather is the attribute of the Egyptian goddess of truth, Ma'at, who weighs the ostrich feather against her scales of reckoning. The other side of the scales holds the heart, the seat of the conscience. The ostrich feather carries this symbolism because unlike birds of flight whose feathers have one side heavier than the other, the ostrich feather is perfectly symmetrical.

Ostrich eggs are balanced on the tops of the pinnacles of Muslim temples in Mali, because the egg is symbolic of the World Egg, and carries an inherent reminder of faith and patience because the ostrich's egg has a long gestation period.

Owl

The Italian word for owl, *strix* or *strega*, also means "witch," and this provides a heavy hint about one aspect of the bird's symbolic meaning. Because the owl is nocturnal, it means that it has access to covert information, occult knowledge, and secrets. It is because of this reason that the little owl is the attribute of the goddess of wisdom, Athena/Minerva, and also explains its appearance perched on top of a stack of books as a symbol of knowledge. The idea that the owl has access to information denied mere mortals is further underlined by the fact the bird can swivel its head an astonishing 270 degrees; quite literally, the bird can see behind itself. Its huge eyes add to its wise reputation.

The links with witchcraft and witchery are also because of some of the owl's habits. It lives a solitary existence, only coming together to breed, and usually separating again once the juvenile owls have flown the nest. An efficient hunter, the owl's feathers are particularly adapted so that its flight is silent, and the bird is able to take ten times the amount of small rodents in one night than a cat. Its killings are often accompanied by an unearthly screeching, which superstitious country dwellers attributed to supernatural causes.

The owl is a symbol of the feminine, the moon, and prophecy. The moon, acting as a mirror of the sun, is itself symbolic of clairvoyant powers, another gift of witches. This gift of second sight, though, generally brings gloomy news, and everywhere the shriek of an owl in the night presages a death. The owl has other unfortunate symbolism connected with it. Since it chooses derelict buildings in which to make its home, the bird is associated with destruction and decay. The owl is also a companion of the infamous witch queen Hecate, goddess of the underworld. The belief that the owl could come and go between the lands of the living and the dead was not restricted to the Romans and the Britons. The same belief exists for Native Americans, for Africans, in China, in Japan, and in India, where the god of death, Yama, is shown with an owl. The owl is a psychopomp, able to guide the souls of the deceased into the afterlife.

RAVEN

The raven is one of the most intelligent of all the birds. To give some idea of its intelligence, if the average IQ for a human being is measured at the 100 mark, then the average IQ of a raven is 138. Its linguistic skills are legendary, and it is possible that the raven can understand as well as imitate human words. It is this intelligence, and the playful nature of the raven, that makes it the ultimate symbol of the trickster.

In some societies, the raven is as important as the eagle, and occasionally this black bird even surpasses the golden one in terms of its symbolic import. Like the eagle, the raven has few natural predators except for humans. Unlike the eagle, ravens will work together for the benefit of the group, and so have come to symbolize the benefits of teamwork.

Even if the raven has never been taught to speak in human languages, its voice carries a surprisingly human inflection and tone. This led to a belief that the bird knew everything, as personified by the ravens that belonged to the Norse god Odin. Called Hugin and Munin, from the words for "thought" and "memory," the birds flew back to the god at the end of every day where they whispered into his ears all the doings of mankind. More sinisterly, the raven is seen as a harbinger of death, as personified in the Morrigan, the great battle goddess of Celtic myth who takes on the form of a raven. The raven is a carrion bird and was often to be seen at the sites of battles, making a grim meal of the bloody remains of the defeated army. The idea of the raven as a bird of malice is promulgated by the Bible story that Noah first sends a raven to find land; the raven never returned, and so was seen to be no friend of man. The dove, sent out next, returned with the sprig of the olive tree and has been a beneficial omen ever since. The ravens at the Tower of London are a symbol of protection par excellence. Birds have been kept in this spot for over a thousand years, due to an ancient legend that the country would be safe from invaders while ravens remain there. Indeed, this idea is so firmly entrenched in the national psyche that when the raven population at the tower dwindled during World War II, Winston Churchill arranged that ravens be "imported" from Wales to keep the country safe.

In Native American belief, the raven is a symbol of the creator and as such is a powerful protector of humankind. Myths tell that the bird not only made the universe but also discovered and looked after the first man. The shape-shifting abilities of the bird are mentioned here, too, and as such, the raven is the preferred bird of shamans, who converse with the birds in order to discover what the gods have in store for humankind.

ROOSTER

The rooster would be easy to overlook as a bird of mystic significance. Nevertheless there's a rich history of magical lore surrounding the bird. Its name, the "cock," says it all, and it's no accident that the name of the bird is the same as a slang word for penis.

The rooster is the ultimate masculine symbol; it signifies the sun, power, pugnacity, and sexual prowess. It appears as the head of the mystical Abraxas symbol. These links with the sun are universal; the frilled red comb on the bird's head looks like sunbeams. Many

Christian churches have the rooster on their weather vanes. This is not only because the cock appears with the coming of physical light and therefore spiritual enlightenment, but also because the bird is a poignant symbol within the faith. It crowed once when Christ was born, again when St. Peter denied Christ, and it will crow again as a warning of the Day of Judgment. According to the Qu'ran, conversely, the end of the world will be upon us when the cock stops crowing.

All the solar power and masculine energy of the rooster made it fitting as a sacrifice to the god Apollo. Later, people believed that they could harness this energy by eating the bird, which explains in part why a bowl of chicken soup is said to have such a fortifying effect.

In the East cockerels are bred specifically to live in and around Shinto temples. The rooster also appears as one of the twelve signs of the Chinese zodiac, where the attributes of people born under the sign include enthusiasm and a sense of humor.

SPARROW

Sadly, the sparrow has latterly become a not-so-secret symbol of the decline in the bird population and is held as an example of what can happen as a result of modern farming methods and the use of chemicals. Nevertheless, for thousands of years the sparrow has held a close place in the hearts of people as a symbol of satisfied domesticity, living in close proximity with us, happy to share space, and being so much a part of the natural landscape as to be virtually unnoticeable. The close relationship between humankind and this small, unassuming brown bird led to a certain species of it being called the house sparrow, and it is used in the Bible as an example of something that is cheap and plentiful, described as being sold "two for a farthing" although nevertheless important in the eyes of God. Here, the sparrow is a symbol of the importance of every living thing, no matter how lowly.

STORK

When parents think that their children are too young to be told how babies are made, the issue is fudged for a while longer, and the child is often told that a stork brings the infant. The image of the bird flying along carrying the baby in a sling is popularly used on christening cards and other artifacts. This affectation seems to exist across the world, even reaching into the mythology of the Plains Indians. The reason is unclear, but it might be because storks will happily live in close proximity to humans.

The stork is famously dutiful toward its parents, so much so that in Rome a Stork Law (Lax Ionia) was passed to ensure that Roman citizens would emulate the bird and take care of their elders.

tion about where the swallow went for the winter months. Aristotle theorized that they hibernated in holes, and an eighteenth-century writer supposed that they traveled as far as the moon.

The swallow was associated with the Egyptian goddess Isis, who was said to change into a swallow at night and fly around Osiris's coffin, singing mournful songs, until the sun arrived back the next morning.

SWALLOW

The migratory habits of the swallow are so reliable that they are a universal symbol of the arrival of spring. Because of this they are a welcome sight and most people regard it as a privilege if the bird chooses to live in close proximity to humans. The Chinese even used to date their equinoxes to the swallow's arrival and departure. The spring equinox is the traditional time of fertility rites, and resulting pregnancies would sometimes be blamed on the girl's eating a swallow's egg. Confucius was allegedly born through this mechanism, which led to his nickname of "The Swallow's Son." There was a great deal of specula-

SWAN

The appearance of the swan, an ethereal, otherworldly creature, floating gracefully upon the calm waters that resemble the spirit world and the eternal feminine, packs a powerful symbolic punch even without any prior knowledge of the myths and legends surrounding the bird that have aided and abetted its significance. Its pure white color, its strength, and its beauty make it a symbol of light, both of the direct light of the sun and the reflected light of the moon.

Despite plenty of evidence to the contrary, the swan is believed to be silent until its moment of death, when its song is said to be the first and last sound it utters.

Therefore, "swan song" has come to mean the final expression of an artist's work, for example, or a late resurgence before the final demise. Curiously, though, the name "swan" comes from an Anglo-Saxon word *sounder*, which has the same root as "sound" or "sonnet."

In the UK, the swan is under the protection of the Crown. This legislation is believed to date back to the twelfth century, and even today only the household of the ruling monarch is allowed to eat the meat of the swan. The swan is the symbol of the poet; druidic bards wore cloaks made of swan's feathers as a shamanic totem to enable them to contact the spirit of the muse. It was because of this that Ben Jonson refers to Shakespeare as the "sweet swan of Avon." In ancient

A Lunar Bird Calendar

Inspired by a concept from Robert Graves's *The White Goddess*, this calendar is based around the thirteen moons contained within a year.

From	To	Bird	From	To	Bird
Dec 24	Jan 21	Pheasant	Jul 9	Aug 5	Starling
Jan 22	Feb 18	Duck	Aug 6	Sept 2	Crane
Feb 19	Mar 18	Snipe	Sept 3	Sept 30	Titmouse
Mar 19	Apr 15	Gull	Oct 1	Oct 29	Swan
Apr 16	May 13	Hawk	Oct 30	Nov 25	Goose
May 14	Jun 10	Night Crow	Nov 26	Dec 22	Rook
Jun 11	Jul 8	Wren			

The entire day of December 23 belongs exclusively to the eagle.

Greece, the swan was the attribute of the Muses and the symbol of Apollo, the god to whom poetry and song belong. Apollo could shape-shift into the form of a swan, and when he was born, seven swans flew around the island of his birth, seven times.

TURKEY

Birds, like other animals, naturally carry their strongest symbolic meanings in their place of origin, which in the case of the turkey is in the Americas.

It is a symbol of fertility and motherhood, and because it lives close to the ground and is the avian opposite of the high-flying eagle, it's sometimes called the Earth Eagle and is representative of the Earth Mother.

To the Toltecs, the turkey was "the jeweled fowl," because of its sparkling colors, and was reserved as food only for festivals and ritual occasions. Nothing of the turkey was wasted; after it had been eaten, the feathers were used as ornamentation, and the bones used to make musical instruments or whistles.

For some tribes, however, most notably the Pueblo, the bird was considered so sacred that it was never eaten but kept for its beautiful feathers alone, which grow back after plucking. Because the bird was felt to be able to communicate with the gods and could intercede on behalf of human beings, in the Pueblo funeral rites whole turkeys were buried along with the corpse, and occasionally these bones are still found. Prayer sticks decorated in a specific way with turkey feathers were given to the families of the deceased.

The Mayans used the emblem of the turkey in their codices, where it indicated fertility. The bird was decapitated in rituals designed to ensure that the gods would favor people with an abundant harvest.

Although the bald eagle was chosen as the national bird of the United States, Benjamin Franklin was far more enthusiastic that the turkey should have this honor. He suggested that the eagle was a bird of "bad moral character" and that the turkey was the more courageous bird.

VULTURE

An archetypal symbol of death and decay, the vulture frequently stars in cowboy movies where it circles ominously, coasting along on the thermals, an indicator of imminent doom. It is true that vultures are scavenger birds but their supposed talent of being able to predict death is unsubstantiated. The Latin name for the bird, *Cathartidae*, has the same root as the word "catharsis," meaning purification, and much of the symbolism of the vulture follows this idea.

The Egyptians, however, relied on a more wholesome aspect of the vulture's character to inform their own symbolic meaning. A notoriously good mother, the vulture personifies the process of birth and the maternal instinct, and is associated with Isis. The goddess is shown enfolded in the wings of a huge vulture, the solar disc behind her. The vulture was so revered that there was also a vulture goddess, Nekhbet, who is depicted with the head of the bird. Vultures were called "Pharaoh's Pets" because they were invaluable in keeping the streets clean.

Native Americans, too, hold the vulture in high esteem and also see the bird as symbolic of both spirit and matter. A feather from the bird, used as a totem object, enabled the shaman to "come back to the self" after shape-shifting ceremonies. The bird is a symbol of purification and renewal.

WOODPECKER

Also called the flicker, the woodpecker is believed to be a magical bird with powers of sorcery and clairvoyance. This may be because its behavior signifies changes in the weather; many of the folk names of the bird throughout Europe reflect this ability, for example *pic de la pluie* or rain woodpecker in France, and *Ragnfagel*, or rainbird, in Sweden.

The knocking sound made by the woodpecker as it burrows into the tree where it makes its home leads to an association with Odin, the Norse god of thunder and also with Mars, the Roman god of war. The image of the bird is seen on Roman coinage because the founding twins, Romulus and Remus, were said to have been given solid food by woodpeckers, after they had been suckled by a she-wolf.

The bird's association with thunder and lightning occurs elsewhere in the world. For example, the Pueblo associate the bird's drumming with the sound of the thunder that is the precursor to rain. Many Native Americans believed that the woodpecker had the skill to be able to avert lightning, and its feathers were used in rituals and ceremonies because of this power. Among some tribes, the woodpecker was believed to have brought fire to humankind.

WREN

Although the wren is tiny, it is known as the "King of the Birds" and symbolizes the power of humility. Despite its size and modest appearance, the wren is one of the most sacred of all birds and has a large role to play in myths and legends, where it is regarded as a magician, a magical symbol, and an emblem of wise intelligence.

In the Celtic pantheon, the bird is the symbol of the Druid, and its names in Irish, Drui, and in Welsh, Drwy, share the same root as the word for "Druid." The royal nature of the bird is accepted all over Europe; in Spain, Germany, Italy, Scandinavia, and France the name for the wren is the same as that for "king." (In the Breton language and that of the Pawnee, however, the word for wren is the same as that for "happy.")

One explanation for this symbolism comes in a story where the eagle challenges all the birds to see which of them can fly the highest; although the wren is ignored as being too insignificant, the smaller bird wins the race when it secretes itself in the feathered ruff around the throat of the eagle. The wren pops out at the opportune moment when the eagle begins his descent, and wins the race by flying a few inches higher than the bigger bird. Therefore, the strength of the wren is in the might of its intellect and wit, as opposed to mere physical brute force and size.

Because of its sacred status, anyone harming a wren should expect dire consequences. Despite this, once a year the rules were lifted, and on St. Stephen's Day, December 26, the Hunting of the Wren took place in parts of the UK, Ireland, and France. The bird was caught, ritually slaughtered, and carried from house to house in a tiny box surrounded by a hoop or bower of flowers. The meaning of this curious ritual is unclear. It may have symbolized the death of winter and the coming of spring, since the wren is highly visible during the colder months of the year as it does not migrate; or it may have been because of a legend that the martyr St. Stephen, about to escape from prison, was caught again when the wren inadvertently alerted the prison guard.

Part Three

FLORA

THE CONCEALED WISDOM
OF THE PLANT KINGDOM

Flora may have been a relatively minor goddess of the Greek pantheon, but was elevated in status since she kindly lent her name to all the world's abundant plant life. Flowers, plants, and fungi constitute one part of this section, and trees the other.

There are perfectly reasonable scientific explanations about how a seed, with the simple addition of the darkness of the soil, water, air, and sunshine, can transform into something as magnificent as, say, an oak tree. However, when those green shoots appear above the ground, that's as close a thing to magic as anything you could ever experience. It's not a surprise, therefore, that the seed itself is one of our most significant sacred symbols.

priate name for the short-lived nature of this small, fragile flower, which symbolizes the transience of life itself. Ovid said that the flower was both "born of the wind, and carried away by it." The flower is popular in funeral wreaths where, again, its symbolic meaning carries a hidden message.

There's a Greek myth, too, which tells the story of the anemone. Aphrodite wept when she mourned the death of her lover Adonis, and as the tears fell on the ground they became anemones. But Aphrodite's sadness didn't last long, and shortly afterwards she took another lover; therefore the flowers also symbolize the ephemeral aspect of love.

ANEMONE

Anemone comes from the Greek *anemos*, meaning wind, an appro-

ANGEL'S TRUMPET

See Datura.

Aquilegia

The aquilegia is an unusual, complex-looking and ethereal flower. It is associated with magical powers, and carries hidden secrets within the elaborate folds and ruffles of its petals.

Aquilegia is associated with two birds that have opposing characteristics. Initially the flower was called the columbine, after the Latin word for dove, *columba*, since its nectar gland is dove-like in shape and because the petals look a little like a circle of doves. But Latin monks renamed the flower the aquilegia from the Latin for "eagle," *aquila*; this is because the curlicued spurs at the back of the petals look like the talons of the eagle. The eagle, of course, is a flamboyant bird, symbolic of kings, emperors, and power. The dove is the diametric opposite of the eagle, a bird of humble appearance associated with peace and love. The dove is the "secret" symbol of the United States and balances the eagle, which is a more overt sign of this nation. Sometimes the columbine is used in religious paintings as a secret symbol for the dove, which in turn represents the Holy Spirit.

Ayahuasca

A tall, climbing forest plant, ayahuasca is the most important plant in the spiritual life of South America, and is carefully used in sacred rituals so that the shaman or intrepid explorer can reach the depths of his innermost consciousness. The benefits of taking the ayahuasca drug as part of a guided ritual are said to enable the celebrant to witness not only his own birth but also the dawning of creation, receive wisdom from the Ancestors, meet the Great Spirit and also be completely aware of being a part of the All.

The word *ayahuasca* translates as the "vine of the soul." The bark of the vine is made into an infusion which is then consumed with due ceremony. Popular shared hallucinations as a result of ayahuasca intoxication include witnessing the appearance of God as a great bright bird.

Basil

Basil leaves are said to contain magical powers, used in both love potions and as a divinatory tool to assess the nature of a marriage or relationship. More practically, the leaves can be used to cure wounds. If a basil leaf is laid on the hand of a promiscuous person it will apparently wither. It is the herb of the Haitian goddess of love, Erzuli.

The importance of basil is a part of Hindu tradition, too, and is partly explained in myth. The goddess Tulasi was seduced by the god Vishnu. When she realized what had happened Tulasi was horrified and killed herself. As a result Vishnu declared that she would be a reminder of faithfulness and purity, and would thereafter keep women from becoming widows. The holy basil that sprang from her ashes became a symbol of love, immortality, and protection. The Sanskrit name for this holy basil is *Tulasi*, which means "the incomparable one."

BELLADONNA

This plant is called "beautiful lady" because the court ladies of the Italian Renaissance used it to enlarge their pupils and so render themselves more attractive; however, this name belies the deadly poisonous nature of belladonna, a member of the potato family. Its other name, deadly nightshade, is far more fitting to its toxic nature. Another sinister aspect of the plant is its association with witches, who used deadly nightshade to bring about hallucinatory visions. As with many poisonous plants, however, there are medicinal benefits to be had from the plant, and one of its constituents, atropine, is a heart stimulant.

BROOM

Because the broom shrub has long straight branches with lots of similarly long straight shoots that point in the same direction, it has been used for sweeping for thousands of years, hence the name "broomstick."

In Latin, the broom is called *Planta genista*, and gives its name to the Plantagenet kings who used it as their emblem.

CAMELLIA

For the Japanese, the camellia is a symbol of friendship, harmony, and grace. However, for the samurai class the flower symbolized death and the fleeting nature of life.

The flower was one of the most sought-after of the nineteenth century, the cause of financial speculation, and very expensive. They therefore became a status symbol that could be enjoyed only by the very wealthy.

The camellia is similar in appearance to the rose, but somehow has a more sedate quality for all its elegant sexuality. It is also a symbol of pride and aloofness, as reflected in Alexandre Dumas Jr.'s novel, *La Dame Aux Camellias*, whose heroine carries a bouquet of white camellias for twenty-five days then swaps them for red ones, as a signal that she is sexually available.

CHRYSANTHEMUM

The chrysanthemum is the emblem of the Japanese Imperial family. The flower is a solar symbol, and its many layers of orderly petals mean that it is associated with longevity and immortality. There's even an annual festival dedicated to the flower, National Chrysanthemum Day, also called the Festival of Happiness. In China, too, the flower is seen as a symbol of vitality.

The flower is an ambiguous mix of restraint and exuberance; it is a show-off, while retaining a certain orderliness and formality. The name comes from the Greek *chrysos*,

meaning "golden," and *anthemum*, meaning "flower."

CLOVER

The clover stands for protection, fertility, and abundance, and if brought into the home serves as a charm to keep away witches. It is worn for the same reason. The clover has three distinctly heart-shaped leaves, both elements that contribute to its benevolent reputation. The shamrock—the form of clover that is synonymous with all things Irish—was known as the *shamrakh* in Arab countries and symbolized the triple aspect of the goddess.

The rare four-leafed clover is a ubiquitous symbol of good luck, and finding one means that the bearer will be able to see fairies and witches, and recognize evil spirits. Accordingly, the four-leafed clover can protect from these creatures, too. The four-leafed clover or shamrock carries all the symbolism of the number four.

COCA

The ancient use of the leaves of the coca plant, which is cultivated primarily in South America, is well known. Mummies dating back to the fifth century AD were buried with a supply of the leaves. When these leaves are chewed, they have a stimulant effect that leaves the mouth feeling numb. The Incas recognized the special qualities of the plant and called it the "food of the gods," reserving its use for sacred rituals. However, the breakdown of the Inca Empire meant that the restrictions surrounding the plant, as a sacred herb, were relaxed. It's possible that Spanish missionaries exploited the use of the coca plant since chewing the leaves masked hunger and meant the Andean Indians' work output increased. Philip II of Spain decided that the drug was essential to the well-being of the Indians but forbade its use in religious practices. It might be said that this edict signaled the end for the coca plant as a sacred herb. But this would not be the last time that people were exploited because of the drug. The coca plant is now arguably one of the most controversial plants in the world.

The source of this controversy is cocaine, the primary chemical compound of the coca plant. Its usefulness as a medicine is unfortunately belied by its recreational use. Cocaine is highly addictive;

not only this, but the value of the drug means that cultivation of the coca plant has profound political and sociological repercussions. It is now U.S. policy to discourage the cultivation of this crop.

DAISY

The scientific name of the daisy is *Bellis perennis*, but it attained its more popular name as a corruption of "day's eye," since it opens at sunrise and closes again at sunset.

In Victorian times, as well as having the association with purity, the flower was a symbol of love; girls would pluck away the petals of the daisy repeating the lines "he loves me, he loves me not" as each petal fell away, and the final petal would give the answer.

The daisy is also a sign of the coming of spring, said to have arrived when nine of the little flowers can be trodden on.

DANDELION

The dandelion is so called because the jagged shape of its petals look like the teeth of a lion; hence, *Dents de Lion*. If this humble little flower were difficult to grow it's likely that it would be highly prized for its beauty; since, however, the dandelion is a common weed, its sensational looks are often taken for granted. In an example of sympathetic magic, because the plant contains a thick milky sap it was believed to be good for the production of sperm.

The dandelion clock, the delicate pompom-shaped seed head of the flower, is associated with old age and the passing of time; children count the number of breaths needed to blow all the seeds away as a method of telling the time.

DATURA

The datura is a jungle plant with beautiful, bell-shaped flowers. There is a (possibly apocryphal) tale that Victorian and Edwardian ladies, sitting in conservatories full of exotic plants from the far-flung places of the British Empire, would place their teacups underneath the datura plant since the moisture dripping from it caused strange and rather pleasant sensations. These ladies may have been shocked to learn that the effects were produced by the psychotropic chemicals in the plant, which makes the datura sacred for

shamans in South America and Mexico, who use it to induce a trance-like state. The seeds are pounded into a paste and washed down with beer.

Datura is highly toxic, having reputedly caused more deaths by poisoning than any other plant; but provided the shaman doesn't take a physical as well as mental trip into the otherworld, he can enjoy up to three days' worth of auditory and visual hallucinations that apparently include conversing with imaginary beings.

GARLIC

Garlic has strong antiseptic qualities and is good for warding off disease. As a vegetable symbol of protection, garlic really is second to none. Its most famous use, arguably, is as a talisman to ward off vampires; the garlic needs to be tied to the bedhead in an attempt to dissuade these demonic creatures.

Like its relation the onion, garlic was believed to ward off snakes, and this could well be because of the efficacy of garlic in treating all kinds of infections. Shepherds in the Carpathian mountains still rub their hands with garlic before milking their ewes; this is a symbolic ritual that has its roots in solid fact, since the antibacterial powers of the garlic can prevent the spread of disease.

Garlic used to be carried by brides as a symbol of good luck, although this practice seems to have died out.

GINSENG

Ginseng is one of the plants accorded magical properties partly because of the appearance of its roots, which look like a human being. In the East, particularly in China, ginseng is revered as being the elixir of life and is called *Panax ginseng* in recognition of its supposed powers of curing all ills. Symbolically, the ginseng plant represents longevity, vitality, vigor, strength, and clarity. Ginseng is also said to be an aphrodisiac and to increase both sexual potency and virility.

GRASS

Often overlooked because it is one of the more prolific plants on the planet, the very mundanity of grass is the factor that elevates its symbolic status. As a litmus, grass is invaluable; dry, brown, and dying grass signifies a drought, whereas lush green grass is symbolic of healthy land and fertility. The Roman army gave a crown of grass, or *corona graminea*, as the highest of accolades to particularly effective warriors; symbolic of the very land itself, this crown was made of grasses, flowers, and weeds pulled from the battle-field. The entire army had to decide whether or not their leader deserved such a high accolade, which was given only after the most desperate of campaigns. Pliny the Elder recorded only nine men who had received this honor.

HEMLOCK

The very word "hemlock" conjures up the idea of poison, but curiously, although the hemlock is deadly for humans, it does not harm domes-ticated animals. The hemlock is symbolic of death, pure and simple, and, famously, was consumed by Socrates. After his trial, Socrates was given the death sentence and it was decreed that he must kill him-self by drinking hemlock. The great philosopher used his philosophical outlook to great effect and drank the hemlock without fuss, even managing to describe his symptoms as the poison gradually overcame him. The whole episode was described by Plato. To this day, the phrase "to drink hemlock" is synonymous with committing suicide.

Hemlock used to be rubbed onto knives and swords to prepare them to kill the enemy, the poison further enhancing the potency of the blade as an instrument of death. The hemlock plant should not be confused with *Tsuga*, the tree genus of hemlock.

HEMP

Hemp is the name for all the different species of cannabis. *Cannabis sativa* and *Cannabis indica* were species that were smoked in many countries all around the world long before the Conquistadores discovered tobacco. Its ubiquity is reflected in its many different names; in India, it is called *bhang* or *ganja* from the Sanskrit words *bhanga* or *ghanjika*; in the Near East it is called *hashish* (incidentally, the origin of the word "assassin") from an Arabic word meaning hemp; in South Africa it is called *dakka*, and the native South American name of *marijuana* was interpreted by the Conquistadores as "Mary Jane." It's called "weed" just about everywhere.

The usefulness of hemp in making fabric is really overshadowed by its use as a narcotic plant. Its use as a ritual substance is well documented, with evidence dating back as far as Neolithic times. A mummified shaman was found in China in 2003 along with a leather basket containing fragments of seeds and leaves. Shamanistic use of cannabis included burning of the flowers of the plant to induce a trance-like state.

Of late, hemp has been adopted as a sacred herb by the Rastafarian movement and the cannabis leaf symbol is often depicted in the Rasta colors of red, green, and gold. It is considered that the use of the herb purifies the soul, clears the mind, and promotes peacefulness.

The Mahayana Buddhist tradition sees hemp as a particularly sacred plant because it is associated with the Buddha, who, so they say, lived on one hemp seed per day as he journeyed toward enlightenment.

IVY

Ivy is traditionally seen as the female counterpart to the masculine holly, and the two plants are paired together symbolically in Christmas and Yuletide songs. Like the vine, ivy has tendrils that enable it to climb vigorously, and, like the vine, ivy is associated with Dionysus. He is often depicted using the plant to bind the nubile young ladies who would otherwise resist his advances. A wreath of ivy used to hang outside shops as a sign that wine might be purchased there.

Ivy was believed to be able to both cause and cure drunkenness, and an old cure for a hangover was to drink vinegar in which ivy berries had been boiled. It should be stated here, however, that most parts of the ivy are poisonous and it is not recommended that you try this remedy, no matter how bad your headache.

Houses with ivy growing on them are seen as being protected by the maternal nature of the plant, but the clinginess of the ivy is viewed as a less attractive female characteristic. It is this same binding tendency that makes ivy an ingredient in love charms.

Ivy appears in the Ogham Tree alphabet where it is called *Gort.*

JUNIPER

The juniper berry is what gives the alcoholic spirit gin both its name and its delicate flavor. In preChristian times the juniper bush was believed to harbor spirits, so offerings would be made to it to propitiate them. Junipers are symbolic of patience since the berries— which in fact are tiny cones—take three years to ripen. Buddhist monks use juniper wood in their sacred temple fires. The wood does not burn very well but gives off an aromatic smoke which is said to aid both meditation and inner visions.

Junipers happily grow in hilly, windswept places so they are symbolic of resilience. There's a legend that the infant Jesus and his parents hid in a juniper bush to escape Herod's soldiers.

Juniper berries are used to aid stomach ailments and are a purgative for worms. The old wives' method of inducing an abortion with a scalding hot bath and a bottle of gin has some truth in it; juniper berries contain a chemical that can cause uterine contractions, and to speak of a girl giving birth "under the savin" (an old word for the juniper) refers to an abortion induced by the plant.

THE LANGUAGE OF FLOWERS

The idea that a posy of flowers could convey a secret meaning, particularly between lovers, was originally an Eastern concept, although the flower as divine messenger is an ancient concept. The Buddha's words manifested as flowers dropping from the sky are an early example. The language of flowers is called floriography, and though this art gives specific meanings to flowers, these meanings do not always tie in with their more generally accepted symbolism.

This idea became popular in Europe (and consequently in America) after Lady Mary Wortley Montagu visited Turkey in 1718. Writing to her friends back home, she described the system she had discovered whereby flowers and other objects were used as a means of communication. This idea, called *hana kotoba*, also existed in Japan. It might seem strange to Westerners to think that the infamous samurai warriors were particularly fond of this art, but its influence was so powerful that samurai families often chose specific flowers as their crests, a similar device to the heraldic coats of arms.

Objects used to convey secret messages apart from flowers included fruits and other food, gemstones as well as valueless pebbles and even coal. Therefore a Turkish love letter was not simply a piece of paper or a bunch of flowers, but a parcel or packet containing a very odd assortment of items.

The lists of flowers and their meanings did vary, and this ambiguity continues today, although some meanings are generic. For example, the red rose is universally accepted as symbolizing love. The following list has been compiled from several different sources.

ACACIA—Secret love, considered bad luck if given to a woman

AMARANTH—Faith, immortality, unfading love

AMARYLLIS—You are sought after, poetry

ANEMONE—Brevity, "go away!"

APPLE BLOSSOM—Preference, better things to come, good fortune

ASPHODEL—Languor, regret, death

ASTER—Daintiness, a talisman of love

AZALEA—Take care, temperance, passion, Chinese symbol of womanhood

BABY'S BREATH—Innocence, purity of heart

BACHELOR'S BUTTON—Single blessedness, celibacy

BEGONIA—Beware, a fanciful nature

BLUEBELL/BELL FLOWER—Humility, constancy, gratitude

BUTTERCUP—Childishness, riches

CACTUS—Endurance, my heart burns with love

CALLA LILY—Magnificent beauty

CAMELLIA—Admiration, perfection, good-luck gift for a man, gratitude

CANTERBURY BELLS/BELL FLOWER—Gratitude

CARDINAL FLOWER/SCARLET LOBELIA—Distinction

CARNATION (General)—Fascination, admiration

CELANDINE/PILEWORT/FIGWORT—Future joy

CHRISTMAS ROSE/HELLEBORUS—Relieve my anxiety

CHRYSANTHEMUM (General)—You're a wonderful friend, cheerfulness

CLEMATIS—Artifice (ingenuity)

CLOVER—Fertility

CLOVER (Four-leaf)—Be mine

CONVOLVUS MINOR/BINDWEED—Uncertainty, tender affection

CORNFLOWER—Delicacy, refinement

COWSLIP—Rusticity, winning grace, healing, youth, pensiveness

CROCUS—Cheerfulness, abuse not, gladness

CYPRESS—Mourning

DAFFODIL—Regard, unrequited love, you're the only one

DAHLIA—Dignity and elegance, forever thine, instability

DAISY—Innocence, loyal love, purity, beauty, respect

DANDELION—Faithfulness, happiness, love's oracle

DELPHINIUM—Big-hearted, fun

DOG ROSE—Pleasure and pain

EGLANTINE/SWEET-BRIAR/ROSA EGLANTARIA—Poetry, I wound to heal

ELDERFLOWER—Zeal

EUPHORBIA—Persistence

EVERLASTING—Never-ceasing memory

FERN—Magic, fascination, confidence, shelter

FORGET ME NOT—True love, memories, remembrance

FORSYTHIA—Anticipation

FOXGLOVE/FAIRY THIMBLES/DEAD MEN'S BELLS—Stateliness, youth

FOXTAIL GRASS—Sporting

FREESIA—Innocence, trust

FUCHSIA (Scarlet)—Confiding love, taste

GARDENIA—You're lovely, secret love, purity, refinement

GENTIAN (Closed)—Sweet be thy dreams

GERANIUM—True friend, stupidity, folly

GERBERA—Innocence

GLADIOLI—Generosity, I'm sincere, flower of the gladiators

GRASS—Homosexual love

GUELDER ROSE/SNOWBALL—Winter

HAREBELL/CAMPANULA—Humility, grief

HEARTSEASE/PURPLE/JOHNNY JUMP UP—You occupy my thoughts

HEATHER (Lavender)—Admiration, solitude

HEATHER (White)—Protection, wishes will come true

HELIOTROPE—Devotion

HIBISCUS—Consumed by love, delicate beauty

HOLLY—Defense, domestic happiness, good wishes

HOLLYHOCK—Fruitfulness

HONESTY/LUNARIA/DOLLAR PLANT/MONEY PLANT—Sincerity

HONEYSUCKLE—The bond of love

HUCKLEBERRY—Faith, simple pleasures

HYACINTH (General)—Games and sports, rashness, dedicated to Apollo

HYDRANGEA—Thank you for understanding, frigidity, heartlessness

INDIAN CRESS/NASTURTIUM—Resignation

IRIS—Your friendship means so much to me, faith, hope, wisdom and valor, my compliments

IVY—Wedded love, fidelity, friendship, affection

JAPONICA—Sincerity, symbol of love

JASMINE—Admirability

JONQUIL—Love me, affection returned, desire, sympathy

KENNEDIA—Intellectual beauty

LADY'S SLIPPER—Win me, capricious beauty

LARKSPUR—Levity, an open heart, lightness, fickleness

LAVENDER—Love, devotion

LILAC (General)—Beauty, pride

LILY (Calla)—Beauty

LILY (Day)—Coquetry, Chinese emblem for mother

LILY (General)—Majesty and honor, purity of heart

LILY (Orange)—Hatred, dislike

LILY OF THE VALLEY—Sweetness, tears of the Virgin Mary, happiness, humility

LOTUS—Estranged love, forgetful of the past

LOVE IN A MIST—You puzzle me

LOVE-LIES-BLEEDING/ AMARANTHUS—Hopeless, not heartless, desertion

LYCHNIS/CAMPION/ MALTESE CROSS—Religious enthusiasm

MAGNOLIA—Nobility, perseverance

MALLOW—Delicate beauty, sweetness

MARIGOLD (Common)—Cruelty, grief, jealousy

MARJORAM—Joy, happiness

MIGNONETTE—Your qualities surpass your charms, health

MIMOSA—Secret love

MINT—Virtue

MISTLETOE—Kiss me, affection, difficulties, sacred plant of India

MORNING GLORY—Affection

MULLEIN—Good nature

MYRTLE—Love, joy, Hebrew emblem of marriage

NARCISSUS—Egotism, formality

NASTURTIUM—Conquest, victory in battle

OAK LEAVES—Bravery

OLEANDER—Caution

OLIVE BRANCH—Peace

ORANGE BLOSSOM—Innocence, eternal love, marriage, fruitfulness

ORCHID—Love, beauty, refinement, Chinese symbol for many children, thoughtfulness

PALM LEAVES—Victory and success

PANSY—Merriment, thoughts (you occupy my thoughts)

The Encyclopedia of Secret Signs and Symbols

PASQUE FLOWER—Unpretentious, you have no claims

PASSION FLOWER—Faith, religious fervor

PEONY—Shame, happy marriage, compassion, bashfulness

PERIWINKLE/VINCA/MYRTLE—Early recollections, pleasures of memories, sweet memories

PETUNIA—Your presence soothes me

PHLOX—Our souls are united, unanimity

PINK (Mountain)—You are aspiring

POPPY (General)—Eternal sleep, oblivion, imagination

POPPY (Red)—Pleasure

PRIMROSE—I can't live without you

QUAKING GRASS—Agitation

RAGGED-ROBIN—Wit

RANUNCULUS—I am dazzled by your charms

RHODODENDRON—Danger, beware, I am dangerous

ROSE (Bridal)—Happiness

ROSE (Christmas)—Relieve my anxiety

ROSE (Dog)—Pleasure and pain

ROSE (Green)—I am from Mars

ROSE (Red)—Love, I love you, respect, beauty

ROSE (Tea)—I'll remember, always

ROSEMARY—Remembrance

ROSE-OF-SHARON—Consumed by love

ROSES (Bouquet of full bloom)—Gratitude

ROSES (Garland or crown of)—Beware of virtue, reward of merit, symbol of superior merit

ROSES (Single full bloom)—I truly love you, simplicity.

RUE—Mercy, pity

SAGE—Domestic virtues, wisdom, great respect, female fidelity

SHAMROCK—Lightheartedness

SNAPDRAGON—Gracious lady, strength

SNOWDROP—Hope, consolation

SOLIDAGO—Success

STEPHANOTIS—Marital happiness, desire to travel

STOCK—Bonds of affection, promptness, you'll always be beautiful to me

SUNFLOWER—Constancy, devotion

SWEET PEA—Departure

SWEET WILLIAM—Gallantry

SYRINGIA/MOCK ORANGE/
LILAC—Memory

TEASEL—Misanthropy

THRIFT (ARMERIA)—Sympathy

TRUMPET FLOWER/ANGEL'S
TRUMPET/DATURA—
Separation

TULIP (General)—Perfect lover,
fame, flower emblem of Holland

VALERIAN—Accommodating
disposition

VENUS FLYTRAP—Caught
at last

VENUS' LOOKING GLASS—
Flattery

VERBENA—Pray for me,
sensibility

VERONICA SPEEDWELL—
Fidelity

VERVAIN—Enchantment

VIOLET—Modesty, virtue,
affection, steadfastness

WALL FLOWER—Faithful
in adversity, fidelity, lasting
beauty

WISTERIA—Welcome

WITCH HAZEL—A spell

WOODBINE—Fraternal love

YUCCA—Yours until death

ZEPHYR FLOWER—Sincerity,
symbol of love

ZINNIA (Mixed)—Thinking (or
in memory) of an absent friend

LILY

Along with the rose and the lotus,
the lily comprises a sacred trinity
of the most important flower symbols in the world.

Not all lilies are white, but
paleness is synonymous with the
flower; we even speak of something as being "lily white." The
lily is therefore a symbol of purity,
innocence, and virginity. The angel
Gabriel appeared to Mary carrying

a lily, and the flower has always been associated with the Virgin. However, both the shape of the lily's petals and its phallic-looking pistils, standing erect from the center of the flower, mean that the flower is a symbol of sexuality and reproduction. So the lily effectively contains both male and female reproductive parts; hence when we see depictions of Mary we can recognize the flower as symbolizing virginity as well as fertility and motherhood.

The lily is the symbol of the goddess, in whatever form she may take, and the Babylonian goddess Lilith—reputedly the first wife of Adam—who was later demonized by the Christian Church, takes her name from the name of the lily or the lilu (lotus). The flower is also sacred to Astarte, whose name in parts of Europe is Eostre, which gives us the word "Easter"; hence the lilies which have become a symbol of this springtime celebration are a secret symbol of a much older association.

Lotus

The lotus is arguably one of the most important flower symbols on the planet, along with the lily and the rose. The lotus can only be grown under hothouse conditions in western Europe, and for a Westerner to see a lotus growing in the wild for the first time can be an astonishing experience. Both the otherworldly appearance of the flower and its growing circumstances make it obvious that the flower is somehow very special indeed. It's therefore no surprise that the flower is one of the eight auspicious symbols in both Chinese and Tibetan Buddhist iconography.

This sensuous and extraordinary flower, with its perfect petals, rises imperiously from muddy swamps, its head above the dirty water. The symbolism applied by generations of Egyptian, Indian, and Chinese sages is obvious. First, the flower rises in complete perfection from the murky primal waters of creation. Next, the flower comes from the darkness into the light, woken by the sun; third, the lotus symbolizes the triumph of spirit over matter and is a metaphor for the journey to enlightenment.

Because the lotus retreats back into the water during the hours of darkness only to rise again above the surface of the water at dawn, the Egyptians saw it as a symbol of death and rebirth.

The tight bud of the flower is a symbol for the universe. The flower is also an archetypal symbol for the vulva, and so is associated with the goddess.

In all cultures the lotus carries within it a reminder of the elements. It has its seed within the earth; it grows in water; the blossom exists in air which also carries its fragrance; and the flower itself is awoken by the sun, and therefore the element of fire which it also resembles, the curious central circle surrounded by the rays of petals. The symbol of the lotus is often partially hidden in mandalas, the petals forming a border that is both symbolic and decorative. The Buddha sits in the center of the eight-petaled lotus, detached from the material world with its cycle of death and rebirth.

In Hindu iconography, the lotus is seen as the base of the earth from which the holy mountains (such as Kailash and Meru) rise. The stalk of the flower is associated with the World Axis which rises up through sacred mountains.

MANDRAKE

Mandrake roots have a very human-looking form, the cause of many odd beliefs about the plant. It was said, for example, to grow where the semen of a hanged man dripped onto the ground. When wrenched from its burial place in Mother Earth, the mandrake would utter such a terrifying shriek that anyone hearing it would die on the spot. The only way to harvest the root was to get a dog to dig it up, causing the unfortunate animal to suffer fatal consequences. In the Harry Potter books, the children that are re-potting mandrake seedlings have to wear protective headphones.

The Egyptians believed that the mandrake was an aphrodisiac and so it also became a love symbol. Since all parts of the plant, if taken in quantity, are poisonous and have narcotic effects, as a love philter mandrake needed to be handled with care. As the emblem of the great sorceress Circe, the plant had particularly powerful magical properties, and was treated with both awe and reverence.

The Greeks used it to deaden the senses of people during surgical operations. Charms made from mandrake roots were sold at a high price during the Middle Ages, and were highly prized because of the perceived danger and difficulty of obtaining the roots.

MISTLETOE

The sacred golden bough of mythology, mistletoe is a mysterious plant, the subject of poem, song, and legend. Its sacred nature is attributable to many factors. It grows only in the sky, and never on the ground, so is closer to the heavens; it is propagated by birds, themselves symbolic messengers of the gods; and its pearlescent berries represent drops of semen, so the mistletoe represents fertility. Mistletoe has

healing properties, too, and is often hosted by a sacred tree.

A parasitic plant, many people assume that oak trees host mistletoe, but in fact, it is much more usual for it to be found growing on old apple trees. Most visible in the winter months when the trees are bare of leaves, bundles of mistletoe look like untidy birds' nests, a scribble in the branches of the tree.

Birds play a large part in the life cycle of the mistletoe. The mistle thrush in particular eats the berries; these are "planted" when they are excreted. In addition, when the birds scrape their beaks on branches to remove excess seeds, the seeds are embedded under the bark where they can take root.

Druids traditionally harvest mistletoe with a golden sickle, a magical tool that represents the sun. It is vital that the plant is not tainted by contact with the ground and care is taken to make sure that it keeps its airy associations intact. It is caught in sheets that are stretched taut around the tree.

As an evergreen, mistletoe symbolizes longevity and immortality, and has become a traditional part of Christmas decorations in the home. However, although holly and ivy have managed to cloak their pre-Christian significance in order to enfold themselves into the mythology of the Church, it has been harder for mistletoe to be absorbed in the same way. The plant is an uncomfortable reminder of powerful pre-Christian practices and beliefs, and is banned in many churches. Despite this, mistletoe is sometimes called *lignum sanctae crucis*, since the Church said at one time that the cross of Christ had been made of mistletoe wood (an unlikely claim for anyone familiar with the fragile stalks of the plant).

Paradoxically, given that the mistletoe is poisonous, it is also called "all heal." Because of its symbolism, it was used to aid fertility problems, but recently it has been found to be effective in circulatory and respiratory problems, as well as possessing anti-carcinogenic qualities.

Initially, people hung mistletoe indoors to ward off evil spirits. The tradition of kissing under the mistletoe is a remnant of its potency as a fertility symbol, and because of the tiny little "x" (kiss) symbol found on the underside of the berry.

NETTLE

The stinging nettle originates in Mediterranean areas, and was spread elsewhere by Roman soldiers who planted it wherever they found the climate to be cold. They would warm themselves by rubbing themselves with the stinging leaves, a practice that might seem odd to anyone who has experienced the pain of the nettle sting.

The nettle is symbolic of healing, protection, courage, and also of exorcism; it was used to ward off ghosts, and in combination with yarrow was said to give courage.

Nettles were used in remote healing; the plant was grasped firmly and the name of the patient spoken out loud, the idea being that the pain was taken on by the person carrying out this ritual.

Nettles were the symbol of the god Thor, and like him, were associated with thunder and lightning, hence its old German name *Donnernessel*. In deference to this, bunches of nettles would be thrown over the roofs of houses to deflect the lightning from the home. A decoction of nettles is said to clear the blood, and has been used as an aphrodisiac.

Nettles make good strong thread, and nettle fabric was used to make the uniforms of the German army during World War I when other material was in short supply.

Orchid

The word *orkhis* is Greek for testicles, named for the shape of the bulb of the orchid flower. Greek mothers-to-be believed that they could control the sex of their unborn child by eating orchid roots; large for a boy and small for a girl.

Because of this reason and also because of the shape of the flower, which looks like the female genitalia, the orchid scores high as a symbol of sexuality and potency. In China, orchids were used as a charm to ward off barrenness; however, to cut an orchid meant that your children might die.

The beauty of the orchid led to it becoming a symbol of spiritual perfection, and the longevity of its flowers symbolizes undying truth.

Pansy

The pansy has gained a reputation as being a flower of remembrance, in part because its name sounds like the French *pensées*, meaning "thoughts." The pansy is subject to much anthropomorphism because its petals resemble a little face.

The old English names for the pansy are "love in idleness" or "heartsease," since it was believed that to carry a pansy would reassure the person that they were loved, truly. Hence the pansy represents loving thoughts.

Parsley

Parsley has always had association with magical powers, and is seen in some countries as an evil plant despite its usefulness in the kitchen. In ancient Greece it was the herb which most symbolized death, and graves were strewn with it. It was served with meat in order to calm the spirit of the slaughtered animal.

Parsley can take a long time to germinate, and it used to be said that it had to visit the devil nine times before the seeds sprouted. If you are brave enough to have parsley in your garden, then it will apparently grow best in a place where the female is more powerful than the male partner. If sowing parsley, the only day on which it can be done that does not throw the immortal soul of the gardener into serious risk is Good Friday, when Satan has no jurisdiction over the soil.

Passion flower

At first glance it might seem odd that this climbing jungle exotic, a flamboyant and unusual flower, should have a Latin name comprised of the words for "suffering flower." However, the passion flower was discovered by the Spanish when they invaded the Inca territories in the sixteenth century, and when they came across it they saw it as a message of approval from God that it was right to convert the native peoples to Catholicism.

A gothic-looking blossom, the passion flower seems to contain within it certain symbols that the Spanish read as being reminders of Christ's suffering, or passion. The central part of the flower looks like a crown of thorns. The innocence of Christ is reflected in its white petals, of which there are ten, the same as the number of faithful apostles. The styles that emerge from the center of the flower represent the nails used in the crucifixion and the five stamens are the wounds endured by Christ.

There are other aspects to the passion flower, though, beyond this strictly Catholic interpretation. Passiflorine, a narcotic substance derived from the plant, induces heavy hypnosis or sleep, and prior to its use as a medicinal plant the passion flower was consumed by shamans who believed that it enabled communion with the unseen world of spirits and gods.

In modern-day Japan, the flower has become a symbol for male homosexuality.

Peyote

One of the holy plants of Mexico, a part of this small, spineless desert plant is consumed as the peyote "button," a small protuberance that is attached to the side of the peyote cactus. The hunt for the cactus itself forms a part of a ritual that has been carried out by the shamans of the area for thousands of years. The psychoactive ingredients in the peyote button include mescaline, which causes vivid hallucinations, allowing the psychic explorer to travel in other dimensions, communicate with animals, and experience the world in a heightened state of consciousness. The peyote itself symbolizes a gateway into another world.

The hunt for the peyote, its ingestion, and the hallucinatory process can take several days. Carlos Castaneda records the whole process in great detail in his "Don Juan" books.

POPPY

Because of the narcotic qualities of some of its species, the poppy is the flower of sleep and oblivion, a reputation it has had for many centuries. The most common opiates—heroin and morphine—come from the opium poppy, *Papaver somniferum*. Morpheus, the Greek god of sleep, counts these drugs among his attributes, as does Demeter in her guise as goddess both of the harvest and of death.

The story goes that the god of sleep made the poppy specifically for Demeter because she could not sleep after she lost her daughter, Persephone. Demeter was so tired that she could not get the corn to grow. After the drugs helped her to sleep, all was well again, and it is still counted as good luck to see poppies in a cornfield.

Because of its reputation as a flower that can either cure or kill, there is an ambiguity about the poppy; some see it as a good influence, and some as evil.

Where the poppy head appears in paintings, it often secretly symbolizes fertility, because of its numerous seeds.

Recently, the poppy has become a symbol of remembrance for those who died during the two world wars. In November, around the time of Remembrance Day, paper poppies are sold to raise funds for bereaved families. The poppy is well suited for this purpose because it grew in profusion in the fields of Flanders. However, the poppy as a symbol of grief for lost warriors is not new; in the *Iliad*, written in the eighth century BC, a description of a dying warrior compares him to a poppy.

ROSE

In common with the lotus and the lily, the rose is one of the most important flower symbols in the

pointed star created by the natural world. Because of its perfection and beauty, the rose is a symbol of purity. At the same time the flower has undeniably sensuous qualities, in both its luxuriant petals and its scent, equating it with female sexuality. Paradoxically, the rose is at once a symbol of life and of death, of heavenly perfection and earthly desire, of fertility and chastity.

world, its influence as a sacred flower pervading all cultures and religious beliefs. The reasons for many of these beliefs is shrouded in mystery, not a surprise given the age of the flower; fossilized roses from 35 million years ago have been found, and wreaths of roses have been found in the most ancient tombs. These days, the rose (particularly if it is red) is the ultimate flower of love, an ingredient in love potions and philters, dedicated to Venus and Aphrodite.

Love is, however, not the only symbolic meaning of the flower. Its beauty springing from the muddy earth is a synonym for the triumph of spirit over matter, an aspect it shares with the lotus.

Like the lotus, the number of the rose's petals carries meaning. The original wild rose, prior to human cultivation, has five petals, an example of a pentagram or five-

The rose is also a symbol of secrecy, perhaps because of the way the petals hide its center, perhaps for some more obscure reason. To speak of something as being *sub rosa*—"under the rose"—means that any information must be kept confidential. Some Masonic lodges and alchemy guilds still conduct meetings with a red rose hanging from the ceiling as a reminder of the private nature of the discussions taking place. There are three roses on the ceremonial apron of the Master Mason, acting as reminders of faith, silence, and secrecy.

The Rosy Cross of the Rosicrucians has a rose at its intersection. Here the rose symbolizes the heart, life, and secrecy.

In alchemy, the wild rose carries rich symbolic meaning, too; it is primarily the sign of the union of opposites, (again because the petals indicate 2 + 3 = 5). Alchemical terminology calls this the "con-junction." The colors of roses are as important within the alchemical tradition as anywhere else and carry the same meanings; the red rose for male energy, passion, love; the white rose for female energy, innocence, purity; yellow for compassion and humanity; pink for friendship and thankfulness; and orange for enthusiasm and optimism. The black rose—which does not exist in nature—is symbolic of death, depression, and loss. Roses have long been associated with Mary, mother of Jesus, and rose windows in cathedrals and churches are her symbol. In India, the Great Mother was called the Holy Rose.

SAFFRON

The spice saffron is one of the most valuable on the planet because of the difficulty in harvesting it; it is comprised of the tiny stamens of a particular type of crocus. Because of its vibrant yellow color, it is associated with the sun and also with wisdom, and carries many of the associations of the actual color which is named after it.

The saffron-colored robes of Buddhist monks are a significant part of their identity. Saffron is also made into a paste that is used to mark the followers of certain castes or divisions within Hindu tradition.

SAGE

Unsurprisingly given its name, sage is said to confer wisdom on those who eat it or who drink an infusion of the dried flower as a tisane. It is also a symbol of longevity, protection, and cleansing.

The sage leaf is a divinatory tool, used in the following simple manner. Write down whatever you desire on the leaf and leave it under your pillow for three nights. If you dream of your desire during this time, then your dream will come true.

Bundles of the herb tied up with cotton thread are used as "smudge sticks"; that is, sticks that are used, ritually, to purify a sacred area with their smoke. The smoldering herb has a medicinal scent. This practice originated with Native American tribes but has spread into many other parts of the world.

STRAWBERRY

The sacred strawberry is one of the fruits that grew in the Elysian Fields, the resting place of blessed souls. There is also strong Christian symbolism associated with the strawberry plant.

The three parts of the leaf are emblematic of the Holy Trinity, and the white flowers stand for the purity of the Virgin Mary and the innocence of Christ. The fruit of the strawberry has neither thorns nor pips and is eaten whole, thereby representing good deeds; the red color symbolizes the blood of Christ. Where strawberries grow at the feet of the Virgin in religious paintings, the plant carries all these different meanings.

The strawberry, in its fruiting stage, is symbolic of fecundity and sensuality, both being aspects of any seeded fruit that are often overlooked by the Christian Church. In the interplay of the sacred and the profane that is an intrinsic part of the allegorical perception of nature, strawberries are symbolic of spiritual development as well as physical sensuality.

As a symbol of vitality because of its bright red color, there was an old belief that eating plenty of strawberries would ensure a long life. It seems that this old wives' tale, as is often the case, has a basis in truth. Recent research shows that strawberries have anti-carcinogenic properties.

SUNFLOWER/ HELIOTROPE

As its name signifies, the sunflower has close solar associations, not only because of its appearance, but also because of its habit of turning its head to follow the course of the sun during its journey across the sky. The sunflower has magical powers, too, and adorned the crowns of Roman emperors, thereby conferring the ruler with the potent power of the sun that the flower held within it. The sunflower was later adopted by the Christian Church to denote the saints, prophets, and apostles of the faith; as the flower follows the sun, so the true believer follows God.

The sunflower was sacred to Native Americans; the flowers were used extensively in celebrations and festivities, and the image of the sunflower was carved into golden breastplates.

The sunflower is a symbol of light, hope, and innocence, and has been adopted fairly recently as a symbol for world peace.

The seed head of the sunflower contains a magical symbol. It shows a perfect example of the golden spiral that has been created naturally. This shape is one of the cornerstones of sacred geometry.

TEA

There are many different kinds of tea, and lots of different herbal decoctions are called by the name of tea; however, "real" tea, the "cup that cheers," is made from the plant called *Camellia sinensis*, a member of the camellia family that originated in India.

There is a story telling how, in AD 1510, the Indian prince Bodhidharma arrived in China to spread the teachings of the Buddha. He swore that he would not sleep until his mission was accomplished. This proved to be an ambitious aim, and although he managed several years of nonstop teaching and meditating, the prince eventually fell asleep. When he awoke he was so angry with himself that he cut off his eyelids, and where they fell the Buddha caused the first tea plant to grow. Tea leaves have an eyelid shape and the herb contains caffeine, which hinders sleep, so the story aptly explains the origins of both the plant and its qualities. Tea's ability to refresh and revitalize was soon realized and its popular-ity spread rapidly. Because it was expensive, it was the provenance of the wealthy, and so tea became a status symbol.

The tea ceremony in Japan is a Zen ritual that aims to remove the ego from the action, and is carried out in accordance with strict guidelines. The English tradition of afternoon tea is not religiously significant but became an essential part of the day after the Duchess of Bedford made it a fashionable habit in the mid-nineteenth century.

TOBACCO

It's impossible to say precisely when people first started chewing, smoking, or sniffing various dried plants, but it's safe to say that we have done all of these for several thousands of years all over the world. The reasons for this are many; for medicinal purposes, as a stimulant, or as a narcotic, for relaxation, and for ritual purposes. However, no herb used in these ways has gained the worldwide popularity of tobacco.

Originating from the Americas, tobacco was used by Native American shamans long before it was "discovered" by the Conquistadores and other Western colonizers. Drinking tobacco juice was a ritual carried out during training for these medicine men, the juice invoking hallucinations or visions. The juice was squirted into the eyes to confer the gift of second sight. Smoking tobacco was considered to be even more profoundly magical an act than drinking it, enabling the smoker to come into direct contact with the spirit world, and passing the pipe of tobacco around a circle of people signified the unity of the group and the shared vision. The ceremony began with the ritual pipe, or calumet, being offered to the sky, then the earth; then smoke was puffed towards the four cardinal points to acknowledge the spirits of the directions and of the elements. The smoke was blown over people to heal diseases and to confer strength.

The tobacco ceremony was carried out with due solemnity in honor of the sacred properties of the herb; however, when it was introduced to Europe in the sixteenth century, people rapidly became addicted to it. Tobacco "drinking," as smoking was called at the time, became a fashionable pursuit, and by 1610 there were as many as 7,000 tobacco shops in London alone.

As with many of the most sacred herbs and plants that were originally designated for use only very occasionally, tobacco is extremely poisonous, and the enormous amount of deaths caused by its consumption could arguably be said to be indicative of a general lack of respect for the magical substances given to us by the natural world.

TOMATO

The tomato—because of its red color and its succulence—was viewed with great suspicion when it arrived in Europe from the Americas in the sixteenth century. A sensual fruit stuffed full of many seeds, the tomato was called the love apple and was believed to be an aphrodisiac, and therefore it incurred the disapproval of the Church as a lewd fruit.

The tomato as a sexual symbol is also common in Africa, and in Bambara territories couples eat them before making love. Women make offerings of tomatoes to the god Faro. The biggest tomato fight in the world, La Tomatina, occurs annually in August in the town of Bunyol, near Valencia, in Spain.

VINE

In Christian symbolism, the vine, with its far-reaching tendrils, represents the Kingdom of God, and is described as such in the Gospels. Although there are many different types of plant that have vine-like attributes, the vine referred to is the grape vine since, of course, grapes give us wine, which is seen as conferring knowledge and immortality.

The vine grows vigorously and has tendrils that both climb and bind, using available surfaces in order to reach the sunlight while using the minimum of energy. In some cultures, including that of the Babylonians, the vine was symbolic of the Tree of Life itself. Indeed, the Latin word for vine, *vitis*, came from the same root as that of "vitality." The Sumerian hieroglyph for "life" was a vine leaf.

The vine is associated with the Greek god Dionysus (or when in Rome, Bacchus). Because vines need to be chopped back in order to grow most vigorously, they are symbolic of renewed vigor after a sacrifice.

The vine appears in the Ogham Tree alphabet where it is called *Muin*.

WORMWOOD

The Greek word for this herb, *apsinthion*, means "without sweetness" and lends its name to the alcoholic liqueur (absinthe) which is made from it and which can cause a disease called absinthism if too much of it is consumed on a habitual basis. A symptom of this disease is complete paralysis. The drink became so problematic during the nineteenth and early twentieth centuries that it was banned, although it is gaining popularity once more.

Because of its bitterness, the plant symbolizes this quality as well as that of grief or of something that is poisonous to the soul. In the Book of Revelation, "Wormwood" is the name given to the star related to a devilish figure that, it is predicted, will lay waste to Israel; the star falls from the heavens and poisons a third of the water on earth. This story is believed to foretell the Last Judgment, symbolized by the poisoning of our waters.

Wormwood was used in magical spells to make the dead rise from their graves, and, rather unexpectedly in view of this, was an ingredient in love philters. The plant is said to confer psychic powers and the gift of second sight.

The Latin name for the herb is *Artemisia absinthum*, showing its association with the goddess Artemis, the huntress and the great goddess of the woods.

WORLD TREE

It's not difficult to see why the tree is universally revered as a sacred, living being. Trees are not only beautiful but also benevolent, providing food in the form of nuts, fruits, and syrups, medicines (aspirin, for example, comes from the bark of the willow), and its timber provides material to build houses, ships, and carriages, as well as weapons and tools. Trees, too, provided the material to make gallows, and people were executed by being suspended from their branches.

The tree combines all the elements within it. It has its roots in the earth, which nourishes it; its sap is the water element, the "dew of heaven," as well as being its life blood; it has its leaves and branches high up in the air. Not only is fire produced when its sticks are rubbed together, but the wood provides fuel for that same fire. One of the most important functions of the tree, however, is its processing of carbon dioxide. The destruction of the rain forests is akin to a vital organ being removed from a human body. These forests are so great that they even create their own atmosphere, as do the coast redwood (or sequoia) forests in northern California. The Doctrine of Signatures—the ancient idea that a plant possesses the qualities of the thing that it physically resembles—makes sense in the case of the tree. Denuded of leaves, the branches look like a huge upturned lung, and indeed, trees are the lungs of our planet.

The idea of a World Tree, a giant tree that grows through the cosmos linking the heavens, the earth, and the underworld, is completely universal, constituting a primal image or archetype, having parallels with the Axis Mundi and the omphalos. This tree represents not only the idea of something that strives toward the heavens, but the life cycle of the tree itself is a reminder of the endless cycle of regeneration; of life, death, and rebirth. The birds that sit in the tops of the branches of this tree symbolize the souls of unborn beings. The symbolism of the tree is far-reaching; it is used to represent the idea of a family;

the Kabbalah itself is imagined as a tree; and in alchemy, the World Tree appears as a naked woman, crowned with sprouting, fruiting branches, wands in her hands, the sun and moon appearing to her right and left.

The inverted tree with its roots in the air, on the other hand, is a sacred symbol that has largely been forgotten. It symbolizes the idea from the Upanishads that the whole universe is an upside-down tree, its roots in the heavens and its branches embracing the earth. The same image appears in Kabbalistic imagery, the ten spheres of the Sephiroth and their twenty-two connecting branches generally represented as a cosmic tree.

ACACIA

The acacia thrives in barren, desert climates, and specimens have endured for thousands of years despite drought and famine. It provides shelter for both animals and people from the scorching heat of the sun, and its leaves and seeds are edible. These characteristics make it a symbol of protection and resilience. The tree also has vicious thorns that conceal the secrets said to be hidden by the tree. The wood of the acacia is particularly hard and durable, close-grained, of a beautiful orange color, impervious to insects, and seemingly incorruptible. This incorruptibility means that the tree signifies purity and its wood is therefore burned only for specific, magical purposes.

The acacia tree was around a long time before the Bible was written, and it is believed that this is what was meant by the Shittim tree mentioned in the Old Testament, the timber of which, plated with gold, was used to make the Ark of the Covenant. One of the trees speculated to have been used to make Christ's crown of thorns is the acacia; ancient kings who were sacrificially slaughtered wore these agonizingly painful crowns. The cross—sometimes described as a "tree"—upon which Christ was crucified, too, is likely to have been made from strong and durable acacia wood. For the Jewish people, the acacia was so sacred that it would never be used for mundane purposes such as furniture.

One of the foremost symbols in Freemasonry, a spring of acacia leaves is laid on the coffin at the funerals of Freemasons in memory of Hiram Abiff, builder of King Solomon's Temple. Hiram had the sprig of acacia laid on his grave as a sign not only of death and resurrection, but as a reminder that, like the tree, Hiram refused to divulge certain secrets. Its evergreen leaf is a symbol of the immortality of the soul, and the acacia, as a symbol of incorruptibility, signifies the purity of Hiram's soul.

APPLE TREE

The apple tree is a tree of the underworld, a tree of immortality, and sacred to Apollo. The mythical Isle of Avalon, meaning orchard (from *afal*, the old Welsh word for apple) is the resting place of Celtic kings and heroes, and one of the places where King Arthur is meant to wait until he is needed to rise once more to protect his people. For Celtic people, the apple tree symbolized the World Tree, the axis of the universe. They considered the apple the most magical of fruits, a fruit of immortality and prophecy. At Samhain, or Halloween, the time of the apple harvest, the fruit has a large part to play in the rituals and celebrations, including divinatory practices.

The apple itself contains a potent magical symbol within. If it is cut across its "equator" (with the stalk at the top), there are five pips inside, contained within a five-pointed star or pentagram. The pentagram, in turn, can be the basis of the golden spiral. The spherical shape of the apple symbolizes eternity.

In the biblical story, when Eve persuaded Adam to eat the fruit from the Tree of Knowledge, she also handed him the pentagram hidden inside the fruit (although the Bible never specifically states that this fruit was an apple). Here, the pentagram stands for the spiritual nature of man, and eating it awakens Adam to new possibilities; the flesh combines with the spirit, and immediately Adam and Eve cover their genitals, signifying sexual awakening. In Gypsy wedding ceremonies it is customary to cut the apple in the way described above, the bride and groom each eating a half of the fruit.

In Latin, the word for apple, *malum*, also means "evil," and reflects the paradox of the apple as a symbol of both good and evil. Although in the *Tales of the Arabian Nights* the apple of Prince Ahmed cures all ills, in the fairy tale *Snow White and the Seven Dwarves*, the eponymous heroine is poisoned by a shiny red apple offered by the witch and falls into the sleep of oblivion.

ASH

Yggdrasil, the "World Tree" of Nordic legends

The ash is one of the more important of all symbolic trees, and it is said to have been the first tree ever created. The plethora of myths and legends about it, which emanate from all corners of the globe, are testimony to its elevated mythological status. Just as the oak is the "King of the Forest," the ash is the "Queen of the Forest," associated with the color and element of silver, and other feminine qualities such as water and the moon. The goddess Nemesis, daughter of the sea god Oceanus, carried an ash wand as a symbol of divine justice. As a counterpoint to this, oaths were taken on spears made of ash wood.

The quality of the timber of our symbolic trees provides clues as to their meanings; ash wood is strong, does not split, and because it is hard and close-grained, it polishes well. In the days when wood was used more often than metal for mechanical objects, ash was used to make axles, the hard-polished wood ensuring the smooth turning of the wheels. Witches' broomsticks, made of ash, helped them to fly quickly through the air, as well as providing a powerful link with the goddess.

Perhaps the most famous ash, and the one that gives the most information as to the symbolic nature not only of the ash but of the tree archetype in general, is Yggdrasil. In northern European mythology, Yggdrasil is the great World Tree, whose roots stretch to the very heart of the earth where the Norns dwell. These are creatures that decide the fate of human beings. The extensive roots of this giant tree also reach down to the underground well, Mimir, which is the source of all the secrets of magical power and mystical revelation. The branches of Yggdrasil stretch right up into the heavens, sheltering the entire universe in its branches, a mythic tree that is the one constant feature of a changing world. Here we see the ash as a symbol of stability.

Because the ash was seen to exist in both the worlds of spirit and matter, it's a symbol of the union of opposites and therefore of marriage. The ash is also a fertility symbol, and amulets of ash wood are said to attract love. Older ash trees sometimes grow or split in such a way that a hole is formed in the trunk; it was customary to pass newborn babies or small children through this hole to ensure their protection or to cure illnesses, showing an aspect of this great tree as the mother-protector and healer. When this ritual was enacted, small tokens of food or coins would be pushed into the ground around the roots.

The ash, or *Nuin*, is the third letter of the Ogham Tree alphabet.

BANYAN

The banyan, also known as the vata tree, the bodhi tree or the Asiatic fig, is one of the trees considered to be the World Tree by the people who revere it.

This tree is particularly special because the Buddha happened to be sitting underneath one when he was suddenly illumined as to his true nature—the word *bodhi* means "enlightened." Although

the particular tree under which he was enlightened is no longer living, a cutting was taken in the second century BC by a Sri Lankan princess, and this tree now grows in Anuradhapura in Sri Lanka, where it is the object of pilgrimage. The banyan can now be found anywhere in the world where Buddhism or Hinduism are practiced, and it is often grown near temples. Although it is sacred, it is said to shelter many different kinds of spirits, and so it is considered unlucky to sleep under one at night.

The tree grows in quite an unusual way, with its roots reaching down from its branches which then take hold in the ground. This is why the banyan is sometimes called the "walking tree." The structure of the tree, which is a little like a strange organic building that casts a deep shade, makes it a perfect place to meet, and village councils in India (whose national tree symbol it is) still meet under these trees to discuss important matters.

BAOBAB

This is one of the oldest and largest of all trees, its gigantic, contorted shape a curiously cartoon-like silhouette against the skyline. The tree seems to be an amalgam of animal, vegetable, and mineral, with a distinct personality of its own. Because of its wrinkly, scored bark, size, and great age, the baobab is sometimes compared to the elephant. A creation myth from West Africa says that all the animals were each given their own tree. The hyena, appalled to be given the baobab, immediately tipped it upside down, which explains the root-like appearance of the branches.

The baobab occupies an important position in the community in places where it is prevalent, such as West Africa and Madagascar. At one time, the people buried their dead in its hollow trunk, no doubt in the hope that this massive, benevolent tree might protect the soul. In addition, when a baobab dies, people still commemorate it with a full-scale wake, according this tree a sacred status that is on a par with a human village elder. When the Kariba Dam in Zambia was built in the 1960s, the people had to evacuate the spirits from the baobab trees before the trees were submerged by water; branches were taken from the trees and attached to baobabs in unaffected areas.

BEECH

Beech woods are shady, magical places, but the trees are most commonly used in hedging these days (one of the tallest hedges in the world, the Meikleour beech hedge in Scotland, is over 100 feet tall). The tree forms nuts that are packed, three at a time, into an outer husk, and although they are edible, they are most commonly used in animal feed. Indeed in medieval times in Europe, pigs were often left to feed in the forest on the "mast"—the collective name for the beech's nuts. The beech, like the ash, often plays the role of "queen" to the oak's "king."

Like the birch, the beech tree is associated with written communication, and thin slices of its bark were used as paper. The name of the beech, *boc* in Anglo-Saxon, shares the same root as "book," a concept also found in German and Swedish etymology. It was an old custom to write a spell or magical charm on a sliver of beech wood, then bury it in the ground and wait for the desired item or situation to manifest itself.

BIRCH

The birch, being fast-growing, is often planted with the saplings of slower-growing trees (such as oak) in order to shelter them as they develop. Therefore, the tree is seen to have protective qualities. Suitably, given that the birch is often the first visible tree in the forest (hence its nickname, the "pioneer tree"), its name *Beth* is the first letter of the Ogham Tree alphabet, and as such it represents the start, the beginning, the birth. Accordingly, birch wood was often used for babies' cradles.

The root of the word "birch" is the same as that of "bright," and appropriately its bark, particularly those of the silver and the Himalayan birch, is both bright, beautiful, and symbolic of purity. This bark does not rot, lending the tree an aura of indestructibility, and the bark is quite flexible and can be written on; it is sometimes used as a parchment for spells. The *Midewiwin*, or Grand Medicine Society of the Ojibwa Indians, uses birch bark rolls to depict the symbols that serve as a reminder of the secrets of their society, and they become one of the most treasured items of an initiate. These birch bark rolls have the same sacred significance as the tracing board in Freemasonry.

BODHI TREE

See Banyan.

CEDAR

In the same way that oak groves were sacred in ancient Greece and throughout Britain, so too were cedar groves sacred in their native locations in the Middle East and North Africa, where similar oracular rites were carried out. The *Epic of Gilgamesh* describes cedar woods as being the dwelling place of the gods. Long-lived, large, dark-hued, and imposing, the cedar—particularly the stately Cedar of Lebanon—is clearly identifiable, being a symbol of longevity and nobility. The wood of the cedar is tough and durable, making the tree synonymous with the qualities of incorruptibility and purity. Its timber was used in the building of the Temple in Jerusalem.

Like all evergreens, the cedar is emblematic of immortality. It is one of the trees which, it is conjectured, was used to make the cross used in Christ's crucifixion; Christ shares the incorruptibility and purity of the tree. Paradoxically the original forest that used to cloak Mount Lebanon has now been reduced to a handful of scattered remnants. Cedar wood has a particularly fragrant scent, which is used in incenses; it is likewise burned by Jewish people to mark the New Year.

CHRISTMAS TREE

The old pagan custom of bringing a living tree indoors in the middle of the dark months of the year and decorating it with candles and trinkets was introduced to Britain by Prince Albert, the husband of Queen Victoria. The idea rapidly caught on. Bringing evergreen vegetation in the form of trees, boughs, and branches from the outside to the inside was a magical ritual, a piece of sympathetic magic, meant to encourage the return of spring and the growing season.

The timing of the entrance and exit of the tree was critical. Any time before Christmas Eve was too soon for the tree to come inside, and all decorations had to be taken down and the tree removed by Twelfth Night, January 6. This tradition, however, does not seem to signify for the department stores who start to display artificial Christmas trees from September onwards.

The Christmas tree is traditionally an evergreen tree, usually a spruce or a fir, which is cut down from the forest. The tree itself symbolizes immortality and everlasting life, and the lights draped on it are a reminder that during the darkest time of the year, lighter days are just around the corner. The Yule Celebrations in northern Europe were echoed in similar rituals in southern Europe. The Roman god Atys or Attis was a savior god whose life story very much parallels that of Christ. Atys was born on December 25 to a virgin mother, and was sacrificed to save mankind, killed beneath a conifer, remaining for three days and nights in his tomb before resurrection. His priests, called *dendrophori* (meaning "tree bearers"), were charged with selecting a conifer from a sacred grove that would be brought indoors in memory of the death and resurrection of Atys, who is also linked with Apollo, the sun god.

Elder

The elder appears in the Ogham Tree alphabet as the 15th letter, called *Ruis*. It is a prolific tree, happy to grow in poor soil and dense shade, although it rarely attains the height or girth of which it's capable; an elder with a 7-foot girth is an unusual sight.

One of the most beautiful aspects of the elder is its flowers. Abundant, frothy heads with hundreds of tiny flowerlets reach toward the sky and fill the air with a heady, distinctive, ethereal scent that can be used to flavor sorbets or cordials, or used to make a delicate sparkling wine. As well as these more worldly uses, the scent of these flowers, if inhaled deeply, will apparently open up the doorway into the realms of the fairies and elemental spirits. The ancients, particularly the Celts and some Native Americans, believed that the elder held the spirit of the "Elder Mother," a great mother goddess or nature spirit that would wreak havoc on anyone chopping down the tree. In England, permission had to be gained from "Old Gal" before a tree could be felled. Witches could shape-shift into the form of the elder, and an old superstition says that if an elder tree is "injured" then the tree would not only gush blood but would revert back into human shape; the witch would bear the same scars that had been inflicted on the tree.

Elm

Sadly, the elm population in both the UK and the U.S. has been decimated by Dutch elm disease, and this lofty, dignified tree, which used to reach an age of 400 years or more, is now considered lucky if it reaches thirty years.

However, the symbolism of the tree is rich, as befits such a beautiful specimen. Groves of elms were sacred to the goddess or the great mother, and some believed that the first woman was created by the elm tree. Such a large tree would be seen as a protective force, and the elm was planted in particular in vineyards to shade the plants and protect the vines. As a result it came to be linked with Bacchus, the Roman god of wine; the vine and the elm were effectively "wedded."

The elm is also connected with death, and the wood was used to make coffins at a time when the tree itself was not so rare. The elm has a special affinity with the elves that are said to guard burial mounds, so the tree was associated with these places.

The size of the elm meant that they made a good marker in the landscape, so much so that they often had pet names, and were used as meeting places. In the U.S. the famous Liberty Tree in Boston, Massachusetts, was a colossal elm beneath which the Sons of Liberty met from 1766 onwards. At the time of the American Revolution, an unauthorized meeting was a punishable offense, but it was relatively easy to meet hidden beneath the branches of such a tall tree. Soon all thirteen colonies each had their Liberty Tree as a place to meet under. The elm itself therefore became synonymous with the ideas of independence and liberty.

FIG TREE

There are many varieties of fig tree, and, wherever they appear and in whatever form, they are revered as the Tree of Life, symbolic of abundance, plenty, and peacefulness.

The tree under which the Buddha received his enlightenment was a species of fig, appropriately called *Ficus religiosa* in Latin. This tree—also called the banyan or the bodhi tree (meaning "enlightenment")—is from the same genus, *Ficus*, as those which in Africa house the souls of dead ancestors.

For Muslims the tree is held to have great intelligence, its consciousness only one step away from that of an animal. So the fig tree is also associated with knowledge; it's no coincidence that Adam and Eve chose to cover themselves with fig leaves after they had realized that they were naked.

The fig tree's milky sap also contributes to its symbolic meaning. Any tree containing a liquid that looks like semen is naturally associated with male fertility. The shape of the fruit of the fig itself, and its many seeds give further emphasis to the idea of male fertility and sexuality. There is also an obscene hand gesture called the "fig," made by sticking the thumb through the first and second fingers of a closed fist.

FIVE PACIFIC GIANTS

The following five species of tree all grow in the northwest of North America on the Pacific coast of both the U.S. and Canada. Apart from the two species of redwood (or sequoia) discussed below, they are among the tallest and largest of all trees. Their common names, however, are slightly misleading. The western hemlock should not be confused with the hemlock; it is quite a different plant from the one that killed Socrates. The Douglas fir is not a true fir at all, the Lawson's cypress is a false, not a true cypress, and the western red cedar has nothing to do—botanically—with the cedars of North Africa, the Middle East, and the Indian subcontinent, such as the Cedar of Lebanon and the deodar.

DOUGLAS FIR

This huge tree—an introduced specimen is the tallest tree in Britain—is named after the Scottish explorer David Douglas, who died in his thirties after being gored by a buffalo in Hawaii that had fallen into a trap that Douglas himself had set. The unusual arrangement of the seeds in its cones is explained by a Native American myth which holds that the three-ended bracts of the seeds are the tail and two legs of a mouse which hid from forest fires in the cone. The Douglas fir should not be confused with two other giant firs with a similar geographical range: the grand fir and the noble fir, which are true firs from the genus *Abies*.

LAWSON'S CYPRESS

The several hundred varieties of this tree make it one of the great symbols of suburbia. Bred by nurseries mainly in Britain and Holland, cultivars of the Lawson's cypress can be seen in most gardens in the West, such has been its success. Varieties can be totally different in character from the vast and brooding wild tree, and come in a range of colors from green through blue to yellow, including dwarf varieties that grow no higher than five feet.

SITKA SPRUCE

Large specimens of Sitka spruce can be found in the old-growth forests of the Pacific Northwest, the closest thing in the temperate world to a rain forest. Covered in mosses and tree ferns, these trees grow to an enormous height—the biggest so far discovered is called the "Carmanah Giant" on Vancouver Island, which is 315 feet tall (surprisingly, it is less than 400 years old). A similarly massive tree, called Kiidk'yaas, which was sacred to the Haida people, was illegally felled in 1997. Tribal elders believed that this act was a sign that the days of their people were numbered.

It is as a symbol of the unchecked advance of industrial-style agriculture that the Sitka is perhaps best known. Around 100 million saplings a year are planted in the uplands of Britain, forming vast, sterile blankets of uniform forest over much of the north and the west of the country. Ecologists who resent the spread of non-native trees in the country see Sitka spruce as the most culpable tree of all.

WESTERN HEMLOCK

This elegant tree, which can reach a height of 200 feet, has boughs which were used by Native Alaskans—particularly the Tlingit people—to collect herring eggs during the spawning season.

WESTERN RED CEDAR

Another enormous tree from the Pacific coast, the western red cedar was particularly sacred to the Native Americans of the region, some of whom called themselves the "people of the red cedar." Its timber was used in the making of totem poles, houses, tools, and canoes. The foliage, when crushed, has a distinct scent of pineapple.

HAZEL

For the Celts, the hazel was the Tree of Knowledge, the nuts of the tree believed to encapsulate great wisdom. In Druidic lore, it is closely aligned to the Salmon of Wisdom, which was believed to have acquired its knowledge from eating magical hazel nuts. Both the Druidic salmon and the hazelnut appear in the fall.

The hazel favors damp places, and this association with water means that the wood makes good dowsing rods, primarily for detecting water in the form of hidden underground wells or springs, but also for finding other things such as mineral seams. These rods were made from coppiced hazel, a forestry practice for which we have evidence from Bronze Age Britain. The combined power of the hazel wood and the perception of the dowser were especially valuable in Cornwall, where they were employed to detect tin. However, given the penalties for harming the tree, selecting the wand or rod from the tree had to be carried out in a specific, ritualistic way, using a sickle. Cutting could take place only at dawn on a Wednesday, since this is the day of Mercury, the god that rules the hazel.

HOLLY

One of the trees most commonly associated with Christmas, like other evergreens, the holly is symbolic of immortality; its red berries stand for life and vitality, as well as for blood. These scarlet berries appear in Christmas songs specifically as the blood of Christ, the redeemer. Both the masculine holly and its female counterpart, ivy, are welcomed into churches, unlike the mistletoe whose pagan origins are less easy to disguise.

The custom of bringing holly boughs into the home in the depths of winter has its origins in the original pre-Christian idea that its prickly leaves sheltered the fairy folk, who were delighted to come indoors at such a cold time of the year.

The Romans also brought holly into the house during the time of the Saturnalia, in mid-December. Holly trees planted close to the home guarded the house and its occupants from evil influences; the spiny leaves of the "male" tree are a symbol of protection. Holly with smoother leaves has more female attributes.

The name of the holly comes from the Teutonic goddess Hole, who was the mother of all unborn children and was responsible for naming them. However, so sacred was the holly that it was also named the "holy tree."

The "holly king" is a symbol of a giant man, constructed from holly, who carries a holly club in his hand. The seasonal counterpart to the oak king, the holly king is the guardian of the midwinter solstice. Holly stands for the letter T in the Ogham Tree alphabet, and its name is *Tinne*. It is ruled by the element of fire.

OAK

Before there were temples and shrines made by humans, the gods were worshipped under oak trees. The oak is particularly sacred to the Druids, who take their name from the name of the tree, *duir*. The word for "door" is a derivative of the same root; the tree symbolizes a door to another world, the *Siddhe*,

able to control the weather and further promulgates its association with the gods, as the rulers of storms and lightning. The fruit of the oak, the acorn, provides nourishment and also carries a rich symbolic meaning all of its own. A giveaway sign of a witch was that she wore a necklace of acorns, since the nut in its cup symbolized the phallus, as well as birth and the womb.

the invisible realm of the Celts that runs parallel to the "real" world. Oak, or *Duir*, is the seventh letter of the Ogham Tree alphabet.

The oak is symbolic of strength (the root of the Latin word for oak, *robur*, is the same as that for "robust"), power, longevity, and protection; it's also a friendly and benevolent tree, proving a useful ally to animals and human beings. A practical use of the oak as a great protector is seen in the many oaks that were used to build the ships that repelled the Spanish Armada from the shores of Britain; there are ancient houses still to be seen with beams that came from these ships.

Because of the great size of the oak, it attracts lightning; this gave it the reputation of being somehow

OLIVE TREE

The gift of the olive, from Athena, the goddess of wisdom, to the city of Athens, meant she won the privilege of having the city named for her. The alternative gift that was offered was a spring of water given by Poseidon, but the water proved salty and unfit to drink. There's an old spell or charm related to this story. To cure a headache, write the name of Athene on an olive and hold it to your head. This will induce the goddess to take away the pain.

The olive branch has long been a symbol of peace and of hope. When Noah sent a dove from the ark to see if land was close, the bird brought back a sprig of greenery believed to have been from the olive tree. This showed that both land and hope were at hand. To offer someone an olive branch is a universal symbol of peace and the desire for harmony.

Olive oil was of primary importance to any people who seldom ate meat since it has high nutritional value. It is therefore considered to be a sacred plant wherever it grows, and in times past to harm an olive tree was a punishable offense. Because olive trees grow to a great age—olive wood is an antitoxin and has protective powers—they are also symbolic of longevity. The olive tree is the most important of all trees in the Islamic faith, and is a symbol of the Prophet Mohammed. Each of its leaves is said to have one of the names of God written upon it.

ROWAN

The rowan stands for the second letter of the Ogham Tree alphabet, *Luis*. Because it's at home in mountainous places and is sacred to the goddess, the rowan is sometimes called the "Lady of the Mountain." It's also called "witchbane" or "witchwood," underlining the belief that rowans act as protectors from witchcraft or malevolent magic. The power of the tree is such that the stake driven through the heart of the vampire to kill it once and for all was meant to be made of rowan wood.

Although the rowan is a symbol of protection—particularly against witches—it's also said that the trees grow in places where they are needed, primarily where witches make their homes (in Britain, the tree was also known as *witchen* or *wiggin*). Witches themselves favored it as a magical tree, using its wood, berries, and leaves in spell-casting and charm-making.

Because the rowan is believed to have magical powers, the wood is among those used for wands and dowsing rods. There's also a charm made of rowan which is particularly efficacious, since it combines the protective powers of the tree with the similar powers of the cross; two twigs are tied together with red thread to make a small amulet. This was used as a symbol of protection over doorways and also over babies' cots to protect the infant from being kidnapped by fairies or other mischievous spirits.

The rowan is also symbolic of psychic powers, and is believed to confer the gift of divination. The berries of the tree possess hallucinogenic qualities, and the wine or simply the juice made from these berries was favored by the Druids in their shamanic practices. Groves of rowan trees were sacred places where oracular practices were carried out, and which were especially powerful in the presence of water.

SEQUOIA

The two species of redwood—the giant sequoia (*Sequoiadendron giganteum*) and the coast redwood (*Sequoia sempervirens*)—are the biggest and tallest trees in the world. The largest giant sequoias are even given names, such as General Grant and General Sherman, and they are the biggest of all single living organisms. General Sherman, the outright champion in terms of size, weighs 1,500 tons, has a volume of 55,040 cubic feet, and achieves a height in excess of 274 feet. The tallest coast redwoods, a more graceful tree than the grizzled giant sequoias, have achieved a height of 400 feet. Inevitably, these trees have become symbols of longevity, but not necessarily of survival. The coast redwood was used extensively for its timber (it is said that San Francisco was built from it) and although the

tree is now protected, there is little more than 3 percent left of the original 500 miles of forest that spread from Monterey to Oregon.

Although the redwoods have not been adopted by any particular culture as being the epitome of the World Tree, they make likely candidates for this sacred status. So tall that their heads are sometimes in the clouds—the upper parts of the coast redwood are so tall that they cannot draw water from the soil, instead surviving by absorbing the sea fogs that roll in off the Pacific—these trees can be virtually impossible to photograph, and usually all we see of them are their feet, with a small human figure dwarfed somewhere in the picture to try to give a sense of the scale. The giant sequoia became known as "Wellingtonia" in Britain, it being seen as a suitable tree to commemorate Britain's most famous soldier, the 1st Duke of Wellington, who had died the previous year. Unimpressed by this attempt to snatch the glory of their own largest tree, the Americans responded by naming it "Washingtonia" after the first president.

Shittim tree

See Acacia.

Vata tree

See Banyan.

Willow

Because of its shape, perhaps, the willow tree has long been associated with death and mourning; one of its varieties—*Salix* 'Chrysocoma'—is even called the "weeping willow." Willow branches were believed to ease the passage of the soul into the afterlife, and were placed on the tops of coffins. Graves were lined with willow branches for the same reason. In ancient Britain, burial places were planted with willow trees to protect the spirits of the dead, and the Greek sorceress Circe had a riverside cemetery full of willow trees; the corpses of men were put into the topmost branches of the trees where they were eaten by the birds. The willow is used in magical rites at Samhain since it helps communication with the spirit world. However, death is not the only meaning of the willow.

The word "willow" comes from an Anglo-Saxon word meaning "pliancy," and willow is the wood of choice in basket making. It's supple and strong, able to make baskets safe enough to hold people underneath a hot-air balloon. Moses was found as a baby floating in a willow basket, hence the tree is a symbol of protection. Witches' broomsticks were traditionally bound with willow that was used to tie the broom to the handle; this practice may have been a nod to the moon goddess, Hecate, who rules both the willow and the moon.

The willow contains a very important chemical constituent, salicylic acid, which is a very effective painkiller. Salicylic acid is the primary ingredient in aspirin, and the meaning behind the willow's folk name of "the witch's painkiller." The willow—or *Saile*—stands for the letter S in the Ogham Tree alphabet.

Yew

One of the longest-living of all trees, certain yews are in existence today that are said to be up to 9,000 years old, although it is difficult to prove these claims definitively.

Because of its great longevity, the yew is a symbol of everlasting life. It grows in an unusual way, too, its new stems growing down the outside of the tree, giving the yew an association with rebirth and regeneration, as the new is born from the old. Adding to this symbolism is its habit of putting in a growth spurt when it is around 500 years old.

So sacred was the yew as a symbol that—to a pre-Christian society—wherever it grew was considered to be sacred ground. It was considered both immoral and illegal to chop down the tree. It is likely that the yew is often seen in church-yards because the church itself would have been built on this sacred ground in the presence of the tree, in an effort to align the incoming Christian belief system with pagan traditions. The association of the tree with death therefore started to overlay its former meaning. Because the berries of the yew are poisonous, they can effectively carry people into the spirit world.

The hollow center of the yew tree is a symbol not only of the power that lies in empty space, but underlines the significance of this tree as belonging, in part, to a spiritual dimension. Recently, the yew as a symbol of life has been shown in a practical and unexpected way. One of the constituent chemicals of the tree, taxol, has been found to be efficacious in curing breast cancer. Yew wood is tough and durable and was used for making shields and spears, and also—using both heart-wood and sapwood to gain extra strength—the famous English longbow that helped the English win the Battle of Agincourt in 1415, at which they were completely outnumbered. Hence the yew is also a symbol of the warrior.

Part Four

FLOWERS OF THE UNDERWORLD

The mystical charisma of minerals, metals, and gems

If you pick up an attractive stone or pebble while walking along the beach, the chances are that you are putting something in your pocket that is as old as the earth itself. However, as Confucius said, "Better a diamond with a flaw than a pebble without," and despite the ancient provenance of both diamond and pebble, it is the sparkling stones, prized primarily for their beauty, which have fascinated us for millennia.

AGATE

A variety of quartz known as chalcedony, the agate comes in many different colors including blue (blue lace agate), and with different patterns and shapes embedded within the stone (such as moss agate and dendritic agate, which has tiny tree designs within it). Some agates are constructed of concentric circles of differently colored pigments, and when these particular stones are cut and polished to show a black or brown inner circle surrounded by a band of white, they are regarded as a symbol of the eye and, like similar talismans, are believed to protect the wearer against the evil eye.

Agates are also believed to protect people and buildings from damage by storms and lightning. Any agate with a naturally formed hole in it is still nailed above the doorways of some rural dairies so that the cows' milk will not be rendered sour by lightning. An added benefit is that this talisman will also keep witches from kidnapping the cows and riding them during the night. Such a stone was also carried by sailors in order to keep them safe at sea and to prevent seasickness. In the same way that agate is believed to have a calming effect on tempests, storms, thunder, and lightning, it soothes human nature too, and an agate worn by (or in close proximity to) a sleeper will ensure a good night's sleep and peaceful dreams.

AMBER

The association with the sun is probably the most powerful symbolic link for amber, and it does indeed look like a trapped sunbeam, especially when the occlusions and faults within the stone catch the light. Many of the uses of the stone reflect this association; amber is said to cheer and revitalize. Amber was also believed to cure all manner of ailments, in particular hay fever, asthma, and other throat and respiratory infections. Because amber was once liquid, small insects can sometimes be found embedded in it and this is the most valuable type of amber as well as being the premise of the film *Jurassic Park* (where dinosaurs were bred from DNA taken from these insects). Like jet, amber burns easily, and it was for this reason that in Germany it was called *Bernstein*, meaning "burn stone." The scent given off by burning amber was believed to drive away evil spirits.

AMETHYST

Amethyst is used to describe lavender/purple quartz crystals, whose sublime color has lent deep meaning to this particular stone, the importance of which is underlined by its appearance as one of the twelve stones set into the breastplate of the High Priest of the Temple in Jerusalem.

The name itself gives a clue as to its symbolic meaning and supposed efficacy. In Greek, *amethystos* means "non-intoxicating." It was said that the stone, placed under the tongue or worn by the drinker, would enable him to consume as much alcohol as desired with no ill effects, and goblets were made from amethyst for the same reason. Amethyst's reputation as the stone of sobriety may be what still makes it a popular choice for bishops (it is sometimes called the bishop's stone) or it may be the color: the high-frequency hues of violet and purple are associated with the spiritual realms. It should be remembered that purple, as a dye, was a costly color to produce and so was reserved for those rich enough or illustrious enough to be able to afford it; yet here was a crystal of that valuable hue, created naturally. No surprise that it was regarded so highly and was seen as a natural symbol of authority.

AQUAMARINE

The name *aquamarine* means "water of the sea," and accurately describes this sea-blue translucent gemstone. Not surprisingly, the stone is sacred to many of the sea deities, and sailors believed that it would bring them a safe passage across the oceans and banish fear during stormy weather.

In the Kabbalah, the aquamarine is linked to the Great Mother, Binah, because of its associations with the sea and the water element. The aquamarine also has protective qualities.

BERYL

See Emerald.

BEZOAR

This is the generic term given to "stones" that have been recovered from the insides of animals, held to have talismanic power commensurate with the creature from which they are recovered. One of the most efficacious uses of the bezoar stone also gives us its name. They are believed to dispel poisons, or at least to provide an antidote to them; *pad-zahr*, in Arabic, means "poison removing," and in time this became "bezoar." The bezoar was introduced to Europe by Arab physicians during the time of the Great Plague although it was also known to, and used by, the Chinese, the Malays, Peruvian tribes, and Indians.

Bezoar stones were carved and set into knife handles, as a way to protect the knife's owner from poisoning. The bezoar was also believed to confer the gifts of youth and vitality, could prevent asthma, and was used as a treatment for the kidneys and the bladder by being ground into a fine powder and made into an elixir.

Black Stone

The reason that Mecca is one of the foremost places of pilgrimage in the world today is because it is home to the black stone, or al Hajar ul Aswad, one of the most holy and sacred items in Islam. The provenance of this stone is unknown, although it is generally believed to be a meteorite. Others claim that it was given to Ishmael, the son of Abraham, by the angel Gabriel. The story goes that the angel that had failed to prevent the serpent from tempting Adam and Eve was trapped inside this stone, a zircon, that was turned black by the kisses of sinners. At the Day of Judgment the angel, released from this prison, would be able to bear witness to all those who had made the pilgrimage to Mecca. Despite the myths, the only thing certain about the black stone is its great age.

Muslims circling the Ka'aba seven times during their ritual pilgrimage will attempt, if they can, to kiss the stone; if this proves impossible they will point at the stone each time they go around it instead. The black stone is regularly anointed with perfumed oil.

The stone is of modest size, measuring approximately twelve inches in diameter. Legend has it that the stone was once pure white, but blackened as it absorbed the sins of mankind. The stone itself is now cracked, damage which may have occurred when it was stolen around AD 930. Others believe it was broken during a siege in AD 638. The stone is held together by a frame of silver which is oval in shape; the entire sacred object resembles a large unblinking eye.

Breastplate of the High Priest

This extraordinary artifact of the ancient world has provided the original source for much of the importance of certain gemstones.

The first high priest of Jerusalem was named Aaron, who lived in 1200 BC. Aaron was the first high priest to wear the "breastplate of righteousness and prophecy," also known as the *Essen*. The breastplate was connected with the mysterious objects Urim and Thummim, which were said to be the powers of judgment and prophecy.

This breastplate had twelve stones, in gold mountings,

embedded into it in a specific sequence that had been described in the Book of Exodus in the Bible. There has been some speculation as to the identity of some of the stones, as many centuries have elapsed since they were first described, and their names have changed.

Set in four rows of three stones each, the gems are described as follows, from the first row working down:

- Sardius (possibly carnelian); topaz; carbuncle (possibly garnet)
- Emerald; sapphire; diamond
- Ligure (possibly jacinth); agate; amethyst
- Beryl; onyx; jasper

Each gem was inscribed with the name of one of the twelve tribes of Israel, and also bears a relationship to the twelve months of the year and the twelve signs of the zodiac. The breastplate itself was tied over the top of the robe-like garment of the high priest.

CARNELIAN

A variety of chalcedony which has a specific orange-red opacity, the carnelian is among the many gems that used to be referred to as bloodstones, because of its color. Its name is said to come either from the karnel cherry, or from the Latin words for meat, *carne*, or heart, *cor*.

The carnelian has always been held to be a protective stone, and is sometimes referred to as the "blood of Isis," again because of its color. As a carved talismanic object, it was placed at the throat of the mummy in order that the protection of the goddess would be invoked in the journey through the underworld. These amulets often had images and symbols—such as the eye, the lion, and the hand—carved into the carnelian. The carnelian which was carved with the symbol of the eye was an efficacious charm against the evil eye.

The ancient Greeks believed that the carnelian could satisfy all the heart's desires; this is similar to Muslim beliefs about the carnelian, which they called the Mecca stone, since it could make wishes come true. The symbolism of the carnelian as one of happiness and bonhomie means that, if placed under a sleeper's pillow, it will bring happy dreams.

* ** *

CAT'S EYE

Any stone which has an occlusion within it that causes light to refract in the same way as in the eye of a cat can be given this title. The actual name given to the process is called chatoyancy. The true cat's eye, however, is a stone called chrysoberyl, which is composed of thin fibers running in the same direction that reflect light in the manner described.

Wherever the symbol of the eye appears in a naturally occurring stone or indeed elsewhere in nature, the object is seen to have protective qualities. The cat's eye stone is no exception. The cat's eye is also used as a charm to counter the effect of spells and sorcery, in particular the malice caused by the evil eye. In Arab regions, it was believed that wearing the stone could render the wearer invisible; something to do with the eye of the stone affecting the sight of the viewer, no doubt.

CHALCEDONY

See Agate.

CHRYSOLITE

See Topaz.

CITRINE

The yellow color of the citrine (a type of quartz) not only gives us the origin of its name but means that it has become symbolically associated with the sun, warmth, and vitality. The stomach area also shares the same association with the yellow section of the spectrum, for example in the system of energy centers called chakras, and so the citrine is believed to be able to cure ailments related to this part of the body.

COPPER

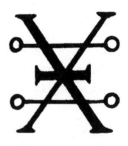

The chemical name for copper— *cuprum*—has the same root as the word for the island of Cyprus, where major deposits of the ore were once found. Cyprus was sacred to the goddess Venus, and so copper was her metal and also the metal associated with the planet which bears her name.

Copper was well known to ancient people and has long been a source of protection against lightning, since copper rods act as conductors and will direct the electricity into the ground. As a result, copper was considered protection against other evil influences. In Egypt, mummies had a copper disc, engraved with magical signs and symbols, placed beneath their head. This disc was called a *hypocephalus*, and made use of the heat-retaining ability of the metal to keep the corpse warm. Even today the use of copper bracelets as an antidote to the aches and pains of rheumatism is widespread. People believe that this works because the skin absorbs minute copper deposits (turning the skin a tell-tale green). However efficacious these copper bracelets may be, there is no definitive evidence as to how they work. Copper is also said to soothe insect stings when laid over the affected area.

Diamond

The Greek word for diamond is *adamas*, meaning both "untamable" and "hard." It gives us the word "adamant" or "adamantine," which is also used as a term of reference to describe the brilliance of the stone. The diamond is the hardest of all minerals, and is used as a measure of the toughness of other stones.

One of the stones on the breast-plate of the High Priest of the Temple in Jerusalem where it was said to shine brilliantly in the presence of truth and innocence, the diamond is not only tough, but extremely beautiful and relatively rare, qualities which make it one of the most costly precious gems. Traditionally it is the stone used in engagement rings as a symbol of betrothal, although the notion that an eager suitor should be obliged to spend a month's salary on the ring for his future wife is nothing more than a cynical ruse, invented relatively recently by a leading diamond house to persuade people to spend their money.

The diamond, therefore, became a symbol of love and commitment, although its use in rings was originally as a protective talisman. Knights and warriors liked to set diamonds into their sword hilts and shields for this reason. But these diamonds did not sparkle in the way we recognize today; they remained as they had done when they came out of the ground. The diamond is so hard that it will easily score a mark on glass, and during the time of Queen Elizabeth I "scribbling rings" were all the rage. These were rings into which a diamond was set with the sharp point facing upwards. The stone was used to scribble messages on windows, usually little love letters or secret messages.

Because of the fire which flashes within a well-cut and polished diamond, the stone is associated with thunder and lightning. In India it is even named Vajra, meaning lightning.

Diamonds are believed to absorb both good and bad energy, and people who use gemstones for healing purposes need to be very careful not to upset the delicate balance of the stone. Some notorious diamonds—no doubt the object of much envy, greed, and sometimes even bloodshed—have curses attached to them and are believed to be "unlucky" in the hands of their owners.

One of the more notorious of these cursed gems is the Hope Diamond. The stone seems to have left a trail of ruined lives and devastation in its wake. The bad fortune surrounding the stone started when it was stolen from the forehead of the statue of the goddess Sita in India, and some believe that the malice surrounding the stone is because the goddess subsequently cursed anyone who touched it. The original thief was reputed to have been torn apart by wild dogs. The diamond passed through the hands of Marie Antoinette and Louis XVI, both of whom were beheaded. It was eventually purchased by a wealthy banker, Philip Hope, and then inherited by his nephew Thomas, who lost his entire fortune shortly thereafter. Next it was bought by Ambul Hamid, a sultan of Turkey, who lost his title and was forced to sell the diamond. It was bought by Evalyn Walsh McLean, wife of an American newspaper magnate. She lost both her fortune and her only son, who was killed in an accident.

EMERALD

One of the most precious of all stones, the emerald comes from the beryl family. A perfect emerald is difficult to find and is therefore extremely valuable, although even the flawed kinds are costly. Its importance as a beautiful and valuable mineral has been acknowledged since ancient times. One of the most famous emerald mines was in Upper Egypt and belonged to the Queen of Sheba. The mine itself was said to be guarded by evil spirits. These emeralds were accorded magical status, and were said to grow, flourish, or diminish according to the seasons, and to change in intensity with the phases of the moon. This belief—that emeralds "ripened"—was also held by the Peruvians, who reputedly had a Temple of Esmerelda, which contained a massive stone, together with lots of smaller stones which were called her "daughters." This temple has never been discovered.

Thoth—also known as Hermes Trismegistus, Hermes, or Mercury, the god of writing, communication, and knowledge—wrote down the secrets of the universe on a great emerald tablet, the Smaragdina Tablet. The emerald is therefore symbolic of arcane information, and carries with it the wisdom of the ancients. Because it was dedicated to Mercury, the emerald was carried as a talisman by travelers to keep them safe on their journey. Emerald talismans were also used to exorcise demons. If given as a gift between lovers (for example as an engagement ring), the emerald would ensure a long and happy life. However, if either partner should be unfaithful, then the emerald would start to fade in its brilliance, so the stone represents truth.

GARNET

Although the garnet can be transparent, green, yellow, orange, ultraviolet, brown, and black (although not blue), it is the red garnet which is the best known. Because it generally has a rich, dark color similar to that of veinous blood, the garnet has long been associated with this vital liquid, and is said to be efficacious in treating bleeding wounds, blood disease, and hemorrhages. The garnet was even believed to have been able to staunch bleeding wounds, and so was used as a protective talisman by soldiers from the Crusades onwards, set into sword hilts and shields.

The name "garnet" comes from pomegranate; indeed, the jewel does look similar to the sparkling seed of this fruit, and is similarly associated with the fertility of the womb.

As well as being able to heal wounds, garnet is also believed to be able to inflict mortal wounds on the enemy. In 1892, when Indian and British troops were fighting one another in Kashmir, the enterprising Hunza tribesmen used spherical garnets as bullets interspersed with more regular ammunition. These jewels, used as weapons, caused many serious injuries or fatalities to the British forces.

GEMSTONE CORRESPONDENCES

Associations between gemstones and the signs of the zodiac, the planets, the months of the year, days of the week, anniversaries and birthdays, chakras and more, tend to be something of a movable feast, varying according to different writers and depending on individual spiritual beliefs. The stones attached to the months and the seasons, for example, differ according to the religion and country of origin of the authority that is consulted. In addition certain stones tend to go in and out of fashion. Adding to the confusion are the changes in the names of stones, as well as alterations to the calendar dates over the centuries that have meant that the traditional stone for one month sometimes spills over into the next.

The following charts give the most popular definitions of these correspondences. The links between planets and their metals are listed toward the end of this section under seven magical metals.

Gemstones and the planets

SUN: Amber, diamond, topaz
MOON: Moonstone, pearl
EARTH: Amber, jade, ammonite
MERCURY: Agate, opal, citrine
VENUS: Malachite, rose quartz, emerald
MARS: Hematite, ruby, spinel
JUPITER: Sapphire, lapis lazuli, turquoise
SATURN: Jet, onyx, coral
URANUS: Opal, amethyst
NEPTUNE: Aquamarine, coral, pearl
PLUTO: Diamond, jade, zircon

Gemstones and the zodiac

ARIES: Diamond, bloodstone
TAURUS: Emerald, lapis lazuli
GEMINI: Agate, citrine
CANCER: Moonstone, pearl
LEO: Peridot, amber
VIRGO: Aquamarine, carnelian
LIBRA: Jacinth, amethyst
SCORPIO: Opal, sapphire
SAGITTARIUS: Turquoise, topaz
CAPRICORN: Onyx, garnet
AQUARIUS: Garnet, aquamarine
PISCES: Amethyst, bloodstone

According to the esotericist and prolific occult author Walter Richard Old ("Sepharial"), 1864–1929, who was the first president of the British Astrological Society, the stones that belong to the birth signs vary slightly from those listed above. He has the ruby belonging to Cancer, the sardonyx to Leo, the sapphire to Virgo, the opal to Libra, the topaz to Scorpio, and the amethyst to Aquarius.

Gemstones and the months of the year

JANUARY: Garnet
FEBRUARY: Amethyst
MARCH: Heliotrope, jasper
APRIL: Diamond, sapphire
MAY: Agate, emerald
JUNE: Emerald, pearl, agate
JULY: Onyx
AUGUST: Carnelian
SEPTEMBER: Peridot
OCTOBER: Aquamarine, beryl
NOVEMBER: Topaz
DECEMBER: Ruby

Gemstones and the chakras

Starting from the crown chakra and working down, the colors of the chakras have a strong bearing on the gems that are said to represent them. In this chart, the first gem listed is said to close the chakra, and the second one will open it.

7 CROWN CHAKRA or SAHASRARA: Amethyst, diamond
6 THIRD EYE CHAKRA or AJNA: Lapis lazuli, amethyst
5 THROAT CHAKRA or VISHUDDA: Aquamarine, blue topaz
4 HEART CHAKRA or ANAHATA: Emerald, rose quartz
3 NAVAL CHAKRA or MANIPURA: Amber, citrine
2 SACRAL CHAKRA or SVADHISTHANA: Jade, ruby
1 ROOT CHAKRA or MULADHARA: Hematite, garnet

Gemstones and the elements

Air: Agate, citrine, lapis lazuli, opal, rose quartz, sapphire, turquoise
Fire: Amber, citrine, fire opal, garnet, heliotrope, ruby, spinel, topaz
Water: Amethyst, aquamarine, coral, lapis lazuli, moonstone, pearl, tourmaline, turquoise
Earth: Amber, ammonite, emerald, jade, jet, magnetite, malachite, onyx
Ether: Amethyst, diamond, opal, pearl, rock crystal, sapphire, tourmaline, zircon

GOLD

Gold, considered to be one of the most precious and beautiful metals

of all, is inextricably linked with the element of fire and with the sun, which it represents both in appearance and in symbolism. In mythology, the passage of the sun is often described as a golden chariot traversing the heavens. Gold has the benefit of remaining unaffected by tarnishing or corrosion of any sort, and so is an emblem of immortality. Even if it is melted or liquefied by heat, gold retains its color and luster. It is surpassed by platinum in terms of actual monetary value, but retains the upper hand in terms of symbolic meaning because of its color and thousands of years of adoration.

Gold has always had magical powers ascribed to it, the ancients believing that it was actually made from sunbeams buried underground. Egyptian mummies of the highest castes were encased in gold, denoting the immortality of the soul. Gold was one of the three gifts brought by the Magi to the infant Christ. And even today, gold

is still the most popular metal for use as wedding rings, because it is seen to confer a long and happy life to the married couple.

Although gold is a symbol of purity because of its physical incorruptibility, paradoxically, gold has also taken on some extremely negative connotations. The striving for gold can cause corruption in men once greed for the precious metal takes hold; as an object of desire it can bring out the very worst in people. The story of King Midas is a case in point. Midas wished that everything he touched be turned to gold, and once Dionysus had granted him this wish, Midas soon realized it was a terrible curse. Unable to eat because his food turned to gold, unable to hug his daughter because she turned to gold, too, Midas eventually asked Dionysus to remove the curse, which he did by having the king wash his hands in the Pactolus River, which is now in modern-day Turkey. The myth not only explains the origin of the gold deposits in this river, but effectively proves the later Shakespearian idea that "all that glistens is not gold."

Alchemists used gold to symbolize the soul, and the search for the Philosophers' Stone also signified the conscious efforts made by them to purify the spirit, since the material stone could be created only in tandem with spiritual growth and development.

HAG STONES

This is a stone that features a naturally made hole in it, and can be made of any mineral, although in Britain the flint hag stone is the most usual sort to find. Also known as witch stones, snake's eggs, adder stones or holy stones, there are all manner of powers ascribed to these objects. In particular, they were believed to be able to protect cattle from witches who would take them out at night and ride them, leaving the farmer to discover the tell-tale signs of filthy, exhausted animals the next morning. The stones would have string or ribbon passed through the holes so that they could be hung above the doorway, where they would handily also stop milk from curdling; this belief was so strong that farmers in some parts of Europe, while milking their cows, would hold a hag stone in such a way that the milk poured through it.

Looking through the hole is said to enable another world to be viewed: the fairy world or the spirit world. Put simply, the solid part of the stone represents the material world, and the hole in the middle, the spirit world, the void, the "no thing." It is for this reason that the wreath, the hoop-shaped floral tribute, is often used at funerals.

IRON

It may be one of the cheapest and most abundant of all metals, but iron has great relevance in both symbolism and the practical application of magic.

Iron is one of the primary constituents of blood, and the metal and the liquid smell similar; therefore, iron has been perceived to be the "blood" or life force of the Earth itself. But it is not only the Earth which has high iron content, since early iron that was used by people originated largely from meteors. In Tibet, this "sky iron" is used for making the singing bowls, the vibrational frequency of which is believed to attract good spirits, and heal both body and soul.

Iron had the reputation of being repellant to witches, ghosts, and other malevolent entities. Numerous folk tales have the supernatural creature being rendered powerless by being struck with iron. When iron appears in the form of the horseshoe, its power is increased because the horseshoe is a symbol of the protective goddess, the crescent moon, the chalice, or the yoni.

JET

Jet is in fact wood that has rotted and been compressed over millions of years. At the end of this process it turns into a stone that is easily carved and, when polished, takes on a brilliant luster. Jet famously comes from Whitby, a little town on the northeast coast of Yorkshire, England, although this area is not the only source of the material.

Because of its color, jet has long been associated with death and mourning (its presence in burial chambers dating back 10,000 years testifies to this). It became very fashionable when Queen Victoria ordered great quantities of jet jewelry that she wore when she was in mourning for her deceased consort, Prince Albert. Victorian Britain was fascinated with death,

and soon the demand for jet jewelry achieved staggering proportions. In 1870 the jet industry in Whitby alone employed 1,500 people. However, the association of jet with death and funerals became so pronounced that the use of the stone was pretty much exhausted once the trend had passed, and the many other properties of the stone were largely forgotten about.

When jet is rubbed with a piece of cloth it becomes charged with static electricity (in the same way as other organically created stones, such as amber) and can pick up small pieces of tissue or lint; therefore jet was believed to attract good fortune. If the jet is rubbed very briskly, it sometimes gives off smoke, which had the power to drive away the demons that were as black as the jet itself. A jet cross nailed to a door would keep out evil spirits and jet talismans were carried to protect the owner from devilish forces.

LAPIS LAZULI

The golden specks which are scattered throughout this beautiful blue stone like stars in a dark sky are in fact flecks of iron pyrites. The color of lapis is what makes it important, and it is ground into a fine powder in order to make the ultramarine pigment used in painting. The ancient Egyptians called this stone sapphire, but from their descriptions we know that it was lapis lazuli to which they were referring.

Blue is a symbol of purity and chastity, and much of the symbolic meaning of lapis lazuli relates to its color. Although many of the stones examined in this section of the encyclopedia are symbolic of fertility and may somehow aid childbirth, the lapis is an exception in that it was used to cause miscarriage, and so was called the "stop stone." An amulet of lapis lazuli was used for this purpose.

The lapis lazuli was sacred to the Egyptian goddess of truth, Ma'at. Since truth is about seeing things correctly, the stone was believed to be particularly potent in treating the eyes. A paste of ground lapis, milk, and mud from the Nile was used to create an ointment. In a nod to its association with the eye, there is also a New Age belief that the stone can help to open the third eye.

* ✳ *

LEAD

A weighty metal, it is no surprise that lead symbolizes heaviness and an oppresive burden. It is the attribute of Saturn, and both the planet and the god (who is often depicted as a grim-looking hunched old man carrying a scythe) share these somewhat morose qualities, from which the word "saturnine" is coined.

In alchemy, lead is described as the "base metal" which will hopefully be transmuted into gold. In order to do this, alchemists made great efforts to free themselves from the limitations of the material world as symbolized by this heavy metal.

LODESTONE

Lodestone refers to a type of magnetite, although the stones have a slightly different crystalline structure one from another. Magnetite is relatively common but the lodestone is rare; in addition the lodestone needs to be electrically charged—by lightning for example—before it acquires the magnetic properties that have made it such an important mineral. The compass was invented because lodestone existed; if this discovery had not been made, then the course of world history would have been very different.

The potential of the powers of the lodestone, which is attracted to the earth's magnetic field, was first spotted by the Chinese, who adapted it to make the world's first compass. From about AD 100 onward, there are references to a "south pointer," most likely to have been a lodestone "spoon," whose curved base would have allowed the stone to spin freely within an indented hollow.

Although exploited initially by the Chinese, the lodestone was also familiar to the ancient Greeks. Pliny the Elder writes of a herdsman, Magnes, whose iron hobnailed boots and the iron tip of his staff attracted pieces of lodestone. Many ancient people believed that stones had souls, and the ability of the lodestone to attract things to it and to cause things to move must have seemed magical indeed, as though the stone had a mind of its own. Accordingly, the stone was given water to drink and iron filings to eat.

Although it was lightning which gave the lodestone its power, it also attracted lightning, so it was not to be carried or worn during a storm. Because the lodestone attracts things to it, it was associated with both attraction and retention; shopkeepers believed that it encouraged customers, for example, and prostitutes used it to attract clients. The temple of Konark, on the coast of the Bay of Bengal in India, is reputed to have had such a huge and powerful lodestone mounted on the top of its sun temple that it caused shipwrecks because the vessels were both drawn toward the stone and because their compasses were affected by it. Rumor has it that the stone was removed by Muslim voyagers, with the result that the temple eventually fell down.

MAGNETITE

See Lodestone.

MERCURY

Mercury is a metal, a planet, and a god. Here we are dealing with the mineral aspect of mercury,

although it's sometimes hard to separate these three in terms of their symbolism. Mercury is one of only four metals which is liquid at room temperature; its name "quicksilver"—suggesting something that is difficult to handle, whimsical, and swift moving (indeed mercurial)—fittingly describes the metal in this state.

Mercury is not harmful when it is in insoluble form; however, as soon as it's in soluble form—as in methyl mercury—it becomes extremely toxic. Lighthouse lanterns float in a circular vat of mercury, and the vapors used to make some lighthouse keepers go mad, although the cause was undiscovered for many years. Similarly, the phrase "mad as a hatter" derives from the insanity suffered by milliners as a result of the use of mercury nitrate as a solution that helped the felt fabric to matt together and so strengthen the material. Symptoms of mercury poisoning include hallucinations, tremors, and dementia.

MOONSTONE

The moonstone is aptly named. Its opalescent, milky semi-opacity really does have a moonlight-like quality. Some stones have a white spot inside them that reacts in a similar way to the occlusions in cat's eye-type stones, in that it appears to move inside the stone. This was at one time believed to be a trapped moonbeam, and the stone used to be called the "astrion," since it was believed to contain light from the stars, which it could collect if it was held up to the night sky.

The links between the moon and the moonstone are further strengthened by the belief that the stone shares the same waxing and waning pattern as its celestial counterpart. Effectively, the moonstone is believed to help the owner to tap into the intuition and psychic powers which have long been considered qualities of the moon.

OLIVINE

See Peridot.

* ** *

ONYX

OPAL

The word *onyx* means "claw" or "nail" in Greek, and the story goes that the mischievous Cupid cut Venus's nails one day while she was sleeping on the beach. Cupid left the fingernail shards scattered around the sand dunes, but the Fates, wanting to make sure that no scrap of the goddess would be wasted, turned the fingernails into onyx stones.

Onyx comes in a wide range of colors, sometimes striated, sometimes plain. The reddish colored onyxes are called sardonyx, which was useful in Roman times for the carving of seals, since the wax never stuck to the stone. Onyx was used in magical rituals to conjure up demons, and it may well be this property that meant that the stone should never be worn at night lest the wearer suffer from nightmares. Hildegard of Bingen recommended that onyx be "soaked" in wine for up to thirty days; the resulting elixir would be used to touch the eyes in order to clear eyesight.

* ✳ *

The iridescence of the opal is caused by the large amount of water retained by the silica from which the stone is made, sometimes constituting as much as 10 percent of its mass. This water content causes the opal to have a higher degree of sensitivity than any other gemstone, a quality which informs not only its physical characteristics but its symbolic meaning too.

Because of its ethereal beauty, the opal has always been a favored gem; its changing colors have also given the stone a distinct personal identity, as though it has a soul of its own. Changes in temperature can affect the opal; a sudden move from a hot room to a cold environment can even cause the stone to crack.

The reputation of the opal as being unlucky seems to be a belief held only by Western people. Sir Walter Scott's book *Anne of Geierstein* may have contributed to this reputation. In the story, Anne is a baroness who wears a precious gem in her hair that is not actually ever named as an opal in the book but that carries its qualities. This stone acts as a perfect litmus for the baroness's moods, flashing red when she is angry and sparkling when she is happy. The story becomes more sinister. Holy water is splashed onto the stone, which shatters; Anne faints, and is found turned to dust like the stone.

The opal's unfortunate reputation is not found anywhere else in the world. Its name comes from the Sanskrit *upala*, which simply means "precious stone." In Greece and Rome, it was called the *paederos*, meaning "precious child," and also *opthalmus*, meaning "eye." Because the opal was associated with vision, this was extended to mean psychic vision and second sight.

Many opals originate in Australia, and when they were first discovered there Queen Victoria was understandably delighted, ordering a large amount of opal jewelry and restoring the gem to favor for a time, despite its reputation in the West.

PEARL

The origin of the pearl, as an irritating piece of grit which manages to get inside the shell of a mollusk, is completely belied by its symbolism, the mythology surrounding it, and above all its beauty.

The name of the pearl derives from the Latin *pilula*, meaning a ball. It shares the same origin as the word "pill." If the diamond is the epitome of the masculine gemstone, then the pearl is equally prominent as a feminine symbol; its softness, its rarity, its gentle luster, and its origins in the sea ensure this is the case.

Pearls are sensitive objects, both physically and in a symbolic sense. They like an even temperature since their high water content makes them liable to cracking or even breaking. In the same way, pearls are responsive to changes in body temperature and to chemicals such as perfumes or hairsprays, and so a dull pearl is said to signify illness in its owner.

The most valuable pearls are those that have formed naturally, and—as with other gems—people have lost their lives trying to attain that elusive large, perfect pearl. But pearls can also be cultivated by the simple insertion of a piece of mother-of-pearl into the host mollusk. These pearls are gathered after three to four years.

The pearl, because of its whiteness and perfection, is a symbol of purity, and is dedicated to the moon goddess in all her forms. Because the moon rules over lovers, pearl, ground into a fine powder, was used to make an aphrodisiac potion.

PERIDOT

Like other green-colored stones, the peridot was referred to as an emerald in ancient times, although it is actually a type of olivine. The name is believed to have originated either in the French word *peritot*, which means "unclear," or from the Arabic *faridat*, meaning "gem." To add to the confusion, in Greek, *peridona* means "to give richness."

A stone that answers the description of the peridot appeared on the breastplate of the High Priest of the Temple in Jerusalem, a mark of the esteem in which it was considered. Both the ancient Egyptians and the Romans treasured the peridot, and it was often used as an amulet, with effigies and inscriptions carved on it. For example, a peridot featuring the image of a vulture would ensure that demons would give the wearer a wide berth. A peridot amulet with a torch depicted on it was believed to attract wealth to its owner.

A necklace of peridots was said to dispel melancholy and make the wearer cheerful and optimistic. Wearing the beautiful green peridot was said to preserve the owner from jealousy; this is probably an instance of sympathetic magic, since green is traditionally the color of envy. As an amulet set in gold, the peridot prevented nightmares and gave the wearer a good night's sleep.

QUICKSILVER

See Mercury.

RUBY

The word "ruby" is synonymous with red; indeed, it comes from the Latin word *rubens*, which has the same meaning. A powerful and valuable precious gem, in India the ruby is called *ratnaraj*, meaning the "Lord of Precious Stones." Hindus call their most precious and valuable rubies "Brahmins," and these particular stones had to be protected from contact with inferior rubies in case of contamination. Further evidence of the stone as a symbol of royalty can be found in the title of the former kings of Burma, who were known as the "Lords of the Rubies."

The color of the ruby plays a major part in its symbolic meaning. They are the color of vitality, the life-giving forces, and passion, and were considered to be so powerful that, if thrown into water, they would make the water boil. The light from the ruby was also said to shine through any cloth wrapped around it, and so it was impossible to hide. This idea of precious stones generating light rather than just reflecting or refracting it occurs time and time again in the writings of the ancients, and a ruby was said to have been set on the roof of the Temple of the Holy Grail so that the Grail knights could be guided toward it in the dark.

The ruby was a symbol of protection, and if a landowner touched all four corners of his estate with a ruby then the land would be protected from lightning and storms, and harvests would be prolific. Similarly, wearing a ruby in such a way that it touched the skin would protect the wearer from ill health, particularly if the stone was placed on the left side of the body since the color of the ruby meant that it was instantly connected to the heart and the circulatory system.

SALT

The sea is full of salt, and so there is an inextricable link between the mineral salt and the element of water. However, salt is frequently produced by allowing sea water to evaporate on the ground, and so salt is also associated with the earth; witness the popular saying "salt of the earth," meaning that a person is good, grounded, and honest.

The cuboid structure of salt is further reason for it to be a symbol of the earth element, as well as making it an emblem of protection. Salt has a practical use as a preservative of meat, fish, and other foodstuffs; it has therefore taken on the same symbolic significance—as seen in rites and rituals—to sanctify and protect holy or magical places. It is used for this reason from cathedral services to the Magic Circle. It is possible that this practice is a residue from a time when blood from sacrificial animals was used for this purpose, the blood being sprinkled with salt to soak it up.

Salt is also able to bring out flavors in any food to which it is added, and was considered to be so valuable a commodity that it was used as currency to pay people for their work; hence the word "salary" from the Latin *salarium.*

Because salt is valuable in so many ways, spilling it is considered to be a bad omen. This is still counteracted by superstitious people, who make a cross in the salt then throw some of the salt over their left shoulder, supposedly into the eye of the devil.

Alchemists say that salt—which represents the human body—is one of the three vital natural ingredients, called the three alchemical principles, and that it forms a trinity with sulfur and mercury.

SAPPHIRE

The sapphire is made from carborudum, the same extremely hard material that goes to form the ruby.

Although the word "sapphire" is synonymous with blue, sapphires themselves can also be yellow, pink, orange, violet or even multicolored. However, the most sought-after and valuable types of sapphire come in the traditional rich blue color.

Because all blue stones used to be known as sapphires, it is sometimes difficult to separate out the mythology that belongs to the sapphire as we know it today. Its blue color gives the sapphire a connection with the sky, the gods, the world of spirit, and it was a favored stone of ecclesiastical ornament because of this symbolism. Added to this is the origin of the word "sapphire" as the biblical *sappur*, which was the name given to the material from which the throne of the gods was made; presumably it refers to the blue of the heavens. As is the case with many of the rarer and more valuable stones, sapphires are thought to be efficacious in medical use. A paste made from finely ground sapphires was meant to cure ulcers and boils when applied to the skin. It was also believed to be an efficacious antidote to poison, as well as being able to clarify the thoughts and aid a good night's sleep. Along with other blue-colored stones, the sapphire was believed to be able to cure eye troubles.

SARDONYX

See Onyx.

* * *

Seven magical metals

The first seven planets recognized by our ancestors continue to have a huge influence on mankind. Other aspects of these links are explored elsewhere, but metals were among the many items that were mystically linked to these planets.

Each of these planets has its own metal. These seven magical metals are silver (the Moon), mercury (Mercury), copper (Venus), gold (the Sun), iron (Mars), tin (Jupiter), and lead (Saturn).

In the Dharmic religions, sacred artifacts (such as singing bowls and temple statuary) are made using a mixture of all seven metals.

Silver

As gold is to the sun, silver is to the moon. It is the archetypal female metal, imbued with connections to the goddess in all her forms. The link is plain to see because the moon appears silver. The superstition of turning a silver coin in the pocket at the sight of a new moon is a throwback to this ancient connection.

In the same way that the moon is a cosmic mirror illuminated by the light of the sun, the mirror is a sheet of glass with a fine layer of silver applied to one side. Silver goblets were filled with water and used for scrying; water is also inextricably linked with silver and the moon. Because evil spirits such as vampires have no reflection, silver gained a reputation for being able to repel and even destroy them; hence the use of silver bullets as the ultimate weapon against these blood-sucking demons.

As a precious metal, silver has been used for making coins since 700 BC, when it was used in the form of electrum. The term "sterling," referring to the monetary currency of the UK, comes from sterling silver; one troy pound of this was the source of the original "pound sterling."

Like the moon, silver is associated with psychic powers and intuition, so the clairvoyant or crystal ball reader traditionally requests the client to "cross my

palm with silver," not purely as a payment, but to help the psychic powers flow.

SULFUR

Along with salt and mercury, sulfur forms the "holy trinity" of substances that are the three vital minerals of nature in alchemy. Indeed, sulfur is an essential ingredient in all living cells. Alchemists believe that sulfur represents the vitality or life force of a person.

A bright yellow chemical, it's likely that sulfur obtained its name from the Arabic word for yellow, *sufra*. Sulfur is sometimes referred to as "brimstone," particularly in the Bible, where the "fire and brimstone" of hell await non-believers and sinners.

TIN

One of the seven magical metals, tin is associated with the planet Jupiter. In alchemy, both tin and the planet share the same symbol.

Tin does not corrode, and is classically mixed with copper to create the alloy, bronze. Tin has been used in this way since at least 3500 BC. The earliest tin mines were those

in Cornwall and Devon in England. In fact, the British Isles were so famous for their tin production that the islands were referred to by the Greeks as the *Kassiterides*, meaning the "tin-producing" lands. Tin and the tin mines came to be associated with the fairy folk or little people that also proliferated in the area, especially those that were believed to live in the underground tunnels that contained the metal.

TOPAZ

Although the topaz can be an amazing blue color, or even pink or red, it is best known as a golden yellow gemstone. The topaz itself is symbolic of something which is hard to find, and it is this quality that gives it its name.

All golden yellow transparent stones used to be called "chrysolite" in ancient Greek, which means "golden stone." The most beautiful chrysolites were to be found, so legend has it, on a place called Serpent Island. Whether this place was real or imaginary was at the time open to conjecture, and Pliny the Elder named this island Topazos, after the Greek word for conjecture—*topazein*. We now know that the island in question is the place the Crusaders called the Isle of St. John and which the Egyptians called Zebirget. The stone was dedicated to the sun god, Ra, since its color and sparkle were reminiscent of the rays of the sun. The inhabitants of this island were given an exclusive license to collect the precious golden stones, which were reputedly visible only in the dark.

The physical qualities of stones often inform their symbolic meaning. Because topaz cools down rapidly after being immersed in hot water, it is believed to have the power of calming frayed tempers and high passions, and of cooling fevers. The stone would be touched to the skin of plague victims in an attempt to cure their ulcers and blisters. The coolness of the stone was also acknowledged by the Indian sages. One of the more peculiar and inexplicable notions concerning the topaz, however, was the idea that it emitted a milky fluid which could be used to prevent rabies.

TOURMALINE

Tourmaline comes in a veritable rainbow of colors. It wends its way through the spectrum, starting with a transparent crystal, and then on to the palest pink, through to peach, yellow, blue, green, brown, red, and all the shades in between. An Egyptian legend held that the stone absorbed the colors from a rainbow on its way through the depths of the earth to the surface, and the stone was sacred to the sun god, Ra. Because of its many hues the stone has a vast array of different names, too. Some tourmalines show colors layered through their core like a stick of rock, and the outer color of this tube-shaped crystal may be a completely different color to those on the inside. Tourmalines like this frequently have pale pink or yellow in the center, graduating to dark green on the outside. These are called "watermelon tourmalines."

The tourmaline has electrical and magnetic properties that make it a useful stone in technical applications. Pliny the Elder wrote of a stone that he called *lychnis*, meaning "lamp," which when heated (either by the sun or by applying friction) could attract straw and other fibrous material. The ancient

Greeks used the tourmaline to help kindle their lamps, while Dutch colonists in Africa—one of the places where the stone can be found—used tourmaline crystals to draw ash from their meerschaum pipes. If the stone is electrically charged and then allowed to cool down, it will have a positive charge at one end and a negative charge at the other. This has made the stone symbolic of harmony and balance between opposing energies.

TURQUOISE

The very finest turquoise stones come from Iran, and so it is no coincidence that the name means "Turkish stone" (Iran used to be part of the Ottoman Empire). One of the qualities symbolized by the turquoise is that of sensitivity. This is because the stone can be affected by changes in the body temperature of the wearer, or by the chemicals in perfumes and sprays.

For the Aztecs, the turquoise was considered to be so sacred that no single person was allowed to own one; they all belonged to the gods, and to the gods alone. The stone was used to decorate the iconic death masks of these people.

When the Mayan empire was effectively destroyed by Cortez, the sacred nature of the turquoise was passed on to the Pueblo people. This "stone of the gods" is also held in high esteem by Native American people. Although its use is now widespread and has become so popular that it has become a symbol of the people themselves, it was originally the preserve of the medicine man and the shaman, who were closest to the gods and so had some jurisdiction over the stone.

WITCH STONE

See Hag stone.

Part Five

SACRED GEOMETRY AND PLACES OF PILGRIMAGE

WHAT IS SACRED GEOMETRY?

Geometry means, quite literally, "measurement of the earth," a term coined by the ancient Greeks. People need to have boundaries and a system for defining space, and geometry fulfills this need. Geometry becomes sacred when it pleases the gods, and in order to accomplish this, a structure has to be designed and built with the conscious aim of creating a harmonious resonance with the natural—that is, divinely created—world. Geometric reasoning provides not only a framework for the solid, material plane, but enables us to measure the movement of the stars and the planets, helping us to understand our own place in the cosmos.

The notion of sacred geometry was not restricted to the ancient Greeks. The elaborate patterns and shapes of Islamic architecture were also influenced by the idea that certain measurements are an inherent part of a divine plan. Gothic and Renaissance architecture follow its tenets too. The influence of sacred geometry extends from the pyramids to latter-day buildings, both secular and sacred. Modern building technologies mean that fluid, organic shapes can now be incorporated into large structures, such as Gaudi's Sagrada Familia in Barcelona, Jørn Utzon's Sydney Opera House, and Norman Foster's 30 St. Mary Axe (widely known as "the Gherkin") in London.

But what of these proportions, and how do they differ from "normal" systems of measurement? The key word is "harmony." This short introductory piece can't claim to be an exhaustive treatise on sacred geometry, but outlines some of the basic principles.

There are certain proportions that the ancient Greeks designated as sacred. Spatial proportions are only one aspect of these measurements; the principles of sacred geometry underpin the harmonics and frequencies of music and color, as well as natural forms. Numbers, like letters, are sacred symbols in themselves, so people already had the basic tools needed to gauge these divine quantities. For our ancestors, numbers and letters were intrinsically connected and certain symbols encompassed both; pi, for example, was also called the golden mean, the golden section, the golden ratio, and the divine proportion.

Golden section

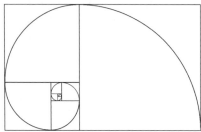

Whatever you want to call it, of all of the many secret signs and sacred symbols this is perhaps one of the most exciting, occurring in the natural world in the most unexpected of places. If you clench your hand, tucking the index finger into the base of your thumb and wrapping the thumb in tight, you create the golden section.

The spiral shapes of shells and ammonite fossils, and the seed heads of sunflowers all obey its mathematical rules. Stylized patterns of unfurling fronds of the tree fern in Maori art are another example. The series of numbers called the Fibonacci sequence provides a sort of instruction manual for the construction of this never-ending spiral shape.

Platonic solids

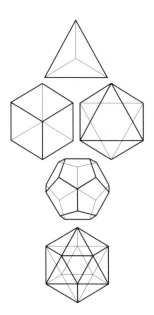

Despite being named after the Greek philosopher and mathematician Plato, there is plenty of evidence that these shapes—said to encompass the four classic elements of earth, air, fire, water, together with the elusive fifth element—had been discovered at least a thousand years before his time. In fact, the first three shapes were identified by Pythagoras.

Plato described his discovery in 360 BC. Because they are related to the elements, the Platonic solids are said to encompass everything within the known universe.

These shapes are regular polyhedrons. That's to say, they are multi-sided, three-dimensional figures whose points or corners all touch the sides of an orb. There are literally millions of irregular polyhedrons, but only five regular ones. Each of the elements is represented by the solid object to which it relates.

Earth is the twelve-edged cube or hexahedron, fitting as a symbol for the solidity of the Earth as a planet as well as a concept. Fire is a six-edged tetrahedron, its pyramid shape appropriately flame-like. Air is a twelve-edged octahedron. Water is a thirty-edged isocahedron.

The fifth element—ether or aether—was identified as such by Aristotle, although it was commonly accepted in the East much earlier. Although Aristotle did not identify the element with the fifth Platonic solid, the thirty-edged dodecahedron, Plato had commented that God used the shape to arrange all the constellations in heaven.

The Platonic solids may not at first appear to be particularly secret or sacred. However, their discovery was of profound importance in our understanding of how the universe works, and the beauty of their regular geometric forms is a great influence on sacred geometry and architecture.

PLACES OF PILGRIMAGE

Inevitably, the buildings that most noticeably follow the principles of sacred geometry tend to be places of worship or tombs, but this isn't always the case, as we'll see when we look, for example, at the hogan and the yurt. Sometimes natural features of the landscape are encompassed as an inherent part of a building, like the church that originally dominated Glastonbury Tor. The use of high places to site temples or other places of worship gives an added value to the man-made structure, not only by making it more prominent in the landscape, but because of the shared symbolism of the altar, the holy building and the mountain itself, that all signify humanity's attempt to reach the divine.

BOROBUDUR

Like other Buddhist structures, the Borobudur follows the form of the mandala (which is itself a diagram of the cosmos) with each of the faces of the square base facing the cardinal directions head on. Seven square terraces surmount the platform at the base—each being successively smaller than the last—so that the building assumes a stepped shape. On the last of the square platforms are three raised circular levels each set with circular stupas numbering 72 in total, and the whole is surmounted by a single, central stupa that appears to skewer the rest of the building into the ground. Each of the 72 stupas contains a statue of the Buddha, although it can only be seen with some difficulty through the latticework. This filigree stonework serves to illuminate the closeness of the worlds of spirit and matter.

Each square side of the temple has a stone staircase leading to the circular levels, symbolizing the earth (the square levels) meeting the heavens (the circular layers).

When viewed from above, the building forms a perfect mandala structure. Even when painted on a flat surface, the mandala provides a compelling aid to meditation; the temple at Borobudur is a living representation of this cosmic map, and pilgrims, moving about the sacred structure, are reminded that their physical lives run parallel to the spiritual tenets of their faith.

CHARTRES CATHEDRAL

One of the most impressive and mysterious of all the cathedrals in France, Chartres is in the Gothic style and was built in the twelfth and thirteenth centuries. However, its site is much more ancient—the ground underneath Chartres is an ancient pre-Christian pagan mound, with a grotto called the "Pregnant Virgin." A Roman temple replaced the Druid temple that was built on the earlier site. Chartres remains an important focus for the specific worship of Mary.

Legend, myth, and mystery stick fast to Chartres. Relatively unchanged since it was completed in the early thirteenth century, there are suggestions that the Knights Templar brought the lost languages, such as the Language of the Birds, and the treasures of Solomon, and secreted them inside the cathedral. It is even rumored that the Ark of the Covenant itself is hidden in the crypt of Chartres. Notably, there are no burial places within the cathedral. Many of these secrets could arguably be held to be an inherent part of the actual material and construction of Chartres, since the early masons were party to the arcanum of sacred geometry and construction methods that inspired the fraternity of Freemasons in the first place. These secrets exist in many dimensions, and include the use of sound, shape, and color, as well as material form.

As there are nine "gates" to Chartres, nine knights were legendarily involved in its design. These were the knights who excavated Solomon's temple in the eleventh century and who returned with its secrets in the first place. In an uncanny echo of the "Pregnant Virgin" grotto that the cathedral stands on,

Chartres boasts possession of a veil, the Sancta Camisia, said to be the one actually worn by Mary when she gave birth to Christ. This veil, given by Charlemagne in 876, was initially housed in an earlier, wooden church that stood on the site, which was destroyed by fire. The Sancta Camisia was thankfully saved, and the main body of Chartres, as it stands today, was completed in just twenty-six years, between 1194 and 1220.

Of the many unique features of Chartres, two of the most talked about are the rose window and the labyrinth, also called the "Road to Jerusalem." Situated on the floor of the nave and effectively functioning as a barrier to the sacred space at the altar, if the western wall of the cathedral were folded down to the labyrinth, the rose window would match its space exactly.

There is one path to the center of the labyrinth, and the center itself is a six-petaled flower that could conceal a Star of David, the two convergent triangles that say "as above, so below." Pilgrims in modern times are more likely to walk the eleven circuits that measure exactly 666 feet to the center, but formerly the journey was taken on the knees, symbolic of the journey to the Holy Land.

The Encyclopedia of Secret Signs and Symbols

GLASTONBURY TOR

The myths surrounding Glastonbury Tor are made even more mysterious because there are so few precise facts known about it. Not only do these myths populate the tor with Druids, Wiccans, fairies, and other spirits, but King Arthur is also said to be buried there, as well as the Celtic gods of the underworld. It seems that the possibilities of this magical place are as colorful, entrancing, and exotic as the imaginations of the pilgrims that go there.

What *is* known, however, is that this imposing conical hill (which is what *tor* means) forms an awe-inspiring silhouette against the sky. Viewed from above, the mound resembles a vulva, so has become a natural icon of feminine forces. The land surrounding the tor was once watery fenland, and so the tor itself would have been an island, a good, easily defended vantage point for the Celts who lived there. Adding to the myth, the area was referred to as Ynys yr Afalon, leading one to suppose that this must have been the Avalon of legend, the "Isle of Apples."

One of the more intriguing aspects of this hill is the spiral path that twists its way around from the bottom to the top of the tor. This path forms seven terraces. There are several explanations for these terraces. Overlooking the mystique of the place for the moment, theories have suggested that they may have had an agricultural use for growing crops, that they were made by grazing animals, or that they were defensive ramparts.

However, the most obvious explanation—given the position and appearance of the tor, and that it was an obvious place of pilgrimage—is that the spiral path served the same purpose as the steps or paths associated with other natural or man-made sacred places that also have seven levels of ascent. People still climb the spiral path of the tor, not only as a physical journey but also as a spiritual one. The seven levels correspond to the seven planets known to ancient people, and with whom the deities were inextricably linked; it's for the same reason, for example, why the ziggurat also has seven levels. In some parts of Wales, it's still the custom to walk to the top of the nearest high place around the time of the Lughnasad festival at the beginning of August.

The existing tower on the top of the tor serves as a bitter punctuation to this sacred landscape. Once there was a fifth-century fort in the same position; this was replaced by a medieval church, St. Michaels, which remained there until 1275 when it was destroyed by an earthquake. The church that was rebuilt some eighty years later lasted until the dissolution of the monasteries; after that the tower was used as a place of execution, and the last Abbot of Glastonbury Abbey was hanged there. All that remains of the tower today is a haunting, roofless ruin.

GLASTONBURY ZODIAC

There are few places in the British Isles—or arguably, anywhere else in the world—that have the mystical charisma of Glastonbury. This is a place steeped in legend, reputedly the focus of the Arthurian tales, and believed by many to be a place where the seen and unseen worlds meet. Dr. John Dee, the renowned magician, seer, and astrologer to Queen Elizabeth I, was fascinated by the place, and he is reputed to have been the first person to propose that a representation of the celestial zodiac occupies the sacred land in and around the town.

Several hundred years later, a woman named Katharine Maltwood elaborated on the idea. Born in 1878, Katharine was an artist and scholar, whose marriage to a wealthy advertising manager, John Maltwood, enabled her to devote her life to art, sculpture, and most of all to her overriding interest in antiquarian matters. In particular, she was intrigued by the story of the purported visit of Joseph of Arimathea to Glastonbury, and by the Arthurian tales. While living in Somerset she made the discovery that would make her famous among future generations of seekers after the esoteric and the marvelous.

In 1929, Katharine claimed that the outlines of the characters of the astrological zodiac were traceable in various earthworks in a ten-mile radius around Glastonbury town, publishing these discoveries in her book, *The High*

History of the Holy Grail. Using large-scale Ordnance Survey maps, the shape of Leo the lion was the first that she noticed. Such was her fascination with the quest that in the 1930s she commissioned aerial photographs—at what must have been very great expense for that time—to be taken of the entire area. Her discoveries caused a sensation that was to be overshadowed by the outbreak of World War II.

Today the idea of the Glastonbury zodiac is treated as fact by some, but others see it purely as a flight of fancy, the product of a vivid imagination and people's desire to associate an even greater meaning and mystery to a place that is already crammed full of the amazing and the fantastical.

GREEN MAN MAZE

There can be few finer examples of a magical symbol hidden in the landscape than the Green Man Maze at Penpont House near Brecon in Wales. Although the term "Green Man" was not coined until the late 1930s, the name perfectly epitomizes the notion of a spirit of nature, living in among the leaves from which he is made. The maze is hidden in a wild and magical part of the countryside, and what's even more surprising is that it was constructed as recently as 2000 as a celebration not only of the millennium but also of the fortieth birthday of the landowner who, with his wife and family, also helped build the maze. That the Green Man can only be viewed in full from above—the viewpoint of the gods—makes it even more intriguing.

The maze was designed by David Eveleigh, specifically in accordance with the principles of sacred geometry. He used dowsing methods to align the Green Man with the points on the horizon of the solstice sun; the design incorporates the ancient sun wheel symbol, as well as a pentagram overlaid on an elven star to give the proportions and structure that form the basis of the design. At the very center of the maze is the root of an upturned tree, a symbol that had significance not only for the Celts but is also mentioned in the Upanishads.

HOGAN

This is the traditional dwelling of the Navajo people of the southwestern U.S. Constructed of timber and earth, the hogan seeks to replicate the home that the coyote and beaver gods made for the first man and woman. These people did not operate with the Western demarcation between secular and sacred space, and the hogan itself is a replica of the cosmos, as straightforward an example of sacred architecture as we are likely to find.

The doorway of this circular, single-roomed house faces east, welcoming the morning sun and receiving the blessings of its rays. This eastern entrance is also favored by certain tunnel-nesting birds, and by wild bees. The hogan has a central hearth. The southern half of the room represents the male element, while the north half belongs to the female. This male–female union is also symbolized in the physical construction of the hogan. The first stage in its building

sees a forked, female log placed toward the north, with a straight male log pointing towards the south, resting in the cleft. These logs demonstrate a strong union between the husband and wife, and make an obvious fertility symbol, as well as providing a solid foundation for their home. A third forked log is placed toward the west, balancing the entrance. The rest of the building is constructed from stacked logs and other materials. Gemstones are secreted among the logs, and the whole might be covered in mud or earth against the elements.

Like any sacred building, the hogan is consecrated before use. This involves chanting from an ancient song called "The Blessingway" that describes the making of the original hogan. A clockwise pilgrimage around the building honors the path of the sun.

MECCA

For Muslims, Mecca symbolizes the actual point on earth where the vertical axis of heaven (and space), and the horizontal axis of human existence (and time) intersect.

The Encyclopedia of Secret Signs and Symbols

One of the most famous of all holy cities, a pilgrimage, or *hajj*, to Mecca at least once during their lifetime is an essential part of the spiritual life of any Muslim. This journey is so significant that it forms the fifth of the five symbolic Pillars of Wisdom, the foundations of the faith. The main focal point of this journey is the Great Mosque, which was built to surround the Ka'aba that stands in the center. This is a large cube-shaped building, built by the prophet Abraham after his wife Hagar found water in the desert at the Well of Zamzam. This well, revealed by an angel, saved their son Ishmael from dying of thirst, and inspired Abraham to build the Ka'aba in the first place. Muslims hold that the Ka'aba mirrors a heavenly house, and that it sits on the site of the first house built by the first man, Adam. It is expressly forbidden for people of other faiths to enter Mecca; the first Western woman to do so was Lady Evelyn Cobbold, who wholeheartedly embraced the faith and performed the *hajj* in 1933 when she was 66. The explorer and scholar Sir Richard Burton had entered the Ka'aba itself in the nineteenth century; aware that the penalty of his discovery would be death, he resorted to subterfuge, disguising himself as a Sufi to gain access.

The origins of the word *Ka'aba* are the same as for "cube," and the dimensions of this granite building are imposing; it is nearly 46 feet high, with sides of 36 feet and nearly 43 feet. The four corners of the Ka'aba point roughly to the four points of the compass, and the building is the focal point for prayer. Wherever they may be in the world, the devout pray towards the Ka'aba, and have special compasses to help align themselves correctly. In the eastern corner of the building is the sacred "black stone," generally accepted to be the remnant of a meteorite and possibly the original reason for the sanctity of the place. Prior to the coming of Mohammed, this stone was the focal point for worship of the goddess Al'Lut. The goddess had seven priestesses, and pilgrims circled the holy stone—which resembled the vulva—seven times in honor of the seven known planets of the ancient world.

MEDICINE WHEELS

We examined the use of the medicine wheel as a graphic device that is a mandala-like focus for meditation in Part One. The original medicine wheel, however, is constructed as a living part of the landscape although, like the stone circles that are in many ways their larger European counterpart, the reasons lying behind their design and construction remain something of a mystery.

The largest of these stone wheels, sometimes called the American Stonehenge, is the Bighorn Medicine Wheel at Medicine Mountain. Situated at an elevation of 9,640 feet, it's an impressive sight, and the plain it lies on is a sacred place in its own right; for hundreds of years ceremonies marking rites of passage were held there by diverse peoples, including the Cheyenne, Arapaho, and Shoshone.

Made from half-buried rocks laid out in the shape of a giant wagon wheel, it has twenty-eight spokes emanating from a hollow-centered central cairn that is about 3 feet tall. Each spoke is 36 feet long, and the whole is 245 feet in circumference. Surrounding this central wheel are six smaller cairns, each with an open side, giving it a C-shaped appearance from above. Like Stonehenge, certain points on the wheel align to the sun, the moon and the planets; specifically, the central cairn and another one on the outside of the rim perform exactly the same function as the heel stone of Stonehenge on the day of the summer solstice. It is likely that each of the twenty-eight spokes represents the days of the lunar cycle. Other lines in the medicine wheel describe earthly demarcations for celestial bodies, including Sirius, Rigel (a star within the Orion constellation), and Aldebaran. The age of the Bighorn Medicine Wheel is indeterminate. The wheel shares the meaning of the circle as a symbol of eternity with no beginning or end, showing the endlessness of the passing of time.

MENHIR

A large, upright standing stone, our ancestors obviously spent a great deal of time and effort to find and quarry the stones, shape their tapered tops, drag them into position, and make them stand upright. But why? Unless they are part of a group of stones, such as a stone circle, there is no consensus of opinion as to what menhirs actually signified.

The word *menhir* comes from two Breton words, meaning "long stone." They are most often seen in western Europe but appear as far afield as Asia and Africa, too. Theories about their function—or symbolic meaning—include, in no particular order:

1. Territorial markers
2. Part of a calendrical system
3. Sites of sacrifice

Until recently, we were not even absolutely sure as to their age. It was believed that they belonged to the Bronze Age (*c.* 3000 BC) but recent evidence suggests that they may be much older.

Any tall, narrow object can serve the function of marking time by means of the shadow, popularly represented as the gnomon that stands firmly in the center of the sundial. It's possible that the menhir may have served this function as well as being a symbol of fertility; there's an obvious phallic nature to these mighty stones.

As with many ancient artifacts, the early Christians had a deep-rooted suspicion of menhirs, and many of them were toppled. Others were explained away as being put there by demonic forces; the Rudston monolith in Yorkshire is one such example. Standing at 26 feet high, the stone weighs at least 80 tons and is believed to be as deep as it is high. The stone stands right next to the tiny village church and local legend says that the devil threw the stone at the church but narrowly missed it because of his poor marksmanship; a conflicting tale says that God threw it, punishing some people who were desecrating the churchyard.

Rudston itself means "cross stone" (*rud stan*), and the stone was apparently "Christianized" at one point with the addition of a cross perched on its top.

NAZCA LINES

The Pampa Colarada desert near Nazca, high up on a plateau between the Andes and the Pacific Ocean, is one of the driest places in the world. Scattered over a vast area of 200 square miles are more than a hundred massive animal shapes. These shapes are so huge that they are fully visible only by the gods, or via a means of transport that the people who created them 2,000 years ago could never have dreamed of: a helicopter or airplane.

It has rarely rained in the Nazca valley during the last 10,000 years, and the shapes that were created by arduously scraping away the topsoil—in much the same way that the similar shapes were made in Britain and elsewhere—are protected from vehicles or footprints. Some of the lines are more than five miles long, requiring an amazing feat of concentration by their constructors to get the form right without ever being able to see the final result. Their work was also carried out in dusty, arid conditions. The shapes include geometric patterns, as well as human figures, a serpent, flowers, a lizard, a spider, and several varieties of bird, including the great warrior god Huitzilopochtli in the form of a hummingbird.

No one knows specifically why these drawings were made. Theories include their use as some sort of calendrical system, or even as landmarks for visiting UFOs. Arguably, the most logical suggestion is that the shapes were made to communicate with the gods, to please them as they looked down to earth.

NEWGRANGE

Situated in the northeast of Ireland, Newgrange is a huge construction dating back at least 5,000 years. As a sacred space, it emulates the idea of the cave as a secret place of ritual, the womb of the earth, a place of death and rebirth.

From the outside, Newgrange is an imposing sight. It comprises a mound of earth surrounded by a stone wall, encircled by numerous standing stones and almost a hundred roughly worked stones laid end to end. The edifice is 36 feet high and almost 300 feet across. Mounds like this were later thought to be the homes of the numinous beings that inhabited the place: earth spirits, fairies, and creatures from the otherworld.

In front of the entrance to Newgrange is a large stone, beautifully engraved with spiral motifs. These shapes would have been chipped into the stone with flint tools, and the precision achieved is remarkable. The spiral symbol is associated with the passage of time and the cycle of the soul through death to rebirth, often depicted as a labyrinth. There is nothing labyrinthine, however, about the innermost part of Newgrange. A long, narrow passageway ends in the main room, a vaulted space with three flat-roofed chambers. Seen as though in an X-ray from above, the passageway and the three chambers form a cross shape. The main "hall" has a roof that's been constructed artfully by stacking stepped stones so that it resembles the basic shape of a beehive.

One of Newgrange's secrets was discovered as recently as 1972. In the roof over the entranceway is a hole that allows a shaft of light to fall onto the triple spiral pattern more than 60 feet away inside the chamber. This happens just once a year, at the winter solstice. Other megalithic monuments are believed to have an astronomical connection, but this feature of the roof at Newgrange plainly proves the point.

PANTHEON

Literally meaning the "Temple to All Gods" in ancient Greek, the Pantheon was conceived around AD 50, at a time when the old deities had not been usurped by Christianity. It was intended as part of Augustus Caesar's plan to rebuild the city in his own image and was erected in honor of the gods and goddesses that had assist-

ed in his rise to power. The temple was not completed, however, until the following century by Emperor Hadrian.

The features of the Pantheon which give clues to its having been constructed following the principles of sacred geometry are the rectangular porch with a triangular pediment sitting squarely on top, the circular shape of the main temple area, the domed roof representing the vault of heaven, the proportions of the building, and the symbols inlaid into the floor. These are among the basic units of measurement that Pythagoras calculated as being part of the harmony of the cosmos and, as such, were believed to have been devised by the Creator. This celestial harmony is reflected in the Pantheon. The measurements of the building are also calculated according to Pythagoras's rules of sacred geometry. The main temple is 145 feet in diameter and 145 feet from floor to ceiling.

The dome of the Pantheon is a particularly magnificent piece of engineering. The internal volume of the main temple is 16,360 square feet and has no reinforcing support. It was only 1,500 years later that the size of its dome was exceeded, marginally, by that of the Church of Santa Maria del Fiore in Florence. Because it is a symbol of the vault of heaven, the dome was a particularly popular piece of design for sacred buildings, and cities vied with one another in a sort of architectural one-upmanship to find new ways of building bigger and better ones.

The dome of the Pantheon is open to the skies, and this opening is called the *oculus*, or "great eye," symbolic of the sun, and is 29 feet wide. The ceiling has graduated ribs that are not only a structural feature designed to lighten the load, but also represent the major planetary gods of Rome: Mars, Venus, Mercury, Jupiter, and Saturn.

Part of the design of the Pantheon—in its original conception as a temple to honor all gods—was the installation of apses, or niches, which contained the shrines of these deities. However, with the coming of Christianity the Pantheon was adapted to the new faith, the shrines were removed, and the building was renamed the Church of Santa Maria Rotunda. These apses now contain the tombs of Italian kings, as well as that of the Renaissance artist Raphael.

PYRAMID

At its most basic, the upward-pointing triangle represents the fire that is the meaning of the word "pyramid" in Greek. The pyramid itself is an incredibly strong construction, both symbolically and practically, with the solid base of the square supporting the four triangles that meet at the peak or axis of the pyramid. The shape is as impregnable and daunting as it looks.

The Pyramids themselves have become a symbol of Egypt, and together with the Sphinx, capture the essence of that country more completely than any modern advertising logo could ever do.

There have been countless books written about the Pyramids, and the symbolism of the shape is not to be confused with any claims of "pyramidology." Essentially, the pyramid represents the axis mountain of the world. This mountain is said to have risen from the waters of creation and represents existence itself. Furthermore, the cavern-like aspect of the Pyramids, in which the bodies of the pharaohs were interred with elaborate rites, represents the natural cave to which early humans were attracted, not only as a womb-like place of refuge but also as a place where religious rites could take place in secrecy. The sloped shape of the exterior of the Pyramids is echoed in their internal passages, which also slope steeply; these angles help the souls of the interred pharaohs ascend to heaven.

We still have a primal belief that the closer we are the sky, the nearer we are to heaven and to the Creator. The shape of a pyramid provides a way for people to achieve this goal. Stepped pyramids culminate in a flat platform where the world of spirit meets the world of matter, the construction acting as a reminder of the convergence of the material and the ethereal. The ancient Egyptians further demonstrated this idea by another symbol, an inverted pyramid balanced on top of an upright one, also known as the "creation sign"; the upper symbol represents inspiration pouring down from the heavens (the chalice shape as a sign for water is an obvious clue), whereas the base pyramid shows aspiration, a striving for the perfection of heaven. This symbol itself repre-sents the same concept as the Star of David: "as above, so below."

ROSSLYN CHAPEL

This small chapel, also called the Collegiate College of St. Matthew, is set in the sleepy rural hamlet of Roslin some seven miles south of Edinburgh, Scotland. It is the subject of intense scrutiny, attract-ing worldwide curiosity as a result of Dan Brown's best-selling novel and the ensuing film *The Da Vinci Code*. In the book, Brown posits that the Holy Grail itself was hidden in the chapel, and that the bloodline of a child born to Christ and Mary Magdalene can be traced directly back to the building.

The crazed excitement and conspiracy theories surrounding Rosslyn mean that fact has become increasingly hard to separate from fiction. Unsubstantiated rumors of the esoteric articles secreted in the chapel include the Ark of the Covenant, the original Stone of Destiny, and even the Holy Grail itself. The mystical charisma of Rosslyn is so powerful, however, that it needs no media frenzy to exacerbate its importance.

The chapel was commissioned by Sir William Sinclair (or St. Clair) in 1446. It seems as though the chapel was the start of a much larger Catholic church, and, like other grand ecclesiastical buildings, was seen as a way for Sir William to accumulate future credits in heaven to atone for his transgressions on earth. It is also rumored that Sinclair's interest in arcana was because he was none other than Christian Rosenkreuz, founder of the Rosicrucian Order.

This small chapel is smothered in elaborate and accomplished stone carvings. These include angels and demons, roses, stars, elephants, pyramids, serpents, plants that were not available in Britain at the time the chapel was built, and many depictions of the Green Man. There are other carvings that retain their secrets despite centuries of investigation and conjecture, along with dozens of Masons' marks as testimony to the anonymous craftsmen that worked on the building.

The 213 stone cubes that seem to represent Chladni patterns—the shapes made when fine powder laid on a taut surface is subjected to certain frequencies—is explained in Part Seven. Among the other features of the chapel, the "Apprentice Pillar" is particularly notable. While the Master Mason was abroad, investigating designs for the pillar, the legend goes that his apprentice dreamed that he himself had carved it. His vision was of such power that he set to work. Upon his return, the Master Mason was so jealous of the ornate pillar that he killed the hapless apprentice with a blow to the head; both characters, and the grieving mother of the apprentice, have been immortalized in stone. This myth seems to have originated in the eighteenth century, and bears some resemblance to the story of Hiram Abiff that lies at the heart of Freemasonry.

At the base of the pillar are eight dragons, from whose mouths emerge vine tendrils that spiral up the pillar. This is said to be a representation of the World Tree. At the top of the pillar is a Latin inscription that translates as:

"Wine is strong, a king is stronger, women are stronger still, but truth conquers all."

There is a plethora of Green Man carvings in the chapel—110 in all—peering out stonily from all directions. The Green Man is an ancient idea of a spirit of nature, found in a similar form all over the world. It is an unusually pagan image to appear so prominently in a Christian place of worship. These carvings appear youthful when they appear in the eastern side of the chapel, gradually aging as they move west with the course of the Sun and the passage of time.

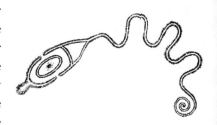

Despite generations of research, it seems that the mysteries of Rosslyn will remain unsolved. Perhaps the biggest conundrum is the juxtaposition of so many seemingly pagan images in the context of a Christian place of worship; perhaps the designers of Rosslyn were wise enough to realize that integration is the surest path to wisdom and understanding. Today, however, the trustees of Rosslyn have a less esoteric problem to solve—how to cater for the recent and dramatic increase in visitors, from 30,000 a year in 2000 to 145,000 in 2014. All these people, crammed into what has been described as a "stone storybook," in a room measuring just 69 by 35 feet.

SERPENT MOUND

Some natural features of the landscape represent mythological creatures or suggest the shapes of animals or birds; others are man-made, and the efforts taken to construct such monuments are a reminder to us of just how important certain images were to the people who designed them.

One of these man-made structures is the Serpent Mound in the northeastern U.S. (The symbolism of the serpent is examined elsewhere in this book.) The mound was built some 2,000 years ago by Native Americans, either the Hopewell or Adena people. The earthwork is built of yellow clay and stones, and takes the form of a 1,253-foot-long snake, its tail end curled into a spiral, and with what appears to be an egg in its mouth.

Although it's impossible to say precisely why the mound was constructed, the primal importance of the serpent as a magical symbol is well documented. It was one of the most important animal symbols not only for Native Americans but for the Celts, Hindus, Assyrians, and others. It has been argued that this serpent represented a particular deity; because the serpent was a symbol of the powers of the earth it would make sense to construct it in such a way that the deities up in the heavens would be able to see it. The creature lies at the edge of a promontory and burnt stones in the center of the "egg" suggest that fires were once lit there. This fire would have been visible for miles around and possibly signified that the snake—the numen of the place—was "awake" and protecting her people. The egg is a symbol of fertility and rebirth, and the spiral at the other end of the tail suggests the coiled power of the energy of the earth.

STONEHENGE

The most impressive single stone circle of all is arguably Stonehenge in Wiltshire, England. The scale of Stonehenge is vast; when it first comes into view its impact, set against the gently rolling backdrop of Salisbury Plain, is breathtaking. Constructed between 3000 and 2100 BC, the standing stones of this megalithic monument were quarried from the bluestone that is found only in the Preseli mountains in Wales, some 240 miles away.

Stonehenge is an evocative place and remains a primary focus for neo-pagan groups, especially at the time of the summer solstice when the "heel" stone of the circle aligns with the rising sun cresting over the horizon. Pagan worship at Stonehenge resumed again after hundreds of years in 1905, performed by the Ancient Order of Druids that was founded in the nineteenth century. For years the site of peaceful pagan worship and a month-long rock festival, in 1985 the infamous incident known as the "Battle of the Beanfield" occurred. New Age travelers converging on the site at the time of the solstice for the free festival were prevented from doing so by the police, some of whom were dressed in riot gear. The incident resulted in smashed cars and caravans, and a great deal of violence toward the travelers.

Access to Stonehenge, especially at the time of the solstice, is now carefully controlled. The stones, however, stand as a powerful symbol of the freedom to choose not only one's gods, but also the way in which they are to be worshipped.

Synagogue

The word "synagogue" means "assembly," and its decor adapts to the circumstances and surroundings of the country and environment in which it is situated.

Prior to the synagogue, hereditary priests, known as *kohens*, officiated in the rites, and the worshippers stayed outside the main body of the temple, making their burnt offerings to God. The rabbis who subsequently officiated at the synagogues were part of a democratic movement; a marked difference between the temple and the synagogue is that, whereas God was believed to reside in the temple, the synagogue is an unconsecrated building. The emphasis of the synagogue is on education, and the study of the Talmud (the Jewish laws and legends) is given priority. Despite this secular angle, however, the synagogue retains its status as a sacred building.

The main focal point in any synagogue is the ark, a box which contains the scrolls of the Torah, the first five books of the Bible that God gave to Moses. Although the ark may be highly decorated, it is distinctly not an object of veneration, and is only important inasmuch as it contains the word of God. The ark is set into a wall that faces the direction of the original Temple in Jerusalem. This symbolizes the fact that although the physical Temple no longer exists, the idea of it remains close, a reminder of the sense of exile. Prayers are often directed toward the coming of the Messiah, which is believed to coincide with the rebuilding of the Temple for the third time.

God is not portrayed figuratively anywhere in the synagogue, a feature shared by Islamic places of worship. Unlike Christian churches, which have highly decorated windows and paintings depicting scenes from the Gospels, the designs and patterns in the synagogue are more abstract and indeterminate.

Yurts and tipis

As the simplest magical symbols often encapsulate the most concentrated meanings, so our most basic dwelling places can often say just as much as the largest or most imposing cathedrals or temples.

The yurt is the portable dwelling belonging originally to the nomad peoples of Central Asia, although the popularity of the structure has extended way beyond this area. The yurt is circular, its walls built from a trelliswork of sticks that concertina together so that they can be transported. Traditionally, the "walls" are made from felt or other fabrics. The dome-shaped roof, or *shangrak*, is also made from wooden lattice and although the rest of the yurt will be replaced over the years, the *shangrak* is something of an heirloom, passed down from generation to generation.

The roof has a central hole that enables smoke to escape from the centrally positioned hearth. The smoke from the fire, ascending through this hole, is symbolic of the Axis Mundi. The smoke carries the prayers and wishes of the yurt-dwellers—as well as offerings of food—directly to the gods.

The tipi is a similarly portable, circular construction that imitated the greater cosmos, although the ground space is more egg-shaped than circular. Three poles, tied together, make a tripod; these three foundation posts represent man, woman, and the Great Spirit. Next, a number of poles are woven together and supported by the junction of the foundation poles. The number of poles depends on the circumference of the tipi. Finally, the whole is covered with a semicircular piece of cloth, made in such a way that smoke flaps can be positioned, using two separate poles, according to the direction of the wind to allow smoke to escape from the central hearth. This central pillar of smoke has the same symbolic meaning as that of the yurt.

Part Six

NUMBERS

THE BAIT THAT ATTRACTS THE MYSTERIOUS

Underpinning the idea of the number as a basic tally device is a profound system of philosophy and symbolism that resonates through the entire world, operating in remarkably similar ways throughout most cultures and belief systems.

This notion, that numbers represent not only physical quantities but also the inherent qualities, laws, and powers of the universe, is very ancient. It is described and explained in various ways, and is reflected in the mystery traditions, including those of the Pythagoreans, Babylonians, and Hindus as well as in the Kabbalah. The form of the number, its conceptual nature, and its symbolic meanings carry sacred and mystical significance, a hidden code that can be cracked to reveal the secret construction of the universe and humanity's place within it.

*   *   *

RELATIONSHIP BETWEEN LETTERS AND NUMBERS

Different disciplines accord slightly different numerical values to the letters of the alphabet, but generally, the following table is applied:

1	2	3	4	5	6	7	8	9
A	B	C	D	E	F	G	H	I
J	K	L	M	N	O	P	Q	R
S	T	U	V	W	X	Y	Z	

Compound numbers are reduced to a single digit.

ZERO

It's hard to know where to put zero. Should it go at the beginning or the end of this section? A magical circle, indeed, it encompasses everything and yet stands for nothing.

The invention or discovery of zero has had profound implications for humanity's development; it was the last "number" to be recognized as such.

Conceptually, zero is the symbol that stands for "no thing." In Buddhism and Taoism, it represents the Void, which existed before Creation, and in India, the word for the concept of zero was *Sunya*, the Sanskrit word for void or vacuum. In Islamic belief, zero represents the essence of divinity, and Pythagoras said that the zero indicated perfect form. However, if zero is placed after a number, then this number is increased tenfold, giving the infinite and limitless possibilities of such a simple symbol as defined by the Kabbalah.

The representation of zero as a blank space appeared in India in the fourth century BC, and the Egyptians, similarly, used a gap to represent the concept. The Babylonians used a pair of slanted lines to represent the zero. The Mayans were using the zero at least a thousand years before anything similar was seen in Europe. In Mayan calendars and codices, the zero is represented by the humble snail-shell, whose spiral form inspired the symbol. The first known use of this shell symbol was around 36 BC. The Romans used the word *nulla*, meaning "nothing," and by around AD 720, this had been abbreviated to the letter N.

There has been fierce debate as to whether zero can really be a number at all; this question so vexed the philosophical ancient Greeks that it caused intense arguments about existence itself and the nature of nothing. Must nothing also be something? How *could* nothing be something?

Zero in the form we know it today, as the oval shape so similar to the Cosmic Egg, was first used in the Indian numerological system and appears in a Jain text dated AD 458. This circular shape is an entirely appropriate symbol for the zero concept, which, like a seed, represents potential and possibility.

The Indian and Greek concepts of zero were amalgamated by a Persian mathematician and scholar named Al Khawarizim, and the zero as we know it today comes from this source.

In the tarot, the zero is the number of the Fool, the card of enthusiasm, innocence, and guilelessness fatalism.

* ** *

THE FIRST NINE NUMBERS

ONE

The straight line is one of the simplest basic symbols. A human being, standing upright, is the perfect representation of the number 1. *Homo sapiens* is the only creature on earth that stands naturally erect on two feet, and the number 1 demonstrates this graphically as well as being a symbolic reminder that humans are unique in the animal kingdom; truly, one of a kind. One is the number of confidence, and of the one God, but it is also the number of the "one-ness" of the many. It is the number of the mythological first man, Adam. It is the World Tree and the Axis Mundi. Turn this line on its side, and it becomes the horizon.

One is generally the number of the individual and the leader. It's often seen as a male, "yang" number, a solar number. This means that the number 1 is also the number of the autocrat and the dictator as well as that of the divine.

Strictly speaking, the Pythagoreans did not regard 1 or 2 as numbers at all. There was a school

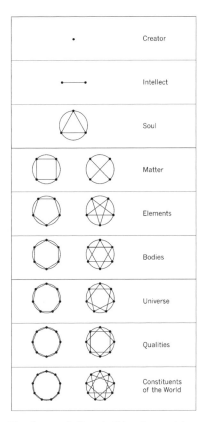

•	Creator
•—————•	Intellect
	Soul
	Matter
	Elements
	Bodies
	Universe
	Qualities
	Constituents of the World

Number symbolism in Islamic mysticism.

of thought that associated 1 with the monad, i.e., the "noble number, sire of gods and men," the whole which is made of many parts. To this school of philosophers, 1 represented the mind, the intellect and hermaphrodism, since the 1 was both male and female. 1 is seen as being full of potential, effectively giving birth to all other numbers.

The phrase "odd one out" implies the eccentric, the maverick, and the one who stands on the fringes of society as a matter of course. It's the number of the only child, the number of the person who will question the rules of a society built to operate around the needs of the many rather than of the individual. 1 is about "out of the box" thinking and lateral solutions.

In the tarot, 1 is the number of the Magician, the secretive loner who has the powers to amaze and confound us.

Two

The vertical line of the number 1 is joined by another, and so makes the form of the Roman numeral II.

The Arabic symbol for 2 does a very interesting thing if you hold it up to a mirror; it forms the shape of a heart, the universal symbol for love and, specifically, two people in love. This is purely coincidental, but is, nevertheless, a pleasing little trick.

The Pythagoreans saw 2, or the duad, as a symbol of opposition and also of audacity, because it had had the cheek to separate itself from the first number. As they revered the 1, or monad, the 2 was despised as a symbol of polarity. If 1 represents the heavens, then 2 is the depths of the seas, which reflected the heavens and therefore 2 was capable of illusion and became associated with Maya, the Great Void. The magi carried mirrors with them as a reminder of this illusion, since mirrors reflect, another quality of the 2.

The number 2 gives us the positive and negative aspects of all things; indeed, without the number 2, positive and negative themselves would not exist. Day and night, light and dark, good and bad, male and female, attraction and repulsion, life and death, these are all encompassed by the number 2. 2 is the number of balance, but is also the number of conflict and split personality. It is the number of the first woman, Eve.

In the tarot, 2 is the number of the High Priestess, underlining the female, "yin" nature of the number that is sacred to all female deities.

Three

As the man and the woman have the potential to create a third, so one and two make three; a neat twist. Now, the third vertical line joins the other two giving us the Roman numeral for three and the potential to make a triangle and a circle, if the points of the triangle are joined up with three arcs.

It's because the number 3 gives us this potential circle—and a new dimension—that it becomes the first true magical number. There are countless examples of groups of three: the Holy Trinity of Father, Son, and Holy Ghost; the Triple Jewel of Buddhism in which Buddhists take refuge—Buddha, Dharma (ultimate truth), and Sangha (virtue)—and also faith, hope, and charity.

Then there's Brahma, Vishnu, and Shiva in the Hindu pantheon, who represent the Trinity that is God; in ancient Babylonia there was Anu, Bael, and Ea (heaven, earth, and the abyss, or hell); there's the Three Wise Men who visited Christ; the three Fates; and the three parts of time, past, present, and future.

There's a satisfaction about things that happen in threes, a feeling of "third time lucky" and the completion of a cycle. Fairy stories often use this device: Goldilocks and the Three Bears, or the three wishes that are often granted by a benevolent super-being such as the genie that pops out of Aladdin's lamp.

The Pythagoreans considered that the number 3 was the first true number. The triad represents the first "equilibrium of unities" and it was for this reason that the god Apollo used a tripod from which to give oracles. 3 was seen as the number of wisdom, understanding, and knowledge.

In the tarot, 3 is the number of the Empress, the embodiment of the female principle that symbolically links the heavens with earth and who carries within her the triple aspect of the goddess as virgin, mother, and crone.

FOUR

Now a new shape can be made which had no way of existing previously. As the third point of the number 3 gave us the triangle, a fourth point gives us the potential not only for the square but also for the cross. The circle of the earth can now be divided, and where the lines of latitude and longitude meet, a cross is formed.

Four is a masculine number and gives us, among countless other things, the number of the cardinal directions, north, south, east, and west; the four evangelists, Matthew, Mark, Luke, and John; the four elements of earth, air, fire, and water, and so on. In the Sufi tradition, there are four gates through which people have to pass on their way to enlightenment.

In alchemy, there are four key ingredients that go towards the making of the Philosopher's Stone; these are sulfur, mercury, salt, and azoth. In the tarot, 4 is the number of the Emperor, the archetypal male figure, the father, the king, the patriarch, who likes to create order and harmony in the universe that is enfolded within the number itself, which holds a hidden secret: if the numbers within 4 are added together (1 + 2 + 3 + 4), the whole adds up to 10, which implies the start of a new cycle, a rebirth or reincarnation. These ten numbers form the holy name, or Tetragrammaton.

In Pythagorean philosophy, the 4 or tetrad was considered to be the root of all things, the perfect, intellectual number. They believed that 4 symbolized God and this theory was explained in a secret and sacred discourse that described the concept of God as "the Number of Numbers" because of the reasons described above.

* ✳ *

FIVE

Now things start to get even more exciting. The dots that add up to 5, if placed symmetrically, give the potential for a five-pointed star (pentagram) or for a five-sided shape (pentagon). The 5, like the 3, is constructed from adding an odd number (3) to an even one (2), thus blending male with female. The pentagram itself is a mystical symbol that also holds within it all the qualities of the 5.

Five is a number of balance, its central dot acts as a pivot for the two on either side. It's also the numerical symbol of a human being, which forms the five-pointed star shape when legs and arms are outstretched, as in Leonardo's famous drawing of *Vitruvian Man*.

In the Western world there are four elements, but in the East there's a fifth, or quintessence, that binds them all together, called ether. Alchemists indicate this with a five-petaled rose in the center of a cross, redolent of the Rose Cross Lamen.

The Pythagoreans held that the pentagram—or pentad—was a sacred symbol of health, vitality, and light. The holy number 10 is divided equally into two parts by the pentad, which also symbolizes the triumph of spirit over matter.

In the tarot, 5 is the number of the Hierophant or the Pope, who represents the face of God on earth.

Six

Six was described by Pythagoras as a "perfect number" because 1 + 2 + 3 = 6; also, 1 x 2 x 3 = 6. God created the world in six days. The hexad was called the Form of Forms and the Maker of the Soul because the harmony of its arrangement was said to symbolize the harmony inherent within the soul. Because of the equally balanced triangles, the two groups of three that comprise the number 6, it is the symbol of marriage. Six is dedicated to Venus as the goddess of love but seems to have no connection with the spiritual nature of love or with the Creator. However, the number 6 gives us the tools we need to make that most powerful of magical signs, the Star of David, which is the embodiment of the phrase "as above, so below."

Because six can be split into two groups of three, it's seen as the number that can go either way, and is as likely to be evil as much as it is good. It's this precarious balance that crops up time and time again in examining the symbolism of the

number. The symbol for 6 itself has ambivalence; flip it the other way up and it becomes a 9. Six is the number of the marriage of opposites, an image and its reflection making up the whole.

In the tarot, 6 is the number of the card called the Lover, and shows a young man at a crossroads trying to decide between two girls of equal merit, although Cupid hovers in the background, bow and arrow at the ready, about to make the decision for him. The image demonstrates perfectly the dilemma that belongs to the number 6.

The witch's curse—or hex—is so called because six represented the number of copulation, the union of the Triple Goddess with her mate. The word itself was the original derivation of the word "hag."

The Egyptian hieroglyph for six shows male and female genitalia, underlining the sexual connotations of this number. For them, 3 was the number of the goddess and 6 when discussing Egyptian gods, since there were many gods. The fairy-tale command "Open, Sesame" is actually a Sufi love charm and "sesame" has been corrupted from *seshemu*, the Egyptian word for intercourse. The symbolic "cave" that needs to be opened is the female genitalia or yoni.

Early Christian authorities deemed 6 as the number of sin because of its association with physical love.

SEVEN

The number 7 is very busy; it seems to be everywhere. The Sumerians and Babylonians identified the seven days in a week, and the number of the traditional planets that give us much of our mythology is seven. There are seven deadly sins, which are balanced by seven cardinal virtues. There are seven orders of angels, seven colors in the rainbow and seven pure notes in the diatonic scale. Seven gives a pivotal point to the indecision of the number 6, rendering it satisfyingly complete and whole.

Very early on, it seems, this number was given special status as a number of completeness and perfection. For the ancient Egyptians, 7 was the number of eternal life. Legend has it that the prophet Mohammed, when in Jerusalem, ascended into the seven heavens and came into contact with the divine, and so the Dome of the Rock mosque was separated into seven sections to honor this experience. Pilgrims make seven circumnavigations of Mecca.

The Pythagoreans called 7 the septad, and said that it was "worthy of veneration." It was both the number of religion (because of the seven celestial spirits related to the seven planets) and the number of life. In the septad, the 3, comprising the mind, spirit, and soul, meets the tetrad, or 4, which is the number of the world. Therefore, the resulting 7 represents the mystic number of humanity as symbolized by the three-dimensional shape of the cube: six sides, with the seventh element the space inside. The sides of the cube represent the directions (the cardinal points plus above and below) with humanity at the center.

The phase of the moon lasts for 28 days, which is 4 x 7. Happily, $1 + 2 + 3 + 4 + 5 + 6 + 7 = 28$.

God created the world in six days, reserving the seventh to rest; therefore the seventh day is a holy day or holiday. This relaxation time also connects God with humanity, proving that even a deity needs a break now and then.

There are seven alchemical operations: calcination, dissolution, separation, conjunction, fermentation, distillation, and coagulation. In the tarot, the number 7 card is the Chariot. The card depicts a young man, a king, in a chariot driven by two horses; this young man knows where he is going and is full of determination.

EIGHT

In general, eight is seen to be a good number, a symbol of cosmic harmony and balance. The inter-cardinal points balance the four cardinal directions.

For Pythagoreans, the 8 or ogdoad was called the "little holy number" and considered sacred for several reasons. The cube has eight corners; also, in the Pythagorean numerical system eight is an "evenly even" number, and the only such number under 10. This is to say that the eight is divided into 2 x 4, and further, into 4 x 2. The serpents that twist up the staff of the caduceus make figure-of-eight shapes.

There are eight trigrams in the *I Ching* that go to make up the 64 hexagrams, itself constructed of 8 x 8. In Hindu belief, each of the eight directions of the earth is ruled over by a god. These eight divinities are related in turn to the eight petals of the lotus that resides, symbolically, inside the skull, a reminder of the microcosm and the macrocosm. Additionally, there are said to be eight qualities that belong to God; these are innocence, purity, self-knowledge and omniscience, freedom from impurities, benevolence, omnipotence, and bliss.

The figure 8 itself forms a symbol called the lemniscate, which is the scientific sign for infinity as well as having the same meaning at a more philosophical level, where it stands for the cycle of birth, life, death, and rebirth in the same way that the eighth day—following the six days of work and the seventh day of rest—denotes the day of renewal and invigoration.

In the tarot, 8 is the number for Justice, again reflecting the universal idea that 8 is the number of balance. It is the first card of the second set of the Major Arcana, reinforcing the idea of 8 as a symbol of renewal.

NINE

As it is 3 x 3, the number 9 has magic status and is a sacred number. For Hindus, it is the number of Lord Brahma, the Creator. It is also the numerological sum of Ba'hai, and so is seen as a symbol of perfection and unity, which explains the use of the nine-pointed star in this faith.

The Pythagoreans recognized the 3 x 3 as the ennead, which is the first square of an odd number. However, because it falls one short of the perfect 10, it was classified as an unfortunate number, sometimes even seen as evil because it is the inversion of the number 6. However, it was also considered limitless since there was nothing beyond it but infinity as represented by the 10, the perfect decad.

Because it is the last single-digit number, there is a sense of completion and wholeness about the number 9. It is for this reason that nine represents achievement and culmination of a task. In addition, nine is the zenith of achievement for a single-figure number. Because human embryos need nine months of gestation, nine is the number of humanity. Humans also have nine physical apertures, symbolizing nine channels of communication with the world. In the tarot, 9 is the card of the Hermit.

It's interesting to note that 666—also described as the number of the Beast—adds up to 18 using numerology, and 1 + 8 is 9. No great evil there, but a simple matter of fact.

TEN AND BEYOND

TEN

The first number that requires more than one digit, 10 is the foundation stone of the digital age, and despite any high-tech connotations, is the number of choice simply because of the number of fingers and thumbs on the hands. This simple fact has also given us the decimal counting system. Happily, the number 10 is infinitely malleable and versatile.

Pythagoras believed that 10 was the most sacred and greatest of all numbers, and the Tetraktys (a shorthand version of the name of God) was devised from it based on the premise that 1 + 2 + 3 + 4 = 10. The decad was a holy number, the first number to need a second part. Pythagoreans took oaths on this sacred number. Ten is a satisfying number, and 10 of anything seems like a complete set; for example, the Ten Commandments. In the Kabbalah, there are ten Sephiroth, emanations from the mind of God that represents the universe and its workings. Ten, in this instance, symbolizes the unity of creation and the synthesis of all things.

The Encyclopedia of Secret Signs and Symbols

The Mayans, however, regarded the number 10 as unfortunate, since it belonged to the god of death (Thoh). In the tarot, the number 10 is the number of the Wheel of Fortune.

ELEVEN

Eleven is considered to be the number of woman, since the female has 11 apertures in her body. The unborn child receives 11 divine powers via these holes. Numerologists consider that 11 is a "master number" that should not be reduced down into a single digit.

However, some traditions are suspicious about 11. If 10 is the number of completion and wholeness, then there is an idea that 11 must be the number of excess and extravagance (an idea perfectly defined in the movie *This Is Spinal Tap*, where the amplifier goes up to number 11). The eleventh hour has a sense of urgency about it. Since the clock runs to 12, then this is that last hour in which something can be done. World War I ended on the eleventh hour of the eleventh day of the eleventh month.

The eleventh card of the tarot is either Justice, or Strength. This card stands at the mid-point of the numbered series of cards.

TWELVE

There are 12 calendar months in a year, 12 signs of the zodiac that guard those months, 12 apostles, 12 tribes of Israel, 12 Knights of the Round Table. As there are 12 months in the year, so the hours of the day are also split into two sections of 12.

In more recent years, the European Union decided to put 12 stars on their flag. This is nothing to do with the number of member states, but an acknowledgement of something that people have long been aware of: that 12 is a number of perfection. This is because 12 is the result of the number 4 (four elements, four cardinal points, four corners of the earth) being multiplied by the number 3 (three levels of the universe, three aspects of any god); i.e., the multiplication of the number of the earth with the number of the heavens. In the tarot, the number 12 is the number of the Hanging Man; suspended from a rope by his foot, this unfortunate soul has the time to contemplate his place in the larger universe.

Thirteen

Are you a triskaidekaphobe? If so, it means that you're one of the thousands (or possibly even millions) of people who believe the number 13 to be unlucky. And some of you may even be among those who refuse to leave the house if the thirteenth day of the month happens to coincide with a Friday. Sometimes the number 13 is excluded from door numbers, or the thirteenth floor will be skipped over and effectively labeled as 14, so deep-rooted is this superstition.

Thirteen has long been regarded by many as an unlucky or inauspicious number. The Kabbalah, for example, says that there are 13 spirits of evil. It's still considered unlucky to have 13 people sitting down to dine because it is a reminder of the Last Supper, where Christ was betrayed by one of the twelve disciples who were eating with him, Judas Iscariot.

However, it's not all black for the number 13. Despite the year being divided up into twelve calendar months, there are actually thirteen lunar months, i.e., thirteen sets of twenty-eight days in a year. Therefore the Mayans regarded 13 as an auspicious number. There is also said to be a secret, hidden, thirteenth sign of the zodiac, Arachne, the spider whose web binds the network of the heavens. In classical antiquity, the thirteenth member of a group was considered to be the leader, the exalted one. Zeus sits at the head of the twelve Olympian deities, for example, in the same way that Christ sat among his disciples or King Arthur with his twelve knights at the Round Table. A coven consists of twelve members plus a leader. The *Apollo 13* Moon landing was beset by bad luck, and an explosion could have resulted in a disaster. However, no one died and the crew returned to Earth safely, so it could be said that the number 13 was lucky for them.

The number 13 is shown in several places on the United States' currency bills, and in this instance there is no hidden sinister meaning; simply, there were thirteen states that joined the original Union.

In the tarot, 13 is the number of Death. This represents initiation and facing fears. Presumably, these fears might include that of the number 13.

FOURTEEN

The phase of the moon is split into two sets of 14; one where the moon is waxing, or growing larger, and one where the moon is waning.

In Freemasonry, the significance of the number 14 has not gone unnoticed, and due attention is paid to the fact that the body of Osiris was reputed to have been cut into fourteen pieces by his murderer, his jealous brother Typhon, and the pieces scattered to the four winds. Isis, Osiris's wife, found the pieces and gave them a more fitting burial. Thus, the number 14 came to be associated with death and resurrection.

A part of the process of resurrection or reincarnation must necessarily be a lack of memory, the idea being that it might not be very constructive for the returning soul to be able to remember what went before. Therefore, 14 is the number of forgetfulness. The ancient Greeks believed that a soul about to be reborn drank the waters of Lethe, which was a river in Hades. Drinking this water caused the soul to forget everything in preparation for its return to an earthly body.

The fourteenth letter of the Hebrew alphabet is called Nun, and in the Kabbalah, this represents the idea of the spirit or soul dressed in the material body. In the tarot, this is equivalent to the card called Temperance; Temperance mixes liquid from a blue jug with that of a red jug. This mixture gives violet, the color of Temperance and the color of the spiritual and the material combined. As chance would have it, Temperance is also the card of reincarnation; the character carefully pours the violet liquid, the spirit, from one vessel to the other.

FIFTEEN

Fifteen is the product of two sacred numbers: 3 x 5. The Sumerian goddess Ishtar was attended by fifteen priests and her city, Nineveh, had fifteen gates. Because Ishtar was the goddess of both war and physical love, her number sometimes has negative connotations although the understanding of the number holds the key to greater spiritual comprehension.

In the tarot, 15 is the number of the Devil, since 1 + 5 gives us the ambivalent number 6, which apparently does not know right from wrong.

However, it's not all bad news for 15. Because each moon effectively waxes for fifteen days, there are fifteen steps to freedom and personal enlightenment in the Passover Seder or meal. To Kabbalists, 15 is the number of energy points that run down the center of the body.

SIXTEEN

Sixteen may be sweet, but as the square of the number 4, it's also powerful, encapsulating four times the strength of the tetrad. Therefore, the number represents the attainment of physical, earthly power. The sixteenth card of the tarot is the Tower, which carries a reminder of the consequences of the arrogance that sometimes accompanies material gain.

SEVENTEEN

Seventeen is an almost universally important number. With few exceptions, it's generally seen to be beneficial, redolent of spirituality and immortality, rebirth and transformation.

Why, though? In understanding the significance of certain numbers, their component elements can provide clues as to their meaning and significance. Seventeen is comprised of 1 + 7 giving the number 8; 1 is the number of the one God, and 7 is the number of completeness and perfection. Eight is the number of cosmic balance and harmony, and these qualities are compounded by the reappearance of the number 8, which is added to 9 to make 17: 9 is also full of rich spiritual significance.

This 8 + 9 is also the number of consonants in the Greek alphabet, broken down into eight semi-vowels or semi-consonants, and nine mute consonants.

In the tarot, 17 is the number of the Star, an auspicious card of the Major Arcana that expresses the notions of rebirth, change, and transformation, in accordance with the beliefs about the number 17 in general. There are exceptions to the universal esteem in which 17 is held, however. For the Egyptians, it was considered unlucky, since Osiris was slain on the seventeenth day of the month. In Rome, the Roman numeral for the number—XVII—is an "anagram" of VIXI, meaning "I have lived," the implication being that the person is alive no longer.

In Japan, the haiku poem is comprised of seventeen syllables.

Eighteen

Eighteen is the number of the moon, in not only the tarot but elsewhere. The moon itself is a symbol of intuition, mystery, and femininity.

There are elements of the eighteenth tarot card that are quite disturbing. The Moon drips blood, and these drips are caught by a ravening wolf and a dog. A crab or scorpion climbs up from the nether regions to join in the feast. These images point to the number 18 as a symbol of the material trying to destroy the spiritual.

However, it's not all doom and gloom for 18. It is, of course, the product of 2 x 9, meaning that the good qualities of the 9 are doubled in intensity. The Sufis say that 18 is a sacred number and so they give gifts in multiples of eighteen. There's also a Hebrew prayer called "Shemone Esre" which means "eighteen," and lists eighteen blessings. This is because, in the system of applying numerological values to letters (gematria) the word for "life" has a value of 18.

In Norse mythology, too, the number 18 has special significance. The god Odin was said to have pinpointed eighteen wisdoms, which correspond to the eighteen consonants in the Elder Futhark runic system.

Nineteen

Numerologically, $1 + 9 = 10$, which in turn is related to 1, so 19 has much of the same symbolism, by default, as these two previous figures.

Nineteen has special powers. It's a prime number, divisible only by itself and 1. Moreover, because it is made up of the first single number and the last single number, there is a feeling of completion about it, a beginning and an end. In the Kabbalah, 19 is the number of spiritual activity.

The Jewish calendar is based around the number 19 because there's a nineteen-year cycle of the moon in relation to the sun. A full moon will occur on roughly the same date every nineteen years. The Babylonians, too, were aware of this nineteen-year cycle.

In the tarot, 19 is the number of the Sun, again referring to its close association with the number 1, also a masculine, solar number. All the goodness associated with the Sun— happiness, honor, success, courage— are also qualities that belong, symbolically, to the number 19.

TWENTY

We can count up to 10 by numbering the digits on both of our hands, and we can count to 20 by including the toes. Therefore, 20 is the number of humanity in many civilizations, including the Mayan. There was an ancient measurement of land based on the space needed to grow enough corn to keep one person alive. This space was 400 square feet (20 squared). The Mayan year was 400 days long, which also corresponded to this measurement, all based on the number of fingers and toes.

In the tarot, the sense of completion about the number 20 is symbolized in the meaning of its card, namely Judgment. The Judgment card stands for awakening, realization, a call to action, and the realization of purpose in life, as pictured by three naked figures, one of which is rising from a grave. These figures are roused to action by the trumpeting angel that floats above them.

TWENTY-ONE

Looking at the component parts of 21, we see that 2 + 1 = 3, which in itself is a magical number, being the first number that broadens our perspective with a new dimension. Add to this the fact that 21 is 3 x 7 (or 7 x 3), with seven being one of the most sacred numbers, and we start to understand something of the significance of this number.

It is no coincidence that the age of majority in many countries around the world was traditionally held to be 21, when, figuratively speaking, the person reaching this birthday was given the "key to the door," symbolizing the responsibility of adulthood as well as an initiatory "unlocking." In the Old Testament, 21 is the number of perfection, and is the number of the attributes of wisdom.

In the tarot, 21 is the number of the World, and the last card of the Major Arcana. The card shows an androgynously female figure, standing within a vesica piscis of laurel leaves. The elements are represented by the images of an ox, an angel, a lion, and an eagle (respectively, earth, air, fire, and water), as are the cardinal points. The whole makes a victorious, triumphant picture.

In the Kabbalah, 21 represents the path of conciliation and the blessings of God.

Twenty-two

There are 22 letters in the Hebrew alphabet, and 22 cards in the Major Arcana of the tarot; this is not a coincidence. In the Kabbalah, these 22 letters are believed to give expression to the universe, and the tarot cards also reflect the qualities of the universe. This notion—that everything in the world is somehow encompassed in the number 22—is also reflected in the beliefs of the Bambara and the Dogon people, who believe that not only is 22 a symbol for the span of time from the creation to ultimate perfection and completion, but that all mystical information is embraced by the symbolism contained in the first 22 numbers. Twenty-two is also the number of books in the Avesta, the sacred texts of the Zoroastrians.

Twenty-three

Known as the Royal Star of the Lion, in purely numerological terms 23 is an auspicious number, announcing help from higher places or people, success, and fame. However, with 23, all is not quite so simple and much of the mysticism surrounding this number comes from a relatively recent source, Discordianism, more of which in a moment.

If 22 is somehow able to encompass the whole of the universe, then what of the numbers that come after it? As its immediate successor, logically, 23 must herald the beginning of a completely new world, a world not ruled by the same harmonious laws as the preceding 22. In addition, 23 comprises 2 (female) plus 3 (spiritual energy), combining to make 5, the number of harmony and balance, reflected nicely by the 23 chromosomes that are each contributed by the male and female during conception.

Discordianism is a modern, "prankster" spiritual movement, which started in 1958, and one of its central tenets is called the "23 Enigma," a belief that everything in the universe and all events are somehow connected to the number 23. The goddess who presides over the Discordians is called Eris, the Greek goddess of strife and discord, who is also known as the Queen of the Night.

* *⁎* *

THIRTY-THREE

Because 33 was the age at which Christ died, this number stands for the Christ-consciousness, which in itself means nurturing, responsibility, higher levels of awareness, and spirituality. It's also the number of the educator and the healer.

In the Sagrada Familia church in Barcelona there is a magic square called the Subirach Square, named for its inventor. The magic sum of this square is 33.

The 33rd degree in Freemasonry is generally held to be the highest degree, although some Masonic orders have further degrees above this one. In this context, 33 represents illumination and freedom from superstition or the received opinion of organized religion.

THIRTY-SIX

In both Tantric and Buddhist philosophies, 36 is the most sacred of all numbers. This is because it's considered to be the number of heaven. Thirty-six doubled (36 x 2 = 72) is the number of earth, and 3 x 36 (108) is the number of humankind. Buddhist and Hindu rosaries have 108 beads.

One of the more mystical aspects of Judaism says that there are 36 "Tzadikim Nistarim," or saintly people, on the earth at any one time. According to the Talmud, if any one of these people were not present, then the world itself would end. These people are unknown to one another, and although they possess magical powers, they are not themselves aware of their special role, which is to justify mankind in the eyes of God. Apparently, when the time comes these chosen ones will know exactly what to do. As it is also believed that these 36 special people are too humble to ever believe that they could be one of the Tzadikim Nistarim, 36 has come to represent humility.

FORTY

Forty, it is generally agreed among most religions and belief systems, is the number of symbolic death, initiation, trial and testing, preparation, and waiting. Both Moses and Mohammed received their "call" from God at this age, as did the Buddha, the very epitome of the idea that "life begins at forty." In addition, Muslims believe that the Qu'ran should be read every 40 days.

It's said to be unwise to attempt to study the Kabbalah before the prospective student has reached 40.

Knowing about the symbolic meaning of this number means that we have a deeper understanding of the 40 days and nights that Christ spent in the desert being tempted by the devil, and the 40 years during which the children of Israel wandered in the wilderness. Other examples of the number 40 that reveal a period of trial or tribulation are the 40 days of the deluge, the 40 days that Moses spent on Mount Sinai, and the 40 days of denial or fasting during Lent.

Among some Native American tribes, a second burial is customary, and this takes place 40 days after the first interment. In Islam, a memorial is held 40 days after a death.

The period of isolation for suspected plague victims during the Middle Ages was set at 40 days, thus giving us the word "quarantine."

FORTY-NINE

The product of 7 x 7, for Tibetan Buddhists, 49 is the number of days that it takes for the dead soul to be reborn into another body.

FIFTY

Do you know why the Olympics are held every four years? It's because the original ancient Greek games were held at Olympia every 49 or 50 moons or "lunations."

The number 50 signifies a new beginning, coming as it does directly after the 7 x 7 cycle, which adds up to 49.

The goddess Kali has 50 skulls in her necklace. Each skull represents a letter of the alphabet.

ONE HUNDRED

The ancient Babylonians worked to a base of 60, whereby anything multiplied by 60 was increased exponentially. We work in a base of 10 (the decimal system), so any given number will be increased likewise. One hundred is, of course, 10 x 10; though when we use the phrase "a hundred times better than/nicer than . . ." it can just mean "a lot" or "many times" more rather than the actual number. Therefore 100 is symbolic of exaggeration. One hundred is also a beautifully rounded number, a satisfying number, and is a number of perfection.

666 ... THE NUMBER OF THE BEAST?

Do you suffer from hexako-sioihexekontahexaphobia? If so, you fear the number 666: the so-called Number of the Beast. If you do, you are not alone; this series of three sixes strikes fear into the hearts of many who encounter it, even causing some people to protect themselves with the sign of the cross, although they may not be entirely sure of the reason why.

This number first occurs, other than as a natural phenomenon, in the First Book of Kings in the Old Testament, and refers to the amount of wealth that came to King Solomon, possibly because of his partnership with the Queen of Sheba. However, much of the superstition associated with this number stems from a chapter in the New Testament Book of Revelation, here quoted from the King James version:

Here is wisdom. Let him that hath understanding count the number of the beast; for it is the number of a man; and his number is Six Hundred Threescore and Six.

[Revelation, 13:18]

Since then, there have been many theories about to whom, or what, this description refers. For Christians, it has come to represent a catch-all idea of an Antichrist, a title conferred at different times to various enemies of the Christian religion, including the emperors Nero and Domitian, Genghis Khan, Napoleon, and Hitler. Even the Roman Catholic Church and various popes have been identified as the Beast.

Recent notions about the meaning of the number result in speculation that it might provide some kind of code whereby the devil will brand people in order that they will be able to buy or sell. Credit cards, barcodes, social security numbers, and microchip technology have all come under the scrutiny of conspiracy theorists, with varying levels of incredulity and paranoia.

It's also interesting to note that the atom of the chemical element carbon, which forms the basis of all life on earth, is comprised of six neutrons, six protons, and six electrons.

The satanic connotations of 666 are ambivalent in the Kabbalah, however, where it is not only the number of the solar demon Sorath, the opposite of the archangel Michael, but it is also regarded as a sacred number that depicts the entire universe.

But the devilish associations of 666 don't give us the true picture of this mysterious symbolic number. It is the number belonging to Hakathriel, also known as the Angel of the Diadem. And in Sacred Geometry, it is called the magic square of the sun. This particular magic square is constructed in such a way that the first 36 numbers add up to 111 on horizontal, vertical or diagonal planes. The entire square adds up to 666, and the number's significance predates the Bible.

The architects of Chartres Cathedral may have known about the earlier significance of this number, since the labyrinth there measures exactly 666 feet long.

Numerologically speaking, 666 adds up to the number 18, which breaks down to 9; given that 9 is known to be the number of humanity, perhaps this simple explanation is what lies behind the biblical quote; 666 refers to the material part of humanity—the "beast"—rather than to the spiritual aspect.

MAGIC SQUARES

The tradition of the magic square is ancient, going back at least as far as 2800 BC. There is a legend from China about people trying to appease the god of a flooding river. The god sent the people a turtle that had a magic number painted on its back, which mystically enabled the people to control the torrents.

Magic squares can be made of either numbers or letters. In the case of the former the numerals are set in a square grid pattern, each column or row of which adds up to the same number. This number is called the magic constant, and has significance in itself; the square format enhances the vibrational power of the series of numbers and also of the magic constant contained within it. The magic square somehow entraps all the potency of the number or letter within it.

The most basic magic square comprises nine squares in three rows of three. Magic squares are believed to have great potency depending on their magic constant, and they are used as charms and talismans, and in the casting of spells. The magic square is created according to the intention of the ritual, and is afterwards then burned, crushed, torn up, or otherwise destroyed, so "releasing" the magic into the world.

Magic squares can become very elaborate, as in the series called the Kameas, which were originally created by the sixteenth-century occultist philosopher Cornelius Agrippa. This particular series describe the magic constant number of the sun, the moon, and five planets. Kameas are designed for sigils to be drawn over them or incorporated into them.

Significant or magical names can be used as well as numbers; there's a satisfying palindromic kind of fun to be had in creating them. One of the most famous is the Sator Square, which features in a number of magical treatises including the Key of Solomon.

There's a magic square at the Sagrada Familia church in Barcelona whose magic constant is 33, the age of Christ at his crucifixion.

1	14	14	4
11	7	6	9
8	10	10	5
13	2	3	15

Part Seven

SACRED SOUNDS, SECRET SIGNS

The intrigue of resonance, letters, and language

This book is, for the most part, comprised of the most important and versatile secret symbols you'll ever see: the letters of the alphabet. Even as your eyes are scanning this page, you are instantly translating the meaning of these curious squiggles that effectively contain all the secrets of the universe. Although the symbols bear no relationship to sounds, nevertheless we hear the sounds that they represent. This section looks at how these signs, sounds, and ideas converge, and also how other signs are used to keep certain information clandestine.

Sound

Everything in the universe has its own frequency, its own vibration. The human ear cannot hear some of these frequencies, but they exist nevertheless. A simple example is the dog whistle that is heard by dogs but seldom by their human owners. Some frequencies are so powerful that they can destroy physical objects; again, a good example is the soprano whose top note is so pure that it can shatter glass. In the Bible story, the walls of Jericho were destroyed not by physical force as such, but by the power of sound. Certain very low frequencies can destroy matter by scrambling molecules.

Each planet emits its own frequency, as does the Earth itself. The natural harmonic of our home planet is said to be F sharp, an idea that was agreed by ancient peoples including the Egyptians (the Great Pyramid "plays" this note) and the Chinese, who called it Hu; interestingly, Native Americans tune their flutes to this note.

Does all this mean that our most secret and sacred symbols are inspired by something that cannot be seen, but only heard? Sounds can only be interpreted by us as written squiggles, and like the wind, we can only gauge this phenomenon by its effect on something else. Arguably, the most important symbol in the world is something that cannot be touched or seen.

WORDS

Many faiths seem to be in agreement with one thing at least: the notion that the primal resonance of a word, or sound, gave birth to the universe. Understandably, the source of this primal sound is held to be divine. In the Bible it's described like this:

In the beginning was the Word, and the Word was with God, and the Word was God.

[John 1:1–3]

In the Qu'ran is written:

Words of Truth that have the power to express the Truth are like flourishing trees whose roots, or branches, or direct meanings are established deep in the earth of the heart, and whose branches, or subtle meanings, reach high into the sky of mystical knowledge.

The power of a word is such that it is considered to be the very seed of creation. The old saying "sticks and stones may break my bones but words can never hurt me" does not take into account the potency of a curse; whether or not its power lies in superstition does not make its consequences any less real. Similarly, a blessing carries with it wishes that are a powerful force for good.

For the Greeks, *logos*—"word"—meant not only the spoken word or phrase, but it was also inextricably linked to the intellectual faculties and ideas. The gift of eloquence belonged to the gods, or gave god-like status to those who had mastery of it. A politician without the skill of oratory will never be a powerful leader. The Druids, for whom the oral tradition lasted long after the "invention" of the written word, had all sorts of charms and rituals guaranteed to confer eloquence: a cinquefoil leaf under the tongue, for example. Learning by repetition was considered the purest way of gaining information; the transference of words from one person to the next was to retain the purest intention of the words, unsullied by the "middle man" of writing.

LETTERS AND WRITING

The journey from primal sound to a deliberate word to written symbol is a mysterious one. In the same way that children learn to draw before they can write, early people's first "writing" was symbolic, a pictorial representation of ideas. The history of writing is well-documented elsewhere, but the sacred and momentous nature of the alphabet is indicated by the universality of stories of its divine invention: Thoth for the ancient Egyptians, Hermes/Mercury in the Greco-Roman tradition, Odin in the Norse myths, and Ogma of the Celtic pantheon. Letters, along with numbers, are the most potent secret signs and sacred symbols of all; their secrets so ingrained into our consciousnesses that we tend to take them for granted.

The letters of any alphabet carry great power; they are not just letters, but calendars, calculators, symbols, and concepts of divinity. It is worth remembering that, not so very long ago, reading and writing were arts reserved for the powerful and priestly castes, because with these gifts came the power of knowledge. These people had the power to transcribe the very word of God. The first printed texts were religious ones. Once people could read and write—and could therefore decide which ideas they preferred—in certain ways, the power of the secular and religious authorities were considerably weakened.

Although writing is a fantastic tool, in some ways it "kills" ideas by giving them a permanent form. Ideas change; revolutionary theories become everyday fact. As with any of the signs and symbols in this book, it is as well to be aware of this when investigating the hidden meanings behind the alphabets themselves.

ABRACADABRA

A B R A C A D A B R A
A B R A C A D A B R
A B R A C A D A B
A B R A C A D A
A B R A C A D
A B R A C A
A B R A C
A B R A
A B R
A B
A

This ancient word may well have been inspired by the Aramaic "Avra

Kedabra"—"I create as I speak"—or words to that effect. However, there are other theories about the origins of this word. In no particular order, then:

1. It was derived from the name of Abraxas.
2. It was derived from the Hebrew phrase "Abreq Ad Habra," meaning "Hurl your thunderbolt unto death" or "Strike dead with thy lightning" (in this case, its efficacy as a charm to ward away illness would make sense).
3. It could be from the Aramaic "Abhadda Kedabhra," meaning "Disappear as this word," which accurately reflects exactly what happens in the charm (because as the word diminishes and finally disappears, so would any malevolent energy).
4. The first letters of the word could be derived from the initials of Hebrew words for Father (Ab), Son (Ben), and Holy Spirit (Ruach Acadsch).

Chances are that this is such a powerful symbol because all of these theories make sense, so it would have universal appeal.

Although most accounts say that the charm was in use until the Middle Ages, there's curious proof of its efficacy in a small thirteenth-century church in a remote valley in Wales in the UK. St. Michael and All Angels Church at Cascob on the edge of the Radnor Forest has an abracadabra charm engraved on a tablet on one of its walls. In the seventeenth century a local girl, Elizabeth Lloyd, was apparently possessed of evil demons, and this symbol was used to drive them away, along with the astrological symbols that are carved below. There's even a possibility that this tablet was made by the alchemist Dr. John Dee, who was astrologer to Queen Elizabeth I, and lived nearby.

ALPHA AND OMEGA

These are the names of the first and last letters of the Greek alphabet. Alphabets in general are believed to hold within them all the secrets of the universe, so the alpha and omega encompass these secrets within a circular whole, a beginning and end, a completion. The Book of Revelation contains the following:

"I am Alpha and Omega, the beginning and the ending," saith the Lord, "which is and which was, and which is to come, the Almighty."

[Revelation 1:8]

These letters are often seen in association with other Christian symbols, inscribed on altars and crosses, for example.

AUM

The aum, or om, is a living symbol and exists, in varying forms and names, in Hinduism, Buddhism, Taoism, and Sikhism. Sometimes it translates as "So be it" and in this, it is similar to the Hebrew "Amen" or the "Awen" of modern Druidry. The aum is the symbol of the Word, the sound that was present at the creation of the universe. This concept is expressed in the yoga sutras of Patanjali, which state "God's voice is aum." The aum is used at the beginning and the end of prayer and is a chant which, when used consciously, helps the chanter to become a part of the All. The notion of such a primal sound is universal.

In the same way that there are three parts to the symbol that contribute to the whole, the aum symbolizes the three gods: Vishnu, Shiva, and Brahma. In yoga, the sound is used as a meditation on the breath and the nature of the universe, and involves all parts of the lungs as it is chanted.

Hindu Aum

Tibetan Aum

Jain Aum

Sikh Aum

Upkar

This last symbol, the upkar, shows how the Sikh "Ek Onkar" symbol has been slightly altered to encompass a sign that has universal meaning as one of healing and protection. Here, the symbol is also the logo for the northern Indian hospital that shares its name. It means "the welfare of all" and combines the symbol of the Red Cross (physical and medical welfare) with the spiritual aspect of the aum.

BISMILLAH

There are different variations of this beautiful symbol, which hides within its curlicues and flourishes the sacred name of God. Bismillah, in Arabic, means, literally, "In the Name of Allah," and it is the first word in the Qu'ran.

Islamic law forbids representations of animals or people, so the calligraphic form has been developed to a high art, as in the Bismillah symbol. "Bismillah" is spoken as a sign of respect before prayer, before meals, and before important undertakings.

BLAZES, TRAILS, AND TRAVELERS' SIGNS

Blazes are symbols that mark trails or tracks. Sometimes the blazes are, as the name would suggest, overt and easily understood; sometimes necessity dictates that the signs are covertly hidden within the landscape so that only the initiate will be able to follow the track.

The former kind of blaze tends to be visually arresting and transcends boundaries of nationality or culture, often used, for example, in tourist destinations. In forests these route indicator signs will usually be at eye level, perhaps painted onto a tree. Of course, it's important that this type of sign can withstand the elements. So there's nothing particularly secret about this kind of everyday signage.

The other kind—the covert kind—is different. Often used by hunters, these signs might emulate methods used by Native Americans. One of the most basic of these signs is a small nick of bark taken from a tree, which marks the trail. The size of these axe blazes vary according to the skill of the maker. The idea is to make them as small as possible yet noticeable to anyone knowing what to look for.

In areas where there are no trees and a trail still needs to be made, inventive use is made of the natural environment. A popular device is to snap a twig on a bush and leave the broken part dangling,

| DOG | WOMAN | WEALTH | KIND-HEARTED WOMAN |

| CAMPING HERE | BE GOOD | IF SICK WILL HELP | SAFE CAMP |

| WELL-GUARDED HOUSE | AFRAID | TELL PITIFUL STORY |

| DANGER | BE PREPARED TO DEFEND YOURSELF | MAN WITH GUN | BAD DOG |

| UNRELIABLE MAN | UNSAFE PLACE | YOU WILL BE BEATEN |

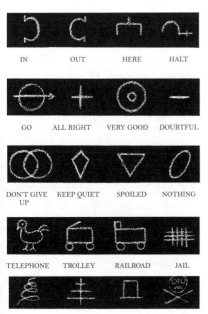

| IN | OUT | HERE | HALT |

| GO | ALL RIGHT | VERY GOOD | DOUBTFUL |

| DON'T GIVE UP | KEEP QUIET | SPOILED | NOTHING |

| TELEPHONE | TROLLEY | RAILROAD | JAIL |

| JUDGE | OFFICER | GENTLEMAN | DOCTOR |

connected by a slim thread of bark. This indicates the trail. If the twig is broken off, the torn end of the twig might indicate the direction to be followed. If the trail is to cover an area of open grassland, a clump might be twisted into a knot; significantly, sometimes more than one knot might be used. Otherwise, stones might be stacked on top of each other or next to each other in a particular way.

The Encyclopedia of Secret Signs and Symbols

SMOKE SIGNALS

A highly effective although highly visible sign, smoke signals can nevertheless carry secrets, and are primarily used by Plains Indians. Making a smoke signal seems to be the dream of every child but it takes time to create the fire needed to make a decent amount of smoke. Here's how to make your own smoke signals.

First, make a very hot and clear fire from as much dry material as you can muster. When the fire is burning well, cover it with damper, green material. Rotten wood is good, too. Then, three or four people each need to take a corner of a blanket, using it to cover and uncover the fire, releasing smoke at intervals prearranged with the people you are communicating with.

Although a funnel of steady smoke will indicate where a camp is, other signals are possible: a steady sequence of double puffs is the equivalent of an SOS.

Throughout history, there have been times when people have needed to cover their tracks or otherwise hide the route they were taking. Romany and nomadic travelers of any sort have each used their own systems of signs and signals to communicate with each other over distances, telling of routes or passing on news. Recently, the cheap availability of mobile phones has meant that traveling people have no problem in meeting up with one another. This wasn't always the case, and not so very long ago it was necessary to have a set of secret signs and symbols, which would enable communication while on the road.

Patrin, or patteran, is the name given to the indicators made by Romany people along their chosen routes. Coming from a Romany word meaning leaf, a patrin could be a drawn sign or a sign constructed discreetly from natural objects found in the landscape: a bundle of twigs, a feather, or a snapped twig.

HOBO SIGNS

During times of extreme economic depression, it has often been necessary for people to leave their homes and take to the roads to find employment in order to survive. Times were particularly desperate during the Depression in the United States in the early part of the twentieth century. Although many saw these destitute people as vagrants, most hobos were desperate for any work they could get; indeed, a hobo differentiated himself from a tramp, who was seen to be unwilling to work. Despite poverty (or maybe because of it) there was a strong bond between fellow travelers and this bond resulted in a series of symbols that could be interpreted by those following, and which could provide hints and tips gained from the experience of those who had gone before.

Although it is hard to date such symbols precisely, it seems that they started from the 1880s and had died out by World War II. The signs were drawn on fence posts, on the sides of the railroad, on paths; in short, anywhere where those on the lookout would notice them. They were usually written in chalk or coal or marked with anything that was readily available.

CHAI

Often seen these days on souvenirs and artwork from Israel, the Chai is the secret symbol that consists of the Hebrew letters het and yod. Together these letters spell "chai," which means "living" and refers not only to God but also to the Jewish people.

The Jewish system of numerology, the gematria, shows that these letters add up to eighteen, which is considered to be a favorable number. Therefore the Chai symbol is also a lucky charm.

DA' WAH

Literally meaning "summons" or "call," the Da'wah is a secret method of incantation, a "call" to a whole mystical tradition, in a similar way that the Hebrew alphabet is far more than a simple series of letters.

Using the Arabic alphabet, each letter has finely tuned associations with the names of God, numbers, the elements, perfumes, planets, spirits and angels. Each letter also has its own nature.

To master the Da'wah the adept must follow a strict moral code and diet. Once the esoteric mysteries of the Da'wah are mastered, they confer a godlike power over the universe.

GEMATRIA

The gematria is a system of numerology where letters and numbers are linked and although this method is used elsewhere, gematria applies specifically to the Hebrew language, and is explained in many mystical Jewish writings.

Although there are 22 letters in the Hebrew alphabet, 27 numerals are needed to express each number up to 999 (1 through 9, 10 through 90, and 100 through 900). The mystical Hebrew numeric system notes that the missing final five letters of the numeral system match exactly with the alphabet's five word-final alternate forms.

* * *

Here is the Hebrew Gematria chart showing the numeric values of each letter:

Aleph	A	1
Beth	B	2
Gimal	C/G	3
Daleth	D	4
Heh	E/H	5
Vav	St/V	6
Zayin	Z	7
Cheth	E/Ch	8
Teth	Th/T	9
Yod	I	10
Caph	K	20
Lamed	L	30
Mem	M	40
Nun	N	50
Samech	Ch/S	60
Ayin	O	70
Peh	P	80
Tzadi	Q/Tz	90
Qoph	R/Rh/Q	100
Resh	S/R	200
Shin	T/Sh	300
Tav	Y/U/Th	400

Some interesting correspondences can arise; in *Math for Mystics*, Renna Shesso points out that the numerical values for "lion," "cheetah" and "tiger" all reduce down to 5. Other words that have the same numerical value share the same qualities, and can be used to reveal still other aspects of the divine.

GREATEST NAME

The Greatest Name generally refers to the most holy and secret name of God, the name that carries the entire essence of divine power. This idea is common throughout many faiths. This name usually encompasses the notion of "light" or "glory." In the Bahai faith the symbol of the Greatest Name is a calligraphic rendering of the phrase "Glory of Glories," or "Ya Baha'ul-Abha."

INVOCATION

At the heart of many magical practices, whether they belong to a conformist religious belief or more pagan tradition, is the idea that calling a name can invoke the spirit or entity that is connected to that name.

An invocation can take the form of a supplication, or a command. Most faiths have a standardized form of invocation—the Lord's Prayer, for example, in Christianity. However, sometimes the invocation of a spirit is an invitation for it to take up residence for a time in a physical host, i.e., possession. This form of invocation or "inviting in" is sometimes the desired outcome of Voudon ceremonies where the spirit, or "loa," is summoned into the body via a series of ecstatic rituals that involve chanting, dancing, and drumming.

In the case of spirit invocation, these entities need to be "bound" or otherwise constrained by means of magical seals or symbols.

"K" IN MAGICK

Sometimes, magic is spelled with a "k" as in "magickal." This final "k" was a conceit introduced by Aleister Crowley at the beginning of the twentieth century, in order to differentiate stage magic and conjuring tricks of a purely mechanical nature with the intentional ritual magic of a supernatural nature that can allegedly cause changes and alter the course of events.

For Crowley, the fact that the "k" is the eleventh letter of the alphabet gave it even more magic(k)al significance. According to the laws of gematria, where each letter has its corresponding number, eleven is the number that corresponds to the realm of the Kabbalah concerning the forces of evil that have to be conquered before the magic(k)al practitioner can truly call himself an adept.

People who are aware of the provenance of this conceit may choose to use it or not, depending whether they wish to align themselves with the teachings of Crowley or any of the mystical orders that he was affiliated to.

KALACHAKRA SEAL

This is a beautiful, elaborate, and evocatively meaningful symbol, a major device within Tibetan Buddhism. It can be seen in monasteries and other holy places and in itself is emblematic of the arcane and occult knowledge into which relatively few lamas are initiated. The meaning of the Kalachakra exists on many levels.

The seal is comprised of a calligraphic rendering of letters, using a script called Lantsa or Ranjana. This secret and sacred script was developed from Sanskrit and is used only for religious scripts, texts, mandalas, and mantras. Many holy documents written in the Ranjana script were destroyed when China invaded Tibet.

The Kalachakra Seal, which is also called the Tenfold Powerful One, contains many elements. Hidden within its curlicues are the seven syllables of the Holy Mantra called the Kalachakra. The mantra is "Ham Ksa Ma La Va Ra Ya."

The remaining three elements that give the symbol its tenfold nature are the crescent moon, the disc of the full moon or the sun, and the flame of fire.

But what does the Kalachakra actually mean?

Both the symbol and the sound of the letters that comprise it are inextricably linked. It is also often drawn in color, as the colors are important symbols in themselves. The syllables are written one on top of the other, and interlock together. The whole stands on a stylized lotus (symbolic of the heart), with the character for "emptiness" and "bliss" set to the left and right, respectively, of the Kalachakra symbol. The framework of the Kalachakra is important, too, and represents a mandala made of flames. This is called the Circle of Wisdom.

If we examine each aspect of the Kalachakra, then, here's what we find.

First, many symbols have an element that is not drawn or shown in any way, but is implied. Here, it's the letter A, which is emblematic of space.

Next, the syllables, including the colors that they might appear as:

- Ham (blue): indicative of formless realms; the vacuum; the spiritual world; bliss; enlightened wisdom; the gods.
- Ksha (green): represents the world of form and desire; the material world. This syllable means the body, the mind, and the power of speech.
- Ma (multi-colored): a reminder of the Holy Mountain, Mount Meru. It relates to the spinal column of the body, which, like the mountain, ascends towards the heavens.
- La (yellow): the grounding earth element.
- Va (white): the element of water.
- Ra (red): the element of fire.
- Ya (black): the element of air.

Collectively, the elements within the Kalachakra represent the spiritual and material life of a person; the elements; the Wheel of Time; the emptiness of the void, and the pregnant seed of creation. It has inspired the calculations of calendars and astrologers.

KAMEA

A particular kind of magic square that is intended to incorporate a sigil. The whole is used as a charm or talisman or as a tool in casting a spell. The kamea is a Kabbalistic invention.

MAGICAL NAME

This is a name given to a newly initiated member into a magical group or cult. A "magical" name is necessarily that which belongs to a magical society, but adherents of many religions will change their name or add a new name to their existing one. Catholics and Muslims, for example, follow this practice, symbolic of belonging and acceptance by the religious community as well as a rebirth into the chosen faith.

* ✳ *

Mani stone

In Tibetan Buddhism, a Mani stone is a stone, pebble or rock inscribed with a mantra, or prayer. The stones are to be found everywhere and serve as devotional offerings. Mani stones appear singly or stacked up in large piles. The most common mantra to be found painted or carved onto the stones is Om Mani Padme Hum, the same mantra which is found on the long pieces of paper inside prayer wheels.

Mantra

This is a sacred phrase or series of sounds that, when repeated over and over, is believed to effect a corresponding spiritual vibration. The mantra has similarities to a prayer except that it tends to be specific to the Dharmic faiths. Whoever chants a mantra becomes unified with the greater cosmos. "Aum," "Om Mani Padme Hum," and "Nam Myoho Renge Kyo" are all examples of mantras. The visual symbol for the mantra is the Yantra.

The mantra does not work if it is translated. It's important that the syllables of the original phrase are pronounced correctly. Like a magical spell, the correct mantra, it is believed, can accomplish anything provided the person chanting it is in the correct frame of mind, mentally and spiritually prepared. The power of certain mantras means that they are taught only with great care to those who are worthy of using them.

Music

The Devil's Chord

Music is truly divine, and legends from all over the world and from all faiths agree that it was invented by the gods.

Pythagoras, like the Chinese before him, knew that music carries the harmony of the cosmos, encompassing the vibrational values of numbers, shapes, and sounds. He called this theory the "Music of the Spheres," a universal symphony of interconnectedness. If sound is the most common unifying factor, then music is the sublime aspect of this connection. The same mathematical rules that underscore sacred geometry also apply to the measurements that rule the harmonic or discordant vibrations of strings played together.

Music can reflect our mood, or can alter it. In myth, music can bring enchanted sleep as well as rousing soldiers to battle. It has much in common with perfume; it is invisible and yet all-pervasive and can be experienced by many people at the same time. Like the scented smoke given off by incense, music plays an important part in sacred and magical rituals, a unifying factor in orthodox religious ceremonies as well as in pagan ones.

In the same way that certain music heralds a change of scene, mood, or action in a film, sometimes music needs to symbolize the presence of evil. The Devil's Chord, or "Diabolus in Musica," consisting of a dissonant and spooky sounding interval such as an augmented fourth, is so evocative of menace that it was allegedly banned from church music in the Middle Ages. An example of what this sinister chord sounds like? Try the opening bars of Jimi Hendrix's "Purple Haze."

Rosslyn Chapel in Scotland, site of much mystical conjecture, recently added a new discovery to its trove of secrets. There is a series of carved stone cubes in the chapel, each with a particular pattern etched onto it. The patterns equate to Chladni patterns. If sand, salt, or some other fine powder is poured onto a taut surface (such as the skin of a drum) which is then subjected to a tonal frequency, the vibrations cause the powder to make symmetrical patterns, including the diamonds, rhomboids, flowers, and other designs that appear on the stone cubes.

The discovery was made after twenty years of research by Thomas Mitchell, whose son, Stuart, has written a piece of music called "The Rosslyn Motet" that is based on the notes encoded in these stones.

Name

A rose, by any other name, as Shakespeare pointed out, may smell as sweet; but would it really still be a rose?

A name carries the essence of the power and spirit of its owner, hence in many faiths the true name of God is a great mystery, shrouded in oblique references and rarely spoken aloud. In the Jewish faith, only the high priest pronounces the name of God. The belief is that the power of the name of God is such that the whole world will be struck dumb if it were shouted out loud, hence the vital necessity to keep it a secret. In Islam, too, there are 99 names of God plus one more, unknown name, the Greatest Name. God and the name of God are identical, and to know all these names enables a person to enter heaven.

The ancient Egyptians felt that the name was a living thing, an inextricable part of the person it described. Often, when people become affiliated to a religion, they are given another name as part of their initiation, a sign of their rebirth, a new identity conferred by allegiance to the faith.

The power of the name is also the reason why, in the Harry Potter books by J. K. Rowling, the name of the arch villain Voldemort is rarely said, replaced instead with "He Who Must Not Be Named." In the fairy tale, knowledge of the name of the gnome Rumplestiltskin will buy power over him. It's an old superstition that a child without a name is somehow without a soul, and is therefore at risk of exposure to evil influences.

In the Celtic lands, the name of a person and their job, occupation, or function was the same. This tradition lives on today, particularly in parts of Wales where the person is described by both name and occupation; Dai the Post, for example.

NOTARIKON

A kind of acronym, this is a method, in Hebrew, of using the letters of a word as the initials for a phrase. This "hidden" phrase generally gives a different way of interpreting the word. Sacred words or the secret names of God were given this treatment, which was a way of hiding their true meaning. These codes are often embedded into sacred texts, hence the importance of preserving the original written form.

A simple example of a notarikon is the word "Amen," which is constructed from the initial letters of the phrase "the Lord and Faithful King."

* * *

OM MANI PADME HUM

This is the most important and profound mantra in Tibetan Buddhism, and the words are engraved onto Mani stones as well as written on the scrolls of paper contained within prayer wheels. The phrase means "Aum, to the Jewel in the Lotus, hum."

These six seemingly simple syllables have a deeper meaning that lies at the very heart of the faith. The resonance is affected not only by the physical components of the mantra but also by the intent of the acolyte. Buddhists believe that not only does the chanter add to his own enlightenment in the process of repeating this magical phrase, but that the consciousness of humanity is raised at the same time.

PONTOS RISCADOS

This is a special sigil, used to invoke the gods (or Orishas) peculiar to the specific magical practices of Brazil. It seems that supernatural beings respond well to such symbols, since they are similar to the magical sigils used by such illustrious luminaries as Aleister Crowley and John Dee. Each entity has its own particular sigil, which is drawn on the ground in special colored chalks as part of an invocation.

SATOR WORD SQUARE

S A T O R
A R E P O
T E N E T
O P E R A
R O T A S

This word square is an ingenious palindromic construction, and can be read in any direction: forward, backward, top to bottom, and bottom to top. The oldest example of it that has been discovered so far is in the ruins of Herculanaeum, an ancient Roman city that was destroyed in the volcanic eruption that also overwhelmed Pompeii in the first century AD. Thereafter, it crops up in all sorts of places: in the cathedral in Siena, in a small chapel near Rennes-le-Château in France, in Malta, Syria, and the UK. It appears on the front cover of the infamous magical tome *The Book of the Sacred Magic of Abra Melin the Sage*, which is considered to be the ultimate guide to the Kabbalah.

Both the meaning and the provenance of the SATOR square are a mystery. Effectively a literary labyrinth that does not yield its secrets easily, it has been claimed as a Christian conceit because the letters can be rearranged in the form of a cross to read thus:

<pre>
                P
                A
                T
                E
                R
P A T E R N O S T E R
                O
                S
                T
                E
                R
</pre>

The left-over pairs of A and O can be taken to mean alpha and omega, the first and last letters of the Greek alphabet.

The literal translation of the square is:

- SATOR: sower, planter
- AREPO: could be a proper name
- TENET: to hold
- OPERA: work, effort
- ROTAS: wheels

Therefore, "Sator, the sower, holds the wheels by his work," or "The sower, Arepo, holds the wheels with effort."

This meaning can be interpreted in several ways, its relevance squeezed into the preferred ideology. The implications of some kind of analogy to sowing and harvesting, death and rebirth cannot be ignored. Scholars have puzzled in particular over the word "Arepo," since it appears nowhere else; it would not be beyond the bounds of possibility that the inventor of this word square put it there because it "fitted" and simply gave it a meaning later. However, it is close to a Celtic word meaning "plow," which aligns nicely with the agricultural references.

Many people believe that the SATOR square is imbued with magical protective properties, the net of elegantly placed words having a depth of meaning that transcends the literal. Dutch settlers in Pennsylvania used it as an invocation to protect their cattle.

SEALS

Magical seals are used in invocations, to bind or otherwise harness the power of an entity or spirit. A seal is a sort of signature for the spirit and the understanding of it by the conjuror is akin to knowledge of a name.

There are dozens and dozens of such symbols, many of them listed in grimoires such as the Lesser Key of Solomon or *Lemegton Clavicula Salomonis* that was compiled in the seventeenth century from much earlier sources. Curious and decorative, these seals are used in ritual magic, often in conjunction with amulets.

SIGIL

Although a sigil is the name applied to a signet or seal that belongs to a fraternity order, as a magical symbol it is less straightforward.

A sigil is a symbol that belongs in particular to the Western tradition of magic. The word itself has its origins in a Latin word, *sigilum*, meaning "seal," and it is a personalized glyph or emblem that carries a specific meaning or intent. The monad of Dr. John Dee, for example, is a sigil.

There is a Hebrew word, *segulah*, which may or may not be related to the sigil, but which describes very well what a sigil actually is. *Segulah* means "a word, action, or item of spiritual effect." This has similar meaning to that of "talisman." Sigils generally appear in a drawn or written form although it is possible for them to be rendered in sound or as a solid three-dimensional object.

The sigil itself sometimes looks simple, sometimes more elaborate, but in either case its design and creation will have a complex series of meanings attached to it. Sigils are frequently made up of lots of different elements; the Norse binding rune is an example of a particular kind of sigil. Astrological signs and their corresponding planets also have their sigils.

The magicians of medieval times used sigils to call up angels, demons, and other diverse spirits.

Each of these entities had its own sigil that represented its "essence," a sort of spiritual autograph or signature, so the sigil was a powerful tool in the right hands—or the wrong ones. Pages and pages of these signatures appear in grimoires and other magical texts, notably in the Lesser Key of Solomon. This anonymously written seventeenth-century work contains a handy at-a-glance guide to the personal sigils of the 72 demons of hell; for the adept, this would be the equivalent of a telephone directory to dial up entities from another dimension. Command of the sigil, combined with correct attention to ritual detail, gives the conjurer power over the being that he is calling upon.

Self-professed adepts Aleister Crowley and Austin Osman Spare famously used sigils in their personal quests of mystical exploration, but the use of sigils is not a thing of the past. Modern practitioners of magic also employ them, and the method of doing so is strikingly simple given their purported efficacy.

STONEMASONS' MARKS

Sometimes small and puzzling marks can be spotted on the sides of old buildings and stone structures. These are stonemasons' marks. In the same way that a painter marks a canvas, a stonemason "signs" his work by means of such a symbol.

Stonemasonry is one of the earliest trades, and any ancient stone building is testimony to the skills of these artisans, whose names might largely be forgotten but whose legacy remains. The Pyramids, the Parthenon, the Pantheon, ziggurats, temples, churches, and cathedrals—all were built by stonemasons.

Despite the difficulty of leaving a signature on a building, the stonemason did not remain entirely anonymous. He often carved a personal symbol into his work, a secret sign that acted not only as an autograph but also as a form of quality assurance. These marks were generally quite angular;

SIGIL MAGIC

The object of the exercise is to cast a spell that attracts the object of your desire, a sort of tool for cosmic ordering. The sigil provides the focus for this spell.

1. Decide what the desired object actually is. Precision is vital. For example, it's not enough to simply ask for money: what if the fortune comes as a result of the death of a loved one, for example?
2. Write down a sentence that expresses the outcome that you want.
3. Now reduce the sentence so that no letter is repeated.
4. Here's the fun part. Reduce the letters down further into shapes. It doesn't matter if some of the letters are upside down, and upper- or lowercase is of no significance either. For example, the letter P also contains within it an I, lowercase L, a C, an F and a lowercase d (if you flip it upside down).
5. Once you have accounted for all the letters, arrange them in a design that pleases you. If you

can draw it in one single stroke and contain it in a circle, so much the better.
6. Next you need to write your sigil on a piece of paper or parchment, with as much due ceremony as you choose to muster.
7. The final part of this kind of sigil magic requires the symbol to be "charged." This can be done by using the symbol as a focus for meditation, and then burning it or otherwise forgetting all about it.

The sigil illustrated on page 461 is the result of the following desire: "*The Encyclopedia of Secret Signs and Symbols* helps people understand one another and makes the world a better place."

This lengthy sentence reduces down to the letters THENCYOPDIAFSRGUKWB.

These letters can be rendered down in lots of different ways but the final sigil can be drawn in one continuous movement and wrapped in a circle.

sometimes runes or runic shapes were used since straight lines are generally easier to scratch into stone then more rounded forms.

In the Middle Ages, most craftspeople had their own guild. These guilds had their own systems of organization that included a certain amount of ritual and ceremony. Each separate guild of stonemasons had a "mother mark" and the individual mason used this as the basis for his own personal signature, which he had to swear not to change.

TEMURAH

Like gematria and notarikon, temurah is a way of rearranging the letters of certain words and sentences in the Bible to give an alternative, mystical meaning. Atbash, for example, is a temurah cipher.

TETRAGRAMMATON

Words carry a great power, and to speak a word out loud "enables" the word. Names in particular carry the most power, and there is no more potent name than the Tetragrammaton.

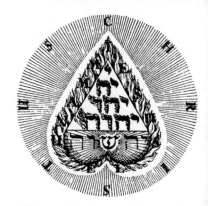

This magical name is sometimes drawn in the form of the earlier Pythagorean tetraktys, a sign that represents the universe.

Quite literally, Tetragrammaton means "four-letter word" in Greek (although it is not to be confused with the popular slang meaning "expletive") and refers to the secret name of the God of the Israelites, written in Hebrew. This name is so holy and powerful that it can never be spoken, apart from just once a year at Yom Kippur by the high priest within the Holy of Holies. To avoid using this name it is referred to as "The Name" or "Elohim" or "Adonai."

The letters of the name are yodh hev vav hev, and God is said to have explained to Moses that the name means "I Shall Be" or "I Am." These letters are pronounced "ee ah ou eh" (hence Jahweh), and will often be seen as a part of magical amulets or talismans.

The actual name of God is said to be 72 letters long and was written on a long slip of paper secreted inside the high priest's jeweled breastplate. When the name was invoked, the jewels would light up in a certain sequence, thereby allowing the priest to communicate directly with God.

WATERMARK

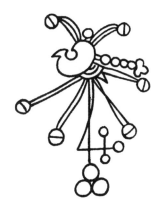

Sometimes, certain terminology is so familiar that we seldom stop to think of its origins.

As a way of hiding a symbol there can be few better ways than the watermark. It is likely that the method of making watermarks was the result of a happy accident. Methods of making paper by hand have altered very little over the centuries; a thin layer of wet pulp is spread over a sieve and left to dry, when the resulting sheet of paper can be peeled from the mesh. If a piece of wire is placed on top of the sieve before the pulp is spread over it, then the image of the wire shows up when the paper is held up to the light because the paper is very slightly thinner at that point. This method is believed to have been discovered by the paper-makers of Fabiano and Bologna in late thirteenth-century Italy.

Papermakers quickly realized that their paper could be protected (from theft, for example) by the use of such a mark, which could also be used as a sign of quality assurance and as an identity for the maker. At the same time, the water-mark might be used to convey a secret message of some kind. Henry VIII of England, for example, commissioned a water-mark for his own supply of paper that showed the image of a hog wearing a miter, to show his con-tempt for the pope.

Although it is almost impossible to prove the mystical use of certain watermarks, it seems as though certain symbols speak for them-selves. These include the paper branded with Rosicrucian symbols that was used by Francis Bacon in letters and in editions of his books that were published privately.

Specifically, his book *The Advancement of Learning* shows his Rosicrucian sympathies in the watermark which includes the initials C.R., standing for the legendary founder of the order, Christian Rosenkreutz.

Papermaking skills were brought to Europe from the East by the Knights Templar and other crusaders returning from the Holy Land, although, as we have seen, the discovery of making watermarks was an accident that happened in Europe. The Cathars—a sect deemed by the Church to be heretical because of their dualist beliefs—were persecuted to the point that they were forced to flee their homeland in France, and were scattered around Europe where they had to make a living in any way they could; papermaking was one of their skills. They allegedly identified one another and kept track of their supporters by means of a watermark used on their "Lombardy Paper." The meanings of these marks are difficult to analyze but their distinctly mystical-looking nature would seem to support this theory.

* ✳ *

Secret scripts and ciphers

As soon as the majority of us were able to convey information to one another by means of reading and writing, we began to invent different sorts of alphabets so that we could still keep some things a secret. It seems that the desire to keep certain information concealed comes naturally to us; even children invent certain changes to their speech or writing that are designed to hide their true meaning.

Necessarily, these secret alphabets and ciphers were often invented by closed societies, such as the Freemasons, or practitioners of magic who wanted to keep information within their own circle of trust. Many of these secret alphabets are mere substitution ciphers, that is, they replace the existing letters of an alphabet with different symbols while retaining the underlying rules of grammatical construction. Others, such as the Enochian script, are true languages in their own right.

Secret scripts, codes, and ciphers are not only the province of sorcerers and magicians. Codes are essential tools during times of war to keep information safe from the enemy.

For example, Navajo was used as a code during American operations in the Pacific during World War II. The complexity and rarity of the language, which was never written and was spoken only by the Navajo tribes and perhaps some thirty others at the time, meant that the Japanese never cracked it. The author Beatrix Potter kept her wry observations about the society and politics of her time to herself, since she invented a code that she used to write her journals from the ages of fifteen through to thirty. Her code was so complex that it was only deciphered some twenty years after her death.

It's worth bearing in mind that our "normal" alphabets are replete with arcane secrets that go way beyond them being mere visual symbols of sounds.

ADAMICAL ALPHABET

See Enochian script.

Aiq Bkr
ALPHABET

This is a substitution, or Temurah cipher, based on the letters of the Hebrew alphabet. The 22 letters of the alphabet are put into a grid of nine squares, meaning that each square will have two characters and some will have three. The letters can be substituted for any in the same square; a simple cipher, but comprehensible only to those that know what to look for. Aiq Bkr is also called the "Kabbalah of Nine Chambers."

ALCHEMICAL
ALPHABET

Secrecy was a fundamental part of any alchemical operation, and the substances and processes of this ancient art were deliberately veiled by sequences of symbols and pictures designed to convey information without using words. Several different alchemical alphabets

appeared in the sixteenth century, simple substitution ciphers based on Roman lettering.

ALPHABET OF
ARROWS

This alphabet is a substitution cipher based on the letters of a mystical alphabet that actually appears to have a proper grammar and syntax all of its own—Edward Kelley and John Dee's Enochian language. The alphabet of arrows appears in a work by Aleister Crowley (see alphabet of daggers).

ALPHABET OF
DAGGERS

A substitution cipher using the letters of the Roman alphabet as a base, this script has little dagger symbols that combine to spooky effect. It first appears in Aleister Crowley's work *The Vision and the Voice*, in which Crowley takes a visionary journey into the realms, or "aethyrs," inhabited by the angels of John Dee and Edward Kelley. The alphabet of arrows follows the same pattern but is a substitution cipher for the Enochian alphabet, and is found in the same book.

ALPHABET OF HONORIUS

See Witches' alphabet.

ANGELICAL SCRIPT

The angelical script shown here is a simple substitution cipher, created by Cornelius Agrippa in the sixteenth century. However, the Enochian script—which is a "proper" grammatical language—is also sometimes called "angelical writing."

ATBASH CIPHER— ZGYZHS XRKSVI

The unpronounceable words in the heading shows "Atbash cipher" written as it would be in its own code. Atbash is a substitution cipher, simple enough to understand but confusing to look at. Imagine the Roman alphabet written normally, left to right, on one line. Then write the alphabet again underneath, this time starting at the right and placing the A beneath the Z. Atbash was originally based on the Hebrew alphabet. One of its uses was to confound any casual inquiries into the inner workings of the Kabbalah.

BINDING RUNE

See Runic alphabet.

CELESTIAL SCRIPT

Among the alphabets that Cornelius Agrippa wrote about, the celestial script is one influenced by the Hebrew alphabet. This script was used to communicate with angelic beings, a use which some students of the occult still practice today. The letters are also used in making charms and amulets.

* ✳ *

COFFIN TEXTS

Coffin texts were the magical symbols and spells written by Egyptians on the coffins of the deceased, their primary function to ensure the survival of the soul in the afterlife.

However, the advent of coffin texts marked a profound social change. Their predecessors, the pyramid texts, essentially fulfilled the same purpose as the coffin texts but were the exclusive domain of royalty. The appearance of the coffin texts meant that almost anyone could have the benefit of the magical commands that carried such power. The consequences, for a society who believed so fundamentally and profoundly in an afterlife, meant that the prospect of a non-exclusive heaven now existed, even if the offer was still only open to those who could afford it.

As well as spells of protection (which might show serpents and other dangerous creatures being stabbed in the back) and charms for a "blessed existence" after death, the coffin texts consisted of maps and descriptions of the Land of the Dead, a sort of guidebook to the afterlife. Perhaps the most famous of the coffin texts was the Book of the Two Ways, which describes the complete journey between the two worlds.

DAVIDIAN ALPHABET

This Arabic script is first mentioned in a book written in AD 855 by an Arab scholar of magical lore. The title of this book translates as the awe-inspiring *Book of the Frenzied Devotee to Learn about the Ancient Scripts.*

Also called Dambudi, the Davidian script is named for King David of Israel whose son, Solomon, was renowned for his wisdom. Even now, thousands of years after his death, Solomon is held in reverential awe by Arabs, and many others, as the greatest magician who ever lived.

The alphabet is imbued, by association, with Solomon's powers. Said to be the father of Freemasonry, Solomon's polymath skills included the ability to understand the language of birds. Stylistically, the alphabet is derived from Hebrew letters. The letters of the Davidian script are believed to be so infused with occult meaning that they are the very embodiment of mystical power. The Arabs that used it referred to it simply as *rihani*, meaning "magic."

ENOCHIAN SCRIPT

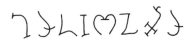

Many magical scripts used in grimoires and other manuscripts as a way of ensuring the secrecy of their contents are actually no more than a cipher, using different symbols to represent the letters of an existing alphabet. Even where Roman and Hebrew letters are used in such a "magical" alphabet, the underlying language is still usually English or Hebrew. However, there are a few exceptions, and the Enochian tongue is one of these.

In the sixteenth century Dr. John Dee (a renowned mystic who was the astrologer to Queen Elizabeth I) and Edward Kelley claimed that angels imparted both the script and language to them. Dee was an extremely well-read and learned scholar, conversant with languages and with a passionate interest in the angelic realms. He was also an extensive diarist, and in his journal, he mentions the angels that God sent to communicate directly with his prophets. Dee was inspired to try to find his own angels since knowledge of their language would be the most powerful tool that any magician could have in his kit. He set about this extraordinary task with the help of Edward Kelley, an alchemist and clairvoyant medium or "seer." Kelley saw the letters in a vision while scrying with a crystal ball. Apparently, when Kelley complained that he could not see the letters properly, the angels caused them to appear on a piece of paper, where they were easy for Kelley to trace before they faded away.

Dee himself didn't refer to the script as "Enochian." He called it "Angelical" or "The Celestial Speech," or sometimes "Adamical," since the angels told him that the language had been taught by God to Adam, who used it to communicate with both God and the angels. It had also been the language used to name all things. The epithet "Enochian" came about because Dee believed that the great biblical patriarch Enoch had been the last person to understand the language.

This arcane tongue had apparently been lost when Adam was banished from the Garden of Eden, a myth that carries a powerful symbolic punch—if mankind can no longer communicate with a divine creative spirit then he is lost indeed, truly cast out. Adam's vague memory of the language is said to have resulted in an early form of Hebrew. During this time, Enoch was the only person who could fully understand the language, but the book he wrote describing it was lost in the Great Flood. This notion, that a divine language existed prior to the Deluge, was a popular one at the time of Dee and Kelley.

There are 21 alphabetical characters in this arcane language and, in common with other angelic scripts, it is written from right to left, although the letters demonstrated above are used as a left-to-right cipher.

Ian Fleming, the author of the James Bond books, suggested that Enochian script be used to flush out evidence of a Nazi conspiracy within Britain during World War II, but the plan never came to fruition.

There could be a strong argument in favor of teaching the Enochian script in schools today, though, since exponents of Enochian magic claim to be able to use it to summon angels and to work with them. There is a downside, though: both the spoken and written language was used extensively by Aleister Crowley's Golden Dawn organization until they deemed it too dangerous. It was therefore abandoned.

GREEK ALPHABET

In common with the Hebrew alphabet, the Greek alphabet is commonly used in magical ritual, although since this classical language isn't taught as frequently as it once was, where it appears in modern grimoires it is more likely to be used as a simple substitution cipher rather than as a fully functioning language system.

Here are the correspondences of the letters of the Greek alphabet with numbers and conceptual meanings.

Whereas the Hebrew alphabet is believed to have been gifted to humankind by God via Moses, the provenance of the Greek language is subject to several different legends. Perhaps the most colorful is that the god of communication, Hermes, invented it after he was inspired by the shapes of the wings of a flock of cranes in flight. In *The White Goddess*, Robert Graves tells us that the letters of this alphabet were kept in crane-skin bags, in homage to the bird. Another story says that the

Greek Character	Letter	Sound	Meaning	Numerical Value	Organ of the Human Body
A	Alpha	A	cattle	1	head
B	Beta	B	demon	2	neck
Γ	Gamma	C	divinity	3	shoulders
Δ	Delta	D	fourfold	4	breast
E	Epsilon	E	ether	5	diaphragm
Z	Zeta	Z	sacrifice	6	belly
H	Eta	E	joy	7	genitals
Θ	Theta	Th	crystal sphere	8	thighs
I	Iota	I	destiny	10	knees
K	Kappa	K	illness	20	shins
Λ	Lambda	L	growth	30	ankles
M	Mu	M	trees	40	feet
N	Nu	N	hag	50	feet
Ξ	Xi	X	fifteen stars	60	ankles
O	Omicron	O	sun	70	shins
Π	Pi	P	solar halo	80	knees
P	Rho	R	fruitfulness	100	thighs
Σ	Sigma	S	psychopomp	200	genitals
T	Tau	T	human being	300	belly
Υ	Ypsilon	Y	flow	400	diaphragm
Φ	Phi	F	phallus	500	breast
X	Chi	Ch	property	600	shoulders
Ψ	Psi	Ps	heavenly light	700	neck
Ω	Omega	O	abundance	800	head

✳ ✱ ✳

three Fates invented the five vowels and the letters B and T. Palamedes, whose other inventions included counting and currency, invented the next eleven letters, while the rest were added by Epicharmus of Sicily, and Simonides.

The Greek alphabet has been extremely influential and is the origin of most European alphabets.

It is also the oldest alphabet that has been in continuous use; the Ionic form still in use today was standardized 400 years before the birth of Christ.

Each Greek letter has embedded into it a sound, a meaning, a number, and a corresponding part of the human body. The esoteric correspondences of the letters of the Greek alphabet mean that it is an effective tool in ritual and in divinatory practices in much the same way as the runes. Gematria, the art of interpreting the numerical correspondences of the letters, shares the same root as the word "geometry," therefore it's not surprising that so many Greek letters are used in the mathematical formulas that are also an essential part of sacred geometry. Like the Hebrew alphabet, the Greek alphabet is believed to hold within it all the secrets of the universe.

HEBREW ALPHABET

The Kabbalah calls the Hebrew alphabet the "letters of the angels." Its sacred provenance is explained in the legend that Moses received it on the top of Mount Sinai in an instance of direct communica-

tion with God. In common with other lettering systems such as the Greek, Runic, and Ogham alphabets, each Hebrew letter has specific concepts embedded into it, both mundane and esoteric. Each letter also relates to a number, giving rise to yet another mystery tradition called the gematria. There is an even more profound aspect to the Hebrew alphabet, though; it is an inseparable part of the cohesive philosophical system of the Kabbalah. The lettering system of the Hebrew alphabet contributes to the encoding of this profound mystery tradition, itself a deeply rooted component of magical custom with tendrils that extend, web-like, throughout diverse esoteric disciplines.

Because of the dual meanings attached to the twenty-two Hebrew letters, it means that they act as a useful everyday tool of communication while having another facet for the initiate. Thus, each letter has secrets hidden within it. These secrets are related not only to the allegorical aspects of the Kabbalah and of the tarot system (the Major Arcana of which relates to the letters of the alphabet) but also includes the planets, the seasons and elements, the days of the week, the stages in the life of a person,

Hebrew Character	Name	Sound	Mundane Meaning	Esoteric Meaning	Numerical Value
א	Aleph	A	cattle	father	1
ב	Beth	B	house	mother	2
ג	Gimel	G/C	camel	nature	3
ד	Daleth	D	door	authority	4
ה	He	H/E	window	religion	5
ו	Vau	V/St	nail	liberty	6
ז	Zain	Z	weapon	ownership	7
ח	Cheth	Ch	fence	distribution	8
ט	Teth	Th/T	serpent	prudence	9
י	Vod	I	hand	order	10
כ	Kaph	K	palm of hand	force	11
ל	Lamed	L	ox-goad	sacrifice	12
מ	Mem	M	water	death	13
נ	Nun	N	fish	reversibility	14
ס	Samekh	S/Ch	support	universality	15
ע	Ayin	O	eye	balance	16
פ	Peh	P	mouth	immortality	17
צ	Tzadi	Tz/Q	fish hook	shadow	18
ק	Qoph	Q	back of head	light	19
ר	Resh	R	head	recognition	20
ש	Shin	Sh	tooth	sacred fire	21
ת	Tau	T	cross	synthesis	22

and their concerns. Additionally, the Hebrew alphabet notably gives the means for the spelling and pronunciation of the names of God.

From all this we can gather that Hebrew was "invented" with mystical intent, each letter representing far more than the sum of its parts. Hebrew reads from right to left, and knowing this makes the letters look a little more accessible for the neophyte. If the meaning of the letters is known then the shapes start to suggest these meanings; for example, the second letter, Beth, means "house," and the letter clearly resembles a picture of a house. However, "house" carries with it other concepts, such as the ideas of "home," "mother," and "domesticity."

Because the Hebrew alphabet carries with it a resonance born of almost 3,000 years of mystical use, it is frequently used in magical texts and grimoires, a handy device for concealing occult knowledge. However, sometimes the authors of these texts are not quite as erudite as they might appear to be, and often Hebrew isn't used as a language but only as a series of symbols, the English language transcribed into Hebrew characters.

HIEROGLYPHS

The pyramid texts are considered to be one of the earliest examples of symbols used with magical intent, employed to inscribe spells that would guide the soul of the deceased into the afterlife. Hieroglyphs are still widely used in magical scripts at least 5,000 years later.

The word comes from the Greek, meaning "sacred carvings" and the symbols were called the "speech of the gods" by the Egyptians. Hieroglyphs consist of pictorial motifs which were used initially for magical purposes, as described above, hence the name.

Mastery of hieroglyphic writing was a complex matter since there were 900 pictorial symbols, and in general it was only the priestly caste that had the skills to access their mysteries. There was a script reserved for common, more secular use called "demotic." This was a simplified form of the hieratic scripts used exclusively by the priests. In AD 391 the Roman emperor Theodosius closed all non-Christian temples, providing the final nail in the sarcophagus for hieroglyphs, whose use had dwindled rapidly even before this time.

The Rosetta Stone, discovered by Napoleon's troops in 1799, served as an invaluable aid to the translation of both hieroglyphic and demotic writing since the same text appeared on the stone in both forms and with a version in Greek, which provided the key to translating the first two.

Many hieroglyphs work according to the principle whereby the sound of the word is symbolized by a picture; for example, both "I" and "eye" could be represented by a picture of an eye. This appears to be relatively simple since it's the kind of code that's seen in children's puzzle books. However, start to compound these pictograms to create longer words and then add in the cultural context of the symbol and the obstacles to the full comprehension of hieroglyphics start to become apparent.

Many of the symbols used in Part 1 of this encyclopedia were originally hieroglyphics whose use as part of an ancient language has expanded into a universal meaning; the ankh, for example, is globally accepted as a symbol of eternal life and of protection. This meaning transcends the barriers of spoken language and culture.

The commonly used hieroglyphic alphabet is based on the values given the hieroglyphs by Sir E. A. Wallis Budge, the renowned Egyptologist. The symbols can be used as a cipher, and appear on magical talismans and amulets.

ILLUMINATI CIPHER

The Illuminati are notoriously well known for a supposedly secret society, despite the fact that an atmosphere of mystery clings to the very name, and there is still speculation about many aspects of the organization. The society, founded by Adam Weishaupt in Bavaria in 1776, is arguably the subject of more controversy and hysteria than any other closed organization. However, an understanding of the social, religious, and political climate at the time of its founding, and Weishaupt's reasoning behind the tenets of his order, might serve to clarify some of the known facts about the Illuminati.

Weishaupt was a former Jesuit and a professor of law at Ingoldstadt University. He has been called a Kabbalistic magician, an ungodly atheist, a fascist, and an anarchist.

Thomas Jefferson, however, called him an "enthusiastic philanthropist." Weishaupt founded the Illuminati from within existing Masonic orders, so effectively it was a society within a society. New and progressive ideas were spreading through Europe at the time, and Weishaupt hoped that the Illuminati would foster an environment for debate and discussion, and chose the name to reflect this ideal of enlightened individuals determined to make the world a better place.

Membership of the society grew slowly, due in no small part to the rigorous study that was demanded of its adherents. However, the idea was that members would rise to positions of power well versed in philosophy and the new progressive ideas, and would therefore be able to influence the creation of an idealized society, and by 1784 the order had extended its influence throughout most of central Europe.

Necessarily, secret scripts and ciphers had a large part to play within the organization, given the Illuminati's known opposition to the religious and political ideals of the time. Members had secret names: Weishaupt was known as Spartacus, for example, and other nicknames included Cato, Hermes Trismegistus, Menelaus, and Agrippa.

They even had their own calendar system, based on an ancient Persian system. Initiates were instructed in a relatively simple substitution cipher, and had to correspond with their teachers in this cipher until such a time as a more elaborate code was taught to the initiates. It is this more complex code that is illustrated on page 477.

In 1785 the Bavarian government banned secret organizations, specifically naming the Illuminati. Weishaupt fled, and instructed the existing lodges to go underground; many members were incarcerated by the authorities. The Illuminati's current fame owes its existence to two factors: first, that the Bavarian government published some of the papers it had seized from the society in 1786; and second, the outbreak of the French Revolution in 1789 and the suggestion that the Illuminati might have had something to do with the troubled political climate of the time.

KAMA SUTRA CIPHER

The encryption code is an ancient device, and one of the first recorded instances appears in the Kama Sutra, which was written in the fourth century BC. As well as the well-known records of sexual positions, the Kama Sutra lists 64 useful skills for women; the housewifely arts, such as cooking and dressing, are listed alongside more unusual talents, including chess, conjuring, carpentry, and perfume making. Also listed is something called "Mlechitta Vikalpa," the art of secret writing, designed so that ladies could conceal their liaisons.

The Kama Sutra cipher is personal to the user, substituting letters of the same alphabet for one another, so is easy to devise but almost impossible to decipher without the key.

KNIGHTS TEMPLAR
ALPHABET

The Knights Templar, whose original mission was to protect pilgrims traveling to the Holy Land, soon amassed terrific wealth. They invented an alphabet based on the segments of the Templar Cross, and used this secret code in their letters of credit.

MALACHIM
ALPHABET

HℋJℋ⊟NℐH

A 22-character alphabet inspired by Greek and Hebrew letters, the Malachim alphabet is mentioned by Cornelius Agrippa in his *Book of Occult Philosophy*. Malachim is a Hebrew word meaning "angels" or "regal" and although not much else is known about it, the alphabet is used among some high degrees of Freemasonry.

MASONIC
ALPHABET

See Rosicrucian alphabet.

Ogham Tree
ALPHABET

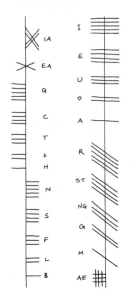

The clue that the Ogham Tree alphabet is a set of sacred symbols is in its name. It is named after the Irish Celtic god Ogma, the deity of learning and poetry who was said to have invented the alphabet itself. Ogham actually means "language."

The alphabet has 25 characters that are all associated with trees and shrubs, hence the alternative name, the Tree alphabet. These "letters" are broken down into sets of five, and the whole is grouped together as a "grove." This is symbolic not only of a collection of trees but also of the sum of knowledge contained in each tree, each smaller part making

a greater whole—it is no coincidence that the Celtic words for "knowledge" and "wood" sound the same.

The trees and shrubs represented by the Ogham symbols vary slightly, but the generally accepted order is as follows:

Tree	Name	Letter
Birch	Beth	B
Rowan	Luis	L
Alder	Fearn	F
Willow	Saille	S
Ash	Nuin	N
Hawthorn	Huath	H
Oak	Duir	D
Holly	Tinne	T
Hazel	Coll	C
Apple	Quert	Q
Vine	Muin	M
Ivy	Gort	G
Reed	Ngetal	Ng
Blackthorn	Straif	St/Z
Elder	Ruis	R
Elm	Ailm	A
Gorse	On	O
Heather	Ur	U
White Poplar/ Aspen	Eadha	E
Yew	Ioh	I
Aspen	Ea/Koad	Ea
Spindle, Gooseberry	Oi	Oi
Honeysuckle, Beech	Ui	Ui
Guelder Rose	Io/Pe	Ia
Pine, Witch Hazel	Ao/Xi	Ae

There seems to be no definite evidence as to the actual origins of the alphabet. Some believed it was based on the runes, and the letters do look similar, although this may be simply because straight lines are easier to engrave onto wood. Several examples of Ogham inscriptions can be found in the British Isles, and all date between the fourth and seventh centuries AD although it's likely that the alphabet is from an earlier date. The only surviving records of it are left on enduring stone, since leather or bark would have decayed over the centuries. There are also some stones showing the Ogham symbols next to Latin letters. These stones were generally used to define ownership and boundaries of land. The inscriptions are read by starting in the bottom left-hand corner, working up, then across the top to the next vertical line of writing.

Sometimes the Ogham script is referred to as the Beth-Luis-Nuin alphabet, in the same way that we use A-B-C. Looking at the chart, it would be easy to suppose that the most obvious name would be Beth-Luis-Fearn; however, the Beth-Luis-Nuin is a throwback to an earlier sequence of trees/letters.

Although the individual Ogham symbols are simple, they represent a more complex whole. As well as having a tree associated with each letter, there was a hand signal, a spirit, and a concept also embedded into it. Like the runes, the Ogham letters are also used as a tool of divination.

Robert Graves extrapolated the idea of the Tree alphabet to make a tree calendar. Because the Druids gauged their months according to the phases of the moon, there are 13 months in this particular system of measuring time.

PASSING THE RIVER

One of the magical scripts based on the Hebrew language and known in Latin as *Transitus Fluvii*, this script is among those described by Cornelius Agrippa in his sixteenth-century work on occult philosophy.

The name may refer to the passage of the Jewish people across the Euphrates River when they returned from Babylon to rebuild the Temple at Jerusalem. Like Hebrew, the alphabet has 22 characters.

PICTISH SWIRL SCRIPT

Another simple substitution cipher based on the 26-letter Roman alphabet, some sources claim that this script is part of some "forgotten" Pictish writing system, but this is unlikely to be the case. It is more likely that Pictish swirl script is a recent invention inspired by the spiral patterns seen on ancient Celtic stonework, for example at Newgrange. The script is given more weight and importance by being linked, spuriously, with an ancient culture. However, Pictish swirl script is used by latter-day practitioners of Wicca in spell-casting and is a good example of a secret alphabet.

PIGPEN CIPHER

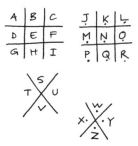

Also called the Masonic or Freemason's cipher, the peculiarly named pigpen cipher is so called because letters are laid out in a grid pattern that resembles a pigpen. The letters are exchanged for the symbol defined by the part of the pen they sit in. The code was devised by Freemasons in the seventeenth century to keep their accounts and correspondence private.

To the uninitiated, the cipher looks rather like a simple graphic design. A good example of it can be seen on the gravestone of one Thomas Brierley, which also contains other Masonic symbols. Although the stone has been damaged in the years since Thomas was buried in 1785, the script appears to read "Holiness of the Lord."

PYRAMID TEXTS

The ancient Egyptians were obsessed with the idea of an afterlife, a concern that informed many rites and rituals. Uppermost in the minds of these people was the idea that the soul should be protected in its journey to the afterlife. As well as the mummy being swathed in an arsenal of charms, amulets and other prophylactic devices, the Pyramids in which the pharaohs were interred were encrusted with magical spells too, all designed to protect the soul on its epic voyage and to appease the gods and other creatures it might meet along the way. Many of the passages in the pyramid texts describe the glories to be enjoyed by the pharaoh in the afterlife.

Among the spells and charms is a curiosity called the Cannibal Hymn that seems to have been designed to warn the very gods themselves about the powers of the pharaoh; this song tells of the pharaoh devouring the deities.

Although the pyramid texts have proved difficult to date with complete accuracy, it is possible that they go back to 3000 BC. This makes them the oldest magical and sacred texts in the world.

ROSE CROSS CIPHER

See Rosicrucian alphabet.

ROSICRUCIAN ALPHABET

Also known as the Masonic alphabet or the Rose Cross cipher, this is a straightforward replacement code. The symbols represent the 26 letters of the Roman alphabet. The alphabet is used by both Masonic and Rosicrucian societies in order to keep certain information a secret to the uninitiated.

The Rosicrucian alphabet is based, like the Aiq Bkr, on a grid system of nine squares, divided up as follows:

ABC	DEF	GHI
JKL	MNO	PQR
STU	VWX	YZ

Each letter is represented by the part of the grid in which it is contained. This is straightforward enough with the first letter in the grid, for example, A. The second letter is denoted by the same part of the grid except with the addition of a dot. The third letter is given two dots. Thus the letter A would be drawn as:

And B drawn as:

ROYAL ARCH CIPHER

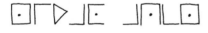

One of the cipher alphabets based on a grid system, the Royal Arch cipher is possibly the best known of these types of codes. Its name refers to one of the degrees within Freemasonry. It is based on a grid of nine squares with two letters in each square, with the remaining eight letters occupying the spaces in an X-shaped figure.

RUNIC ALPHABET

ᚠ ᚢ ᚦ ᚨ ᚱ ᚲ ᚷ ᚹ
ᚺ ᛁ ᛏ ᛃ ᛈ ᛉ ᛇ ᛏ ᛒ ᛖ
ᚷ ᚺ ᛗ ᛘ ᛩ ᚲ ᚨ ᛦ ᛨ

Also known as the Futhork (or Futhark) alphabet for the same reasons that the sequence of letters on a keyboard is sometimes called Qwerty (i.e., because the order of the first few letters spells the word), the divinatory properties of the runic alphabet have been explored extensively, although the letters were used for secular as well as spiritual purposes. The oldest script symbols of the ancient Germans, runes were used in Britain, Scandinavia, and Germany before the Latin alphabet superseded them. Unfortunately, the early Christian Church destroyed many runic inscriptions, although there are still fine examples of markings on ancient artifacts, standing stones, etc.

The word "rune" comes from an Old English or Norse word meaning "mystery," "secret," or "whisper." There's also a Finnish word, *runo*, meaning "song." The runes themselves were considered to be of divine origin, in common with other alphabets.

The Scandinavian epic poems, the Eddas, describe how the god Odin brought the runes to mankind after a strange ritual whereby he hung from the great ash tree, Yggdrasil, for nine days until he saw the runic symbols reflected in the water below. This story has parallels with the tale of Edward Kelley's discovery of the Enochian script by scrying with a crystal ball. Such was the power of the runes that it was said that they could bring the dead to life. Therefore it's likely that knowledge of the runes was an esoteric matter initially restricted to an elite few, in common with other alphabets, the knowledge of which gave great power. Ancient texts, in which runes are given magical powers, confirm this theory. The supernatural powers of Odin himself, which included the ability to fly, shape-shift, bring the dead back to life, and to see into the future, were all a result of his ability to understand the runes.

The shape of the runes is very distinctive. They are constructed of upright parts called staves, and diagonal lines. Notably, runes have no horizontal lines. This is because they were initially scored onto wood, and horizontal lines are more difficult to cut into the grain. Later, the symbols would be engraved onto rock and stone. Tacitus, the Roman historian, wrote a book in AD 98 called *Germania* about the lands and customs of the German people, and in it, he mentions the tradition of augury or divination by "lot," which happens to be another meaning of the word "rune." It would appear likely that Tacitus is describing runes when he speaks of small pieces of wood, generally cut from fruit trees, which were scored with distinguishing marks and tossed onto a white cloth. The pieces were then analyzed to decide the will of the gods, although, it has to be said, the available information as to just how the runes were used as a tool of augury is sketchy.

There are several different runic systems but the one which is seen most often is the oldest version, known as Elder Futhark. The alphabet consists of 24 symbols, each of which encapsulates a small universe of meaning. Every rune carries not only a sound and a shape and a name of its own, but also has both a mundane and a mystical meaning (which enables the alphabet to be understood on many levels) and is connected not only to a god or spirit but also to an idea or concept.

Adding to the layers of complexity in understanding the runic code is the fact that each individual rune can translate into a word or phrase that would have carried significant conceptual meaning to the people who invented them. For example, whereas "a," "b," and "c" are nothing but symbols that indicate a sound, the first three letters of the runic alphabet—"faro," "gurus," and "purses"—are complete words in themselves, meaning "cattle," "aurochs," and "giant" respectively. In order to understand the runes, the skilled reader needs to step back in time and intuit the concerns of the people that invented them; top of the list of priorities would be basic survival, food supply, and protection from enemies and the elements. On top of this, each rune also has a complete story associated with it.

The material used for making the runes had significance, too. Ancient people believed that everything on the earth was alive and animated with a spirit, and so the stone, wood, or leather on which the runic symbol was engraved would itself have contributed to the sacred status of the object. The runes were used for spell-casting, to bring healing and fertility, and to influence the tides and the weather. They were used to curse and to remove curses, to protect, and to assist in both birth and death.

Runes are arranged in groups, called *aett*, plural *aettir*. The Elder Futhark consists of three *aettir* of eight runes.

Here is the list of correspondences and meanings for the characters of the runic alphabet. The first group of 24 runes is the Elder Futhark, arguably the most used runic system.

✳ ✷ ✳

RUNE	NAME	TREE	ELEMENT	DEITY	MEANING
First Aett					
ᚠ	Feoh	elder	fire/ earth	Freya	cattle; movable wealth
ᚢ	Ur	birch	earth	Thor	auroch; the power of wild cattle
ᚦ	Thorn	oak	fire	Thor	a giant; attack and defense
ᚫ	As	ash	air	Odin	Yggdrasil; the primal sound, aum
ᚱ	Rad	oak	air	Ing	a vehicle; a journey; action
ᚲ	Ken	pine	fire	Heimdall	fire; a torch; a beacon
ᚷ	Gyfu	ash/elm	air	Gefn	sacred mark; a gift to the gods
ᚹ	Wyn	ash	earth	Odin	joy; harmony with the flow of events
Second Aett					
ᚺ	Hagal	ash/yew	ice	Urd	ice or hail; transformation
ᚾ	Nyd	beech/ rowan	fire	Skuld	necessity
ᛁ	Is	alder	ice	Verdandi	icicle
ᛃ	Jera	oak	earth	Freya	the cycle of time; fruition
ᛇ	Eoh	yew/ poplar	all	Ullr	yew tree; regeneration; longevity
ᛈ	Peorth	beech	water	Frigg	womb; fate or destiny
ᛉ	Elhaz	yew	air	Heimdall	defense; the splayed hand
ᛋ	Sigel	juniper	air	Balder	sun; triumph over the darkness

✳ ✷ ✳

The Encyclopedia of Secret Signs and Symbols

RUNE	NAME	TREE	ELEMENT	DEITY	MEANING
Third Aett					
↑	Tyr	oak	air	Tyr	sky; justice
ᛒ	Beorc	birch	earth	Nerthus	regeneration; the breasts of the earth goddess
M	Ehwas	oak/ash	earth	Freya	an intuitive bond (as with horse and rider)
ᛗ	Manu	holly	air	Heimdall/ Odin/ Frigg	humankind; humanity
ᛚ	Lagu	osier	water	Njord	the womb; the sea; the balance of opposites
ᚷ	Ing	apple	water/ earth	Ing	potential; male energy
ᛟ	Odal	hawthorn	earth	Odin	land; property
ᛞ	Dag	spruce	fire/air	Heimdall	balance; night/day; black/white, etc.

The next set of runes, the fourth *aett*, is called "the *aett* of the gods," and is sacred to the Norse deities called the Aesir. This particular set of five (not eight) runes was developed in Britain.

So far, we have 29 runes. Around AD 800, the Northumbrian Anglo-Saxons added four further runes: Cweorth, Calc, Stan, and Gar. These form the first four runes of the final group, which is sometimes referred to as the fifth *aett*.

The final five runes have known meanings, but are rarely used.

RUNE	NAME	TREE	ELEMENT	DEITY	MEANING
ᚪ	Ac	oak	fire	Thor	oak tree; the acorn and future potential
ᚩ	Os	ash	air	Odin	mouth; speech; the primal sound of existence
ᚣ	Yr	yew	all	Odin/ Frigg	yew tree; bow
ᛄ	Ior	ivy	water	Njord	Jormungand; the World Serpent
ᛠ	Ear	yew	earth	Hela	dust; death; the grave; an end and a beginning

Rune	Name	Tree	Element	Deity	Meaning
ᛆ	Cweorth	bay/beech	fire	Loge	funeral pyre; a ritual bonfire
ᛌ ᛦ	Calc	maple	earth	Norns	grail; cup; something that is full, and yet empty
ᛥ	Stan	witch hazel	earth	Nerthus	sacred stone
ᚷ	Gar	ash/spindle	all	Odin	spear of Odin
ᛪ	Wolfs-angel	yew	earth	Vidar	wolf-hook; used to capture wolves; hence to bind
ᛏ	Ziu	oak	air/fire	Tyr	thunderbolt; justice
ᛂ	Erda	elder/birch	earth	Erda	Mother Earth; protection, enclosure
ᛨ	Ul	buckthorn	air	Waldh	turning point
ᛋ	Sol	juniper	fire	Sol	the sun

BIND RUNE

The bind rune is constructed for specific magical or ritual purposes. It is a combination of two or more runes that together make a sigil or symbol that is more than the sum of its parts. The Skulds Net, or Web of Wyrd, is a bind rune.

SIG RUNE

The Sig or Sigel rune is also called the Sun rune and represents a sunbeam. However, when it is tipped slightly it resembles either the letter S or a lightning bolt shape. As such, it was doubled up and used in Nazi insignia and its meaning changed to "Victory" from the German *Sieg*.

SKULDS NET

See Web of Wyrd.

THEBAN SCRIPT

See Witches' alphabet.

TREE ALPHABET

See Ogham Tree alphabet.

WEB OF WYRD

A bind rune comprised of three upright staves, with two sets of three diagonal lines criss-crossing to form an orderly trellis, the Web of Wyrd holds within it every single rune symbol and, therefore, all possibilities for the past, the present, and the future.

The Web of Wyrd is a reminder of the laws of cause and effect, or karma. It tells us that all actions, however small, affect each other and that everything is connected. The web predates the coming of Christianity in the West, and is related to an era when time was thought of as cyclical rather than linear.

Although it is a commonly held misconception that "wyrd" means the same as "weird," meaning strange, it doesn't. Wyrd carries the same root as the word for "worth," or "to become." Recently, certain scientific theories have been expounded which seem to prove the interconnectedness of every single thing in the universe. James Lovelock's Gaia Hypothesis is a notable example, showing that this Norse concept, which is so ancient as to be impossible to date, is as valid today as it was several thousand years ago.

WITCHES' ALPHABET

The Theban script or Alphabet of Honorius is also called the witches' alphabet because of its popularity in Books of Shadows, where it's used to encode magical spells. The alphabet is first mentioned by Johannes Trithemius in his *Polygraphia*, published in the early part of the sixteenth century. Cornelius Agrippa, a student of Trithemius, also describes it in his *Three Books of Occult Philosophy* published in Antwerp in 1531. The Honorius in the alternate title is Honorius of Thebes, who wrote a learned tome on magic called *The Sworn Book of Honorius*.

Trithemius was an interesting character. Made a Benedictine abbot at the age of 21 in 1483, he also had a reputation of being a magician, a reputation borne out by his book *Steganographia*. This remarkable work was about black magic and the use of spirits as a means of long-distance communication. The book itself was written in code, and the works of Trithemius formed the cornerstone of the Golden Dawn society almost 500 years later.

It's possible that the witches' alphabet started out as a Latin cipher used by early tenth-century alchemists to keep their discoveries secret. The 26 letters of the alphabet are substitute symbols for the Latin alphabet and so anyone conversant with the script—most likely to be another witch or wizard—would be likely to be able to translate it with no problems, thus rendering questionable its efficacy in disguising certain spells or charms.

WRITING OF THE MAGI

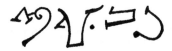

Said to have been invented by Paracelsus in the sixteenth century. Paracelsus was an alchemist and occultist who, like Cornelius Agrippa, was an acolyte of the influential Trithemius (see Witches' alphabet). The script was used by its inventor to inscribe or engrave the names of angelic beings on amulets, which were used for healing or protection. Not much is known for certain about how Paracelsus invented this script but it is likely that it was inspired by other occult alphabets of the time.

Part Eight

THE BODY AS A
SACRED MAP

In an attempt to comprehend the deeper mysteries of the universe, ancient people understandably started with the most accessible and easily definable thing that they knew—themselves. This means that the human body, with its head in the stars and its feet on the ground, is the most universal of all sacred symbols. Our ancestors believed that humans held all the secrets of the universe within their physical bodies, both inside and out.

ADAM'S APPLE

The Adam's apple is actually a protruding piece of thyroid cartilage that develops at puberty, but only in the male. It is so called because it is said to symbolize the piece of the apple of knowledge that got stuck in Adam's throat after Eve, encouraged by the serpent, coaxed him into eating the fruit.

ARM

Arms convey the idea of strength and protection. They also stand for safety and justice, as in "the strong arm of the law."

Some deities have more than the usual two arms. Brahma, for example, is depicted with four arms to show his omnipotence. Shiva, too, shows innumerable arms as a symbol of his action, energy, and accomplishment. This idea— that the arms signify activity— was shared by the Egyptians, and they used the arm to convey this concept in their hieroglyphs.

BLOOD

Blood and its color are inextricably linked, one the symbol of the other, the red standing for life, energy, vitality, and the element of fire and (by association) the sun: all the attributes of blood too.

For early people, the link between the color and the life-giving properties of blood were so powerful that some burial rituals included the corpse being daubed in red powders and unguents, an example of sympathetic magic in the hope that the red color would be enough to restore the soul to life. An example of this can be found in the ritual burial of a young tribal chieftain at the Paviland Caves in South Wales.

Blood is symbolic of the idea of kinship, and to speak of a "blood line" refers to generations of the same family. The term "blue blood" as a description of the aristocracy came about because the veins of the nobility showed through their pale skin because they were unused to manual labor or exposure to the elements.

Menstrual blood, since it comes from that most sacred of places, the womb, is accorded with particular magical power and is symbolic of feminine energy and the moon. This particular blood was used in rites and ceremonies since it was believed to have the most potently charged magic of any kind of blood. Tantric practices say that a man can become spiritually empowered if he drinks menstrual blood. This is symbolic of him accepting female power in addition to his own male energy. Blood is used as ink in magical rites, to imbue certain words and names with vitality.

Ritual spilling of blood, in the form of sacrifice, was believed to propitiate the gods, and where blood is deliberately spilled on the earth—as in some of the ancient harvest rituals—it is believed to bring fertility. Similarly, we speak of the spilling of blood during a war as being a sacrifice to the greater good, a noble and courageous act.

One of the major symbolic elements of the Christian mass is the sharing of the blood of Christ. The red wine held in the chalice is believed by some Catholics to change into the actual blood of Christ by the act of transubstantiation; for Protestants, it is enough that the wine is symbolic of the holy blood.

BONE

As well as giving structure to the body, bones survive for a long time after death, and so are imbued with magical properties. Symbolically, bones carry the essence of the creature that they were once a part of, and there's a curious but relatively common belief that somehow or other an intact set of bones can be remade into a live body.

The human body contains one bone that has particular relevance as a sacred symbol, and its name gives it away. In Latin, *sacrum* means "sacred," and the bone of the same name is the large, curved, and heavy one that sits at the base of the spine. This particular bone was sacred for the Greeks, too, who called it the *hieros osteon*. *Hieros* means not only "sacred," but "temple." *Osteon* means "bone." Therefore this sacred bone acts as a temple to other sacred parts of the anatomy, namely the reproductive parts. In ancient Egypt the bone was sacred to Osiris and as the "seed" bone was the key to resurrection, since it protected the semen.

Because of its size, the bone is one of the very last in the body to rot, along with the skull. For this reason—its longevity—the bone was used as a vessel during religious and magical rites and rituals.

BREAST

Clearly, the breast is the symbol of motherhood, the female principle, comfort, nourishment, and abundance. It is also a symbol of beauty and of fertility. The breast is the first point of contact for the newborn baby as he suckles his first food, milk, hence the primal nature of the breast as a symbol. The Egyptians believed that the stars of the Milky Way were milk spilling from the breasts of the moon goddess, who was the source of all the other stars, too. The right breast is said to represent the sun, and the left, the moon.

In Hebrew, the word for "breast" is the same as for "girl" and also "liquid measure." This indicates the idea of the breast as a symbol of restriction, since any measurement must necessarily be finite.

CHAKRAS

Chakra is a Sanskrit word, meaning "wheel" or "circle," and refers in this instance to a series of subtle energy centers that rise up along the length of the spine. The chakras are said to spin, and are envisaged as lotus flowers (another name for them is the "lotus centers"). Each chakra/lotus is a different color and has a different number of petals according to each particular chakra's meaning and function, in relation not only to the body, but to the mind and spirit too. Meditation and yoga are believed to help balance the chakras, which in turn promotes good health. Any depiction of the chakras contains the symbol of the great serpent Kundalini curled three and a half times at the base of the spine, which relates to the primal creative energy that rises up through healthy chakras when a person is ready to be awakened to such an experience.

CLITORIS

Effectively the clitoris is the female equivalent of the penis, reacting to stimulus in the same way by becoming engorged with blood and super sensitive. It is interesting to note that the clitoris is perceived as representing the male element in the woman, in the same way that the foreskin represents the female element in the man.

The controversial operation of female circumcision—sometimes called female genital mutilation—is something that has been carried out for centuries, particularly in Egypt and other parts of Africa. The reasons for it have remained unchanged. The operation ranges from the relatively simple removal of the hood of the clitoris to the removal of all external genitalia.

There are numerous reasons reported for this operation. The

removal of the clitoris means that the sexual desire of the female will be decreased, and the procedure is thought to promote chastity, as is the stitching up of the vaginal opening. In societies where clitoral circumcision is traditional, then it is considered the "correct" thing to do, and sometimes hygiene is given as the reason. The removal of the clitoris is also performed as a rite of passage, carried out at puberty. Some believe that the sexual satisfaction of the male is increased if the female is circumcised.

For cultures where clitoral circumcision is not the norm, the practice is viewed as symbolic of the subjugation of women, who, it is presumed, are treated as second-class citizens by having the capability for sexual arousal removed.

EAR

Before it was common for people to be able to read and write, the way to receive information was aurally. Therefore, the ear is symbolic of knowledge and also of memory.

However, the shape of the ear as well as its function give clues about other aspects of its symbolic significance. It is shaped like a spiral or a whirled shell, a shape not dissimilar to that of the vulva; therefore, the ear is also a symbol of birth. This analogy is carried a step further in depictions of the Virgin Mary receiving the message of the Holy Spirit, in the form of a dove, through her ear. This idea— that she could receive the spirit in the same way that she could hear a sound—also promulgates the idea of the virgin birth.

Piercing the ears is an ancient practice that is still carried out all over the world, and these piercings have often been used to carry a secret code. For example, the Bible speaks of a pierced ear as being a sign of servitude or subjugation. However, wealthy Romans would pierce their ears so that their earrings could provide one more indicator of their wealth. Sailors pierced both their ears in the belief that this would give them better eyesight.

EYE

The symbolism of the eye occurs in so many places and in so many different forms that its pervasiveness symbolizes the All Seeing Eye itself. The eye is closely associated with the idea of light and of the spirit, and is often called the "mirror of the soul." When a person dies one of the first things that is done is that the eyes are closed, a timeless gesture that signifies the departure of the essence of life. Generally, the right eye is considered to be the eye of the sun, the left, that of the moon.

The eye represents the "god within," for example as the "third eye" whose position is designated by the small dot called the bindhu above and between the actual eyes. The Buddha is always depicted with this third eye. Here, the eye signifies the higher self, the part of a person's consciousness that is ego-free and can guide and direct them. Whereas the eyes are organs of outward vision, this "eye of wisdom" directs its view internally as the "eye of dharma" or the "eye of the heart."

As an occult symbol, the unlidded eye has its origins as the symbol of the Egyptian goddess of truth, Ma'at, whose name was synonymous with the verb "to see"; therefore the concepts of truth and vision were closely aligned. The same eye symbol appears as the Eye of Horus, or Udjat. This stylized eye, with a brow above and featuring a curlique underneath, represents the omnipresent vision of the sun god Horus, and is a prominent symbol within the Western magical tradition where it represents, among other things, secret or occult wisdom. This eye was painted on the sides of Egyptian funerary caskets in the hope that it would enable the corpse to see its way through the journey to the afterlife.

The All Seeing Eye, the eye within a triangle with rays emanating from the lower lid, is used not only in Freemasonry (where it stands for the "Great Architect of the Universe," for external vision, and also for inner vision and spiritual watchfulness) but in Christian symbolism too.

The eye symbol is used as a charm, painted on the sides of humble fishing boats, in order to protect the boat from the evil eye and to somehow confer this inanimate object with the power of sight of its own, a notion which follows exactly the same reasoning behind the practice of the Egyptians painting eyes on the coffins of their dead. Belief in the evil eye is ancient, referred to in Babylonian texts dating back to 3,000 years before Christ. This is the idea that some people can curse an object (or a person) simply by the act of looking, as though the eye itself can direct a malevolent thought.

It is a mark of the profound belief in the concept of the evil eye that there are so very many charms said to protect against it.

FOOT

Footprint of the Buddha

The foot is a symbol of strength, stability, and resolve (after all, we need them to support the rest of our body), and of our connection with the earth—again, the reasons for this are obvious. When we say that someone has his feet firmly upon the ground, we mean that the person is down-to-earth, sensible, and practical.

The feet have always been used as a way to measure something; the old Imperial measurement of a "foot" was based on its average length, 12 inches. Pacing out any distance helps us to measure something, and in the same way that we might work out the dimensions of more prosaic things, both Buddha and Vishnu measured out the universe: the Buddha by taking seven steps in each direction and Vishnu by taking just three strides, across the earth and the heavens.

The Footprint of the Buddha—or Buddhapada—is a popular symbol for Buddhists, showing the soles of the Buddha's feet imprinted with other items of symbolic importance, such as the eight auspicious objects. The Buddha Footprint is used as a symbol to indicate the places he visited during his life on earth.

In the yogic tradition, it is considered the height of rudeness to point the soles of the feet in the direction of the guru or even at his image.

In China, the practice of foot binding was popular for a thousand years. At the age of six or even earlier, girls' feet were wrapped tightly in bandages so that the bones would break. The muscles atrophied, and the feet stayed tiny; a three-inch foot was considered perfection, and was called the "gold lotus." No one is entirely sure how this custom started. It may have been in an attempt to emulate a concubine who danced in silk-wrapped feet. Bound feet became a symbol of wealth and power, since only the rich could afford to keep a woman who was unable to walk. The custom died out after it was banned in 1911 by the government of the Republic of China.

FORESKIN

The process of removing the foreskin, called circumcision, could be considered to be an act of mutilation, although evidence of it goes back to the Stone Age. However, for many, this operation is considered to be correct practice and in the best interests of the man or boy concerned.

There are various explanations for circumcision. Aside from any particular religious or spiritual ideas, it is believed that the removal of the foreskin is a hygienic practice, and may prevent sexually transmitted diseases and genital cancers. Evidence for these claims is not, however, conclusive. To apply a more symbolic meaning rather than a practical reason, then, for some the cutting away of the foreskin is a statement of detachment from the sexual and material self and signifies a cutting away of God's bond with matter, in the same way that a baby's umbilical cord is cut. There is also a sacrificial element to circumcision: to propitiate the gods with the removal of a part of the body which is, after all, essential to the survival and continuation of the human species.

Circumcision may be best known as a Jewish practice, but it is also carried out by other people, such as the Dogon and the Bambara in Africa. These tribes believe that the foreskin embodies the material form of the female soul in the man, and this anomaly is rectified by its removal, thereby restoring full masculinity to the man. In the Jewish faith, the foreskin is removed as a sign of God's covenant with the people of Israel. It is obligatory, according to religious law, for all Jewish males to be circumcised, unless it could put their life at risk. Carried out on the eighth day after birth, January 1 is known as the Feast of the Circumcision in the Roman Catholic religious calendar since this is the day on which Christ would have had the procedure.

As a holy relic, the foreskin of Christ is a potent symbol. Remarkably, as many as 18 "Holy Prepuces" appeared around Europe in the Middle Ages.

HAIR

Hair, the crown of the head, has always been believed to hold an essence or life force that is inextricably attached to, and a part of, its owner, even when the owner is separated from the hair. Therefore a strand of hair is an essential ingredient in magical spells to gain power over someone. This ancient belief actually has solid roots; a small clump of hair can tell an analyst which vitamins and minerals the person needs. It is still considered bad luck and potentially dangerous to let hair fall into the wrong hands.

To have unruly hair is to indicate a separation from conventional society, a sign of someone who flouts the rules, whose ideas are different from the norm and whose long hair is a symbol of freedom from the constraints of society. This is not a recent symptom of societal changes but predates the time when people wore flowers in their hair in the 1960s and 70s. Traditionally, witches and wizards had unruly and disheveled hair and lived apart from their neighbors, as did the hermit, whose long robe and tangled hair are an archetypal uniform. The "mad professor" who teeters between genius and insanity is given away by his hair, which stands on end.

In Greek and Hindu mythology, the gods and goddesses who have the wildest, most disheveled hair are the ones who are the most dangerous or who have demonic qualities. Medusa, for example, whose head was a mass of writhing snakes, is a fine example of a continual bad hair day.

Our hair is a symbol of our individuality, and to make someone cut or shave his hair is to wield power over that person. If a man joins the army or is imprisoned, the taming of his hair is one of the first things to take place. Here, the cutting of the hair implies uniformity and discipline. Similarly, in Roman times one of the signs of slavery was short hair. Gaul remained independent so its people retained their flowing locks and were known as the Gallia Commata ("Hairy Gauls"). A ritual shaving of the hair indicates purity and a fresh start, and it's an almost unconscious ritual to cut one's hair at life-changing moments.

Because long, flowing hair is a sign of virility, power, and the material world, a shorn or shaven head is a sign of worldly renunciation. Religious ascetics often follow the tradition of shaving the hair. The tonsure of the monk or priest is a sign of spiritual devotion. This ritual shaving is not restricted to men; some nuns and particularly orthodox Jewish women shave their heads as a symbol of the rejection of worldly and sensual matters. St. Paul recommended that women cover their hair when inside churches since spirits were meant to be attracted to loose, uncovered hair. Hairstyles can tell us a lot about people, particularly in traditional societies. In India, to wear the hair in two plaits is the sign of an unmarried woman. Conversely, in Russia, a single plait was a sign of virginity, whereas a pair of braids was the hairstyle of the wife.

HAND

Word origins frequently give clues as to the nature of objects and ideas. The Latin word for hand is *manus*, which carries the same root as the word, among others, "manifestation"; a clear indication that to be "manifest" is to be held in the hand or created by the hand.

The hand is possibly one of the most accessible and expressive parts of the human body. We shake hands as a sign of greeting; we can use our hands to make signs and symbols, to gesticulate and to communicate. In the Kabbalah, the left hand of God signifies justice, and his right hand, mercy. Blessings and benedictions are given with the right hand. To give someone your hand is to imply trust, for example when we speak of giving someone's hand in marriage. When we meet someone we shake each other's right hand; this is a sign of friendship and trust and also shows that neither person is wielding a sword.

This right–left symbolism of the hand occurs several times. The right hand is associated with cleanliness and the left, with dirt, and in some countries to offer something with the left hand is seen as an insult.

Hands, as an extension of the will and of the intention, carry a great power. In the practice of "laying on of hands," they are used as agents of healing energies.

HAND GESTURES

The silent eloquence of hand gestures and signals can speak volumes. The "V for Victory" sign, palm forward, index and middle fingers extended, is recognized all over the world, and the pejorative version of the same sign, palm turned around, is also universally understood. There's an apocryphal story about the origins of this particular signal. During the Hundred Years War, the bow and arrow were the major offensive weapons. The English were famous for their skill in handling the long-bow, and if they were captured, the French chopped off the index and middle fingers that were used to pull back the bowstring. Therefore, the gesture, as a signal of taunting defiance, was born.

The meanings of certain hand gestures can alter according to where in the world they are made. A good case in point is the *mano fico* or "sign of the fig," made by thrusting the thumb between the middle and index fingers of the curled hands. The "fico" may have been a good-luck charm for both the ancient Romans and for modern Brazilians, but elsewhere in the world the gesture is not only insulting but also threatening. The *mano cornuta*, or "horned hand," also has a dual meaning. The index and little fingers are straight, while the thumb curls around the other two fingers. This signal is also called the "goat's horns" and while it may be an ancient sign used to ward off the evil eye by emulating the horns of the devil, others see it as a mark of allegiance with evil forces. If the sign is made behind someone's head, surreptitiously, then this indicates that the person's partner is cheating on them; it refers to the horns of the goat, an animal that has a particularly lascivious reputation.

The Japanese beckoning cat or Maneki Neko uses a welcoming gesture that is recognizable everywhere, whether made by feline or human. The palm is at shoulder height and facing outwards. There's another beckoning sign that uses the index finger, curling repeatedly in a hook-like gesture as though to reel something in. This gesture asks the person to come close.

The sign of benediction or blessing is universal, too. Here, the index and middle fingers are extended while the others curl into the palm. This signal is first registered in use by the Romans, who used it as a sign to gain attention or to indicate that the user was going to speak, a more elaborate version of the "hand up" signal used by schoolchildren who want to answer a question in the classroom. This ancient hand gesture is used to bless holy water, wine, bread, or other items; its use transcends religious boundaries and is used by the pope as well as those of a more pagan persuasion, such as Druids and Wiccans.

The clenched fist is a symbol of power, of unity. It's a sign of victory and defiance, and power is held closely in the hand.

The crossed fingers signal is a universal sign of hope or of good luck, generally used when some wish is expressed aloud. The signal has one of two meanings. First, the cross is a protective gesture that averts the evil eye. Second, any bad luck is "trapped" in the cross shape. However, if someone tells a lie, he might surreptitiously make this gesture, making sure that it cannot be seen, to avert any bad luck involved in the telling of the lie.

The "thumbs up" signal has come to mean approval, whereas the "thumbs down" sign means the opposite. Although the gestures are regularly used by makers of epic gladiatorial movies to signify decisions over the life or death of a gladiator, their origins are indeterminate, and may actually date back to a time when the thumb print was used to seal documents.

MUDRAS

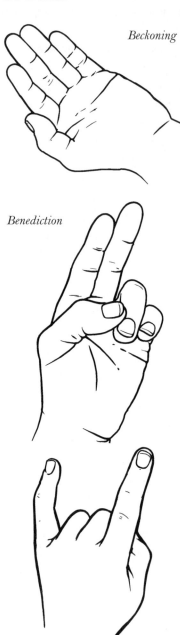

Beckoning

Benediction

The cornus

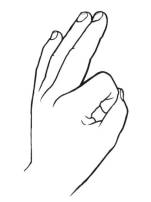

Chin Mudra OK sign

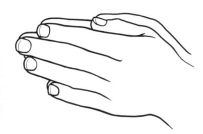

Prayer/Namaskara Mudra

Mano fico

being pleased. It also means "seal," "sign," or "mark." Mudras are hand signals, but with a more sacred nature than the secular gestures described above. They have spiritual meanings not only because of their intention, but because each part of the hand and the fingers is dedicated to a deity. Mudras are used in yoga and dance as well as in religious pictures and statuary. Images of the Buddha, for example, generally show his hands in the silently eloquent gestures that are rich in meaning.

When used in yogic practices, mudras not only help to focus the mind on abstract ideas and the intention behind the pose or *asana*, but experts say that the movements themselves have a direct connection to the nervous system and can help with breath control, etc.

Each of the fingers itself carries several different symbolic meanings. They are dedicated to each of the five elements: the thumb is space, the index finger is air, the third finger represents fire, the fourth water, and the little finger earth.

Some universally accepted gestures have their origins in these sacred signs. For example, the Chin Mudra is effectively the same as the "OK" sign, symbolic of approval, or

The Sanskrit word *mudra* is derived from the verb *mud*, meaning "to please," with the inference being that the gods are the ones that are

The Encyclopedia of Secret Signs and Symbols

"all is well." Here, the tips of the index finger and the thumb close in a circle. The other three fingers are straight. Because in Hindu belief the thumb represents the universal spirit and the index finger represents the individual spirit, the circle made when the fingers touch is symbolic of the self that meets the universe, making a circle of completion or wholeness.

Another mudra that is known universally is the Anjali Mudra or the Namaskara Mudra. Again, Westerners will recognize this as the gesture of prayer, both hands together at chest level. The touching palms represent the connection of spirit and matter. The gesture also seals and contains energy. Often accompanied by a bow, the word *namaskara*, or *namaste*, means "I bow to you."

HEAD

The head and the heart operate in tandem as the logical and the emotional aspects of the body as a sacred map. The head is symbolic of the intellect, the mind, wisdom, reasoned thought, and of a ruling power or the "top" of something—for example, the head of state.

The head and the face are the most easily identifiable parts of the body, and so were considered to be a great trophy in more war-like times. The head, removed from the body, means instant annihilation. For a warrior to return with the actual head of his enemy meant that he also somehow acquired the potency of that enemy; the head was a status symbol of war and would sometimes be preserved in oil so that there would be no doubt as to both the identity of its owner and the certainty that he was dead. In the same way, the head of an animal is considered to be the most valuable trophy of the hunter, a gross display of humanity's dominion over the animal kingdom, and the more savage the animal, the more kudos accorded to its killer.

However, in myth, not all decapitated heads were rendered lifeless. This is in accord with the ancient notion that the head contains the real seat of the soul, the essence of the person and of life itself. It follows, then, that these disembodied heads carried great wisdom and therefore could act as oracles. In the Celtic tale of Bran the Blessed, Bran is decapitated but his head continues to be able to talk lucidly, and tells his people that he needs to be buried at the White Hill in London; so long as the head remains there then Britain will be protected from invasion. The White Hill is now called Tower Hill.

Heart

Physically, the heart is responsible for keeping the blood flowing around the body at a regular pace. Symbolically, it has come to represent so much more than this simple pump-like action. In the same way that the head represents the wisdom born of knowledge and learning, the heart contains the wisdom of feeling and empathy. The heart is symbolic of compassion, love, and charity.

The heart symbolizes the very center of the being, both physical and spiritual, and has been twinned with the soul since time immemorial—even before the Egyptian "heart-soul" was weighed by Ma'at, the goddess of truth. As the last organ left in the mummy, the ideal heart was meant to be as light as a feather—Ma'at wore the ostrich feather that has equally balanced fronds as a symbol of justice. The heart should not be weighed down by misdeeds or untruths.

This idea of the heart containing the "home" of God is symbolized by the Kabbalistic image of the inverted heart that contains the letters of the Tetragrammaton, the secret name of God.

In Islam, the heart is symbolic of the inner life of a person, of meditation and contemplation. Called the Qalb, in the Sufi Islamic sect the heart represents not only God's mercy but is believed also to contain the essence of God, controlling the physical organs of the body as well as the thought processes.

If we look at the shape of the heart, it's rather like an inverted triangle, and indeed, this is a simplified heart symbol. The heart is also sometimes represented as a chalice or, in ancient Egyptian hieroglyphs, as a vase; in all these instances we see the heart as a receptacle. The heart shape is also similar to the shape of the female pubic mound or the yoni; the cuneiform symbol for woman is heart shaped and is likely to be based on the same body part.

The heart became associated with love relatively recently, in the Middle Ages, and today the stylized heart symbol is synonymous with both the word "love" and the concept, and is most prevalent around the time of St. Valentine's Day on February 14.

Hymen

The Greek word for "veil." In the secret symbolism of the sacred body the hymen refers to the membrane that stretches across the vulva before it is pierced, traditionally, the first time that the female has penetrative sex, with the result that her virginity, or maidenhead, is no more. This physical veil is rent, symbolically, at the wedding when the bride lifts the veil that is part of her bridal attire. The cutting of the cake, too, by the newlyweds is also a symbol of this physical act.

In the Greek Pantheon, Hymenaeus was the god of weddings. He was also a deity of both youth and song, and gives his name to the "hymn," which actually started out as a specific wedding song rather than the generalized religious song that it has come to mean today.

Leg

As the pillars that support the rest of the body, the legs are symbols of strength and stability. Further, because they enable us to get from place to place, effectively removing barriers, they are symbols of communication and of locomotion. When we say that something "has legs" we mean that it is full of potential, and will endure.

The symbol for both the Isle of Man and Sicily, the triskelion of three conjoined legs (also called a Trie Cassyn) is of ancient origin. The symbol appears on fifth-century BC coins from Asia Minor, and appears in connection with the Isle of Man from the thirteenth century onwards. It also appears some 300 years earlier on coins, minted in honor of the Nordic King Analuf, who governed both the Isle of Man and Dublin. Like other triskele forms, these three Manx legs are a solar symbol and, significantly, must always appear to be "running" in a clockwise direction since the reverse is considered a malevolent symbol.

Navel

Leonardo's picture of the perfectly proportioned Vitruvian Man shows the navel as being in the exact center of the picture, and indeed the navel—as the omphalos—represents not only the center of the human body but also the center of the universe. These navel symbols are to be found in various places all around the world, usually in the form of large stones with a domed top, with one of the most famous being at Delphi, center of the worship of Apollo. In India the navel takes the form of the lingam. The navel is the point of contact between the mother and the unborn child and so has sacred significance as the place where spirit and matter meet.

In yogic practice the navel corresponds to the very center of transformational energy and is a point of concentration and meditation, hence the phrase "navel gazing" to mean someone who is lost in thought.

NIPPLE

The nipple has conflicting symbolism; it is an erogenous zone and a sign of sexual arousal but also of motherhood. In some countries the sight of an erect nipple under clothes is considered to be offensive, and in Japan special plasters are stuck over them so that they don't show.

Piercing the nipples, among some tribes, was a sign of strength and virility. In Central America nipples were pierced as a rite of passage, from puberty to manhood. Piercing the nipples as a fashion statement is nothing new: there was a trend for it in the late nineteenth century, and chains would sometimes be stretched between the nipples.

NOSE

The nose is a symbol of intuition; to be able to "sniff something out" or to speak of something that "smells wrong" indicates use of the predictive faculties. Additionally, scents and perfumes are extremely evocative and carry information that can be analyzed only by the nose. This information goes beyond the bounds of language and straight to the part of the brain that stores memories—the oldest and most primitive part.

The nose is also the organ that takes in oxygen and then expels it, and because breathing is a sacred spiritual act, the nose is similarly seen as imbued with spiritual properties.

Several tribes that rely on hunting for survival, including the Yakut in Siberia and the Tungus in the Altai regions, believe that the nose or snout of an animal contains its spirit, because the nose is the instrument of the breath and breath and spirit are closely associated. Therefore the snout would be set aside as a totem, used as a charm to protect homes and possessions.

PHALLUS

The phallus is a symbol of male energy and creativity, and as an extrapolation of the idea of man as being made in the image of God, it's also the symbol of the life-giving principles of the male deity. The phallus is a symbol of resurrection and new life, given the different states of the penis being "asleep" or "awake."

The phallus is symbolized in many forms, most of them obvious although not necessarily erotic. The phallus is essential to life. Trees, towers, standing stones—all have their phallic connotations as symbols of strength, support, and also as the foundation of life and the universe, and the phallus is sometimes referred to as the Tree of Life. The omphalos also has phallic connotations although strictly speaking this is a symbol of the navel as the center of the world.

In ancient Rome, jewelry representing the phallus was believed to give protection against the evil eye. And in Greece, the god Priapus is depicted with an oversized phallus as a mark of his power and virility, giving us the word "priapic."

SEMEN

Semen is symbolic of the seed of potential, not just of new life but also of new ideas and innovations. The Roman physician Galen said that semen actually originated in the brain, and this notion was generally accepted until the Middle Ages.

Because semen contains the very essence of male power and of life itself, it is a potent ingredient in some magical spells. Aleister Crowley, for example, was fond of using his ejaculatory fluid to "charge" certain aspects of his magic(k)al endeavors. Even today, certain practitioners of folk magic will harvest semen—perhaps storing it in the freezer until needed—in the hopes that it will imbue a spell or charm with virile potency.

SKIN

As the outside layer of the body and its largest single organ, the skin is symbolic of protection. We use the terms "thick skinned" or "thin skinned" to mean someone who is either completely insensitive or over-sensitive.

For a shaman, wearing the skin or pelt of an animal will help him absorb the power of the animal itself. It also implies dominance over the animal that had to be hunted in order to get the skin in the first place. Skins of sacred animals are often made into bags to contain certain magical items.

In humans, in less enlightened times than now, differences in skin color resulted in gross misunderstandings and prejudice. Fair skin was regarded as a symbol of wealth since the owner was presumed not to have to subject himself to manual labor; conversely, dark skin carried the opposite meaning.

Soul

Mind, body, and soul: the essential trinity that describes what we are. The soul, though, is a difficult thing to quantify; does it exist outside the physical body, and if so, in what form? The belief in a "ghost" that leaves the body at the moment of its physical death is a concept that transcends religious and cultural belief and is closely linked with the breath as the essence of life. The Latin word *animus*, the Greek

anemos, and the Sanskrit *aniti* all mean "breath" or "air," and refer to the soul, literally, as an animating factor.

That the soul is immortal is also a deeply rooted idea, but there are many different beliefs about it. The soul can somehow be recycled (reincarnation), or else becomes part of a collective "oneness" that is a part of the godhead. Some believe that there is a heaven or a hell that the soul is sent to, depending on its actions during its earthly existence. Others believe that the disembodied soul can somehow haunt the places that it has known while locked into the corporeal body, occupying a sort of parallel universe. Some cultures explain these different aspects of the soul by assuming that each person has several different sorts of spirit; a good example is the Buryat belief. The Buryats are an ethnic Mongolian people who believe that one soul goes to heaven or hell, one remains on Earth as a mischievous spirit, and a third reincarnates in another body.

Birds and winged creatures such as moths or butterflies are believed to contain the soul of a dead person, the wings here symbolizing the idea of transcendence.

Throughout history people have tried to identify the seat of the soul within the body. Once, people believed that it was lodged in the heart. The seventeenth-century philosopher René Descartes placed it squarely in the pineal gland, the small gland in the brain that, among other functions, produces melatonin. In yogic practice and metaphysical belief the pineal gland is associated with the third eye, a mysterious inner eye that can somehow be awakened, resulting in telepathic communication.

That the soul can somehow be bought or sold is an idea that is so old that it is impossible to determine where it first came from. Catholic missionaries used to amass collections of souls that had been "saved." If the soul is sold to the devil, on the other hand, the person loses his shadow and his reflection, both aspects that are linked to the concept of the soul or spirit. To be described as having no soul means that the person is less than human, bereft of passion, emotions, or a conscience.

Spinal column

The backbone of the human body, the spinal column is symbolic of the World Axis and also of the World Tree. In Tantric belief systems, the column of energy that rises up the spinal column through the chakras, symbolized by the great serpent Kundalini, carries the same symbolism as the staff of Asclepius.

The spinal column symbolizes strength, hard work, and moral fiber. The spine also represents the ladder that ascends to the heavens and back down again.

Sweat

At the most practical level, sweat is symbolic of hard work. But on a spiritual level, sweat is imbued with the spirit of its owner and so is considered to be a magical substance, and can be used in spells as an energy charge.

The saunas of northern Europe may have health benefits, but they were originally used as a way to enrich the spirit by ritual purification. The sweat lodge rituals of Native American tribes, too, are carried out as part of a greater ceremony that involves fasting and chanting. Heated rocks in the center of the lodge (which is crammed with as many naked or scantily-clad people as space will allow) have cold water poured over them, generating a considerable amount of steam. The sweat is considered to be an offering to the sun god.

TEETH

A good set of teeth is a sign of youth and health, an attractive attribute, and also a status symbol, which many people spend a lot of money to acquire. Conversely, to lose one's teeth is a sign of old age and decrepitude.

Symbolically, it's said that a smile that shows the teeth originates in the baring of the teeth to warn off a potential enemy. Certainly, to show the teeth in such a way that the lips are curled back is a threatening gesture.

When the milk teeth of children fall out in order to make way for the permanent teeth, these little teeth are "bought" by the fairies in order to assuage the child for the loss. The actual milk tooth itself carried something of the essence of the child and is a potent magical object, which should be hidden lest it fall into the wrong hands. The power of the tooth, which carries the energy of the creature it originally belonged to, is reflected in the teeth that are worn as decoration by warriors. To be "armed to the teeth" means to carry as many weapons as is humanly possible.

The wisdom tooth holds sacred significance. The Irish Druids would perform a spell designed to bring about poetic inspiration by putting the thumb on the wisdom tooth, biting down hard, and then dedicating a song or poem to the gods. Long teeth, too, are regarded as a sign of wisdom, because older people have longer teeth (due to their gums receding), and it is commonly supposed that with age comes wisdom.

TESTICLES

To have "balls," one of the many slang words for testicles, means to be courageous, strong, audacious, and upfront. The testicles are a symbol of potential generations to come since they contain semen. The Latin word *testis* means "little witness" and an oath or "testament" (a word that shares the same root) would be sworn on the testicles as acknowledgement of their vital role, i.e., swearing on the lives of one's (future) children and grand-children.

The Greek for testicle is *orkhis*, and orchid flowers are so named because their shape is similar to that of the organ.

THUMB

The opposable thumb is one of the crucial body parts that separate humans from the rest of the animal kingdom in that it enables us to grasp objects. The thumb is considered to be masculine, and a phallic symbol, and also equates to God; in yogic practice the thumb is associated with the male element of fire.

The thumbs-up symbol, meaning agreement or approval, dates back to the Middle Ages, where two parties reaching an agreement would squeeze their thumbs together; hence the gesture came to be a sign of harmony. Movies about ancient Rome that use the thumbs-up/thumbs-down gesture to save or end the life of the gladiator, however, are likely to be using the gesture spuriously; there is no evidence to show that this signal was used for such a purpose.

The "rule of thumb" refers to a vague measurement, an estimate. The thumb is roughly an inch long so is a useful tool for guesstimation purposes.

VAGINA

There is mystery and ambiguity surrounding the vagina symbol. The word itself comes from the Latin for "sheath" or "scabbard." It represents a gateway or a cave, a place of hidden knowledge and secret treasures. The vagina gives birth to the child, and yet appears to swallow the penis, a fact which has caused it to be a symbol of both fear and desire among men. The "vagina dentata" is the most terrifying representation of all vagina symbols, the toothed vagina that could potentially bite off the penis. This frightening extra feature belongs to the legendary succubus of the Middle East.

The vagina is symbolically represented by the vesica piscis, the sacred gateway through which spirit joins the world of matter, and in essence by the yoni, the Hindu representation of it as the bowl or receptacle from whence springs the male lingam or phallus.

WOMB

As the sacred place where new life is gestated, and therefore the ultimate symbol of the mother, the womb carries powerful symbolic meaning and there are many different representations of it.

The womb is a natural place of safety and security, of dependence, and it is seen as deep, silent, and nurturing. It's a place of contemplation, of spiritual and physical growth, and of potential.

Because the entrance to the womb is cave-like, then the cave in the natural world is also a symbol of the womb, the Earth Mother, and the place where hidden mysteries are kept. Extrapolating further, the temple is the man-made symbol of the womb; no surprise that the Sanskrit word for "temple" is the same as that for "womb."

The Egyptian ankh, the tau cross with the circle on top, could be construed as a womb symbol; it is not only the same shape but also carries connotations of the cycle of life and rebirth. Both the labyrinth and the spiral, too, can be interpreted as secret signs of the womb.

YONI

Although the yoni is effectively a symbol of the vagina, there's a subtle difference in the inference. Vagina comes from a Latin word meaning "sheath," i.e., the receptacle for the penis, whereas yoni is a Sanskrit word meaning "divine passage" or "sacred temple." The child was considered as being born from a yoni of stars, the passage of stars that are effectively the constellations that are in the sky at the time of birth. In Hindu temples, the lingam/yoni is an important symbol of the harmonic balance between the male and female energies.

Part Nine

RITES AND RITUALS, CUSTOMS AND OBSERVANCES

We use certain rites, rituals, customs, and observances to mark key moments in our lives. These tend to split into three categories. First, there are the key events in our own lives, such as being named or getting married. Then there are commemorative events in the history of a people. Finally, there are the events that punctuate the seasons. Many of our customs reflect this universal desire to mark the passage of time and the turning of the Wheel of the Year. The many different ways in which we like to bring light into the darkness of midwinter is a good example of this, such as Christmas for Christians (although this festival has become so popular that it has extended way beyond any boundaries of faith) or the Diwali festival of Indian culture. It's interesting to see how aspects of these seasonal festivals change as the religion varies, although the fundamental reason behind them remains largely unaltered.

BIRTHDAY

The actual day of a birthday is believed to have a bearing on the characteristics and prospects of a person, because of the astrological sign and numerology associated with it. The phrase "many happy returns" refers to the return of the sun into the planetary house it occupied on the original day of birth.

Certain ages are marked with some sort of rite of passage, although some of these "special" birthdays tend to be a movable feast and can vary in different places. For example, in the West the twenty-first birthday used to signify the "age of majority" or adulthood; this has since been changed to eighteen. In many Asian countries, the fourteenth birthday is the day on which the child symbolically becomes an adult. This logically ties in with puberty.

In the West, people optimistically suppose that "life begins at forty," whereas in Japan the fortieth birthday is called *shoro*, meaning "the beginning of old age," since this was the age that Confucius ceased his traveling. However, the Japanese forty-year-old need not be filled with gloom for long; he can look forward to his sixty-first birthday, called *kanreki*, marking the completion of a sixty-year cycle. Therefore the lucky sixty-one-year-old Japanese birthday boy or girl wears a red kimono and matching hat and is "new born" on this day.

CHRISTMAS

To understand the true meaning of the festival we now call Christmas we need to delve back into the mists of antiquity.

Once, December 25 was the day on which people celebrated the birthday of the Phrygian sun god, Attis. He was venerated far and wide, and was said to have been born in the country that is now Turkey. However, Attis was superseded by another god, with an uncannily familiar life story. This new god was born on the same day as Attis, in impoverished circumstances, to a virgin mother. He died, and was subsequently resurrected. The tenets of his faith included the notion of a brotherhood of man and the promise of eternal life in return for adherence to a pure moral code. This faith proved very popular among Roman soldiers, who spread the word even further into Europe during the course of their campaigns.

So, this new god must have been Christ? Wrong. It was Mithras.

In Mithraism, December 25 was called *Dies Natali Invicti Solis*, "The Birthday of the Unconquered Sun." It seems as though the need to inject a little brightness and cheer into the darkest time of the year, when the wheel of time carries us through the winter solstice, is symbolically more important than any of the divine beings that have successively blown out their birthday cake candles at this time. The Birthday of the Unconquered Sun is really the most apt description for what has come to be known as Christmas.

Despite meaning "Christ's Mass," this holiday is celebrated all over the world whether people are Christian or not. December 25 is for most the zenith of the festivities, although the change from the Julian to the Gregorian calendar has resulted in a 14-day anomaly, and for some January 6 is the "true" Christmas.

Prior to Christianity the Anglo-Saxons called this generic mid-winter festival *geol*, the precursor to Yule, a name still used by those who might wish to distance themselves, or the festival, from any Christian connotations. Some of the customs of *geol* still prevail, most notably the Yule Log. Although its appearance these days is more likely to be a log-shaped cake covered in plastic holly and lopsided robins, the original was more imposing. It was a gargantuan chunk of a tree, which had to be found rather than chopped down. This tree was then dragged to the largest fireplace in the area where it burned for the duration of the festivities, a symbol of light and heat in the darkness and a welcome reminder of the sun. The Yule candle signified the same thing. Like the log, the bumper size of the candle was important because it needed to burn for a long time. Christian churches adopted this tradition, too, using giant candles that towered over the congregation as a symbol of spiritual illumin-

ation. Today, the largesse of this mammoth torch has shrunk down into the Advent candle, marked into 24 neat segments that burn politely from December 1 onward.

As well as emulating earlier Anglo-Saxon traditions, Christmas revelries owe a great debt to the Roman festival of the Saturnalia. This was the time that Saturn, the god of time, was loosened from his shackles, gifts were exchanged, and the world turned upside down as servants and masters swapped places, a quaint custom adopted as the Lords of Misrule. Saturn effectively reappears again in the starring role of Father Christmas, benevolent dispenser of gifts to all and sundry but to children in particular. He pops up again at New Year as Old Father Time, looking old, care-worn and surprisingly skinny despite the excess of mince pies and sherry, dressed in sack-cloth and carrying a sickle.

The enthusiasm for Christmas celebrations waned from the period of the Reformation, due in no small part to the puritanical Church authorities frowning on their excesses as being "papist." Christmas was actually banned in England in 1647, and though there were areas of defiance, the celebrations dwindled. Hard to imagine now, but by the early nineteenth century there was a very real possibility that the festivities might be forgotten entirely. However, they were revived by Charles Dickens, whose story *A Christmas Carol* is still considered by many to be the very epitome of the Christmas message; a concentration on goodwill to all men, a time for families, and generosity of spirit.

Despite a general (although sometimes uneasy) tolerance toward the liberal sprinkling of pagan practices that encrust what's loosely accepted as the birthday of Jesus, many churches have managed to overlay the heathen symbolism of the festival with Christian values, no mean feat considering they hijacked the heathen celebrations in the first place. The practice of bringing greenery into the house is a good example. The holly tree not only provides a home to nature spirits, but its prickly leaves are also phallic symbols of fertility. However, holly also symbolizes the crown of thorns worn by Christ at his crucifixion; the red berries, his blood. A cup made of ivy is said to prevent drunkenness, hence its association with Bacchus, an influential deity during the gluttony and largesse of the Saturnalia, but these links seem largely to be overlooked by the Church. Mistletoe, however, with its overt sexual symbolism (the berries look like semen and of course it's traditional to kiss underneath hanging sprigs of the plant) has pagan roots so powerful that it still manages to resist Christianization, and so is still banned in many churches. The Christmas tree itself originated in mainland Europe, a way of venerating the spirit of the World Tree by bringing it into the home and decorating it. Although German enclaves in the UK already had their decorated trees, when Prince Albert, consort of Queen Victoria, brought one into the royal household then the custom really took off. Purist Christians excuse the tree by turning it into a symbol of the cross, or "tree," that Christ died upon.

Sharing food is an important focus of the Christmas celebrations. What's on offer for dinner alters according to the dictates of fashion and availability, but meat tends to figure prominently on the menu. The early mince pie contained meat, unlike today's mixture of vine fruits and spices, and they were shaped like the manger that Christ was laid in, sometimes with a pastry baby on the top. The traditional cannonball-shaped Christmas pudding, however, is a relatively recent tradition, adapted in the seventeenth century from a thick plum porridge. The pudding, traditionally, should be made from thirteen ingredients, one for each of the apostles and one for Jesus. The practice of putting charms and trinkets into the Christmas pudding might be dying out, but the charms that people tried not to break their teeth on used to have a specific symbolism of their own. These traditional bibelots included a boot, a bell, the thimble, a ring, a wishbone, button and horseshoe, as well as the silver sixpence. The boot signified travel, the thimble a happy but single life, and the ring, marriage.

DEATH

Although people may never again aspire to the immensely elaborate funeral preparations of the ancient Egyptians, whose obsession with the idea of the afterlife informed much of their culture, the disposal of the body of a dead person is, nevertheless, an important rite of passage. Arguably, any funeral preparations and rituals are carried out as much to comfort the living than as a guaranteed assurance of any great certainty about anything that might follow.

Ultimately, the body is the symbol of the person that remains behind after the spark of life has left it. As such, the ritual of its disposal is an important part of human life, a sign of respect for the body, effectively the grail that contains our spirit. These rituals tell us a lot about the philosophies of the people that take part in them.

Thinking about what must follow the physical death of the body has preoccupied us since the dawn of time, a longing for something "else" that caused Paleolithic people to daub their corpses in red ocher in the fervent hopes that the color alone, the same as the life-giving blood, would somehow restore life or bring back the soul. Famously, the Egyptians buried their dead with everything they might need in the next life; who can say that they were deluded? People who subscribe to the idea of former lives often seem to have enjoyed an episode as an ancient Egyptian.

Opinions about what happens after death differ widely. Cultural and religious ideals don't give any answers either, since the tenets of any single faith can exist on different levels according to the sensibilities of the individual. A fundamentalist Christian, for example, might believe in a heaven that belongs to a virtuous soul and is "up there," and a hell belonging to the lower regions that an "evil" one will be dispatched to. However, such a simplistic idea leads to profound metaphysical problems as to the nature of good and evil in a faith system in which a fundamentally benevolent deity is believed to have created everything in the first place. It's also interesting to note that reincarnation of some sort was the generally accepted belief in most countries of the world prior to the coming of Christianity, whose idea of a punishment/reward system could be used as a political tool.

But what of the rites that accompany death? The way that bodies are disposed of often has an underlying practical nature that has as much to do with topography and climate as any deeper meaning. Burial, possibly one of the most popular forms, dates back 200,000 years and remains of burial mounds appear all over the world. Cremation, or disposal by flames, is the preferred method in India and Japan. Some burial methods prefer to preserve the corpse for as long as possible, using elaborate and highly secure coffins, whereas others, such as those of orthodox Jews and Muslims, prefer that the process of decomposition happens as quickly

as possible, the body being wrapped in a simple shroud. In common with the ancient Egyptians, some bodies are buried alongside possessions that the owner enjoyed in real life, and as archaeological finds these objects have given us a great deal of insight into the lifestyles and interests of our ancestors.

However, what future archaeologists might make of such eccentric burials as that of Mad Jack Fuller, buried in a 25-foot-high pyramid in the grounds of the village church in Sussex, England, is anybody's guess. Jack is allegedly clothed in full evening dress, seated at a table with a roast chicken and a bottle of claret, the floor around him covered in shards of broken glass to stop evil spirits from stealing his dinner.

The positioning of Jack's corpse might be unconventional, but most Christian burials see the corpse flat on its back, arms crossed over the chest, oriented east–west to emulate the layout of a church. Muslims are buried with the face turned towards Mecca, and in some ancient cultures warriors were buried upright, presumably to show their readiness to do battle, even in death. Suicides were sometimes buried upside down, as a continuance of punishment; perhaps losing the mortal soul was not considered pain enough. A further punishment for society's deceased miscreants was to be buried in unconsecrated ground, itself symbolic of being outside conventional society that somehow made the soul vulnerable, since the body was laid to rest outside the safe confines of Church-approved earth. The corpses of souls that might be prone to restive activity in the afterlife were buried at crossroads, to confuse them.

Arguably one of the most exotic and dramatic ways of disposing of a body is in the ritual of the sky burial. Believed to have been practiced initially by the Zoroastrians and once common in Tibet, here the corpse is left to the elements, often on high places such as specially constructed buildings called Towers of Silence. Sometimes, the corpse is carefully dismembered and thrown to the vultures, considered birds of rebirth. The body here is thought to be simply an empty vessel, nothing to do with the soul that has departed. The custom of the sky burial is itself dying, though, because of the vast expense of the ritual.

One of the universal rituals that follow a funeral, no matter what faith or culture, is for the living to enjoy some sort of feast afterwards. This is not only a celebration of life, but harks back to the ancient practice of sin-eating. This is where the transgressions of the departed person are "eaten" by the guests at the funeral, thereby allowing the soul to rise, unencumbered, to heaven. In fact, as recently as the nineteenth century there were still "professional" sin-eaters in the UK, likely to be an impoverished and starving person, who would eat the bread and ale passed to him over the corpse, and accept a coin. These actions symbolically transferred the sins of the dead person to the sin-eater.

The idea of death in general, rather than of human death in particular, is celebrated in different ways around the world. The old Celtic festival of Samhain, which falls at the end of October when the new moon is closest to earth and therefore the veil between the worlds is perceived to be at its thinnest, is these days more popularly celebrated as Halloween, and tallies with Walpurgisnacht in northern Europe. The Mexican Day of the Dead, held at the same time of the year, is one of the more colorful expressions of death, with gaudy skeletons cavorting in the streets, death-head candies, music and dancing, and a great deal of revelry.

EASTER

Although Easter is one of the most significant festivals in the Christian calendar, more often than not the religious side is overlooked in favor of a more secular celebration. Moreover, some of the symbols of Easter are distinctly at odds with one another. How does a chocolate bunny, for example, have anything to do with the resurrection of Christ? The fact is that the Easter celebrations are an interesting amalgamation of the old pagan celebration of spring and fertility, the Passover, and the death and subsequent resurrection of Christ.

Most countries in the world that follow Christian traditions use a word for Easter that is based on the same word as for the Passover, Pesach, from the Paschal Lamb that was sacrificed at this time; only in Britain, Germany, and in some of the Slavic territories is this not the case. It's possible the Last Supper that Christ shared with his disciples was in fact a Passover meal. The Paschal Lamb, with its halo and banner, is also symbolic of Jesus Christ, who like the lamb was sacrificed to the greater good. Lambs, of course, are first seen gamboling around the fields in the spring, so no symbolic anomalies there.

The timing of Easter varies from year to year. Easter Sunday, the main focus of the event that celebrates the Crucifixion and Resurrection of Christ, falls on the first Sunday after the full moon following the vernal equinox on March 21. And so Easter can either be "late" or "early," and the date can vary anytime between March 22 and April 25.

Eostre, or Ostara, was a pagan goddess of spring and fertility, celebrated around the time of the spring equinox. Because rebirth is a recurrent motif in many pagan religions, the death and resurrection of Christ slotted nicely into an already-existing theme. Eostre is the root of the word estrogen, the female hormone, and the egg, as a powerful symbol of potential new life, is celebrated at Easter in the chocolate eggs given to children. The Easter celebrations take place over three days, the first of which is Good Friday. Preceding Easter is Lent, a forty-day period of abstinence and fasting. After such abstinence, chocolate eggs are a welcome reward.

FASTING

The Bible, the Qu'ran, the Upanishads, and the Mahabharata all advocate fasting, and indeed, most faiths embrace the ritual as part of a spiritual discipline. This is possibly due, in no small part, to the fact that not eating can induce hallucinations and a feeling of light-headedness akin to religious ecstasy. Fasting, too, is a shamanic practice, undertaken to help initiates communicate with the spirit realms. Some people claim that fasting is as good for the body as it is for the spirit and advocate an annual "detox" that may have perceived spiritual benefits. It may be that our ancestors also felt that giving the body a rest from heavy foods was beneficial.

The strictures regarding what does and does not constitute a fast are, to pardon the pun, something of a moveable feast. For example, some Roman Catholics might say that fasting involves refusing everything except water; others will see it as abstinence from meat, or they might eat just one solid meal per day. Eating fish rather than meat on Fridays is a fast. There's a very rigorous form of fasting peculiar to the Catholic Church, called a Black Fast. This entails eating just one small meal a day and abstaining from all animal products, including dairy. However, this severe form of fasting could also be used by less scrupulous people as a spell to curse

enemies. One Mabel Brigge was even executed in 1538 for "performing" a Black Fast against Henry VIII and the Duke of Norfolk, which signals the power of such a seemingly simple action that can have devastating consequences: refusing to eat.

HALLOWEEN

Halloween is the abbreviated term for All Hallows Eve, the day before All Saints Day. This was the Church's attempt to associate their own saints with the time of the pagan spirits. Today it is personified by the image of the witch, abroad at night on her broomstick with her black cat perched alongside. Witches can also make boats from undamaged eggshell halves, apparently, and so are sometimes seen abroad on the seas using this unusual method of transport.

Every country around the world celebrates its dead in some way. Halloween is one of these celebrations. Effectively it's a Christian hijacking of the older Samhain festival, one of the festivals that form the eight-spoked Wheel of the Year in the pre-Christian Celtic world, the cross-quarter day that marked the feast of the dead. A night of the living dead is celebrated in all parts of the world at about the same time, a symbol of the end of the harvest, the "closing down" of the year, and a time of death. It was the traditional time when the animals were brought in for the winter, and so it seemed appropriate to welcome the dead back, too. Bonfires were lit at this time in order to guide the dead back to the world of the living, and bells were rung.

This is the time of year when the veil between the worlds of the living and the dead is at its thinnest, the ancestors are honored and their spirits are believed to be able to communicate with the living more easily now than at any other time. Divination, in the form of necromancy, séances, etc., is likely to be more effective now than at any other time too. There are certain rituals that guarantee entry into the other world. One of these is to find a tumulus or similar place that has fairy associations, and run nine times around it.

Kiss

A kiss can be a symbol of erotic love, or a symbol of union. The Romans defined three different types of kiss: the *osculum*, or the kiss on the cheek; the *basium*, or the kiss on the lips; and the *suavium*, the deep involved kiss, or colloquially the "snog," of lovers. To kiss someone means to mingle not only saliva but also breath, which itself is akin to the spirit of life. It's no coincidence that immediately after the marriage vows are taken, the celebrant tells the bride and groom that they can kiss. The mingling of their breath symbolizes the fact that the couple breathe the same air, a sign of the union of their marriage in a physical and spiritual sense.

Kissing the ground is a sign of affection toward, and union with, a territory. In Christian services, the Kiss of Peace is a sign of recognition that might take the form of a kiss or a handshake. Kissing the feet is a sign of respect and obeisance.

Kisses can be used as a symbol of greeting, or alternatively used to say goodbye. Kissing a religious icon shows loyalty and respect; kisses are also used for good luck, for example, the gambler who might kiss the dice before throwing them.

In the Bible, the kiss that Judas gives Christ is a sign of betrayal, immortalized as the Judas Kiss. The kiss of death means the final blow, an action that can destroy something or bring it to the end.

In the Harry Potter books, this is the name given to the terrible spell cast by the Dementors, who kill their victims by sucking their souls out of their mouths.

The kiss of the Mafia, sinisterly, means death, and the kiss of the devil means eternal damnation.

Marriage

Marriage, in the greater scheme of things and particularly in alchemy, can represent the union of two opposing principles, primarily those of male and female. For Christians, the marriage of a man and a woman also symbolizes the union of the believer with the Church.

This idea, that a marriage can signify the union of a human being with his or her God, is extant in many different cultures. The Catholic nun is called a "Bride of Christ." In the ancient cultures of Greece, India, and East Asia, temples were dedicated to the practice of sacred prostitution, part of an antique fertility ritual wherein sexual intercourse, a "sacred marriage," was practiced for a religious purpose. In Hebrew, the word for "harlot" originally meant the same as "shrine prostitute," effectively, a holy woman. Times have changed.

These days, a wedding between a man and a woman is packed with symbolism, some of which is sacred, some more saucily secular. The veil worn by the bride, lifted by the groom, not only symbolizes the removal of her virginity but her introduction to a new state of being. The shared cutting of the cake, the knife held by both bride and groom, is another phallic allusion. The wedding ring is a symbol of eternity.

In neo-pagan wedding ceremonies, such as the handfasting, the symbolism of tying the hands together speaks for itself.

Naming

A name carries with it great magical power, since the word itself contains the essence of the person it belongs to. Therefore, the naming ceremony is an important rite of passage everywhere in the world, whether it is viewed as religious or secular; effectively, a name is an identifying symbol that someone will carry about with them, generally, for the rest of their lives.

There's a general superstition that a child without a name is somehow vulnerable, susceptible to being kidnapped by the fairy folk or similarly mischievous spirits. This is because the name is also a part of the soul, and therefore to have no name is somehow to have no soul either.

The Hindu naming ceremony is one of the most important rite of passage ceremonies. It's usual for the numerology of the child's name to be carefully calculated to harmonize with its date of birth.

Naming ceremonies that happen later in life—as in the Catholic confirmation ceremony—mark a deeper allegiance to the faith by the addition of a name that has meaning to the faith. The confirmation ceremony is just that; the candidate confirms the promises that were made by his parents or guardians at the time of the first naming ceremony (usually called a Christening within the Christian Church). People who join other faiths or cults later in life might undergo a renaming ceremony, as a way of wiping out the old personality in favor of the new one.

It's not just humans who have names. The naming of a boat is considered to be very important, too, since the vessel will be responsible for the safety of its occupants. In particular, the renaming of a boat can be fraught with danger, as to change its name risks incurring the immediate displeasure of the gods of the elements.

VALENTINE'S DAY

The original Valentine was an amalgamation of two or three different men, all named Valentine, and all martyred to the Christian cause; one of them was either martyred or buried in Rome on February 14. However, a certain amount of "spin" was necessary to make St. Valentine fit convincingly as a replacement for the existing pre-Christian Lupercalian excesses. A story was put about that Valentine defied Emperor Claudius's decree that fighting men should not have sexual relations in case their strength was sapped. The emperor was not in favor of the new religion and to be a Christian at this time was hazardous to the health, but Valentine continued to proselytize despite the sentence of death that hung over the heads of anyone caught doing so. Later, he presided over illicit Christian weddings. According to another legend, prior to his execution, he fell in love with the jailer's daughter and left her a note with the words "from your Valentine" written on it.

Part of the Lupercalian festivities included the young men drawing lots for available young women; these couples then spent time together during the festival, with sex the main agenda. The Church invented a lottery, too, although it was a slightly tamer version. People pulled the names of various Christian saints out of the hat, and then attempted to emulate these worthies for the rest of the year. Understandably, this custom failed to excite people's imaginations as much as its saucier forerunner and drawing lots to put couples together started again in the fifteenth century, a sort of medieval version of speed dating, except faster, although its intentions were supposedly more innocent than those of the Lupercalia. Despite this, it proved very difficult to suppress the memory of the Lupercalia, and today the Church rarely celebrates St. Valentine. However, as a secular celebration of love and romance Valentine's Day is a great success. The heart, as the major symbol of love, is seen everywhere at this time.

WHEEL OF THE YEAR

Reference is frequently made to the Wheel of the Year, particularly among Druid, Wiccan, and other neo-pagan groups. Effectively, the Wheel of the Year is the name given to the continual cycle of festivals that take place during the course of the year.

The symbolism of the wheel reflects perfectly the cyclical movement of the seasons and the orbits of the stars and planets. The seasons of human life are reflected in the same way, its key events corresponding to the changing seasons.

The names of some of these eight festivals vary according to the tradition, although all mark key moments in the year. Also, the festivals have been adapted to encompass, for example, Christian beliefs, but generally the spirit and substance of them remains relatively unchanged. It's interesting to see how the same conceptual marking of time takes different forms wherever people happen to be around the world marking the planting and harvesting of the crops, the solstices, and the equinoxes.

Here, then, is a Wheel of the Year drawing some parallels between the ancient festivals and the newer Christianized interpretations of them.

* * *

* ✳ *

Month	Festival	Faith	Meaning
February 2	Imbolc Candlemas	Druid/Wicca Christian	For the Scots, the ancient start of the year; new beginnings
March 20/23	Ostara Alban Eiler Easter	Wiccan Druid Christian	Spring equinox Death and resurrection of Christ (a movable feast, sometimes held in April)
May 1	Beltane	Druid/ Wiccan	Blossoming, fertility
June 21	Midsummer solstice Alban Heruin	Wiccan Druid	Height and midpoint of year
August 1	Lughnasadh Lammas	Druid/Wiccan Christian	Marriage, harvest, sacrifice, baking of the first loaf
Sept 23	Mabon Alban Eleud	Wiccan Druid	Autumn equinox
Oct 31	Samhain All Hallows Eve	Wiccan/Druid Christian	Union of the two worlds, death
Dec 21	Yule Alban Christmas	Wiccan/ Druid Christian	Winter solstice, the turning of the year, death and birth of the sun, birth of Christ

* ✳ *

The Encyclopedia of Secret Signs and Symbols

Part Ten

THE NATURE OF THE DIVINE

THE ULTIMATE SYMBOLIC EXPRESSION OF HUMAN POTENTIAL

Putting aside the notion of a single supreme being for the moment, it seems logical to suppose that the vast pantheon of gods and goddesses from all cultures and societies are an extrapolation of human potential, yet another way that we've discovered of defining the universe and our place in it, projecting our own qualities into the sky and the landscape around us, and amplifying these qualities into divine beings.

When we consider how much time our ancestors must have spent gazing up at the heavens, it's not really surprising that many of our gods and goddesses emanate from the sky. All the planets of our solar system have the souls of the immortal personages that share their names. Other aspects of the natural world are deified, too. Animistic religions believe that every tree, rock, mountain,

and body of water has its presiding spirit. Many of these old gods were absorbed into the Christian faith as saints, since a multitude of different gods were at odds with their one jealous God. The ones that were impossible to absorb were, quite literally, demonized, turned into malevolent, ungodly beings. Pan, for example, the powerful nature god venerated for thousands of years, bears a distinct resemblance to the devil.

Our gods represent archetypes and work on two levels. They not only manifest inside us, but we also project ourselves onto them as external phenomena. In the movie *Castaway*, Tom Hanks's character, Chuck Noland, stranded on an island, finds a volleyball in a box, and after an accident in which Chuck cuts his hand, the imprint of the blood forms a "face" on the ball. The volleyball becomes an

The Encyclopedia of Secret Signs and Symbols

531

icon, personalized with a character that is even able to "remind" Chuck of the whereabouts of a coil of rope. Our ancestors similarly projected characters and thoughts onto the effigies of their gods.

The adventures and escapades of many of our deities read like the biographies of cartoon super-heroes. They walk on water, they fly, they hurl thunderbolts about in the heavens, they can shape-shift into animals and birds. It's notable, too, that the qualities of the gods repeat themselves in characters from different cultures. The great multi-talented divinity that the ancient Egyptians called Thoth, for example, appears in the Celtic myths as Lugh, in Greek mythology as Hermes, and as Mercury for the Romans.

Many deities have jurisdiction over the elements and the weather as well as features of human endeavor that have a life-or-death element, such as fishing, the hunt, or the harvest. Therefore, it was important to keep these beings happy, something that was achieved by ritual obeisance and sacrifices. Let's go back to the sticky subject of that supreme being. Overriding all these divine superpowers is the idea, for many, of a universal spirit, a pervading life force that we are all a part of and that is a part of us. For the purpose of argument, we'll call it the Thing. The problem starts when we start to give the Thing a name, because then the very Thing that cannot be compartmentalized becomes segregated by the nuances of language, even ascribed a sex as either "male" or "female," mother or father. The idea is that the Thing is beyond personification, and yet we personify it and put words into its mouth; in the Book of Exodus, God is quoted as saying "I am that I am."

Yet we constantly find references to a nameless god. The Celtiberians, who lived in north-central Spain and northern Portugal both before and during the time of the Roman Empire, went out every full moon and danced in front of their doors in homage to this nameless god. Like the Celtiberians, the Aztecs also worshipped a god that was so powerful as to be beyond having a name that we could comprehend. Inasmuch as names carry great power, the fact that there are either many names of God, or none at all, is a reminder of the paradoxical nature of a concept that wordy descriptions only serve to confuse even further.

There is no need for there to be a massive divide between the worshippers of many gods, and those who believe that only one god should be venerated. In the Hindu pantheon, for example, it is very clear that the many gods of this faith are separate aspects of the One; all parts of a mosaic that reveal the bigger picture to the observer who is able to stand back far enough to see it. Essentially, worshippers of more than one god fall into the category of pagans, a word whose origins are quite innocuous, coming from the Latin *paganus*, meaning "villager" or "rustic."

THE TRIPLE GODDESS

Pagans, Wiccans, and New Age affiliates often refer to the Triple Goddess, but what exactly does this mean? The idea is ancient, appearing in translations of Egyptian magical papyri, but was really popularized after the publication of Robert Graves's *The White Goddess* at the end of the 1940s.

It's not uncommon for the goddess to appear as a triad. The Fates of Greek myth and the Norns of Norse legend fall into the category. Alternatively, one deity can appear in three aspects; perhaps the best-known example is the goddess Hecate, who appears as maiden, mother, and crone. Selene, the moon goddess, appears in three aspects that reflect the phases of the moon: new, waxing/waning, and full. You might think that should count as four aspects of the moon, but the waxing/waning part counts as one because it is the idea of change, as opposed to the seeming stasis at either end of this process. The moon is seen to be a female energy exactly because of this mutable nature.

The ancient origins of this threefold idea are reflected in the triple aspect of the Christian male deity, the Father, the Son and the Holy Ghost.

THE AMERICAS

AZTEC DEITIES

Huitzilopochtli

Coatlicue

In a similar way to Native American gods, the major Mexican gods belonged to the directions; their domiciles were in the four quarters. In the north lived Tezcatlipoca, in the south Huitzilopochtli, in the east Tlaloc, and in the west, Quetzalcoatl.

The most important of these gods, arguably, was Huitzilopochtli, the great warrior god whose name meant "The Hummingbird that Comes from the South," or "from the Left," a euphemism for the underworld, and associated with the element of fire. His ferocity meant that he was the subject of much worship; the figure of a giant hummingbird appears in the figures of the Nazca Lines. This god was born fully armed and immediately avenged all those who had believed that his mother, Coatlicue, had become pregnant by dishonorable means; in fact, Coatlicue, like the Virgin Mary, was extremely pious. One day while she was sweeping the temple, an archetypal symbolic "message from the gods" fell on her head in the form of a small bundle of hummingbird feathers, and shortly afterwards she realized that she was expecting a child, its divine provenance assured.

Coatlicue herself is an important personage within the Aztec pantheon. Her name means "Mother of the Gods," a fitting title for a goddess that gave birth to the stars and the moon. Wearing a skirt made of serpents and a necklace of human hearts and skulls that she might have borrowed from Kali, the great Indian deity, Coatlicue is the great earth goddess who, again like Kali, is the creator as well as the destroyer.

The three other gods of the elements and directions have equally exotic stories. The northern god, Tezcatlipoca, was the sun god, the positive aspect of whom was that he ripened the harvest, the negative that he also brought drought. Appropriately, Tezcatlipoca sometimes appeared as a shadow or as a jaguar. At night, he stalked the earth in a gray cloak.

Tlaloc, the eastern god, governed the mountains and water in all its forms. He watered the earth with four vast jugs of liquid, and each of these jugs symbolized the different aspect of the seasons: growth, blight, frost, and destruction. Tlaloc was the deity to whom most sacrifices were made. Horrifically, babies were purchased in order to be killed in his honor. The babies were cooked and eaten by the priests. The more the babies and children wept, the better the sacrifice was considered to be.

The western god, Quetzalcoatl, is personified as a snake/bird and, like the Greek god Hermes, has many talents. He was patron of every art and craft and the inventor of metalworking, a civilizing influence on humankind. Quetzalcoatl decided to leave his people, driven out by other gods. He burned his house and hid his treasure and headed east into the rising sun, promising to return. When the Spanish invaders appeared in the Aztec lands, wearing glittering breastplates, they were hailed as the returning Quetzalcoatl and the emperor Montezuma welcomed them with gifts. One of these gifts included the famous snake mask, made of precious turquoises.

INCA/PERUVIAN DEITIES

Prior to their conquest by the Incas, the Peruvians of ancient times had a totemistic religion, worshipping animals, plants, and stones whose names they also took. This animal worship even extended so far as to suppose that animals were their godlike ancestors. Their protective spirits were called *huacas*.

The Incas brought with them a worship of the sun that replaced the earlier totemistic beliefs. The sun god, Apu Puncha ("Head of the Day") was the ancestor of all Incas, and had a human form with a flaming golden halo. The moon goddess, Mama Quilla, was the wife of Apu Puncha. Like her husband, she was represented as a human figure with a silver halo, like moonbeams. Her main role was as the protector of married women.

Other heavenly divinities that surrounded the sun god and the moon goddess were the rainbow, Cuycha, and Catequil, the deity of thunder and lightning, his sling and mace echoing the traditional weapons of storm gods. Children were sacrificed to Catequil and twins were venerated, believed to belong to him.

In contrast to other cultures, the planet Venus was personified as a masculine deity, advisor to the sun and the protector of girls and the moon goddess. All the other planets were the handmaidens of Mama Quilla. The Pleiades was the most respected constellation since it was the great crop-protector.

The earth was personified as the Great Mother, Pachamama; so no difference here from many other belief systems.

NATIVE AMERICAN DEITIES

Manitou

It is not possible, here, to take more than a cursory glance at some of the deities that belong to some of the many Native American peoples. However, there are over-arching tenets that seem, largely, to apply to all tribes.

One of these notions is that of a universal presence, a sexless all-pervasiveness that is similar to the One God or Brahman in Hindu belief. Called the Great Spirit, this largely benevolent supreme being governs the Happy Hunting Grounds, a place similar to the Christian concept of heaven. Indeed, the underlying idea of the

Great Spirit meant that the notion of a single, paternal Christian God sat quite comfortably with many tribespeople. There is even a legend of the Great Spirit's gift of a set of inscribed stone tablets similar to those given by God to Moses.

Native American beliefs are essentially animistic; that is, they believe that every aspect of the natural world has its own spirit, sometimes called the Manitou. Totem poles are the personification of this idea. A key idea, for the Hopi and Pueblo, is the existence of Kachina, the "life bringer." A Kachina can be a physical object or being as well as a conceptual idea of a "life bringer." A Kachina has its own spirit; a poor analogy would be to say that the "Christmas Spirit" is a kind of Kachina. Kachinas are honored with dolls that are used to explain the concept to children, in songs and dances, and are personified as Kachina masks.

Here is a brief look at some of the deities of the Native American pantheon.

Iyatiku is a corn goddess of the Pueblos. Like Demeter she emerges from the underworld, the place from which all of humankind is also born, underlining her aspect as an icon of fertility. The food that she provides sprouts from pieces of her heart that she plants across all four quarters of the world. As befits a mother goddess, a cave or cavern is included among the symbols that represent her.

Muut belongs to the Cahuilla culture, and is the goddess of death, personified as an owl. The Cahuilla saw death as simply a necessary part of life; as such Muut is a benevolent deity who guides souls into the afterlife.

Originally a deity of the ancient Hopi Indians, Kokopeli is a fertility god, encompassing the very embodiment of the creative force. He's portrayed as a dancing, shock-headed figure. Earlier, less sanitized versions of Kokopeli portray him with a prominent phallus, symbol of the male creative force that is echoed in the flute that he plays. Sometimes feared by young girls because of the babies he distributes from the sack on his back, Kokopeli similarly organizes the reproduction of animals, in particular those that are hunted.

The magical power of Kokopeli's musical abilities is renowned. With his flute, he can chase away the winter and herald the spring, as well as calling on the fructifying rains. He has been around for a long time—the first effigies of Kokopeli date back to AD 1000. Recently, he has enjoyed a resurgence in popularity, dancing his way across T-shirts, baseball caps, and other souvenirs of Native Americana.

The Horned Serpent, which goes under numerous other names, is a key god in Native American mythologies, venerated in the landscape at the Serpent Mound, for example, as well as in innumerable pieces of rock art and cave paintings.

CELTIC DIVINITIES

What we know of Celtic beliefs comes down to us from written accounts preserved since the Middle Ages, and in some of the descriptions of the Romans who invaded the Celtic territories. The landscape of the Celts extended through a large area and included parts of Spain and France as well as southern Britain, including, of course, Ireland and Wales. This Celtic landscape is still liberally sprinkled with evidence of the old beliefs; their earthworks and burial mounds are significant symbols in the landscape themselves. The horned god, Cernunnos, is a major Celtic divinity, as is Dagda.

DAGDA

Dagda, a deity from Ireland, was the father of all the gods, written about in the stories of the Tuatha de Danaan, "The People of the Goddess Dana." Dagda was not one of the most attractive gods; he appears ugly and pot-bellied, wearing the rough clothes and rude sandals of the peasant. Dagda carries a club so colossal that it drags along the ground, making furrows and dykes. Dagda's other great tool was a magical cauldron that never emptied; this cauldron appears time and time again in myths, and one of its symbolic meanings is of eternal life. Dagda is a fertility god, and in common with other gods had to undergo a challenge. His was a curious one. He had to eat a vast quantity of porridge that appeared in a crater. This happened on November 1, the time of the greatest feasts of the year, the old New Year that coincides with Halloween or Samhain. One of Dagda's more attractive skills was as a harpist, the beautiful tunes he plays orchestrating the turnings of the seasons.

HORNED GOD

There are several different interpretations of the symbol for the horned god, one of the better-known being the "upside down" pentacle. The uppermost two points do look a little like horns. The manifestations of this ancient deity are many: Cernunnos in Celtic tales, the Greek god Pan, the Egyptian Aamon. With the coming of Christianity, the old pagan horned gods were lent a more sinister image than their previous reputation as the male aspect of the nature god. The horned god was turned into the devil.

LUGH

One of the major Celtic gods, when Lugh asked to become a member of the celestial elite called the Tuatha de Danaan he was asked what skill he could contribute. When he replied that he was a carpenter, the response was there was a carpenter already. Therefore, Lugh volunteered his services as a smith; again, the Tuatha already had someone with this skill. However, the persistent Lugh put all his cards on the table and offered his talents as a warrior, harpist, historian, poet, and sorcerer, all skills that underline the multi-talented nature of this god. In this, Lugh has close parallels with Mercury/Hermes/Thoth. There was no single person in the Tuatha with all these skills, so Lugh was admitted.

A more advanced and sophisticated god than Dagda, he had more elegant tools than the other god's giant club. Lugh had a spear and a sling. Lugh was a god of light, a solar deity whose immortality has been assured in place names such as Lewes, on the south coast of Britain, and even in England's capital city London. Lyons and Loudon in France, and Leiden in the Netherlands, also show the importance of the god. Lugh is honored with the festival of Lughnasadh at the beginning of August, which later became absorbed into Christianity as Lammas. Lughnasadh marked the beginning of the harvest, a time for weddings and handfastings. In modern Irish, the god gives his name to the month of August, La Lunasa.

RHIANNON

Rhiannon's name derives from Rigantona, which means Great Queen, the same meaning as the Morrigan.

The Welsh/Celtic goddess is aligned so closely with the Roman Epona that it is likely that they are one and the same. Both are associated with horses, underlining the ineffable importance of the creature.

Rhiannon first appears in the Mabinogi, the Celtic hero-myths. She is introduced as a beautiful woman, dressed in a golden gown, seated on a snow-white horse. Pwyll, the hero, tries to catch up with her but this proves impossible despite the seemingly relaxed pace of Rhiannon's horse and the speed of his own mount. Eventually he calls out to her, and she stops to speak. It seems that she's been promised to another but is handily in love with Pwyll, so they prepare to marry. The labyrinthine tale that follows, which in the original Celtic tradition would have been passed on orally rather than written down, involves magic, shape-shifting, and the birth of a son that disappears. The six women who were meant to be taking care of the child panic after his disappearance, and squarely frame Rhiannon. When she awoke, she was daubed with the blood from a puppy and surrounded by its bones. Rhiannon is accused of eating her baby, and despite her protestations, she is punished, forced to tell her story to every passing stranger and to carry them on her back if necessary; Rhiannon is changed into a horse.

As well as horses, Rhiannon is also associated with otherworldly birds, and inspired the Stevie Nicks song "Rhiannon." The Birds of Rhiannon sing so beautifully that they not only send the living to sleep, but also raise the dead. Both horses and birds are psychopomp creatures, that is, they conduct the souls of the dead on the journey to the underworld.

There is a white horse carved into the landscape at the Iron Age hill fort of Uffington, in the south of England. It may be that this horse was carved into the landscape in honor of Epona/Rhiannon.

EGYPTIAN DEITIES

The ancient Egyptians had many gods, many of them hybridized humans/animals. Animals themselves were deified and accorded due reverence, the more dangerous the animal the greater its worship. The crocodile god, Sobek, for example, had its own city, Crocodilopolis. The pharaoh was also considered to be as one with the gods, and was deified after his death.

The nine gods of Eliopoulos, the City of the Sun, were Atum, Geb, Isis, Nut, Osiris, Nephthys, Set, Shu, and Tefnut.

ANUBIS

This Egyptian god has close parallels with Hermes, whose ubiquity is reflected in different gods from cultures all over the world. This close association would see the god later renamed Hermanubis. Like Hermes, Anubis also has the caduceus as his attribute.

Anubis symbolizes his status as a conductor of souls by his head, which is that of a jackal, a creature that is also a psychopomp. Anubis presided over the process of embalming, considered essential if the soul were to have any form of life after death. Funerary prayers and offerings were made almost exclusively to Anubis.

Anubis had been abandoned by his mother, Nephthys, and was adopted by Isis. Isis, Osiris, and Anubis shared the same father, Ra, the sun god. When Osiris died, it was Anubis that invented the funeral rites and the all-important process of mummification. Known as the "Lord of the Mummy Wrappings," Anubis also had the ability to take the hand of the deceased and guide them toward the judges who then weighed his soul.

Isis

The Greeks rendered the name of the Egyptian goddess Eset as Isis. She was considered the supreme mother goddess, parent of all the other deities. As such, she personifies all the qualities of the other goddesses. Both the sister and consort of Osiris, her contribution to the civilization of Egypt was to teach spinning, weaving, and the grinding of corn to the women, and the art of healing the sick to the men. She also introduced the idea of marriage and therefore domesticity. This would make it appear that, like the Roman Hestia, Isis had started out her journey as a goddess of the hearth, but in a legend that reinforces the power of the knowledge of a magical name, when she learned the secret name of the sun god, Ra, she became his equal. Drops of her blood gave life to every living creature in the universe. The ankh, a magical symbol of rebirth, belongs to Isis. Her name has been used in tandem with mystery cults and secret organizations—the Fellowship of Isis, for example.

The fame of Isis spread far and wide and was not restricted to Egypt. Her influence even extended as far as the Rhine. She was called, like Mary the mother of Christ, the Star of the Sea. However, in the sixth century AD her temple at Philae was turned into a Christian church. Like the Eleusinian mysteries that celebrated the goddess Demeter, elaborate festivals were held in honor of Isis that similarly taught initiates the secrets of death and rebirth.

Isis brought another great revelation to mankind. This was the art of embalming, and therefore of eternal life. When his brother cut Osiris's body into fourteen parts, Isis painstakingly reconstructed the body. The only missing part was his penis, which had been devoured by a crab. Thereafter, this creature was cursed in Egypt.

OSIRIS

Again, the Greeks have given us the most familiar name of one of the most important gods of Egypt, Ousir. Initially a god of nature, Osiris is identified with other gods who die and are reborn again. Egyptians worshipped him as the god of the dead, which helps explain the fascination with all things morbid. As with other mighty gods, his power is indicated in the sheer number of his names. More than a hundred are listed in the Egyptian Book of the Dead.

Osiris was the eldest son of the sky goddess, Nut, and the earth god, Geb. His grandfather was Ra. His sister, Isis, was also his queen; thus the pair symbolize the perfect union of male and female energies. Osiris proved a civilizing influence, teaching his people the arts of agriculture and dissuading them from cannibalism. His ways were gentle and just, a lover of music who invented two different kinds of flute. Osiris's power spread far and wide, his civilizing influence having a profound effect throughout Asia.

There was a cloud on the horizon, though, in the form of his jealous brother, who assassinated him. We have already explained how Isis painstakingly reconstructed his body. Osiris manifested in numerous animal forms; Onuphis, the bull, the Ram of Mendes that inspired the curious tale of the Goat of Mendes, and in the Benu bird which has similarities to the phoenix, also a bird of death and resurrection. Osiris was celebrated in his own mystery cults that, like the Eleusinian mysteries, instructed its acolytes in the secrets of death and rebirth.

GRECO-ROMAN DEITIES

Mount Olympus, in Greece, is a sacred mountain archetype and the home to the mighty beings that are called collectively the Olympians or the Dodekatheon (twelve gods). Twelve is, of course, a sacred number belonging not only to the number of solar months in a year but is also the number of fulfillment. So, who were this divine dozen? Although there were more than twelve beings that lived on top of the mountain, the twelve principal ones are:

2. Hera: The Mother. Consort of Zeus, queen of the gods, personification of the maternal aspect, ruler of marriage and motherhood.

1. Zeus: The Father. Like Odin, a god of thunder and king of all the gods; his kingdom, the sky itself. Dispenser of justice, his word is law.

3. Poseidon: The mighty god that rules over the sea. Also has dominion over horses and earthquakes.

4. Ares: Not to be confused with Aries, Ares is the god of war and bloodshed. The two are sometimes confused, though, especially since Mars, the planet of war, rules the astrological sign of Aries.

6. Hephaestus: Ruler over fire and forges, Hephaestus is the blacksmith of the gods, making magically empowered weapons.

7. Aphrodite: Goddess of beauty, love, and sexual desire.

5. Hermes: The messenger of the gods, whose distinctive attribute is his winged sandals and the caduceus he holds. Scribe and recorder to the gods.

8. Athena: Goddess of wisdom, often accompanied by an owl as a sign of her sagacity and access to occluded information.

10. Artemis: Goddess of the hunt, often depicted with a quiver of arrows and a bow. Artemis is also the moon goddess and the goddess of virgins.

11. Demeter: Goddess of the harvest, agriculture, and fertility.

12. Hestia: Goddess of the home and the hearth.

9. Apollo: The glorious sun god, governor of light, music, poetry, and beauty.

The family relationships of these gods are labyrinthine. Zeus, Poseidon, Hera, Demeter, Hestia, and Hades were all siblings. Hades, as god of the underworld, does not figure among the Olympians although he is of course a key god; his realm is the world of the dead that lies in the nether regions, not on top of a mountain. Persephone, too, spends some of her time with the other gods but also belongs to the underworld where she spends four months of the year. Hermes, Hephaestus, Artemis, Apollo, and Ares are children of Zeus by various mothers. Athena was born from the forehead of her father Zeus, and Aphrodite was born from the castrated phallus of the sky that existed prior to the Creation.

The Romans adopted many of these Greek gods and their qualities, adding them to their own deities to form a Greco-Roman pantheon. The table below shows the Greek deities with their Roman counterparts:

Greek	Roman
Zeus	Jupiter
Hera	Juno
Poseidon	Neptune
Ares	Mars
Hermes	Mercury
Hephaestus	Vulcan
Aphrodite	Venus
Athena	Minerva
Apollo	Apollo
Artemis	Diana
Demeter	Ceres
Hestia	Vesta
Hades	Pluto
Persephone	Proserpina
Dionysus	Bacchus
Eros	Cupid
Chronos	Saturn
Coelus	Uranus

DEMETER/CERES

The cereals we eat as part of our breakfast take their name from the Roman goddess Ceres, whose Greek counterpart is Demeter. It was this goddess who gave humanity the secrets of agriculture, a pivotal skill that has had a profound effect on humankind, the cultivation of plants itself a perfect symbol for a different kind of cultivation as humans made the transition from savage to civilized.

Any deity who has jurisdiction over the crops and fertility understandably holds immense power, and the worship of Demeter was the primary focus of the Eleusinian mysteries that celebrated the profound secrets of death and rebirth. The winter season was explained, lyrically, as signifying Demeter's journey to the underworld to seek out her lost daughter, Persephone; during this time, she neglected her earthly duties and so all the plants and vegetation disappeared.

The cereal and grain crops, which were this goddess's gifts to humankind, gave us bread, a staple item that nourishes on two levels, spiritual and material.

HECATE

Hecate is the great Greek queen of the underworld and the moon goddess who is often among those that are referred to as the Triple Goddess. Famously, Hecate is also the queen of the witches, and has two opposing aspects. She is the benevolent goddess that brings prosperity, protects sailors at sea and ensures that farmers reap a bountiful harvest. However, she also has a terrifying, demonic aspect as the goddess of the dead, associated with ghosts and nightmares, mistress of sorcery, and summoned by incantations.

As well as personifying the three phases of the moon's cycle (new, waxing/waning, and full) she also embodies the three parts of the universe; heaven, hell, and earth. As befits the sorcerer queen, Hecate rules over spells, charms, and enchantments; she sends demons down to earth to torture men; she haunts crossroads, graveyards, and tombs, often appearing with her pack of hellhounds. Symbolic of the dark side, Hecate is also a symbol of the subconscious mind, the hidden depths that are full of fear and swarming with monsters.

HERMES/ MERCURY

Hermes appears in a number of guises, as befits a god with trickster tendencies. His talents are numerous, his attributes diverse. His Celtic equivalent is the god Lugh, who is referred to by Julius Caesar as "the inventor of all arts and crafts." He also appears as Thoth, the great Egyptian god who invented writing and was the scribe of the gods, as well as the judge of the human soul and mediator between man and god. In yet another guise, there are parallels with the great angel Metatron. The word "Mercury" shares its root with *mercator*, "merchant," indicating his interest in marketing and trade.

The most immediately recognizable symbol that belongs to Hermes is his winged sandals, indicating swift movement and the powers of flight. This makes him an effective messenger of the gods. Originally he moved between Zeus and the gods of the underworld, Persephone and Hades, so was able to move easily in and out of different worlds, the world of the living and of the dead; he is also a god of the dead. In his guise as the ibis-headed Thoth, he is also the patron of science and literature, inventions, and wisdom. His trickster skills make Mercury the god of thieves, too. Communication of all kinds belongs to this god, his image used, for example, by telecommunication companies.

This versatile deity also appears as Hermes Trismegistus, the founding father of alchemy. The magical gifts that Hermes Trismegistus brought to humankind include the divinatory arts as well as music. The great Emerald Tablet that is the cornerstone of the Great Work in alchemy is a riddle, written in such an oblique way that it has several interpretations. It is said that Mercury brings our attention to great mysteries, but also gives us the means to unravel these mysteries. In Greek myth, Hermes made the first lyre, constructing it from the shell of a tortoise and using the guts of a sacrificed bull for strings.

He also made the first flute, which he swapped with Apollo for lessons in magic as well as a golden caduceus, another of his attributes.

JANUS

Many deities from one religious discipline will have a counterpart with very similar attributes in another. However, Janus, a Roman god, appears to be unique although there is a link between him and the Greek god Chaos. As the god of doorways, Janus's defining feature is that he has two heads. As well as this distinction, he also carries a key, to lock and unlock the doors and gates he guards, and a stick to drive away anyone who had no right to cross the threshold.

Because he is the god of gates, Janus is, by extension, ruler of arrivals and departures and of communication. He is also god of beginnings and has jurisdiction over the daybreak, effectively allowing the sun to enter through the eastern gate of the sky. At the time before the creation of the universe and all the elements were a formless mass, Janus was called Chaos; after their separation and the coming of order, his name changed to Janus, but he still rules the time of transition. The month of January was named for Janus, who looks back to the old year and forward to the new. Janus also inspired the title of janitor, the earthly ruler of doorways and corridors. He was honored on the first day of every month.

PERSEPHONE/ PROSERPINA

Persephone is one of the underworld or chthonic deities, the consort of Hades, its king. She is the daughter of the harvest goddess, Demeter. Before she was kidnapped and carried off into the underworld, Persephone was named Kore or Cora, meaning "the maiden." She appears in some accounts as the daughter of Zeus and Demeter but occasionally Styx, the nymph of the underworld river, is named as her mother.

Accounts of Persephone's story vary. According to one, she was gathering flowers in a field when the ground beneath her feet opened up and she was abducted by Hades. Demeter abandoned all her duties in order to look for her daughter. During her time in the underworld Persephone was induced to eat a seed from the pomegranate, itself a symbol of fertility and sexual awakening and a euphemism for the loss of her virginity. However, because she had broken the obligatory fast that should be observed by those in the underworld, she was tied to Hades, and when her mother found her again she had to promise to spend part of the year with him. Persephone, therefore, is symbolic of seasonal change.

The symbols attached to Persephone that allow us to recognize her are the pomegranate, the bat, and the narcissus flower. Worship of Persephone was a key feature of the Eleusinian mysteries. Incidentally, fairy tales also advise against eating anything from fairyland, since by accepting such food the person is trapped there.

THE HINDU PANTHEON

The system of Hindu deities is vast and complex, a multi-layered society of gods and goddesses that encompass a colorful spectrum of personalities. The concept of karma, the rule of cause and effect based on cosmic harmony and balance, is fundamental to Hinduism. The deities themselves are either aspects of the supreme being (Brahman), or more personalized, human representations of it (Bhagavan), or otherwise they are Devas, powerful in their own right. The stories of the Hindu deities are many and varied, and to confuse matters even further, each has different aspects of his or her divine self, such as appearing with, or riding on, an animal, when the beast becomes the "vehicle" of the god.

The Brahman has three aspects. As the creator, it is Brahma. As the preserver, it is Vishnu. As the destroyer, it is Shiva. Each of these three aspects has aspects of its own, but all come back to one supreme being that has neither gender nor age: Brahman. Having said that, the gods and goddesses themselves are distinctly gender affiliated. The male gods are called Devas, the female goddesses Devis. Use of this epithet for humans acknowledges the divine being within. The Devas and Devis appear in the paintings, art, and statuary that thickly cluster all manifestations of Hindu culture.

Hindus affiliate themselves to the aspect of the supreme being that most appeals. Notwithstanding, there's a mutual respect for all the gods and for people's right to choose.

Sometimes, gods take on human form in order to assist humanity in some way. These beings are called avatars, and in many ways equate to Christ who similarly came to earth to help mankind toward ultimate enlightenment and the journey to God. In contrast to Christianity, where Christ is believed only to have come to earth the one time, in Hinduism the avatar can reincarnate repeatedly, as and when necessary. One of the most famous avatars is Rama; the stories in the Ramayana are about his adventures, and the Bhagavad Gita is the collected spiritual wisdoms of Krishna, the avatar of Vishnu.

Each of the Devas or Devis has a particular attribute that identifies it, and gorgeously elaborate stories explain these attributes. Ganesh is the popular elephant-headed god that removes obstacles, and Lakshmi is the goddess of good fortune, often appearing in shops and business places and attracted into the home by the elaborate rice powder rangoli drawings at the threshold of houses. Sarasvati is the goddess of learning, inspiring students and teachers alike.

It is true to say that these divine beings and their attributes are symbols of humanity's own qualities and an excellent way for human beings to focus on their skills, a way of externalizing what is within and a means of focus. Psychologically speaking, Hinduism is a very clever system designed to bring out the best in people. Ramakrishna, the Hindu saint, studied many other religions including Islam and Christianity, and wisely observed that "the truth is One; the wise call it by various names."

GANESH

We've already mentioned Ganesh as the remover of obstacles. Although Ganesh is also the deity of intelligence and wisdom, the obstacle-removing ability makes him one of the most popular gods

of the Hindu pantheon. It's worth remembering that Ganesh can also place obstacles in the way of people as a form of education. But how did he come about his curious hybrid appearance? There are several versions of the story.

As guardian of the gate of his mother Parvati, in his enthusiasm to do his job properly, one day he tried to prevent Shiva, his father, from entering. The result was that the young man's head was cut off. Shiva decided that the head of the first passing animal should replace his son's human head. This animal happened to be an elephant. Ganesh was restored to life with the addition of this unwieldy head, and given his name, which means "elephant head." Ganesh sometimes appears standing on a rat or a mouse, an unlikely "vehicle" that was given to him by a contemptuous demon. However, the mouse itself is a symbol. The word "mouse" comes from the Sanskrit *musaka*, which means "thief," because mice steal valuable grain. The mouse itself, therefore, is an obstacle that needs to be overcome.

KALI

Kali, as the Hindu goddess who is not only a protector and a loving mother but also a vengeful destroyer, has parallels with Hecate from the Greek pantheon.

Kali is instantly recognizable; her name means "dark," and her appearance is quite fearsome. She appears with dark blue or black skin, long disheveled tresses of black hair, furious red eyes, sharp teeth, a protruding tongue and her distinctive necklace of human skulls. Sometimes she wears a skirt made of human arms. She herself has four (or sometimes ten) arms; in common with other divinities that have supernumerary limbs or heads, this signifies superhuman powers. Kali is often depicted standing over a corpse. In each of

her four hands, she carries a sword, a severed head, a trident or *trishul*, and a *kapala* or skull cup that catches the blood from the head.

Like Hecate, Kali frequents the places of the dead, cremation grounds in particular. Her consort Shiva, who is also associated with these places, has his skin colored white from the ashes of the corpses. His pale skin contrasts with the black skin of Kali, the two contrasting shades a reminder of opposing forces. As befits a goddess with such frightening associations and with a reputation for violence, Kali is treated with awe, respect, and not a little fear. She symbolizes death as well as salvation. In her more benign aspect, however, she appears as a smiling figure, hands raised in the boon-giving gesture, young, generous, beautiful, and maternal.

In Tantric practices, Kali is revered as the most powerful of goddesses, and has her own meditation symbol or yantra, featuring in the center of the inverted triangle or yoni symbol. She is held to be the divine essence of the mother goddess, the highest reality and the female element, known as Shakti. Her universality means that she rules over all five of the elements.

To come face-to-face with Kali is to face the reality of death, and all the symbolism of this goddess acts as a reminder of the need to come to terms with this reality.

SARASVATI

Sarasvati is the wife of Brahma, the god of gods who created the world. The goddess of wisdom, knowledge, and music, Sarasvati often appears with a stringed musical instrument called a vina. She is also identified by her beauty and her four arms, the supernumerary limbs, themselves symbols of power, also represent the four aspects of learning: intellect, mind, ego, and alertness.

Sarasvati, as befits a feminine deity, is a water goddess and was in ancient times also personified as a river that bore her name, which is now dried up. A swan sometimes accompanies Sarasvati. This bird, if offered a mixture of milk and water, would select only the milk, therefore symbolizing discrimination. Adherents to the Sarasvati cult make offerings of honey to their goddess, because honey is synonymous with perfect knowledge.

Sarasvati gave a great gift to humanity—the alphabet.

Norse/Teutonic Pantheon

Interestingly, the gods of Norse/Teutonic mythology were never really considered as being immortal, but were humans with super powers. There were two tribes of gods: the Aesir, or ferocious warrior gods, and the Vanir, deities of a more peaceful and benevolent disposition. The two tribes unified to fight the giants.

Freya was particularly fond of lovely things. Once, when she found four dwarves making a gorgeous necklace, her desire to possess it was so great that she readily agreed to sleep with all of them in return for it.

She can be recognized by a small falcon, which often accompanies her. She also had a cloak of feathers, which enabled her to fly.

Freya

Freya was so lovely that she was the constant source of attention from the other gods. As befits a person of such beauty, Freya ruled over love, fertility, and beauty. She was also the leader of the Valkyries, and as such she escorted fallen warriors back to the banqueting halls of Valhalla.

Wotan/Odin

Wotan/Odin is the chief god of the Scandinavian pantheon. His attributes are numerous and seemingly conflict with one another; he is not only god of war and death, but also of poetry, prophecy, ictory. His name comes same root as *wuten*, which o rage," and the idea of y surrounds the god. He god of thunder, heard on ny nights raging in the sky n his army of slain soldiers. otan was the god invoked by the Saxons and the Angles when they invaded Britain in the fifth century, and his influence was all-pervasive.

How do you recognize Wotan? To humankind, he often appears in the guise as a simple traveler, wearing shabby clothing and a wide-brimmed hat. However, when he appears in his true form he is a magnificent sight. He rides Sleipnir, his ultra speedy eight-legged horse that can gallop across water as though it were solid earth, and he is accompanied by two ravens, Hugin and Munin (Thought and Memory), who report back to him every evening the events in the lives of men. As if all this were not remarkable enough, Wotan has only one eye. He gave away the other to Mimir, the demon that lives

in among the roots of Yggdrasil, the World Tree, in exchange for a drink of water from the well of wisdom that sprung up from the base of the tree.

Wotan is eloquent, speaking in verse. Like Mercury whom the Romans likened him to, he brought language to his people, apparently dangling upside down in a tree for nine days and nights, pierced with his own spear, in order that he should learn the secrets of the runes. This curious ordeal was akin to a shamanistic rite of passage that would guarantee his own resurrection. Wotan rules the same day of the week as Mercury, too— Wednesday (Wotan's day), which equates to Mercredi (Mercury's day) in French, of course.

Wotan rules over Valhalla, the Hall of the Slain, where dead warriors are brought by the Valkyries, under the command of their leader Freya, in order to prepare themselves for the final battle, Ragnarok, which will mark the end of the world.

VOUDON

Many of the deities of the Dahomey people of Africa, from Benin, appear in the Voudon religion, which is an amalgam of beliefs from West Africa with Christianity. One of Voudon's creation myths shares similarities with the idea of the creation of the world in Judaism and Christianity, but whereas the Abrahamic God apparently needed six days to create the world, the primary Dahomey deity, the androgynous Mawu Lisa, needed only four. On the first day the world was made; on the second, all plant and animal life was brought into being. On the third day, humans were given intellect and languages; and on the fourth day, the far-sighted god created technology.

In Voudon, there are many different loas, or spirits that have attained a godlike status. These loas are able to possess the human body, which is the aim of many of the trance-inducing ceremonies of the faith. The spirits split into two categories: the Rada, who offer protection and guidance and are generally seen to be quite benevo-lent; and the Petro, who forgiving, and more ass with the darker side of Vo magic. Each loa has aspects both in its personality.

ERZULIE FREDA DAHOMEY

Erzulie is a family of such loa spirits, with Erzulie Freda Dahomey being a very "girly" sort of entity, much concerned with romance, dancing, flowers, beauty, and love. Often portrayed wearing three wedding rings, one for each of her husbands, Erzulie Freda Dahomey is further identified by the heart symbol and by the feminine colors of gold and pink. Erzulie Freda Dahomey is the embodiment of the feminine spirit, which means that she also has a dark side, the Petro side. Balanced against her coquettish playfulness is an aspect that is lazy, jealous, and spoiled. In this aspect she is depicted with a child in one arm and holding a knife.